BROKERING EMPIRE

BROKERING EMPIRE

*Trans-Imperial Subjects
between Venice and Istanbul*

E. NATALIE ROTHMAN

CORNELL UNIVERSITY PRESS   ITHACA AND LONDON

First published 2012 by Cornell University Press
First printing, Cornell Paperbacks, 2014

Printed in the United States of America

Library of Congress Cataloging-in-Publication Data

Rothman, E. Natalie (Ella Natalie), 1976–
Brokering empire : trans-imperial subjects between Venice and
Istanbul / E. Natalie Rothman.
p. cm.
Includes bibliographical references and index.
ISBN 978-0-8014-4907-9 (cloth : alk. paper)
ISBN 978-0-8014-7996-0 (paper : alk. paper)
1. Venice (Italy)—Relations—Turkey—Istanbul.   2. Istanbul
(Turkey)—Relations—Italy—Venice.   3. Venice (Italy)—
History—1508–1797.   4. Turkey—History—Ottoman Empire,
1288–1918.   I. Title.
DG676.97.T9R69 2012
303.48'245311049618—dc23   2011037686

Cloth printing   10 9 8 7 6 5 4 3 2 1
Paperback printing   10 9 8 7 6 5 4 3 2 1

To Tamouz

Contents

CONTENTS

PART IV *Articulation*

Acknowledgments

Trans-imperial in conception and transnational in execution, this project has incurred many debts along the way from manuscript to print. In fact, so many that I am certain to miss someone. I would therefore like to begin by asking for a blanket dispensation and to express my profound gratitude to all the individuals and institutions whose kindness and generosity have sustained me over the years and thereby made this book possible.

This book began at the University of Michigan, where I had the great fortune of learning from wonderful teachers and fellow students in the Doctoral Program in Anthropology and History. Ed Murphy, Chandra Bhimull, Monica Patterson, Sarah Arvey, Caroline Jeanneret, Jenny Gaynor, and Danna Agmon provided a stimulating and collegial environment for graduate studies. I thank especially Fernando Coronil and David William Cohen for their leadership and vision for the program, and for exemplifying a model of critical scholarly engagement with the history of the present. I am equally grateful to Ann Stoler, who taught me about the politics of comparison; Dena Goodman and Webb Keane, both of whom carefully critiqued multiple drafts; Pat Simons, whose sharp comments prodded me to stronger interpretation; and, last but not least, Diane Owen Hughes, my doctoral advisor, whose unfailing support and intellectual openness and breadth have been truly inspiring. I owe to her more than I can easily express.

Since leaving Michigan, I have happily settled into the life of a junior faculty member at the University of Toronto. The transition from graduate school to the tenure track was greatly facilitated by the sound advice of Dan Bender, Franca Iacovetta, and Ken Mills, who guided me through the intricate mysteries of UofT (and the academy more generally). My deep gratitude goes to them and to Bill Bowen, chair of the Department of Humanities at the University of Toronto Scarborough, for his vision and leadership in very trying times, and for his unfailing encouragement of junior faculty. I extend another enormous thank you to the entire staff of the UTSC Department of Humanities, and especially to Monica Hretsina and Laurel Wheeler, for their tireless work at keeping an unruly group of academics more or less functioning!

In Toronto, I have benefited enormously from the warm welcome and enduring support of colleagues across the university, including Konrad Eisenbichler, Rick Halpern, Mark Meyerson, the entire UTSC History group, and my fellow early modernists in the graduate Department of History, Jane Abray, Ken Bartlett, Paul Cohen, Ken Mills, and Nick Terpstra. Dan Bender, Katherine Blouin, Frank Cody, Girish Daswani, Naisargi Dave, Drew Gilbert, Jens Hanssen, Andrea Muehlebach, Katie Larson, Bhavani Raman, Srilata Raman, and Jayeeta Sharma have seamlessly compounded close friendship with deep intellectual engagement. I am equally thankful to the many undergraduate and graduate students in my courses on Venetian and Mediterranean history and historiography who continuously challenge me to think in new ways about how early modern mediation and alterity have impacted our own world.

My intellectual debt over the years to various mentors, formal and informal, is too great to repay here. I thank Gadi Algazi, my MA advisor and friend, whose unwavering commitment to scholarship and activism, to the study of the past and the transformation of the future, continue to inspire me. Benjamin Arbel taught me most of what I know about Venice, the Mediterranean, and the craft of archival research. Benny was the one to suggest that I look at Venetian *suppliche* (petitions to the government) as a genre through which to consider how non–elites engaged officialdom in the early modern period. His painstaking scholarship and endless patience at reading multiple drafts saved me from quite a few embarrassing errors. My immense gratitude is only hinted at in the notes of this book, so I would like to acknowledge here the intellectual generosity, hospitality, and friendship that he and Housni al-Khateeb Shehada extended to me in Tel Aviv and in Venice. In Toronto, I have benefited in more ways than I can describe from the mentorship and friendship of Natalie Zemon Davis. Her passion for history, enthusiasm for bringing scholars together, and commitment to social justice are inimitable. I hope this book reflects some of what I have learned from her over the years.

As is the case with all academic labor, this project would not have materialized without substantial institutional support. The bulk of archival research for this book was funded through a generous research award from the Mellon

Foundation/Council on Library and Information Resource (CLIR). I am grateful to Abby Smith and Susan Randolph from CLIR for their support and advice on archival research. At the University of Michigan, Ethel Thoms of the Rackham School of Graduate Studies showed great flexibility and understanding as fellowship officer. Michael Schoenfeldt and Karla Taylor, former directors of the Medieval and Early Modern Studies Program, were exceptionally supportive of my research and secured funding for supplementary trips to and from the Venetian archives, and for an Italian paleography course at the Newberry Library in Chicago. James Boyd White, Don Lopez, Linda Turner, and the postdoctoral fellows made for a stimulating year as an associate fellow with the Michigan Society of Fellows. Sheila Williams and Lorna Altstetter in the History Department, and Diana Denney of the Doctoral Program in Anthropology and History provided outstanding assistance and invaluable advice throughout my time at Michigan. Their competence and cheer made all the difference in the world. At Toronto, I have benefited from the wise advice of Sarah Scott and her colleagues in the Research Services Office. A research leave from the University of Toronto and a year-long research fellowship at the Newberry Library in Chicago provided much needed focus as I prepared the manuscript for initial submission. Many thanks to James Grossman, Diane Dillon, and Leslie Kan in the Research and Education Office, Carla Zecher at the Center for Renaissance Studies, Doug Knox, Paul Gehl, Robert Karrow, James Akerman, and the entire Special Collections staff. A special acknowledgment goes to my fellow fellows during 2008–9, and particularly to Edward Muir, Diana Robin, Holly Pickett, Carmen Nocentelli, and Sam Truett for their friendship and scholarship. Book revisions were also supported by a Connaught Start-Up grant from the University of Toronto and a Standard Research Grant from the Social Sciences and Humanities Research Council of Canada.

Research for this book was greatly facilitated by the assistance of knowledgeable and dedicated staff in numerous archives and libraries, including the Biblioteca Marciana, the Museo Civico Correr, the Biblioteca Querini-Stampalia, and the Archivio Storico del Patriarcato di Venezia. At the Archivio di Stato di Venezia I benefited greatly from conversations with Giustiniana Migliardi O'Riordan, superintendent of the Veneto archives, and from the thoughtful suggestions and kind assistance of state archivists Dott.sse Sandra Sambo and Michela Dal Borgo. A special acknowledgment is due to archivist Dott. Giuseppe Ellero of the Archivio delle Istitutuzioni di Ricovero e di Educazione (IRE), who shared with me his vast knowledge (and invaluable card index) of the archives of the Pia Casa dei Catecumeni. At the Università Ca' Foscari, I was fortunate enough to discuss aspects of my work with Piero Brunello, Giovanni Levi, Reinhold Mueller,

Gherardo Ortalli, Maria-Pia Pedani, Dorit Raines, Boghos Levon Zekiyan, and the late Giorgio Vercellin. I am grateful to all of them for their encouragement and advice at a very preliminary stage of this project. Away from the archives, Maria and Paolo Vianello substituted as parental figures and made sure my stay in Castello was as pleasurable as possible.

My deep gratitude to Charles Beddington, Charles Cator, and Anne Wakely of Christie's UK, who were exceptionally helpful in securing permission to reprint the cover image and in providing a digital copy of the original, now in a private collection. I also gratefully acknowledge the kind assistance of Jack Zawistowski of the Manuscript Division of the Royal Library/National Library of Sweden; Dott.ssa Agata Brusegan, conservatrice (keeper) of the Archivio Storico IRE; and the staff of the Archivio Storico del Patriarcato di Venezia and the photography services department at the Venetian State Archives in securing digital copies and permissions to print images from their respective collections. Federica Ruspio and Emanuela Brusegan Flavel have been very helpful in coordinating such digital copies and permissions in Venice, and I am truly indebted to them for their timely assistance. I also thank Bryan Skib, coordinator of Graduate Library Collections at the Harlan Hatcher Graduate Library at the University of Michigan, and the capable intercampus and interlibrary staff at the UTSC library for securing microfilms and rare books for this project.

During my stay in Venice I made several friends who introduced me not only to the wonders of the archives, but of the city as well. They include Jana Byers, Georg Christ, Giacomo Corrazzol, Vera Costantini, Holly Hurlburt, and Monique O'Connell. A very special thank you to Maartje van Gelder and Federica Ruspio, whose deep knowledge of the archives and continued friendship over the years have made an enormous difference.

Drafts of virtually all chapters were presented at various forums over the years. I am grateful to Patricia Fortini Brown and participants in the weekend seminar "Artifice and Authenticity: The Ambiguities of Early Modern Venice" at the Folger Institute in Washington, DC, for their valuable advice and encouragement at a very early stage of this project. The workshop on "Trade, Colonies and Intercultural Contacts in the Venetian World, 1400–1650," organized by Benjamin Arbel at Venice International University provided a wonderful opportunity to interact with colleagues and revisit the *Serenissima*. Dan Goffman and participants in the Great Lakes Ottoman Studies Workshop at DePaul University in Chicago opened up the door to sustained engagement with Ottomanist colleagues. Sections of the book were also presented as lectures and conference papers at the University of Michigan, the University of Toronto, the University of Minnesota, Delhi University, Harvard University, the Newberry Library, the Comparative History Workshop in Niagara-on-the-Lake, Ontario, and at annual meetings of the Renaissance Society of America in New York and San Francisco, the American Historical Association in Seattle, and the Middle East Studies Association in Montreal. I thank all the organizers and participants for allowing me to discuss my work in progress in such congenial and productive settings.

Over the years, many scholars across three continents have discussed with me the ins and outs of this project, and provided much valuable advice, including Virginia Aksan, Karl Appuhn, Linda Carroll, Elizabeth Cohen, Tom Cohen, Filippo de Vivo, Eric Dursteler, Rembert Eufe, Gilles Grivaud, Elizabeth Horodowich, Sam Kaplan, Sally McKee, Laurie Nussdorfer, Mary Pardo, Chris Pastore, Leslie Peirce, Zvi Razi, Giorgio Rota, James Shaw, Stefanie Siegmund, Patricia Thompson, Ebru Turan, and Bronwen Wilson. I am thankful to all of them for their intellectual generosity. Numerous other friends and colleagues were kind enough to read and comment on the manuscript, in parts or in whole, including Gadi Algazi, Megan Armstrong, Naor Ben-Yehoyada, Palmira Brummett, Natalie Zemon Davis, Jens Hanssen, Dafna Hirsch, Katie Larson, Ken Mills, Edward Muir, Georgios Plakotos, Ato Quayson, Sean Roberts, and Daniel Smail. My profound gratitude to all of them. I have tried my best to incorporate their suggestions and address their critiques and concerns. All remaining faults are, of course, my own.

Parts of several chapters have been published previously in different form, and I thank the University of Michigan Press and Routledge for permission to use portions of the following two articles, respectively: "Genealogies of Mediation: Culture Broker and Imperial Governmentality," in *Anthrohistory: Unsettling Knowledge, Questioning Discipline,* ed. Edward Murphy, David W. Cohen, Chandra D. Bhimull, Fernando Coronil, Monica Eileen Patterson, and Julie Skurski (Ann Arbor: University of Michigan Press, 2011), 67–79; and "Becoming Venetian: Conversion and Transformation in the Seventeenth-Century Mediterranean," *Mediterranean Historical Review* 21, 1 (June 2006): 39–75.

As this project reached its final stages of transformation from a manuscript into a book, it has benefited enormously from the editorial guidance of John G. Ackerman, Karen Laun, Susan Barnett, and Julie F. Nemer at Cornell University Press. I thank them sincerely for their exceptional support and patience.

My dearest friend Tijana Krstić introduced me to Ottoman historiography a decade ago, and has continued ever since to be my surest and wisest sounding board. I cannot begin to thank her and Tolga Esmer for their friendship, stimulating conversations, and wonderful hospitality in Chicago, Istanbul, and Budapest. I am enormously grateful to my family, in all its transcontinental, multigenerational, multi-household configurations. Their love and intellectual curiosity, not to mention practical support over the years, have made the process of completing this book infinitely more pleasurable. An especially warm thank you to my mother, Hannah Rothman, for her love of beauty and knowledge, and for not letting the physical distance diminish our bond, and to my father, Zamir Havkin, who taught me much about intellectual conversation, political engagement, and careful craftsmanship. A special honorary mention is also due to my aunt and uncle, Hilla Havkin and Rami Rudich, who graciously hosted a rambunctious toddler and her parents for the final month of editing this book. My greatest debt is to my soul mate, Alejandro Paz, for his wisdom and love, for being my fiercest critic and staunchest advocate. Finally, to our daughter, Tamouz Andrea Paz, the proverbial priority changer, whose infinite ability to distract me from work is truly awe inspiring: May you grow to find pleasure in interpreting this world, while also striving to change it!

Frontispiece: The Molo and the Riva degli Schiavoni looking East (before 1718). The ethnic and class heterogeneity of the Venetian commercial sphere, as perceived through early modern eyes, is palpable in this *veduta* (cityscape), one of dozens painted by the Venetian artist Luca Carlevarijs (1663–1730). The painting depicts a promenade teeming with mariners, porters, artisans, and merchants, some of them wearing visibly foreign dress. The bustling commercial scene is flanked by the ships and boats moored at St. Mark's basin, as well as two iconic Venetian architectural elements, the winged lion atop a granite column adorning the Molo, the ceremonial landing spot for official visitors, and the façade of the ducal palace, the political nerve center of the Venetian state. Carlevarijs's cityscapes typically feature "oriental" figures alongside well-to-do locals in scenes that emplace commercial conviviality across class and ethnic boundaries in highly public spaces, be they the market at Rialto or St. Mark's square. The enormous contemporary popularity of this genre suggests how such sites were central to experiencing the links between trade, brokerage, and alterity. Private Collection. Reproduction: Copyright © Christie's Images Limited, (1997). Reproduced with permission.

Illustrations

Abbreviations

ASPV	Archivio Storico del Patriarcato di Venezia
AdC	Avvogaria di Comun
AIRE	Archivio delle Istituzioni di Ricovero e di Educazione, Venice
ASVe	Archivio di Stato di Venezia
b.	*busta*, box/volume
BNM	Biblioteca Marciana, Venice
c.	*carta*, page
cod.	*codice*, codex
CDd	Catecumeni, Documenti diversi
CRb	Catecumeni, Registri battesimi
fasc.	*fascicolo*, fascicle
fol.	folio
MCC	Museo Civico Correr, Venice
reg.	*registro*, register
SU	Santo Uffizio

All archival documents cited in this book are located in the Venetian State Archives (Archivio di Stato di Venezia, ASVe), unless otherwise noted. (See the bibliography for a list.)

Note on Usage, Names, and Dates

In transcribing and translating early modern archival documents I have opted to avoid modernizing the text as much as possible, as my aim is not to increase legibility but to give the reader a sense of the style (including orthography and punctuation) of the original. The only exceptions to this rule are the following Venetian and Latin words, which have been Anglicized for ease of reading:

f. filius/filia	son of, daughter of
olim	formerly (often refers to a convert's prebaptismal name)
q. quondam	son of a deceased father (sometimes a patrician)

Personal names as they appear in the sources have not been standardized or Anglicized. Thus, in the following pages the reader will encounter quite a few people named Zuane and Zorzi (rather than Giovanni and Giorgio or John and George), even as many of them hailed from regions far beyond the Venetian empire.

Similarly, place names are given, at first mention, in the form used in the original source. They are followed in parenthesis by the current Anglicized name or, in its absence, the current local name. Subsequent references are in the current form only, as are the place names on the map. Given the tumultuous, plurilinguistic history of the region, and the contested nature of toponyms, the reader is reminded that present-day designations, territorial divisions, and so forth, do not correspond to those distinguished by early modern states and subjects.

The Venetian calendar began on March 1. References in the footnotes maintain the original dates of the documents and, when these differ from the Gregorian calendar, are marked by m.v. (*more veneto*). Thus, February 25, 1599 m.v., corresponds to February 25, 1600, according to the Gregorian calendar. Dates in the body of the text have been updated to follow the Gregorian calendar.

BROKERING EMPIRE

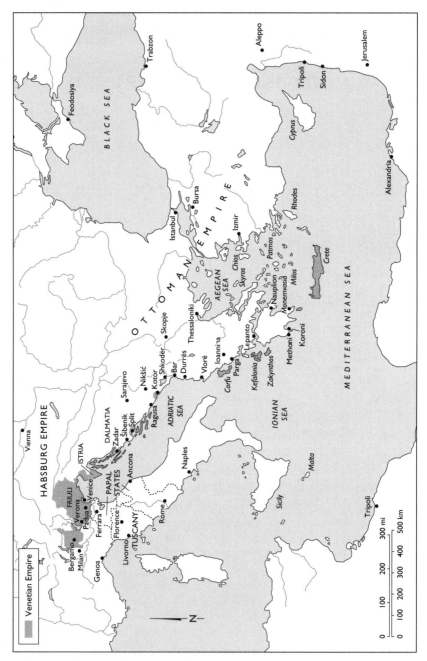

Map of the Mediterranean showing the Venetian Empire, c. 1620

Introduction

"In Venice, all are foreigners who are not Venetians"—such were the caustic words of Cornelio Frangipane (1508–1588) on concluding a visit to the city sometime in the 1550s.[1] A nobleman, a lawyer, and a poet, Frangipane hailed from the Friuli, one of the most economically deprived and war-ravished Venetian colonies, situated on the Venetian-Habsburg-Ottoman frontier.[2] His embittered comments notwithstanding, Frangipane was a staunch supporter of the Venetian cause. A few years earlier, in 1545, he presented an official address upon the election of doge Francesco Donà, in which he "exalted the city of Venice for its balanced form of government, its rule by many, its liberty, tranquillity, and sagacity, and especially its prudence."[3] Indeed, although he was a self-proclaimed foreigner, Frangipane's rigid juxtaposition of "Venetians" and "non-Venetians" actually voiced a metropolitan elite perception of Venetian society itself as serene and cohesive, free of tensions and political strife.

1. "Tutti sono forestieri in Venezia che Veneziani non siano" (Frangipane 1858, 14).
2. As a buffer zone between Venice and its Habsburg and Ottoman neighbors, the Friuli, some 100 miles northeast of the Lagoon, was well known for its impoverished rural populace, and it served as a steady source of labor migrants—especially women—to staff Venetian industries, services, and domestic labor sectors ever since its conquest in 1420. On Friulian working women and men in early modern Venice, see Chojnacka (2001, 87, 91, 95–96).
3. Quoted in Feldman (1995, xx). On Frangipane's work in the broader genre of patriotic panegyrics, see also Muir (1981, 14–17); De Vivo (2007, 21–23). For a biographical sketch, see Cavazza (1998).

Such an image consolidated in that exact same period into an emerging myth of Venice, institutionalized through myriad state projects, including the writings of Venetian patricians and their interlocutors abroad.[4]

A few decades later, another visitor to the Lagoon, Thomas Coryate (c. 1577–1617), an English traveler, painted a rather different picture of Venice. "There," he declared, "you may see many Polonians, Slavonians, Persians, Grecians, Turks, Jewes, Christians of all the famousest regions of Christendome, and each nation distinguished from another by their proper and peculiar habits."[5] Whereas Frangipane lumped all non-Venetians together, Coryate instead emphasized the diversity and multiplicity of clearly demarcated and highly organized "nations" in the Venetian metropolis, each self-conscious of its difference from all others. Coryate's depiction rendered Venice as a welcoming and receptive hub, where subjects hailing from far-flung places did not simply find their place but gave the city its unique character. Frangipane's Venice was a lightning rod for republican unity and civic virtue; Coryate's Venice was a beacon of tolerance in an internally segmented structure. This image of Venice, too, was to have a long afterlife.

Indeed, both Frangipane and Coryate partake in mythic visions of Venetian society and state that informed both their contemporaries and later generations of historians. Frangipane's enigmatic aphorism presents a unified Venetian social body; in contrast, Coryate's suggests multiple, orderly, well-bound, and perduring categories of ethnic belonging. Each author captures one dimension of Venetian mythic self-representation while ignoring the numerous contradictions and ironies inherent in Venetian legal structures—a self-proclaimed republic controlling extensive colonial territories, each with its own layers of accumulated customary law, and a fiercely endogamous patrician oligarchy ruling over polyglot urban and rural populations not only on the Italian mainland but also in the Adriatic, Aegean, and eastern Mediterranean. Neither observer addresses the fraught questions—which had preoccupied jurists for centuries—of who was a Venetian, and whether and

---

4. As James Grubb notes, the myth of Venice identified the glory of the city with its formidable republican institutions and rigid social hierarchies, and was premised on the double notion of "a unified and civic-minded patriciate, guardian of the common good" and "a populace actively involved and fiercely loyal" (1986, 73, 44, 49). Like other aspects of the myth of Venice, the claim of the city to republicanism was promoted as late as the sixteenth and seventeenth centuries to counter its characterization by some political rivals as an oppressive oligarchy. On the myth and its myriad articulations, see Finlay (1999); De Vivo (2004); and, more recently, Fenlon (2008). For a classical discussion of the nature of the Venetian political system and its shifting representations—republican and otherwise—in European political thought, see Bouwsma (1968). See Bowd (2000) for a useful overview of the state of the extensive historiographical debate regarding the myth of Venice in general and Bouwsma's thesis in particular.
5. Coryate (1611, 175–76).

how this status might be inherited and acquired by descent; by birth in the city; or through long residence, loyal service, and the cultivation of civic pride.[6] Moreover, Frangipane's and Coryate's acceptance of a timeless distinction between self-contained "nations," be they Venetian or other, flies in the face of numerous projects that sought to redefine who might belong in the city—and how. Such projects were not the exclusive purview of metropolitan jurists, legislators, and political commentators. Definitions of belonging were shaped through, and in turn helped shape, a range of social actors and institutions in Venice, its colonies, and beyond. It is through the dialectical relationship between such actors and institutions that boundaries around categories of membership were drawn and redrawn.

In this book, I explore the complex networks of alliance and interest, hierarchies of authority, and modes of interaction between the various groups and individuals that helped draw political, religious, and linguistic boundaries in early modern Venice. Such networks engaged—and with time transformed—contemporary patrician notions of social order premised on rigid legal hierarchies, civic unity, and Christian *communitas*—all constituent elements of the fabled myth of Venice as a serene and cohesive society, free of tensions and political strife. In tracing these networks, I underscore how various articulations of belonging and foreignness were engaged by, among others, émigrés from Venetian colonies and borderland regions, redeemed slaves returning from the Ottoman Empire, converts from Islam or Judaism, and merchants and diplomats who regularly traveled across the Venetian-Ottoman frontier. I refer to these social actors collectively as *trans-imperial subjects* and trace their role in several sites in defining *foreign* and *local*, *Muslim* and *Christian*, *Turk* and *Venetian*, *Levantine* and *European*, and *East* and *West* in early modern Venice.[7] Throughout, I capture the ways in which trans-imperial subjects straddled and helped broker linguistic, religious, and geopolitical boundaries across Venetian and Ottoman imperial domains.

CULTURE BROKERS

The figure of the culture broker has long intrigued social theorists. As early as the 1930s, Chicago School sociologists sought to understand the plight of the bicultural marginal man. By the 1950s, anthropologists were optimistic that Latin

---

6. On shifting juridical conceptions of Venetian citizenship, see Kirshner (1973, 1979).
7. Although the term *transnational* has become fashionable, the actors studied in this book and the polities and societies they traversed had very little to do with nations, except in the specific late medieval and early modern sense of diasporic groups of merchants, students, and so forth, whose homogeneity was not pregiven but forged precisely through their mobility. See Ho (2004).

American and African village teachers would be able to mediate the local and national cultures in the (post)colonies. In the 1970s, economists and urban planners were captivated by the phenomenon of middleman minorities, who operated successful small businesses in the otherwise collapsing U.S. inner cities.[8] And since the 1980s, historians have highlighted the complex roles of colonial intermediaries in the fraught dynamics of accommodation between the rulers and the ruled within a host of imperial settings.[9] In each of these cases and others, it was assumed that ethnic minorities had a special predisposition to act as culture brokers. Despite important differences in method and scope, scholars across the humanities and social sciences fixed their gaze on certain intermediary groups because they either enjoyed interregional contacts or could be understood to be "mixed," whether such mixing was understood in terms of race or, by mid-century, culture.[10]

Less teleologically, many scholars now agree that cultural mediation has occurred historically in what Mary Louise Pratt famously termed *contact zones*, defined as "social spaces where disparate cultures meet, clash, and grapple with each other, often in highly asymmetrical relations of domination and subordination."[11] Although Pratt's formulation fruitfully calls attention to the inter-imperial and colonial conditions under which cultural boundary-making has often taken place, it also reinforces a rather partial understanding of these very conditions. Cultures do not simply "meet, clash, and grapple" on their own. Moreover, that two cultures are "disparate" is not a pregiven fact but part of an ongoing process of boundary maintenance that unfolds in specific sites and institutions, through the efforts of precisely those who purport to mediate and bridge them.[12] How trans-imperial subjects acted as intermediaries who articulated difference along such unfolding boundaries is the subject of this book.

The historical study of cultural mediation has been most prominent in the historiography of the New World empires, where it is generally understood to

---

8. For an overview and specific references to theories such as marginal man, middleman minorities, and the ethnography of culture brokers in so-called plural societies, see Rothman (2010).

9. The literature on colonial intermediaries is vast. For some suggestive examples that address both European and other premodern imperial contexts, see Richter (1988); Austen and Derrick (1999); Robinson (2000); Cohen (2003); Jasanoff (2005); Metcalf (2005); Županov (2005); Elson and Covey (2006); Lawrance, Osborn, and Roberts (2006); Raj (2007); Flores (2009).

10. On the process by which interwar social science increasingly substituted *culture* for *race*, see Degler (1991); McKee (1993); Wolf (1994); Jacobson (1998).

11. Pratt (1992, 4).

12. In the famous words of Fredrik Barth, "categorical ethnic distinctions do not depend on absence of mobility, contact and information but do entail social processes of exclusion and incorporation whereby discrete categories are maintained *despite* changing participation and membership in the course of individual life histories … Stable, persisting, and often vitally important social relations are maintained across such boundaries, and are frequently based precisely on the dichotomized ethnic statuses" (1969, 9–10). See also Lamont and Molnár (2002).

have taken place between members of radically different societies and in the context of a dramatic power imbalance. But, as scholars of the Atlantic world increasingly emphasize, New World empires were themselves highly complex and multilayered, shaped in important ways by prior—and ongoing—inter-imperial rivalries in the Old World. It is on the proverbial center of the Old World, the Mediterranean of the sixteenth and seventeenth centuries, that I focus here. By examining the links between shifting notions of East and West, specific groups of trans-imperial subjects, and their institutional settings, genres of writing, and matrices of competing interests, I underscore the role that intermediaries played in fixing the boundaries of the objects they are purported to mediate. Ultimately, I trace to colonization, state formation, and inter-imperial rivalry in the early modern Mediterranean some of the genealogies of our own analytical vocabulary of *in-betweenness, transculturation, diversity,* and *mixedness.*

In focusing on trans-imperial subjects, I have two aims. On a conceptual level, I explore alternative ways for thinking about mediation, against the tendency to presuppose a priori clearly demarcated cultural units. On an empirical level, I "provincialize Europe"—conceptually as well as spatiotemporally—by exploring its articulation in relation to other religious, linguistic, and geopolitical categories (e.g., "Christendom," "Islam," "the Turk," "Franks," and "the Levant") and in specific institutional sites. In developing this frame, I have benefited from the shared epistemological insights of postcolonial critique and Subaltern Studies.[13] Yet, as several scholars have underscored, these critical perspectives risk reaffirming an Occidentalist view of Europe as a preexisting, unproblematic, and coherent fact engaged in a variety of colonial projects elsewhere.[14] In this book, I instead investigate several moments in Europe's becoming, in a region where distinguishing between "Europe" and "non-Europe" was (and is) politically fraught and highly contested.

Since the mid-1980s, interest in early modern cultural mediation has been driven by postcolonial scholars' reassessments of what was once called European discovery, as well as by anthropologists' and historians' interest in the genealogies of modernity and modernization.[15] It is ironic that much of the debate about early modern encounters, although acknowledging its debt to Edward Said's pioneering *Orientalism,* has ignored the *locus classicus* of Orientalism—the Mediterranean—and focused instead on South and East Asia, the Pacific, and, most paradigmatically,

13. Chakrabarty (2000); Dirlik, Bahl, and Gran (2000); Cooper (2005).
14. See, for example, the cogent critiques in Carrier (1995); Coronil (1996); Bracewell (2005); Mishkova (2008).
15. Pioneering works by Caribbean scholars Fernando Ortíz (1995 [1940]) and Eric Williams (1994 [1944]) paved the way for much better-received studies by metropolitan scholars on the cultural dimensions of the colonialism/capitalism nexus in the Americas, including the historical forays of Eric Wolf (1982), Sidney Mintz (1985), and other anthropologists.

the Atlantic.[16] Early studies of interactions between Europeans and indigenous peoples have thus tended to emphasize the brief and circumscribed nature of first encounters, such as raids or exploratory voyages, and the contrasting and (presumably) mutually unintelligible epistemologies of the peoples these encounters brought into contact. Such studies were crucial for exposing the cultural specificity of European practices, denaturalizing what earlier generations of scholars often took to be a universal rationalism.[17] Yet the formulation of a sharp, preexisting, and absolute dichotomy between "European" and "non-European" epistemologies came at a cost. Empirically, the centrality of the Mediterranean as a template for early modern discourses of cultural difference has been relatively ignored.[18] Conceptually, this dichotomy cannot account for the sustained nature of most colonial engagements and for the role of intermediaries in calibrating and recalibrating the boundaries of the very units they claimed to mediate. Indeed, the very adoption of the vocabulary of *hybridity, indigeneity,* and *syncretism* to describe cultural engagement has laced some postcolonial historiography with its own variety of cultural essentialism, implying that prior to any given encounter cultures were somehow homogenous, historically stable, and self-contained.

More recently, scholars have placed greater emphasis on the multifaceted, ongoing, and reciprocal nature of cultural mediation in early modern empires.[19] Still the process by which the intermediaries themselves articulate imperial categories of difference is only rarely thematized. Indeed, a growing tendency among scholars of mediation is to accept intermediaries' claims to be "in-between" at face value rather than to interrogate that very claim as itself a rhetorical move, part of the process of mediation.[20] In paying closer attention to the perspective and practices of intermediaries themselves, I cautiously follow Georg Simmel's definition

---

16. Margaret Hodgen's (1964) pathbreaking survey of early modern anthropology has little to say about European engagements with the Ottoman Empire, its people and institutions. Later discussions of early articulations of alterity similarly leave out the Mediterranean as a space of encounter. See Hodgen (1964); Todorov (1984); Bitterli (1989); Taussig (1986); Trouillot (1991); Schwartz (1994).

17. Gerbi (1985); de Certeau (1986); White (1991); Gilroy (1993); Mignolo (1995); Sahlins (1995); Seed (1995); Trouillot (1995).

18. For a discussion of how sustained interactions affected Renaissance travel literature on the Levant and mitigated the alterity of the region through the notion of "familiarity," see Tinguely (2000, 13–14). For compelling perspectives on the place of the Mediterranean in early modern semiotics of difference, see Rubiés (2000, 251–307); Fuchs (2001, 2006).

19. Wolf (1982); Greenblatt (1991); White (1991); Abercrombie (1998); Dubois (2004); Pardo (2004); Silverblatt (2004); MacCormack (2007); Raj (2007); Flood (2009).

20. See, for example, the Re:Enlightenment Project statement, which defines *mediation* as "everything that intervenes, enables, supplements, or is simply in-between" (www.reenlightenment .org/reenlightenment-project-new-york-university-and-new-york-public-library). For a cogent critique of the spatial metaphor *in-between* as an apt description of the positionality of intermediaries and a suggestive genealogy thereof, see Tymoczko (2003).

of the *stranger* as "a member of the group itself, an element whose membership within the group involves being outside it and confronting it," while taking exception to the notion that the boundaries of any group are fixed and pregiven.[21] Indeed, rather than presupposing that trans-imperial subjects were positioned "in-between" a priori distinct societies, I prefer to focus on how trans-imperial subjects operated as members of multiple social formations and on how in their sustained interactions across linguistic, religious, and political lines they helped shape—and were in turn shaped by—shifting imperial boundaries.

A MULTICULTURAL MEDITERRANEAN?

The recent interest in cultural mediation in the Mediterranean is due in part to Peregrine Horden and Nicholas Purcell's magisterial *The Corrupting Sea*, which characterizes the Mediterranean as a "mediator and boundary, [a] zone of transition and agent of comparison and differentiation."[22] The debate sparked by *The Corrupting Sea* has productively refocused on the shared elements and continuity between the different imperial formations of the region while insisting on its highly fragmented nature, thus making it hard to speak of a unified all-encompassing cultural frontier.[23] Ever since Fernand Braudel's classic *The Mediterranean and the Mediterranean World in the Age of Philip II*, first published in 1949, tropes of contact, circulation, and exchange have retained their popularity among Mediterranean historians. Yet Mediterranean historiography has rarely addressed the intermediaries themselves. To the extent that they have been noticed at all, intermediaries have been celebrated primarily for importing a set of rarefied intellectual or artistic objects (texts, artworks, styles, and techniques) from East to West. More recent scholarship, although rich in formal analysis, still tends to focus on specific canonical artwork and to bracket the interactive aspects of all mediation, ultimately producing more or less mechanistic accounts of artistic, intellectual, economic, or technological influence as the brainchild of individual genius.[24] On the whole, these forays into questions of Mediterranean cultural mediation have yet to integrate more fully either Ottoman or nonelite semiotic practices into a broader system of relations.

The growing interest in Mediterranean cultural mediation has stimulated a reappraisal of the role of colonial ventures in the emergence of late medieval and

---

21. Simmel (1971, 144). Compare Pym (1998, esp. 184–85).
22. Horden and Purcell (2000, 460).
23. Horden and Purcell (2000, 25). This debate has fruitfully involved not only early modernists but classicists and anthropologists as well. For a sampling of their various positions, see Marino (2002); Purcell (2003); Harris (2005); Brummett (2007a).
24. For a critique of this model of unidirectional importation of passive objects from East to West, see Grabar (2003).

early modern Italian regional states. Here, too, a strong division of labor still obtains between the study of metropolitan political history, with some gestures to the important territorial dimensions of such polities, and the study of Italianate Mediterranean empires, including the Genoese, Pisan, and, of course, Venetian. To be sure, the economic, military, diplomatic, and administrative histories of specific colonies have been mapped out in great detail, particularly for the Crusades period and its aftermath.[25] But medieval and, even more so, early modern Mediterranean history is still often written as case studies of specific colonies, in which metropolitan society, if it figures at all, is but a distant force.[26] This compartmentalization has much to do with the more recent past of the region, where dozens of nation states have sought to resurrect "their" histories. As Benjamin Arbel notes, the long neglect of Mediterranean colonial history may also have much to do with the fascist legacy of Italy.[27] Perhaps as a reaction to the unabashedly imperialist Italian scholarship of the interwar period, the history of Italian colonialism was avoided for many decades and has only recently received more critical attention.[28] Be that as it may, a more integrative account of the place of the Mediterranean colonies within the early modern processes of state formation is yet to be written.[29]

Colonial projects shaped Mediterranean metropolitan societies in fundamental ways. Not only did conquest place Catholic colonizers in control of sizable Eastern Christian, Jewish, and Muslim populations, but it also brought them into direct and sustained engagement with Mamluk, Ottoman, and other Islamicate societies, whose methods of managing religious and ethnolinguistic differences diverged significantly from those of Catholic Christendom.[30] Before their Atlantic counterparts, then, the medieval and early modern Mediterranean colonies served as important laboratories for the elaboration of ethnic difference.[31]

25. References to works on specific colonies are scattered throughout this book. See also the specific contributions in Fernández-Armesto (1987); Balard (1989); Abulafia (1993); Balard and Ducellier (2002); Vatin and Veinstein (2004); Fourrier and Grivaud (2006).
26. A notable exception is the pioneering lifework of the Freddy Thiriet (1921–1986), French Byzantinist, on the medieval Venetian maritime empire. For other integrative studies, see Balard (1978); Arbel (1996); and, more recently, O'Connell (2009).
27. Arbel (2004). See also Gourdin (2004) for a recent critique of the Eurocentric thrust of much scholarship on early modern colonization in North Africa.
28. Pergher (2007) and the bibliography therein.
29. Even as late as 1996, Kirshner's comprehensive historiographical collection of essays on *The Origins of the State in Italy, 1300–1600*, authored by leading Italian and U.S. scholars in the field, left out entirely the role of Mediterranean colonies in the rise of the state.
30. Kunt (1974); Goffman (1994); Shuval (2000); Kafadar (2007); Barkey (2008); Peirce (2010).
31. Thiriet (1959, 258); Fernández-Armesto (1987); Arbel (1989b, 1995b); Karapidakis (1992); Georgopoulou (1996); McKee (2000); O'Connell (2004); Epstein (2006). The idea is implicit already in the pioneering work of Charles Verlinden (1954, 1970), although not theorized as such.

Our growing appreciation of the sustained encounters in the medieval and early modern Mediterranean in general, and of the significant continuities between Venetian and Ottoman colonial regimes in particular, raises new questions about how relations between the two empires shaped Venetian society. Following Braudel's lead, economic historians were among the first to explore the complexity of Venetian-Ottoman engagements and to emphasize the centrality of Venice in the trade system of the eastern Mediterranean.[32] Although Braudel and his followers have sometimes been accused of cutting off Venice too sharply from transalpine Europe, other forms of insularity have plagued Venetian historiography with even greater consequences. Until fairly recently, historians of Venetian society and culture have focused on the city proper to the almost complete neglect not only of its Mediterranean colonies but of its Italian hinterland as well.[33] This metropolitan focus was guided by historiographical fashions that privileged the study of urban economies over rural ones. It was also prompted by the lingering effects of the republican myth of Venice, which identified the glory of the city with its formidable civic institutions and rigid social hierarchies.[34] This neglect went hand in hand with a periodization that emphasized the geopolitical alignment of the city with transalpine Europe as early as the fourteenth and fifteenth centuries.[35] Although acknowledging cultural and institutional continuities with Byzantium, standard histories of Venice well into the 1980s still implicitly took the lagoon city to have always been part of a self-conscious West, a front line against a threatening, alien East.[36] Such narratives, which presupposed the Catholicism and Europeanness of Venice, have made its wavering alliances with Rome and Istanbul, as well as its well-documented Lutheran sympathies, into historiographical "problems" that begged explanation.

32. See especially Tucci (1957); Luzzatto (1995 [1961]); Lane (1973); Ashtor (1983); Arbel (1995a); Jacoby (1997). For a sustained, critical elaboration of Braudel's notion of Mediterranean unity, see Horden and Purcell (2000).
33. Even a recent general survey of Venetian history, while decrying the insularity of Venetian historiography and aiming to "explain Venice on the basis of the places where it became Venice," devotes only four pages specifically to the Venetian overseas empire (Crouzet-Pavan 2002, xi (quotation), 9, 86–89). For a historiographical reflection on the relationship between metropolitan Venice and its mainland territories, see Casini (2002). For an earlier emphasis on the imperial dimensions of Venetian statecraft, and their significance for the power and endurance of the myth of Venice, see Mallett and Hale (1984, esp. 212). For a recent integrative study of Venice and its hinterlands in one analytical frame, see Appuhn (2009).
34. Cochrane and Kirshner (1975); Grubb (1986, esp. 73); Martin and Romano (2000).
35. Lane (1973); Muir (1981, 24).
36. The examples are too numerous to cite here and, in general, reproduce some version of the "clash of civilizations" narrative. See, for example, Fondazione "Giorgio Cini" (1971, 86).

How does the picture change by revisiting the relationship of Venice with both Byzantium and transalpine Europe? A growing consensus among historians, art historians, and historical geographers suggests that it was not until the seventeenth (and some argue, the eighteenth) century that Venice took its final, decisive "turn westward." Several arguments have been marshaled to support this view: Venice's lingering attachment to and affinities with Byzantium[37] and its keen interest in the aesthetic and intellectual traditions of medieval Islam;[38] the notoriously undecided political and military stance of Venice toward the Ottoman Empire;[39] the permeability of religious and social boundaries between Venetian and Ottoman colonial subjects;[40] and Venetian merchants' involvement in kinship and commercial networks that extended throughout the eastern Mediterranean.[41] Of great significance here is also the recent recognition of the Ottoman centrality to sixteenth-century European intellectual and artistic life.[42] Even a cursory look at mid-sixteenth-century Venetian political theory reveals the extent to which Ottoman statecraft—as perceived through the mediation of Venetian ambassadors' reports and humanists' historiographical writings—was at the heart of debates about military organization and recruitment, civil bureaucracy, and fiscality.[43]

Recent scholarship has also underscored how embedded the early modern Ottoman state was in inter-imperial systems. Rather than simply comparing early modern Ottoman and Western European states as if these were self-contained civilizations, Ottomanists now emphasize connectivity and convergence, and seek to understand how intensive and ongoing engagements with members of other societies (and of differentially situated members within Ottoman society) shaped emerging cultural categories of difference and sameness.[44]

This analytical shift has wide-reaching implications for the study of mediation in the early modern Mediterranean. The Ottoman Empire can no longer be treated as an external force or at best as a marginal appendage to the grand narrative of European history. Nor can it be considered as a fixed, looming Other, whose outsider status was unmitigated and unchanging. Such a historiographical shift

---

37. Mueller (1972, 76); Romano (1987, 91); Nicol (1988); Brown (1996); Georgopoulou (2001).
38. Howard (2000); Pastore (2003, esp. 94–96).
39. Preto (1975); Libby (1978); Goffman (2002).
40. Bracewell (1992); Housley (1996); Greene (2000).
41. Kafadar (1986); Arbel (1995a); Imhaus (1997); McKee (2000); Dursteler (2006).
42. Jardine and Brotton (2000); Mack (2002); MacLean (2005).
43. Libby (1978, 111); Valensi (1993); Meserve (2008). On Venetian military recruitment and organization modeled on contemporary Ottoman practices, see also Mallett and Hale (1984, esp. 50).
44. Necipoğlu (1989); Kafadar (1996); Berktay (1998); Goffman (2002); Imber, Kiyotaki, and Murphey (2005); Barkey (2008). See also Subrahmanyam (1997, 2007).

compels us to redraw the boundaries of our units of analysis. It suggests that the comparative study of the Ottoman Empire and other early modern polities should be supplemented by transregional studies that can take into account the actual movements across boundaries of both people and signifying practices.[45] Integrating the Ottoman Empire into narratives of the early modern Mediterranean further requires a move beyond the paradigm of influence in conceptualizing the relationship between cosmographies and cultural practices that both defined and defied political borders.[46]

TRANS-IMPERIAL SUBJECTS

The prevailing image of Venetian society as composed of "three orders of inhabitants," namely patricians, citizens, and plebeians, dates to the sixteenth century. Myth-making Venetian elites themselves created this rigidly oversimplified model.[47] Like Frangipane and Coryate, this decidedly Veneto-centric model also defined different juridical and social categories in relation to a presumably stable metropolitan self. Such a vision ignores the many colonial subjects who sojourned in Venice, and whose status in the city was mediated by competing hierarchies of wealth, gender, age, and juridical standing. It also glosses over the dramatic changes over time in the qualities, requirements, and privileges associated with being Venetian.[48] Most important, it is Veneto-centric in positing the city as a telos, as a point of (purposeful) arrival, when in fact for many it was one of several points of reference in complex life trajectories that straddled numerous locales, often across empires. To capture the inherent physical mobility and sociolegal ambiguity of such sojourners and their strategies in negotiating their multiple roles, I explore here how trans-imperial subjects straddled linguistic, religious, and political boundaries and, in the process, helped calibrate distinct categories of difference.

But what, exactly, are trans-imperial subjects? To better understand the concept, it is worth looking at each of its components in turn. The prefix *trans-* refers to the ways in which subjects regularly mobilized their roots "elsewhere" to foreground specific knowledge, privileges, or commitments to further their current

45. For a general introduction to the conceptual and methodological aims of braided histories and histoire croisée, see Davis (2001) and Zimmerman (2008), respectively.
46. See, for example, Algazi (1997, 2005).
47. Cochrane and Kirshner (1975); Pullan (1999); Raines (2006).
48. Put simply, Venice was for many centuries a Byzantine colony, an outpost in the westernmost fringes of the Eastern Empire. Only gradually and retroactively did the mythographers of the city come to celebrate it as independent from birth and as quintessentially republican.

interests. *Trans-* further denotes the dispersion of kin and patronage ties across imperial frontiers, characteristic of many socially mobile families in the early modern Mediterranean, as well as individuals' dual residence and/or extended sojourns in multiple locales.[49]

Following recent work in this field, *imperial* here points to the production and management of alterity as essential to early modern imperial regimes.[50] *Imperial* also serves as a reminder of the claim made by several early modern sovereigns—not least of whom was Ottoman Sultan Süleyman the Lawgiver—to universal God-sanctioned rule. The term thus highlights the significance of religious authority for legitimizing temporal power and for cementing lines of presumed political attachment and loyalty. In the context of the ongoing rivalry between the two Mediterranean claimants to universal empire, the Habsburgs and the Ottomans, confessional affiliation became a key criterion of imperial classification, asserted with renewed vigor in the late sixteenth and seventeenth centuries.[51] Thus, imperial subjecthood increasingly came to imply certain religious as well as political bonds, potentially at odds with individuals' actual juridical status. For example, for Ottoman Catholic subjects sojourning in Venice the perceived misalignment (from a Venetian perspective) between their political subjecthood and their confessional identity could provide ample grounds for insisting on their loyalty to the Venetian (Catholic) cause.

Finally, the term *subjects* evokes questions of subject position and subject-making, which have been at the heart of myriad imperial projects. The choice of "subjects" here, as opposed to "persons," "selves," or "individuals" is not accidental. It points to the entwining of confessional and juridical affiliation in early modern constructions of subjecthood, and turns us away from a notion of autonomous individual self-fashioning outside of sociohistorical constraints. Further, attending to subjects rather than citizens is meant as a critique of a still-current historiographical teleology that seeks the precursors of modern citizenship in the early modern republican city states (of which Venice serves as a cherished prototype). The focus on subjects allows us to recognize the strong imperial (alongside oligarchic and republican) dimensions of Venetian governmentality, and the ways in which decidedly colonial institutions, spaces, and genres constituted specific subject positions. It was precisely in this context that trans-imperial subjects *qua*

49. For a case study illustrating the strategic dispersion of family members across the Venetian-Ottoman frontier, see Wright (2006). For a general discussion of strategies of mobility and employment across political boundaries in the early modern Mediterranean, see Greene (2007).
50. Subrahmanyam (1997); Muldoon (1999); Barkey (2008).
51. On the aspirations to universal empire in the context of early modern Mediterranean imperial rivalry, see Necipoğlu (1989); Fleischer (1992); Ágoston (2007); Turan (2007); Krstić (2009). For examples of the strategic use of religion as an argument for juridical reclassification by various trans-imperial subjects, see Greene (2002, 2007); Fleming (2007). See also chapter 6.

Venetian and Ottoman subjects played a vital role in shaping lasting juridical and ethnolinguistic categories.

The concept of trans-imperial subjects thus underscores the need to understand the perspective of those who were caught in the web of complex imperial mechanisms but who at the same time were essential to producing the means to calibrate, classify, and demarcate imperial alterities. In particular, it calls attention to how these subjects articulated the actual location of sociocultural boundaries, the prototypical centers of different categories, and the meaning of their own "in-betweenness." In other words, rather than take the categories that subjects purported to mediate as an analytical a priori, the concept of trans-imperial subjects allows us to explore how these subjects themselves elaborated and naturalized certain key categories (e.g., "Christendom," "Islam," "the Turk," "Franks," and "the Levant") and their boundaries. And, rather than anachronistically celebrate the early modern Mediterranean as a site of multiculturalism, the focus on trans-imperial subjects enables us to consider how both consciousness of alterity and the technologies for regulating it played out in the context of rivalry and tacit collaboration between Ottomans and Venetians.[52]

The concept of trans-imperial subjects also serves to remind us of the often forgotten degree of institutional overlap between the imperial domains these subjects straddled. For example, certain notions of membership and belonging that trans-imperial subjects helped shape in early modern Venice paralleled in important ways contemporary Ottoman understandings of how a foreigner could be transformed into a subject through extended residence, local marriage, and religious conversion.[53] Such correspondences demand that closer attention be paid to the politics of comparison inherent in the claims that trans-imperial subjects made about the commensurability (or incommensurability) of political systems and social practices.[54]

Seen in this light, the much-celebrated multicultural Mediterranean begins to look like an early modern "native category," albeit by another name.[55] A multiplicity of languages, customs, and religions has been a long-standing trope in representation and self-representation of Mediterranean societies, indeed, in the very essentialization of Mediterraneanness.[56] It is evident—as in Coryate's pithy description with which I began—in a range of early modern genres, including

52. On the Ottoman and Habsburg empires as composite monarchies, see Adanir (2003); Goffman and Stroop (2004); Subrahmanyam (2006). On diversity in the Mediterranean, see Horden and Purcell (2000, esp. 396–400).
53. For a discussion of these processes and the changing vocabulary developed by Ottoman statecraft for dealing with foreigners, see Goffman (2007, 63–65).
54. On imperialism and the politics of comparison, see Stoler (2001).
55. Goffman (1990); Greene (2000); Hoerder, Harzig, and Shubert (2003); Vitkus (2003); Dursteler (2006); Husain and Fleming (2007).
56. One of the earliest modern scholars to propose the Mediterranean as a coherent field of historical inquiry, George Sarton (1936), focused precisely on its supposed "unity in diversity."

travel narratives, costume albums, cartographic compendia, missionary and diplomatic reports, and bilingual dictionaries.[57] Such genres, intended for publics both
at home and abroad, affirmed multiplicity both within and across empires.

As this list of genres suggests, conceptions of borders and boundaries developed not only on the geopolitical frontier. Administrators and travelers played an
important role in bringing metropolitan discourses of governmentality to the borderlands, but they also promoted the circulation of texts, objects, and people that
ensured the material presence of the borderlands in the metropole. Coryate's description of ethnic multiplicity in Venice is echoed in a recent review of Venetian
historiography, which suggests that Venice is now often celebrated as a "multicultural metropolis," where "diverse ethnic subcultures of Greeks, Germans, Jews,
Turks, and Armenians liv[ed] in relative harmony."[58]

I posit the Venetian metropole not as a beacon of multicultural tolerance but
as a node in a much broader trans-imperial field of power. From this perspective, the city of Venice cannot be detached from the larger region in which early
modern categories of difference were formed and transformed, and which spanned
Venetian and Ottoman, colonial and metropolitan territories alike. By situating
trans-imperial subjects in this field of power, I call attention to the enduring relevance of both for any analysis of early modern processes of cultural boundary-
making.

In focusing on trans-imperial subjects, it is obviously not my intention to suggest that subjects whom I define as trans-imperial were somehow conscious of
such a category, let alone of their membership therein. Nor do I wish to privilege
any particular subjects—colonial, metropolitan, or trans-imperial—as possessors
of a priori knowledge of the Venetian-Ottoman field as a whole. On the contrary, I see the productive role of trans-imperial subjects precisely in their ongoing
engagement with multiple institutions and perspectives. Trans-imperial subjects
played a vital role as imperial boundary-markers. *Markers* here is to be understood
in both its senses: as agentive subjects who (re)established boundaries through
their practices and as objects used by others to assert their respective domains of
authority. Indeed, trans-imperial subjects both participated actively in the calibration of certain concepts and were embedded in structures, institutions, and genres
that constrained their action and gave it shape. As I suggest in the following pages,

57. See, especially, Wilson (2005, 2007). Consciousness of this sort was not a unique development of
the early modern period, of course, yet its coupling with particular imperial regimes of subject-making
is significant. These arguments are postulated suggestively, but briefly, in Subrahmanyam (1997).
58. Martin and Romano (2000, 8).

viewing early modern empires from the emergent perspectives of those crossing and transgressing imperial lines is analytically productive—but not because imperial centers were necessarily weak or inchoate. Rather, their articulation and consolidation depended precisely on the semiotic labor of those who moved across them, whether physically or vicariously, through texts.

Trans-imperial subjects made repeated claims to knowledge and membership of an elsewhere. Yet, for their claims to be heard, they already had to possess knowledge of and exercise some form of membership in Venetian metropolitan institutions. It was this unique position that allowed them to perform mediation in the first place. But the concept of trans-imperial subjects raises further questions. To the extent that such subjects operated within complex and shifting political and sociocultural contexts, how were their trajectories and categories constitutive of broader discourses about place, subjecthood, and social membership? How do their performances of mediation challenge not only a bifurcated vision of metropole and colony, self and other, but the very mapping of social position onto space? Venice and Istanbul, two important nodes of early modern diplomacy and trade, can be understood only as nestled in wider networks of kinship and religious ties, as well as circulating texts, people, and commodities, through which categories of inclusion and exclusion were formed and transformed. That trans-imperial subjects were central to processes of boundary-making in the early modern Mediterranean underscores the extent to which systems of meaning-making in the region interpenetrated and overlapped over their long histories. Understanding the specific trans-imperial trajectories of early modern mediation thus helps document the emergence and consolidation of boundaries that became so natural over time that their very historicity is sometimes forgotten.

Studying the relationship between early modern trans-imperial subjecthood and emergent, localized forms of imperial classification and boundary-making, from the bottom up requires attending to the complex and often conflicting objectives of trans-imperial subjects themselves. To this end, I divide the book into four thematic parts: the first three each charts the trajectory of a specific trans-imperial group (commercial brokers; religious converts; and dragomans, diplomatic interpreters) and the fourth addresses their multiple interactions. Throughout the book, I trace how trans-imperial subjects participated in specific Venetian institutions, thereby helping to articulate competing claims about what is "East" and what is "West" and how to tell them apart. I examine not only the elaboration of cultural categories but the ways in which people occupied distinct institutional roles between two imperial centers, how they practiced civic membership and localness.

SPACES OF ENCOUNTER

Recent developments in early modern historiography have allowed scholars to refocus on oral face-to-face interactions and the written genres associated with them as prime sites of knowledge production and sociopolitical contestation. Once relegated to the status of popular curiosities—the proper domain of folklorists and antiquarians—gossip, rumor, petitions and supplications, unauthorized (and often unattributable) copies of official documents, pamphlets, and broadsheets are now receiving careful attention from historians interested in the rich social texture of political interaction. These historians have shown that speech and its control were central to how early modern knowledge regimes operated, to how power was consolidated and contested.[59] Debates about the origins of modern publics have benefitted from studies of associational life in early modern Italy, which have emphasized gathering places, such as the piazza, or main thoroughfare, as sites of interaction for people of different estates, through which notions of belonging and foreignness were negotiated (see the frontispiece). As Christopher Black notes, Tomasso Garzoni's *Piazza Universale* (1585), with its listings of all possible occupations and gradations of social status, is emblematic of this growing recognition of space as constitutive of new kinds of public.[60] The chapters of the present book build on this rich scholarship on the relationship between emerging publics and the early modern state.[61] Taking my cue especially from recent studies of the interface between orality and literacy, I consider market squares and the halls of government as crucial sites of sociopolitical interaction in Venice, Istanbul, and their extensive borderlands.[62] In focusing on these paradigmatic spaces of encounter, I am able to see how multiple interactions among transimperial subjects, local elites, and Venetian and Ottoman state institutions did not simply reflect the preexisting classificatory systems of officialdom but played an active role in shaping these very systems and their hegemonic categories.

Explicitly public spaces of encounter are of key significance for this study, but so too are homes and other sites that have retroactively been classified as private. Studies of modern empire have shown that imperial subjecthood was characterized by the importance of the intimate as "a social and cultural space where racial classifications were defined and defied, and where relations between colonizer and colonized could powerfully confound or confirm the strictures of governance

---

59. Davis (1987); Cristellon (2003).
60. Black (2001, 79).
61. On early modern urban public space, see, for example, Ingersoll (1985); Davis (1994); Trexler (1994); Chittolini (1995).
62. See, especially, De Vivo (2007); Horodowich (2008); Ghobrial (2010).

and the categories of rule."[63] Early modern households were similarly central for the articulation of categories of difference, albeit with other valences. This is especially true of certain kinds of composite, "patrimonial households" that combined domestic and bureaucratic functions, and often brought into regular contact members of different social groups, conjoined in a hierarchical structure.

In addition to marketplaces, courtrooms, and the halls of government, I highlight the importance of composite households as spaces of encounter in their own right. Composite households brought into sustained interactions a variety of subjects across juridical, ethnolinguistic, religious, gender, and age divides, thus producing the intimate ties on which trans-imperial networks often relied. The Venetian diplomatic and commercial spheres illustrate this point. They were among the primary sites where trans-imperial subjects interacted with one another, with Venetian and Ottoman metropolitan elites, and with a broad cross-section of the populations of the two empires. The commercial sphere encompassed—and was constituted through—residential homes, their attics and kitchens, as much as through city squares and markets. Similarly, the household of the Venetian bailo (or resident consul) in Istanbul functioned not only as a node for the circulation of political information but also as the place of residence and primary socialization for a diverse group of boys and men, including both Venetian citizens and colonial and Ottoman subjects.[64]

In this book, I thus consider how interactions between trans-imperial subjects and Venetian and Ottoman elites coalesced around spaces that could serve simultaneously for both domestic and public social functions, such as embassy compounds, brokers' households, patrician palaces, the "Turkish" Exchange House, and the Holy House of Catechumens. In thinking about such sites of interaction between trans-imperial subjects and their interlocutors, it is essential to recognize that households were not understood by their members as inherently private. As feminist critics have argued, the notion of separate public and private spheres fails to explain the historical complexity and variety of understandings of both categories, particularly before the nineteenth century.[65] Rather than as fixed properties of certain sites or practices, public and private may better be understood as relative positions reproduced recursively across a continuum of sites.[66]

---

63. Stoler (2001, 831). See also Taylor (1992); McClintock (1995); Chatterjee (1999); White (2000).
64. The bailo was the resident Venetian commercial representative in the Byzantine (and later Ottoman) Empire and the consul of the Venetian merchants residing there. In practice, he often functioned as Venetian ambassador to the Porte. On the bailo and his household, see Bertelè (1932); Dursteler (2006).
65. Davidoff and Hall (1987); Fraser (1991); Vickery (1998).
66. Gal (2002). *Recursivity* is the ongoing "projection of opposition, salient at some level of relationship, onto some other level." Irvine and Gal (2000, 38). See also Gal and Irvine (1995, 974).

By going beyond representations and juridical definitions of *citizenship* and *subjecthood* to study how people inhabited different roles spatially and temporally, I underscore the extensive interaction and interdependence between Venetian and Ottoman societies. By attending to the domestic arrangements of trans-imperial subjects, I show how central the household actually was to the contestation and transformation of early modern notions of foreignness. Patrician officialdom (and many modern economic historians) understood commercial brokers as agents of the state, operating in an anonymous marketplace composed of discrete actors. Challenging such an understanding, in the first part of the book I explore how trans-imperial brokers and their clients often acted in concert, forging ties across linguistic, religious, and political boundaries. Similarly in part II, I show how religious conversion, often understood by historians as a process of profound transformation of the self and as the utmost expression of modern individuality, operated rather as a highly public form of juridical subject-making in early modern Venice, elaborated by specific institutions that produced converts as social types. In part III, I attend to the making of a cadre of Venetian diplomatic interpreters in both Istanbul and Venice and underscore the extent to which political loyalty depended on the channeling of affect in the domestic sphere. Finally, in part IV, I consider several key moments in the institutionalization of Ottoman difference in seventeenth-century Venice. By paying close attention to specific interactions among commercial brokers, converts, interpreters, and the Venetian Board of Trade over the taxation of Ottoman merchants and their confinement to a particular institutional home, I suggest how linguistic (in)competence became a marker of foreignness and what this tells us about shifting conceptions of difference and sameness across a broad political, confessional, and ethnolinguistic spectrum that encompassed Venetian, Ottoman, and even Safavid territories and subjects.

SCOPE, CHRONOLOGY, AND GENRES OF DOCUMENTATION

In an effort to understand how trans-imperial subjects inhabited composite households and moved across them, I examine here a watershed period in the history of the Mediterranean, roughly the century from the Battle of Lepanto in 1571 to the end of the War of Crete in 1669. Traditionally, Venetian historiography has focused overwhelmingly on the fifteenth and early sixteenth centuries, an era that was seen as the heyday of Venetian political institution-building as well as an artistic Renaissance.[67] In this framework, the Battle of Agnadello

67. Typical in this regard is Frederic Lane's magisterial *Venice, a Maritime Republic*, first published in 1973 and still viewed by many as the most comprehensive synthesis of Venetian history. Although not strictly chronological, Lane's narrative essentially ends in the 1580s. His discussion

(1509) in which the League of Cambrai dealt a decisive blow to Venetian forces and occupied—for a short period only—large parts of the Venetian mainland empire, was often noted as a defining turning point in Venetian history.[68] The reconsolidation of Venetian rule on the Terraferma in the wake of the War of the League of Cambrai spelled a radical transformation of the Venetian patriciate, its refashioning as landed aristocracy and withdrawal from its previous point of pride, the Levant trade. Agnadello also signaled for many the imminent decline of Venice, leading to the initial articulations of the myth of Venice as a more-or-less conscious ideological response by Venetian political and intellectual elites.[69] An eerily parallel periodization long dominated Ottoman historiography, in which the death of Sultan Süleyman the Lawgiver (the Magnificent) in 1566 conveniently marked the passing of the glorious classical age of the empire.[70]

The reigning interpretation of the second half of the sixteenth century as the starting point of the imminent decline and fall of both the Venetian and Ottoman empires authorized a prolonged historiographical neglect of the seventeenth century. More recently, however, historians have revisited the seventeenth century to reassert Venetian centrality in the forging of an emerging European public.[71] New scholarship also suggests that early modern Ottoman society was not (as previously held) fundamentally insular, regressive, or too preoccupied with its Safavid opponents to the east to concern itself with its neighbors to the west. Rather, the very emergence of an Ottoman classical synthesis during the long reign of Sultan Süleyman (1520–1566) is now attributed to an intense engagement by a range of Ottoman elites with a variety of Hellenistic, Byzantine, humanist, and Tridentine intellectual traditions, which were essential to the empire's transformations in the

---

of the seventeenth, eighteenth, nineteenth, and twentieth centuries focuses almost exclusively on changing banking and shipping methods. Combined, the chapters in which these four centuries are addressed (among other periods) take up only one-quarter of the volume. Another major synthesis, David Chambers's *The Imperial Age of Venice* (1970), is explicitly limited to the two centuries from 1380 to 1580, so that the loss of Cyprus serves as a synecdoche for the end of the Venetian Empire as a whole. For a critique of the "decline and fall" paradigm in Venetian historiography implicit in these and many other works, see Cochrane and Kirshner (1975).

68. After invading the mainland territory of Venice, the forces of the League of Cambrai defeated the Venetian forces near Agnadello on May 14, 1509. This prompted the temporary loss of virtually all Venetian possessions on the Italian peninsula and led to continued warfare in the Venetian and Milanese hinterlands throughout the next decade.

69. The economic crisis, from which Venice never fully recovered, was due, according to that school of history, to its inability to compete effectively with the Portuguese in the Asian spice trade and to the "betrayal" of the patriciate, which transferred its investment from trade to agricultural enterprise on the mainland. For a critique, see Grubb (1986, esp. 62–63).

70. For a useful review of the literature, see Inalcık and Kafadar (1993); Peirce (2004); Woodhead (2008). See also Tezcan (2009) for a different grounding of the prevailing periodization.

71. On the importance of Venice to the emergence of Europe-wide publics, see, among others, Infelise (1997, 2001, 2002); Wolff (1997); Muir (2007); De Vivo (2007); Horodowich (2008).

decades following its defeat of the Mamluk Sultanate in 1516–17 and subsequent incorporation of Syria, Egypt, and the Hejaz.[72]

As a result, the later sixteenth and seventeenth centuries have begun to receive much greater historiographical attention. The Battle of Lepanto in 1571, in which the Holy League (the papacy, Spain, and Venice) defeated Ottoman naval forces, is now studied less for its military and more for its ideological repercussions. In particular, historians emphasize the crystallization of a myth of Catholic unity against a common Muslim foe.[73] After Lepanto, the Ottomans were no longer seen by their European rivals as invincible.[74] Nor, for its part, could Venice claim to be the main European power in the Mediterranean. Economic historians also emphasize both the (short-lived) rejuvenation of Venetian-Ottoman trade in the second half of the sixteenth century and the important transformation of these trade relations in the wake of new competition from the merchant companies of the northern seaboard powers, including the English, Dutch, and French.[75]

By focusing on the late sixteenth and seventeenth centuries, this book thus contributes to a reassessment of Venetian-Ottoman relations in a broad Mediterranean context. Although delimited by two wars, the century from the Battle of Lepanto to the end of the War of Crete was in fact marked by sustained Venetian-Ottoman political and economic negotiation, aided by the development of new diplomatic institutions. In addition to the Battle of Lepanto, 1571 also saw the incorporation of Cyprus, formerly a Venetian colony, into the Ottoman state. Almost a century later, in 1669, another important Venetian colony, Crete, also fell under Ottoman rule after a protracted twenty-five-year war.[76] These conquests led to an influx of colonial émigrés to the Venetian and the Ottoman metropoles and introduced new trans-imperial actors into both the commercial and the diplomatic spheres. In the century after Lepanto, ultimately failed efforts

72. On the expansion of Ottoman cultural horizons during Süleyman's reign and in the post-Süleymanic period, see Fleischer (1986); Aksan (1995); Dankoff (2004); Hagen (2004); Casale (2010); Krstić (2011). See also Peirce (2004, 22) and the bibliography therein.
73. On the political and military repercussions of Lepanto, see Hess (1972). On some of its ideological dimensions, see Stouraiti (2003). Papers by Bronwen Wilson, Helena Szepe, and Iain Fenlon in a panel on "After Lepanto, Martiality and Memory" at the 2006 annual meeting of the Renaissance Society of America also indicate new scholarly attention to the reverberation of this battle in Venetian visual arts, music, and liturgy.
74. On the consequences of this changing perception from an Ottomanist perspective, see Murphey (1993).
75. Goffman (1998); Eldem (1999); Greene (2002); Fusaro (2003). Braudel (1972, 291) already cautioned against the idea of an absolute Venetian economic decline in the early seventeenth century.
76. On the transition from Venetian to Ottoman rule on Cyprus, see Kyrris (1989); Jennings (1993); Costantini (2004). On this process on Crete, see Bierman (1991); Greene (2000).

of Venice to preserve its territorial integrity and commercial supremacy in the Mediterranean prompted a closer realignment with transalpine Europe.

The same century witnessed the ambiguous embrace by both Venetian and Ottoman political elites of projects of social disciplining and doctrinal orthodoxy that were the hallmark of the Age of Confessionalization. The myriad processes that historians have dubbed confessionalization, including the ideological hardening of religious boundaries and the growing collaboration between Church institutions and centralizing territorial states, combined to heighten individuals' consciousness of the need to align their religious and political affiliations.[77] Although the fine points of doctrine and liturgy were of little interest to most trans-imperial subjects, strong confessionalizing tendencies on both sides of the frontier decisively shaped their interactions with a range of institutions and their ability to intervene in evolving discourses about the relationship between piety and statecraft.[78]

The period 1570–1670 marked not only Ottoman maritime expansion at Venetian expense but also a watershed in how the Ottoman state and society were represented in Venetian print—and, given the predominance of the Venetian printing press, in European print culture more broadly. What was once seen as a fearsome but imitable model of monarchy had become a tyrannical and despotic anti-Europe worthy only of rebuke.[79] This transformation, I suggest, was informed in part by the sustained interaction of metropolitan elites in both the Venetian and Ottoman imperial centers with a range of trans-imperial subjects.

Thus, in this book I do not simply trace the genealogies of representations of the Ottomans to specific groups of trans-imperial subjects. Rather, I chart a gradual shift over the sixteenth and seventeenth centuries from an essentially juridical-commercial discourse of difference to a predominantly ethnolinguistic and religious one, inflected by practices of conversion that intimately linked political subjecthood with confessional membership. Rather than viewing religious and ethnic identities as primordial, I show how both confessional membership and linguistic (in)competence were articulated in specific institutional spaces (but

---

77. For clear overviews of the historiographical debates on early modern confessionalization, see De Boer (2001); Boettcher (2004); Brady (2004). See also the extensive 2005 H-Net forum on the topic, www.h-net.org/~german/discuss/Confessionalization/Confess_index.htm.
78. For a compelling argument for an Ottoman "age of confessionalization," see Krstić (2009, 2011). On the theological and intellectual frame of the early involvement of Venice in the religious wars of the sixteenth century, see Gleason (1993); Martin (1993). See also Wright (1996) and Schutte (2001) on the specifically Venetian flavor of confessionalizing state-Church dynamics in the early seventeenth century.
79. On the changing representations of the Ottomans in early modern Venetian print culture, see Valensi (1993); Soykut (2001); Çirakman (2002); Höfert (2003); Rubiés (2005); Meserve (2008).

not in others) as grounds for specific concessions, as part of broader claims to be-longing and foreignness. This shift took place through myriad local processes of boundary-marking undertaken by subjects across Venetian and Ottoman domains. These microhistorical processes, in turn, both contributed to and were con-strained by the changing relationship between the Venetian and Ottoman polities in a wider Mediterranean context. The interplay between these differing levels of analysis informs the book throughout.

My focus on the period 1570–1670 is also warranted by the survival of con-sistently comprehensive documentation from a range of institutional archives. Petitions to the Venetian Senate, which form the documentary base for much of the discussion in chapters 1, 5, and 7, are preserved systematically only from 1563.[80] Fairly complete transcripts of trials by the tribunals of the commercial bro-kers' guild, the subject of chapter 2, survive only from 1590. The same is true for notarial and baptismal records from the archives of the Pia Casa dei Catecumeni, a major institution for the conversion of Jews and Muslims in early modern Venice and the subject of chapter 4.[81] The genres of renegades' reconciliation deposi-tions in front of the Holy Office (Inquisition) and converts' *examina matrimonio-rum*, introduced and analyzed in chapter 3, are typical products of post-Tridentine Catholic reform from the second half of the sixteenth century onward.[82] And although both dragomans and commercial brokers were active in Venice much earlier, most of the texts they composed survive only from the 1570s onward. In addition, over half of the archival corpus of earlier dispatches from the maritime colonies of Venice was destroyed by fire in the 1570s.[83]

Of these wide-ranging genres of documentation, petitions (It. *suppliche*) are of special importance. These served as the main vehicle through which early modern subjects engaged officialdom.[84] Particularly in imperial societies such as Venice with its vast territories, complex sociojuridical hierarchies, and diversified institu-tional practices, it was the malleability, contestation and recalibration of concep-tual categories that typified practices of petition writing by trans-imperial subjects and others. The fact that supplicants did not necessarily pen their own petitions but sometimes employed the services of experienced scribes should not be seen as a problem. On the contrary, this study uses petitions not in an attempt to recover authentic subaltern "voices" but to understand how categories were articulated

80. Tiepolo (1994, 890).
81. Ellero (1987).
82. The first extant Venetian *examina matrimoniorum* are from 1592; very few reconciliation depositions by Christians of Muslim background survive from before the seventeenth century.
83. Schmitt (2001).
84. See Nubola and Würgler (2002); Millet (2003); Luebke (2005) and the bibliography therein.

through the ongoing interaction between subjects and the chanceries of official-dom.[85] That the composition process involved other actors proficient in the genre does not fundamentally change the premises.[86]

Another aspect of Venetian officialdom should be mentioned in this context. To preserve its authority, the Venetian oligarchy relied on a republican myth, predicated on the double notion of "a unified and civic-minded patriciate, guard-ian of the common good" and "a populace actively involved and fiercely loyal."[87] This tension between oligarchic and republican assumptions about the relation-ship of the state with its subjects made supplication a powerful vehicle for articu-lating different (and at times conflicting) expectations about the role of a patrician ruling caste. Genres such as petitions perpetuated the idea of the patriciate as the benevolent and attentive custodian of the state, but also placed specific claims on this benevolence. A careful reading of these petitions shows not simply their usefulness for hegemonic elites but, rather, how they functioned as interactive instruments for the elaboration of specific subject-positions and their concomitant claims and counterclaims.

Of special interest are collective petitions, in which signatories claimed to speak on behalf of an entire group and therefore delineated the authorized bound-aries of the group. Given the saliency of ethnic boundary-marking to both early modern Venetian statecraft and modern scholarship, petitions written on behalf of ethnic collectivities offer a particularly illuminating genre through which to examine the calibration and recalibration of ethnolinguistic and geopolitical cat-egories. By observing how certain categories emerged and proliferated in both the petitions and the texts produced by officialdom, we can examine how increased visibility naturalized and authenticated authors' claims to speak on behalf of cer-tain collectivities while other categories of groupness became obsolete.

In paying close attention to petitions submitted by trans-imperial subjects and the responses they received from specific magistracies, I also seek to challenge the image of institutional continuity produced by Venetian documentation pro-cedures. The following chapters show how institutional change sometimes coin-cided with the transformation of classificatory schemes to facilitate the emergence of new categories, such as the "Levantines." My analysis is premised on the idea

---

85. On Venetian chanceries in a Mediterranean context, see Wansbrough (1996, 77–78).
86. In the absence of any detailed studies about the provenance, education, and work practices of early modern Venetian scribes, this crucial dimension of Venetian governmentality remains to be explored. For useful insights on the procedural aspects of petitioning the Venetian government, see the appendix "Suppliche in Venice" in Davis (1991, 181–95).
87. Grubb (1986, 44, 49). On patriarchy and the Venetian state, see especially Sperling (1999b); Chojnacki (2000); Raines (2006).

that, to be successful, supplicants already had to partake in the ongoing constitution of the Venetian social order. Whether juridical subjects of the Venetian state or not, the ostensible foreignness of trans-imperial subjects was undermined already at the moment of its enunciation.

To understand how paternalism, republicanism, and citizenship itself were redefined through the interaction—which petitions both produced and presupposed—between supplicants and officialdom, in part I, "Mediation," I focus on petitioning and related practices among trans-imperial subjects active in the Venetian commercial sphere. I explore their growing role in institutionalizing how foreignness was brokered. I also identify an important juridical moment in the articulation of discourses about Ottoman difference at the height of Venetian commercial triumphalism in the mid-sixteenth century. In chapter 1, I consider the commercial activities of a range of trans-imperial subjects, including converts, returnees from Ottoman captivity, and Jewish, Armenian, and Greek commercial brokers in Venice. I examine the development of commercial brokerage itself as a key link between the state and the marketplace, as well as between local and foreign. After outlining the emergence of the brokers' guild and confraternity, I analyze how differently positioned trans-imperial subjects petitioned to become brokers, what audience they imagined for their petitions, and what notions of Venetian society they invoked in them. In chapter 2, I then look at the trials of unlicensed brokers heard by the tribunals of the brokers' guild. By unpacking the arguments put forth by trans-imperial defendants and their accusers, I trace competing notions of what constituted foreignness and how it could be mediated (and mitigated) through brokerage. Brokers and merchants were linked through trans-imperial bonds of affect and patronage that followed neither juridical definitions of belonging nor the ethnic solidarity presupposed by much modern scholarship.

In part II, "Conversion," I connect a second, religious moment in the discourses about Ottoman difference to the multiple processes of confessionalization and (re)sacralization of statecraft across the Mediterranean at the turn of the seventeenth century. Whereas commercial brokers blurred the line between the Ottoman foreign and the Venetian local, religious converts, despite their precarious position in society, became ideological signs of the potential transformation of foreigners into Venetian subjects. Yet, in an effort to transform Muslims and Jews into proper subjects of the Serenissima, converts' Venetian patrons were constrained to acknowledge their protégés' lingering ties to their former communities. In chapter 3, I examine different genres of converts' life narratives to suggest the contrasting ways in which Muslim, Jewish, and Protestant converts to Catholicism articulated the process of conversion and the converted self and how they envisioned the relationship among religious conversion, juridical subjecthood, and political loyalty. In chapter 4, I explore converts' long trajectories after baptism through a detailed study of a charitable institution for the conversion of Muslims and Jews to Catholicism, the Pia Casa dei Catecumeni (Holy House of Catechumens), established in Venice in 1557. I show how baptized Muslims and Jews, two paradigmatic others of the Venetian state, became constitutive elements of long-standing Venetian networks of patronage that often extended to the Venetian maritime colonies and beyond the Ottoman frontier. In chapters 3 and 4, I explore how conversion operated as a project of metropolitan subject-making in the context of both the strained Venetian-Papal relations in the post-Tridentine era and the ongoing Venetian-Ottoman rivalry. The project of conversion that was elaborated in partnership among lay members of charitable institutions, the Holy Office, Jesuits, and the Venetian state helped specify the religious domain as fundamental for the proper constitution of new Venetian subjects and, therefore, as a prime locus of Ottoman difference.

In part III, "Translation," I trace a third, ethnolinguistic moment in discourses about Ottoman difference, concurrent with the political-economic shift of Venice from a commercial to a territorial state in the 1630s. This period saw the consolidation of dragomans (diplomatic interpreters) as specialized professional intermediaries between Venetian and Ottoman political elites. Indeed, the age of dragomans coincided with Ottoman imperial expansion at Venetian expense in the eastern Mediterranean. As ethnolinguistic and religious categories came to correspond less and less with juridical status and political alliance, new categories referring to Ottoman subjects proliferated in the discourses of Venetian officialdom. These categories are linked to the rise of specific cadres of diplomatic and commercial dragomans in the Venetian state bureaucracy. In chapter 5, I examine the emergence of the office of dragomans, first in the Venetian bailo's house in Istanbul and then in Venice. Through a close reading of dragomans' petitions and the official responses to them, I trace recruitment, training, and employment of this cadre and underscore the inherent tension between loyalty and transcultural competence in Venetian dragomans' careers.

Finally, in part IV, "Articulation," I examine the interactions among Venetian dragomans, commercial brokers, converts, and Ottoman merchants and state officials. I explore how trans-imperial trajectories and social ties combined with inter-imperial institutional milieus to produce new categories of ethnolinguistic difference and how such categories entered official genres of the Venetian state, giving them unprecedented saliency. In chapter 6, I follow the shifting Venetian tax legislation to show how fiscal policy coalesced with the interests of specific dragomans and brokers to articulate new ideas about linguistic incompetence as the quintessential property of foreign and, especially, Ottoman and Safavid merchants. I further illustrate how, by assuming the linguistic helplessness of certain foreign merchants, Venetian officials reinforced the association of brokerage with bilingualism and thus ultimately furthered the claim of converts, redeemed slaves, and other bilingual trans-imperial subjects to be ideal intermediaries between supposedly mutually unintelligible and clearly demarcated groups. In chapter 7, I then trace the genealogy of the categories "Turks" and "Levantines" to institutionalized practices of mediation in the commercial sphere and explore how the defining properties and prototypical centers of these categories shifted, both over time and synchronically, from one institution to another. Using case studies of two petitioning campaigns, one over the taxation of "Levantine" merchandise and the other over the forced relocation of Ottoman and Safavid Muslim merchants to a designated exchange house, I document how the categories "Venetian" and "Ottoman," "European" and "Levantine," were picked up and recalibrated within specific institutions in Venice and beyond.

By looking at how specific trans-imperial groups articulated categories for discussing what is properly Venetian or Ottoman, and by examining how juridical, religious, and ethnolinguistic categories intersected with assumptions about gender, estate, age, and profession, I show the multivalence of claims about difference within specific institutional sites. I underscore how, by positing cultural difference, early modern trans-imperial subjects also positioned themselves within an emergent set of relations between Venice and Istanbul, which were themselves nested in the more complex networks of relations that we now call the Mediterranean world.

PART I

Mediation

1

Trans-Imperial Subjects
as Supplicants and as Brokers

The goal is not to make clearer how the violence of order is transmuted into a disciplinary technology but rather to bring to light the clandestine forms taken by the dispersed, tactical, and makeshift creativity of groups or individuals already caught in the nets of "discipline."

—MICHEL DE CERTEAU (1988, xiv–xv)

In early August 1573, word reached the Holy Office of a teenage slave named Zorzi who had run away from the house of his patrician master.[1] According to the initial deposition, Zorzi, formerly a Muslim, had been baptized and had received communion and other holy sacraments. But now, having gone into hiding in the attic of a house "where several Turks live," he had allegedly returned to Islam ("tornato a far Turco") "having shaved his head and dressed as a Turk in order to go secretly to Turkey." Five days after Zorzi's escape, his master, Marcantonio Falier, visited Zorzi's place of hiding.[2] He was met by an uncooperative landlord, a Greek commercial broker named Francesco di Demetri Lettino but better known by his nickname, Frangia, and his wife, Giulia. The couple claimed complete ignorance of Zorzi's whereabouts, but Falier persisted in demanding that his slave be returned. That

---

1. Established in 1547, the Venetian Holy Office was a highly autonomous chapter of the Roman Inquisition, administered by clerics who for the most part came from the Venetian patrician ruling class. For a bibliography on this well-studied institution, see Ruggiero (2001, 1142 n3).

2. Marcantonio was one of the six sons of Domenico Falier (1492–1564) and Chiara Contarini, a patrician couple of rather modest means. The couple married in 1541, which suggests that in 1573 Marcantonio was a fairly young man. In visiting the slave's place of hiding he brought along some friends, including his brother Luca (b. 1545), himself a young man who had not yet embarked on a career. This suggests either Marcantonio's even humbler position (and possibly younger age) or his sense that a group visit might command more respect. On the Faliers, see Targhetta (1994a, 1994b).

evening Frangia sent Zorzi to spend the night at a friend's house nearby, and the following morning Zorzi was unceremoniously returned to his master.[3]

Despite this "happy ending" from Falier's point of view, and the apparent restoration of Venetian social order, the Holy Office did not drop the case. Rather, it arrested Frangia and opened a lengthy investigation, in the course of which the inquisitors interrogated not only Zorzi but also Frangia, Giulia, and their eighteen-year old son, as well as neighbors and friends of the family.[4] Their depositions reveal the deep tensions between how inquisitors and witnesses drew moral, religious, and social boundaries between Venetians and Turks, Christians and Muslims, masters and slaves, and merchants and brokers. They also underscore the important role of diffuse networks of trans-imperial subjects in defining belonging and foreignness in early modern Venice.

Frangia's inquisitorial trial is exceptional among the archival traces left by early modern Venetian commercial brokers. The overwhelming majority of documents conserved in the archives of the Venetian brokers' guild concern legal attempts to regulate the activities of commercial brokers in the market. Indeed, the Venetian state entrusted brokers with the important task of mediating between foreign and local merchants. Venetian law envisioned brokers—ideally, if not in practice—as loyal Venetian citizens, impartial and vigilant agents of the state, who should note down their transactions in a special notebook, collect taxes and duties from foreign merchants, and protect the latter's interests vis-à-vis less than scrupulous trading partners.

Unlike the archives of the brokers' guild, examined later in this chapter, the record left by Frangia's inquisitorial trial underscores the extent to which the marketplace and the home were—and are—intermeshed and the importance of domestic arrangements and personal ties in forging alliances between commercial brokers and their clients. Indeed, these testimonies reveal a complex set of interests, hierarchies of authority, and modes of interaction between locals, localized foreigners (such as Frangia himself), and Ottoman sojourners. Such interactions clearly violated the mythic representation of a perfected Venetian social order premised on Christian morality and civic unity in the face of religious and political Others. Moreover, rather than bringing into contact the supposedly preexisting categories of "Venetian" and "Turk," Frangia and his household members were active participants in shaping these categories.

The unique position of Frangia and other trans-imperial subjects in the Venetian commercial sphere is well attested in the unfolding testimonies in his trial in summer 1573. The testimonies—including those by Frangia, Giulia, Zorzi,

---

3. From the opening statement in Santo Uffizio, Processi, b. 35, fasc. 12 (Aug. 15, 1573), fol. 1r [henceforth, SU 35]. All translations are mine unless otherwise noted.

4. For more details on this trial and the people involved in it, see Rothman (2010).

the Ottoman merchants, and their slaves—underscore the embedding of such localized foreigners in extensive social networks in Venice and beyond. As important, they suggest the transgressive nature of the witnesses' domestic arrangements, at least from the point of view of Frangia's patrician interrogators.[5] Such arrangements belie a simple parsing of their milieu into "Venetians" and "Turks," and reveal the role of long-settled émigrés, such as Frangia and Giulia, in facilitating a range of interactions across linguistic, religious, and juridical boundaries.

Indeed, key evidence regarding the prevalence of transgressive domestic arrangements was provided by the escaped slave himself. In his testimony, Zorzi claimed that he had planned to go back to the Ottoman Empire in the hope of finding his Christian Bulgarian parents, whom he had not seen since he had been kidnapped as a young boy. He was encouraged to escape from his Venetian master, he said, by several friends in similar circumstances. All of them had purportedly managed to escape Venice on board a ship heading for Izmir just a few days earlier. They were all aided not only by Ottoman merchants and their slaves but also by Frangia's family.[6]

From the beginning of the proceedings, then, Zorzi presented himself as reluctant to abide by the rules governing Venetian domestic slavery. Rather than endorse his new identity as a baptized slave, he asserted his wish to return to his ur-identity—not that of an Ottoman Muslim convert but that of a kidnapped Christian boy. To that end, he related how he had recruited an extended network of accomplices, crossing spatial, social, and religious boundaries. His professed desire to reunite with his parents was, moreover, a powerful indictment against his current servile state, challenging the legality of his very enslavement.[7] To befriend Frangia's tenants, the Ottoman merchants, and secure their assistance in his escape, Zorzi implied he was even willing to "reactivate" his Muslim past and resume Muslim bodily practices such as having his head shaved and wearing a white turban.[8] It is impossible to determine what exactly transpired between Zorzi and his Ottoman-

5. Like Zorzi's master, the inquisitors sitting on the case were themselves, for the most part, Venetian patricians.

6. SU 35, Zorzi's testimony (Aug. 15, 1573), fols. 1v–4r.

7. In theory, if not in practice, Venetians were not supposed to trade in—and certainly not to possess—Christian slaves. Although slaveowners overlooked this moral dictum as a matter of course when it came to recent converts to Christianity, they found it harder to ignore when a slave could prove he or she had been born to Christian parents. Not surprisingly, slaves in Venetian households commonly claimed in inquisitorial depositions to have been kidnapped from Christian parents at a tender age.

8. Early modern Venetians widely regarded head shaving and the wearing of "Turkish" clothes as signs of conversion to Islam. Significantly, Ottomans similarly held a change in dress to be a sign of a convert's new religious affiliation. See Minkov (2004, 127). For the relationship between outward appearance and presumed inner spiritual transformation in early modern Venice, see also Head (1990); Wilson (2003).

Turkish hosts in Frangia's house, but we can assume that Zorzi was convincing enough in invoking his Muslim background for the merchants to collaborate in his ultimately unsuccessful attempt to return to the Ottoman Empire.

Just as Zorzi's testimony pokes holes in patrician representations of a perfected Venetian social and religious order, other witnesses similarly undermine notions of a stable domestic order. Throughout the trial, Frangia sought to present himself as the master of an orderly household and to assert his authority over his wife, children, and tenants. But two revelations seriously compromised his claims to authority: that the keys to his house were actually kept by his Ottoman tenants and that as a broker-landlord he was utterly dependent on the translation skills of his tenants' slaves because he himself did not speak a word of Turkish.[9] Not only did these slaves possess vital communicative skills, but their friendship with a diverse group of young slaves, servants, and apprentices across the city gave them broad social access, belying their presumed isolation. Furthermore, these slaves apparently exerted enough authority to conduct Zorzi's ceremonial head shaving. This act transgressed not only religious but social hierarchies. It mirrored and reversed Zorzi's baptism by his patrician master only eighteen months earlier, an important ritual enactment of ownership and supposed spiritual transformation.[10]

Thus, to act as a broker, Frangia depended on a much larger network of intermediaries. The testimonies of his wife, his son, and his neighbor reveal the extent of this network. The position of Frangia's wife, Giulia, emerges as particularly ambiguous in that she only partially adhered to the religious and moral boundaries sanctioned by Venetian officialdom. Supposedly subordinate to her husband's commands, she deftly negotiated with Zorzi's master and knowingly lied to him about his slave's whereabouts. More broadly, she was in daily contact with her Ottoman tenants about eating arrangements and may have tacitly collaborated with them not only in Zorzi's case but in hiding other runaway slaves in her house as well.[11]

The inquisitorial record further allows us to explore some Venetian officials' implicit concerns regarding brokers' persons and profession. From the start, Frangia's dual social position as both a Venetian civil servant and an ethnic Greek could raise suspicion of political as well as religious subversion.[12] As if his Greekness were not enough, Frangia rented rooms to Muslim Ottoman merchants in clear violation of

---

9. SU 35, Frangia's testimony (Aug. 20, 1573), fols. 6r–6v.
10. On religious conversion as a practice of subject-making by the early modern Venetian state, see chapters 3–4.
11. SU 35, Frangia's testimony (Aug. 20, 1573), fol. 5r.
12. On the triadic relations among Greeks, Latins, and Muslims in the early modern Mediterranean, and specifically on Venetian anxieties regarding Greek-Ottoman collaboration, see Greene (2000).

laws that forbade anyone, save for licensed hoteliers, to lodge foreigners. Brokers were specifically warned against doing so in an effort to monitor foreigners' presence in the city and to secure revenue from the tax collected through licensed hoteliers. This was a repeated point of contention because brokers were ideally placed to offer newly arrived foreign merchants lodgings and other services.[13] Brokers, in turn, frequently claimed ignorance of the law and insisted that they were in fact doing merchants a favor by welcoming them into their homes.

The ban on brokers' lodging of foreign clients was increasingly linked to religious concerns and to restrictions on Muslim Ottoman merchants' freedom of residence to curb "scandals" occasioned by the cohabitation of Christians and Muslims (see chap. 6). Indeed, beyond an obvious concern over Zorzi's planned escape and ostensible apostasy, inquisitors questioned the moral well-being of Frangia's family itself and located it precisely in the crossing of social and spatial boundaries. During the interrogations, inquisitors repeatedly asked Frangia, Giulia, and their son about the nature of their interactions with their Ottoman Muslim tenants. Inquisitors wanted to know who cooked the tenants' food, what kind of food it was (in particular, whether tenants ate meat on Friday, a clear sign of religious transgression), and whether the family and the tenants had ever eaten together. Giulia was particularly careful in her replies, assuring her interrogators that no contact through food (let alone through the sociability presupposed and reenforced by commensality) had taken place between her family and her tenants. Concern over food restrictions and their transgression typified attempts by the Holy Office to expose and uproot heresy, and Giulia was clearly conscious of the link between the violation of Catholic food restrictions and ostensible heresy.[14] Her detailed answer about what her tenant had given her to cook for dinner on Friday evening when Zorzi was discovered in the attic suggests she was well aware of what her interrogators were after: "He eats meat every day, and we don't eat meat, neither on Wednesday nor on Friday for any reason, and it is true that he gave one of my little girls, who is four years old, a pumpkin roll, and I told her not to eat anything with grease or meat, so the cat ate it in the pantry."[15] Giulia

---

The profession of Venetian commercial brokerage became increasingly ethnicized and suspect in the wake of the loss of Cyprus (in 1571) because many migrants from the lost colony were granted license to exercise the trade.

13. Arti, b. 517, fasc. 1, fol. 2v (June 26, 1497). See also Urban Padoan (1990, 18); Manno (1995, 127); Costantini (1996).

14. On the interest of the Venetian Holy Office in food consumption as an index of religious (un)orthodoxy in the age of confessionalization, see Head (1990).

15. SU 35, Giulia's testimony (Aug. 22, 1573), fol. 13r. Abstention from meat on Wednesday and Friday would not have marked Giulia and her family as Catholic as opposed to Greek Orthodox but simply, in this case, as neither Lutheran nor Muslim, the two major concerns of the Venetian Holy Office at the time.

thus emphasized that she deemed the food that her tenant had given her little daughter worthy only of the cat and in the pantry, out of sight. On the other hand, the fact that her tenant offered food to the girl at all may well suggest that affective ties between the tenants and property-owners in this case went beyond polite greeting on the staircase.

As this case suggests, brokers operated at the interface between the state and trans-imperial subjects, between the mercantile and artisanal sectors of Venetian society, between government institutions and the market, and between rich and poor (see also the frontispiece). They were of key importance to the very constitution of these categories, their boundaries, and their possible mediation. Moreover, against patrician understandings of the marketplace as composed of anonymous actors, commercial brokers and their clients often forged ties that crossed religious, linguistic, and political boundaries and that challenged the very assumptions of merchants' foreignness and helplessness. This challenge and the shifting nature of ties among brokers, the Venetian state, and an inter-imperial commercial sphere are particularly noteworthy once we consider the growing predominance of trans-imperial subjects among the ranks of this profession—which included Christian converts; Jewish, Armenian, and Greek-Orthodox Ottoman and Safavid subjects; redeemed slaves; and émigrés from Venetian eastern Mediterranean and Adriatic colonies, among them war refugees and veterans.[16] Indeed, although in 1497 the brokers' guild was instituted as the exclusive purview of Venetian citizens, by 1670 guild membership had come to include a large minority of trans-imperial subjects.

Venetian law assigned to commercial brokers a twofold role: aiding foreign merchants in their negotiations with other merchants and exacting taxes from them on behalf of the state. Both these tasks ideally took place in the marketplace and were premised on the widespread legal notion that foreigners were "poor in relational resources" and hence needed special protections.[17] But as Frangia's case suggests, the commercial interactions of brokers and foreign merchants consti-

16. Cypriots and other Venetian colonial subjects moved to the metropole in increasing numbers in the wake of the Ottoman conquest of Cyprus in 1571, hoping to restore their wealth, if not their status. The relationship between the Venetian colonial nobility, who sought repatriation in Venice, and the tightly guarded oligarchy that ruled the republic was fraught with tensions. According to Benjamin Arbel (personal communication), following the Ottoman conquest of Cyprus many Cypriots presented themselves to the Venetians as the descendents of Venetian nobles. For a fascinating discussion of attempts by émigrés from Crete to reclaim their Venetian patrician ancestry in the sixteenth century, see McKee (2000, 76); O'Connell (2004).

17. Cerutti (1995, 452).

tuted part of a much broader range of domestic arrangements, alliances, and affect. Although Frangia was the only licensed broker in his household, other people, chiefly his wife and daughters, assumed key intermediary roles as well and performed various tasks that redefined authority, familiarity, and community.

To address the differing understandings of mediation and foreignness invoked by the various actors in the Venetian commercial sphere, in this chapter I consider the mass introduction of trans-imperial subjects into the profession of commercial brokers. I explore how trans-imperial subjects petitioned the Venetian government to gain employment as brokers and, more broadly, how they claimed membership in metropolitan Venetian society while in fact expanding the meaning of such membership well beyond the boundaries of legal citizenship. Their means was a specific genre—the *supplica* (letter of supplication, or petition).[18] By analyzing this particular genre of writing, it becomes evident how trans-imperial subjects' sense of their relationship to the Venetian state shaped their narratives of supplication, in other words, how the crafting of their petitions depended on how petitioners understood their pasts, on how they envisioned their futures (as commercial brokers and as metropolitan subjects), and on how they sought to make these pasts and futures compelling to the patrician interlocutors who were ultimately to adjudicate their cases. By paying close attention to these petitions' narrative frames, we can therefore gain a better understanding of how they articulated subjecthood in relationship to the political economy of early modern Venice and, more broadly, to the imperial and patrician dimensions of early modern statecraft.

Before we enter their world, it should be noted that this chapter is not meant as a comprehensive history of early modern Venetian commercial brokers, which

18. The corpus examined in this chapter includes virtually all petitions for employment as commercial brokers conserved in the Venetian State Archives for the period 1563–1670, the first hundred years for which such petitions survive systematically. Generally, petitions to the Venetian government are organized in two main series: *Collegio, risposte di dentro* (for petitions referred to magistracies within Venice, starting in 1563) and *Collegio, risposte di fuori* (for petitions referred to magistracies outside the city, particularly the army, starting in 1554). I thank Dott.ssa Sandra Sambo of the Venetian State Archives for pointing out to me this division and its limitations. Significantly, the two series, despite their names, do not include the actual *risposte* (the formal reports that magistracies produced in response to petitions) but, as a rule, only the original petition and a summary of the resolution by the College on which magistracies the petition should be referred to, if at all. Some magistracies, however, did keep records of their *risposte* in separate series, which can sometimes be cross-checked with the petitions to which they refer. The Venetian Board of Trade, Cinque Savi alla Mercanzia, kept a particularly extensive archive of its responses (*Cinque Savi alla Mercanzia, Risposte*). This genre merits a separate study about the voicing of supplicants' narratives in the writings of officialdom. For a general introduction to Venetian petitioning practices, see Davis (1991, 181–95).

still awaits a full study.[19] Instead, I explore here brokers' contribution to a cultural transformation—the consolidation of new geopolitical and ethnolinguistic categories and sensibilities.

WHAT IS A BROKER?: A VIEW FROM VENICE

With the expansion of long-distance trade in the late Middle Ages and throughout the sixteenth century, commercial brokers, who mediated between sellers and buyers, became ubiquitous in Mediterranean commercial hubs. Historians are divided as to the provenance and antiquity of this institution. Some nineteenth-century historians suggested it was of Roman origin.[20] Others link its emergence to the growth of urban economies in the thirteenth century.[21] Still others have underscored the expansion of cross-Mediterranean trade in the wake of the Crusades and the establishment of enduring Genoese and Venetian mercantile colonies in the eastern Mediterranean as equally important factors in introducing the profession of commercial broker to the Italian peninsula. Known in Arabic as *simsar,* it appeared in Italian sources as *sanser* (Venetian), *sensale,* or *mezzano* (Tuscan).[22] Whereas legal traditions and commercial practices clearly varied across time and space, the institution of commercial brokerage itself was shared throughout the early modern Mediterranean, Indian, and Atlantic Oceans, exhibiting some strong structural similarities across various inter-imperial trading hubs.[23]

19. Indeed, although I have benefited greatly from the growing literature on the history of early modern markets, financial institutions, and international commerce, as well as from several magisterial studies of the medieval Venetian economy by Gino Luzzatto (1995), Frederic Lane and Reinhold Mueller (1985), and others, the transformation of Venetian economic institutions from the second half of the sixteenth century on is far less studied, perhaps due to the paradigm of crisis and decline that dominated the field for a long time. This allows for only tentative remarks about the role of brokers in the economic transformation of that period. For pioneering studies of the seventeenth century, see Sella (1961); Rapp (1976); Lanaro Sartori (1999); Lanaro (2006).
20. Pertile et al. (1894, 692).
21. Van Houtte (1936, 106).
22. See Abulafia (1993) on Italian merchant colonies in the medieval Mediterranean; Colin and Becker (1999) on brokers in medieval Arab societies; and Cortelazzo (1989b) on the etymology of *sanser/sensale.* But see also Van Houtte (1936, 115) for a cautionary note against assuming that the Arab institution of *simsar* was imported to Europe with all its original functions intact.
23. On early modern inter-imperial trade generally, see Curtin (1984); Curto and Molho (2002); Trivellato (2009); Aslanian (2010). For specific case studies of brokers in places other than Venice, see Qaisar (1974); Beg (1977); Pearson (1988); Bornstein-Makovetsky (1989); Das Gupta (1991); Colzi (1998); Farolfi (1998); De Matteo and Schisani (1999); Bolognesi (2000); Vigiano (2001); Cohen (2003). For an overview of brokerage-related commercial law in the various Italian city-states, see Lattes (1884); Pertile et al. (1894, 692–96).

Regardless of the (probably multiple) origins of the institution, evidence for the operation of brokers in Venice, as in other commercially oriented city-states, dates back to the thirteenth century.[24] Some brokers, such as those operating among Jews and in the Fondaco dei Tedeschi (German Exchange House), were presumed to cater to clients of particular provenance (although this was not necessarily the case). Most brokers operated near the Rialto Bridge, the Venetian marketplace and commercial nerve center, and were known simply as *sensali ordinarii di Rialto* ("regular brokers of Rialto"); and many of these brokers exhibited little specialization in either clientele or commodities, with the exception of grain, whose brokers were supervised by the Officio alle biave. Otherwise, the only noticeable official distinction obtained between the Rialto commercial brokers, on the one hand, and bond and bill brokers on the other. By the fifteenth century, even this distinction eroded in practice; whereas "a certain ambiguity of roles was normal ...; operators in each distinguishable category of manipulators of money, for example, might also lend money under some guise, often illegally, or deal at least occasionally in bullion as well as in worked silver and jewelry, tasks that we might expect to find only among goldsmiths."[25]

Despite important continuities with their medieval predecessors, the incorporation of Venetian brokers into a guild and a confraternity in 1497 marked a dramatic shift in their social composition and duties.[26] It was through the institution of a guild and consequently their subjection to much tighter state supervision in the sixteenth century that brokers' activities, in the words of one scholar, "transcend[ed] the field of private economic relationships ... into the sector of public law."[27] In this sense, the jurisdiction of the Board of Trade over the brokers' guild after centuries in which individual brokers were required to report

24. Luzzatto (1995, 103). See also Vercellin (1979, 1980) for path-breaking studies of commercial brokerage in early modern Venice.
25. Mueller (1997, 26). It was only in 1571 that the *sensali di cambii* (bill-of-exchange brokers) were allowed to form a separate guild and confraternity, modeled explicitly on that of commercial brokers; Cinque Savi, Seconda serie, b. 13, fasc. 274 (October 24, 1571). This situation differed in other cities. In Bologna, for example, each broker had to announce in advance which commodities he would deal with and was then subject to regulation by the guild active in that sector (Farolfi 1998, 310). Such guild membership, however, did not necessarily prevent brokers from brokering other commodities. As Antonella Astorri (1988, 391) notes in her study of Girolamo di Agostino Maringhi, a late fifteenth-century Florentine broker and member of the apothecaries' guild, his account books listed over fifty different kinds of merchandise.
26. Arti, b. 517, fasc. 1, c. 2r. I discuss the relationship between the guild and its confraternity in chapter 2.
27. Astorri (1988, 392).

to different government agencies, such as the Ufficiali alla messetteria[28] or the Visdomini al Fondaco dei Tedeschi,[29] marked an important change. It was, no doubt, part of the concerted effort by the Board of Trade to centralize Venetian commercial policies, to facilitate long-distance trade, and to attract foreign merchants to the city.[30]

Although the Board of Trade did not participate in electing guild-member brokers,[31] it had a strong say in virtually all legislation regarding brokerage and supervised brokers' ongoing activities. The board also exerted substantial influence over the granting of brokerage privileges, which allowed noncitizens to engage legally in brokerage without becoming guild members. In fact, petitions for appointment as brokers by privilege were regularly referred to the board for appraisal, and the resulting reports often carried great weight in the ultimate government decision.

This is not to say that prior to the sixteenth century brokers had no role in bringing the Venetian marketplace under the sphere of government control. As Reinhold Mueller argues, already by 1422 brokers were required to register each transaction so that the brokerage tax (*messetteria*) could be correctly applied.[32] Yet, until the Senate decreed the election of one hundred brokers in September 1503 (see fig. 1.1) and guaranteed these brokers' monopoly over commercial brokerage in Rialto, virtually anyone could operate as a broker in Venice, and there was no mechanism in place to enforce the collection of brokerage taxes.[33] Indeed, the main reason cited by the Senate for capping the number of brokers, making citizenship a prerequisite for appointment, and incorporating brokers in a guild was precisely the "great number of foreign brokers [who] do not care about

28. The Ufficiali alla messetteria, established in the thirteenth century, were initially in charge of collecting all brokerage taxes. With the establishment of the Board of Trade in the sixteenth century, their jurisdiction was substantially reduced to the collection of tax on the sale of real estate, such as "mills, plots, marshes, swamps, houses, ponds, forests, ships, and sailing equipment" (Da Mosto 1937, 198).

29. The Visdomini al Fondaco dei Tedeschi, established in 1268, supervised all economic activity in the German Exchange House, including the operation of brokers on its premises (Da Mosto 1937, 189).

30. On the establishment of the Board of Trade as part of the reorientation of the Venetian Republic as a territorial state in the sixteenth century, see Lanaro Sartori (1999, 86).

31. This was the purview of three other magistracies: the Provveditori di Comun, the Consoli dei mercanti, and the Ufficiali alla messetteria.

32. Mueller (1997, 519).

33. The number of guild members was deemed insufficient already by the Ufficiali alla messetteria, which was able to pass a Senate law in December 1503 (that is, only three months after the first bill) to increase the number of regular brokers to 150. This number was raised again to 190 in 1560. See Consoli dei mercanti, b. 58, fasc. "Per li magistrate a stampa," c. 11 (Dec. 21, 1503); c. 18 (May 26, 1560).

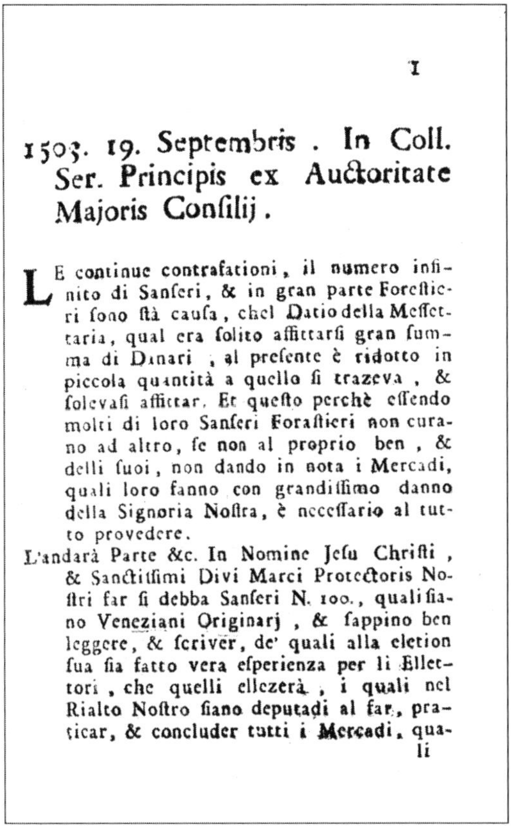

1503. 19. Septembris . In Coll.
Ser. Principis ex Auctoritate
Majoris Confilij .

L E continue contrafationi , il numero infi-
nito di Sanferi, & in gran parte Foreftic-
ri fono ftà caufa , chel Datio della Meffet-
taria , qual era folito affittarfi gran fum-
ma di Dinari , al prefente è ridotto in
piccola quantità a quello fi trazeva , &
folevafi affittar. Et quefto perchè effendo
molti di loro Sanferi Foraftieri non curano ad altro, fe non al proprio ben , &
delli fuoi, non dando in nota i Mercadi,
quali loro fanno con grandiffimo danno
della Signoria Noftra, è neceffario al tutto provedere.
L'andarà Parte &c. In Nomine Jefu Chrifti ,
& Sanctiffimi Divi Marci Protectoris No-
ftri far fi debba Sanferi N. 100., quali fiano Veneziani Originarj , & fappino ben
leggere, & fcriver, de' quali alla eletion
fua fia fatto vera efperienza per li Ellet-
tori , che quelli ellezerà , i quali nel
Rialto Noftro fiano deputadi al far, pra-
ticar, & concluder tutti i Mercadi, quali

Figure 1.1 *Decree for the election of one hundred brokers from among Venetian citizens by birth (1503). ASVe, Consoli dei mercanti, b. 58, fasc. Magistrati a stampa, c. 1. Reproduction: author, by permission (num. 17/2011) of Ministero per i Beni e le Attività Culturali.*

anything but their own property, [and therefore] fail to note down the transactions they conclude, with the greatest damage to Our Signoria."[34]

Legislators were clearly concerned about brokers' loyalty and hoped to turn them into an effective mechanism of surveillance over foreign merchants, hence the requirement of literacy ("must know how to read and write well"), which

34. "Et questo perchè essendo molti di loro Sanseri Forastieri non curano ad altro, se non al proprio ben, & delli suoi, non dando in nota i Mercadi, quali loro fanno con grandissimo danno della Signoria Nostra." Consoli dei mercanti, b. 58, fasc. "Magistrati a stampa," cc. 1–10 (Sept. 19, 1503). This was not a new problem. As Luca Molà (1994, 130 n52) shows, already in 1365 the Great Council sought to address the problem of foreign brokers who, it was argued, came to the city without their families and resided in the houses of their merchant clients, by making citizenship *de intus* a prerequisite for exercising the trade of broker (Maggior Consiglio, Deliberazioni, reg. Novella, c. 107v (June 28, 1365)). Similarly, according to David Jacoby (1999, 55, 65), late medieval state assessors in Venice, who also acted as official brokers in charge of collecting the brokerage taxes, included at least seven Greeks and numerous Jews.

was stipulated in the original preconditions for elections into the guild in 1503 and repeated in guild statutes in 1551.[35] The law further urged members of the brokers' guild:

> under sacrament to be solemnly given them by our *Governatori delle Intrade* [customs officers], to search, inquire, and investigate all those who do, practice, or conclude any business, either in Rialto or in the *Fondaco dei Tedeschi*, who are not regular brokers and registered in the above mentioned confraternity, under punishment to those who in any way presume to do, practice, or conclude any business, either in Rialto or in the above-mentioned Fondaco, of 300 *Lire di piccoli* [36] to be divided in half between the above-mentioned confraternity and the accuser. And if those to accuse him are brokers they shall remain secret, and if the accuser is not a broker, and is fit to enter in his place, [he may do so] without further election, and [the accused] beyond the said punishment must remain in prison behind bars. Those transgressors and falsifiers shall be punished.[37]

Oaths to uphold guild regulations and to actively pursue, report, and denounce fraudulent colleagues were a staple of many Venetian guild statutes as early as the thirteenth century.[38] But, given the potential loss of public revenue in the case of brokers, the government did not shy away from outright bribes in an attempt to secure their loyalty. To discourage brokers from engaging in trade on their own, the government gave guild members an exemption from all levies save for a 10 percent tax on import customs (*intrada*). In ex-

35. Marco Ferro, a jurist who compiled Venetian law in the eighteenth century, adds that "the merchants need these people [brokers], because their notes serve as proof in court, being considered commonly as a kind of incontestable public document" (1779, 676). Similarly, in early modern Bologna, "[brokers'] records gave contracts legal and probative value in judgment" (Farolfi 1998, 307). Yet several lists of guild members that bear their signatures clearly attest to many brokers' difficulty with signing their name, indicating that the requirement of literacy was only nominally observed.

36. A *lira di piccoli* was one of several silver coins that served as currencies of exchange in medieval and early modern Venice. These loosely corresponded to a set of gold currencies of account. In this period, 1 Venetian gold ducat was equivalent to 6 lire, 4 soldi of account, or 124 soldi in all (Molà 1997, iii). For an introduction to the baffling world of the Venetian money market, see Lane and Mueller (1985).

37. Consoli dei mercanti, b. 58, fasc. "Magistrati a stampa," c. 8 (Sept. 19, 1503).

38. Mackenney (1987, 25–26).

change, brokers were required to annually pay 100 ducats to the Governatori dell'Intrade.[39]

Such efforts to secure brokers' loyalty and impartiality proved less than successful. According to Venetian law, brokers had to be present at all transactions involving foreign merchants, ostensibly to ensure the payment of customs as well as to prevent foreigners from being defrauded. Their presence was also meant to allow an increasingly nervous government to keep track of the activities of foreign merchants. Yet brokers were never mere agents of governmental will. The repeated legislation requiring that brokers be impartial, that they refrain from engaging in any commercial activity on their own, and that they submit periodic written records of all transactions in which they were involved underscores precisely their partiality.[40]

Similarly, the documentation brokers produced of their activities was never simply an unmediated, transparent reflection of the economic transactions in which they were involved. In fact, it is precisely brokers' failure to submit written reports of the transactions in which they had been involved that led the government to attempt various solutions that ultimately produced some of the guild archives. In 1511, the *Consoli dei mercanti* required brokers, sellers, and buyers to sign their names in a special register immediately on concluding a deal. The register was to be kept by the brokers' guild. In 1560, the Board of Trade reduced from ten to three the days allowed between the conclusion of a transaction and its reporting by the broker, in the hope of curbing "the many frauds" supposedly occasioned by the ten-day hiatus. In 1586, the board threatened to dismiss brokers failing to note transactions in their books. Finally, in 1641 it required brokers mediating transactions with Ottoman merchants to note all sales in their notebooks and to have the seller and buyer cosign (or stamp, if illiterate) these notes as well. All transactions were to be reported to the board within eight days.[41]

These concerted but ultimately unsuccessful efforts to subject brokers to the reason of state have been frequently overlooked by historians. To the extent that brokers' textual production has caught scholars' attention at all, it has been taken at face value, as objective documentation of the activity in the marketplace. Brokers' writings, in other words, have been treated as transparent windows on

---

39. Arti, b. 520, fasc. 2, unpaginated (Sept. 19, 1503). Later legislation periodically changed brokers' taxation. In 1645, for example, the brokers' guild petitioned to be exempted from one of two taxes to which they were subjected at that time, the *decima & annata* and the quota of oarsmen. They were exempted from the former on June 4, 1646 (Arti, b. 520, fasc. 2, unpaginated (April 27, 1645)).

40. Lattes (1884, 107).

41. Consoli dei mercanti, b. 58, fasc. "sanseri," c. 10r (Jan. 28, 1510 m.v.); fasc. "Magistrati a stampa," cc. 18–19 (May 26, 1560); fasc. verde, c. 9v (May 5, 1586); Arti, b. 520, fasc. 2, unpaginated (Dec. 17, 1641).

to economic reality, equally serviceable to early modern rulers and to modern scholars.[42] But, as will become clearer shortly, brokers did not simply document an independent reality external to their actions. Rather, their activities—including their documentary practices—helped to shape that reality. It is to brokers' documentary practices that I now turn.

TRANS-IMPERIAL PETITIONERS AND THEIR RHETORICS

Trans-imperial subjects were avid petitioners, and their frequent petitions for brokerage privileges shed much light on emerging early modern understandings of the relationship among brokerage, citizenship, and subjecthood. Supplicants insisted on their own membership in Venetian society by underscoring Christian and civic virtues, by invoking a history of loyal service to the state (both their own and their ancestors'), and generally by insisting on the paternal responsibility of the state for the well-being of its least-fortunate subjects. The rhetorical strategies that characterize each subset of this admittedly diverse group of trans-imperial subjects reveal important differences in how supplicants' notions of civic membership and social boundaries were articulated in the life stories they narrated to support their cases.

As already noted, the prevalence of noncitizens among Venetian brokers was certainly not a new development in the sixteenth century. But only with the incorporation of brokers into a guild and their subjection to more rigorous gov-

---

42. For example, one scholar claims that already by the thirteenth century "the State could verify prices ... for government officials mediated all (legal) transactions in Venice no later than 1225. It was illegal to transact without the intervention of *sensali della messetteria*... . The *sensali* made sure that sale taxes were paid and that merchants did not break the law" (González de Lara 2001, 24). Such a view misses not only the fact that many transactions escaped the purview of the state but also that brokers were very rarely dutiful and disinterested executors of governmental policy. Indeed, their actions reflected several, often conflicting, interests, including their own and those of foreign merchants. Unfortunately, a positivist approach to brokers' documentation is far from unique to Venetian historiography. Oscar Gelderblom and Joost Jonker have noted that the early seventeenth-century charter of the Amsterdam guild of sworn brokers (*Makelaars*) "included an official obligation to keep a register of all the transactions arranged, and the brokers' data served both as raw material for the official commodity price current, and as proof for the price of particular goods on the market at a specific time" (2003, 13). In a similar vein, Edward Stringham (2003) analyzes the Amsterdam-based broker Joseph Penso De La Vega's polemical text *Confusion de Confusiones* (1688) as an unmediated reflection of financial practice. But see Jonathan Israel's reminder that among the key factors that De La Vega listed as affecting the stock market were "the designs and machinations of the stock exchange dealers themselves" (1990, 414). See also Israel's (1990, 419) comments on De La Vega's intended audience and purposes, which highlight the author's self-consciously polemical intentions and Kellenbenz's (1996) discussion of De La Vega's literary training.

ernmental supervision did the issue of noncitizens among the ranks become an identifiable problem that the authorities sought to address through legislation. Historians have noted the general attempt by the sixteenth-century Venetian government to curb what was often perceived as foreign "takeover" of the city's guilds.[43] In approving the statutes of the brokers' guild in 1503, the Senate decreed that all guild members must be citizens by birth.[44] But three months later, when guild membership was increased from 100 to 150, the Great Council stipulated that the 50 additional brokers could be either "Venetians or others who have resided in the city for fifteen years."[45] Even these residency requirements did not remain in effect for long. In the course of the sixteenth century, the condition of formal citizenship for brokers was repeatedly overlooked and eventually was waived almost entirely.[46] The increasing prevalence of brokerage by special privilege (i.e., by non–guild members) obviated such requirements altogether.

Yet the process of supplicating for and obtaining a privilege for nonguild brokerage should not be seen as separate from the processes of the brokers' guild incorporation. It was precisely the new closure and institutionalization of brokerage that necessitated the procedure of supplicating for individuals to operate as

43. According to Anna Bellavitis (2001, 40) after 1520 foreigners could enter the offices of guild stewards (*gastaldi*) and judges only if they were the sons of foreigners but had been born in Venice, formally naturalized, and married to a Venetian woman. This requirement was eventually enforced on all guilds even when it contradicted their own statutes. But, as Luca Molà notes with regards to the silk guild in 1537, "While guild officials in fact decided to exclude all foreigners from admission to the guild and from apprenticeship ... they were unable, or unwilling, to impose the same rule on the various classes of artisans, whose survival—in Venice as elsewhere—largely depended upon the steady, and always welcome, influx from abroad" (1997, 100).
44. Consoli dei mercanti, b. 58, fasc. "Magistrati a stampa," c. 1 (Sept. 19, 1503). See also Ferro (1779, 677).
45. Consoli dei mercanti, b. 58, fasc. "Magistrati a stampa," c. 11 (Dec. 21, 1503). This was still more restricted than the fifteenth-century legislation, which allowed anyone who had resided in the city for ten years to operate as a broker in Rialto and which waived residency requirements altogether for certain other types of brokers. A summary of a Senate resolution in the matter from January 22, 1435 m.v., appears in Consoli dei mercanti, b. 58, fasc. verde, cc. 1r–v.
46. In 1519, the three Provveditori di Comun, the commission in charge of electing new members of the brokers' guild (and, significantly, also in charge of generally supervising the guilds and naturalizing foreigners), decreed that "all these foreigners, who have petitioned to become regular brokers, who have taken a Venetian wife in accordance with the decree made by the Great Council on July 5, 1517, can benefit from the decree that they can be brokers, and therefore can be voted and elected by this College, as if they were citizens by birth" (Arti, b. 517, fasc. 1, c. 26). The case of Battista Garibaldo, a broker who in 1553 was threatened with having his license revoked due to the fact that he was Genoese, is telling. Garibaldo argued that his having taken a Venetian wife qualified him as a citizen. The Board of Trade accepted his arguments and renewed his license (Cinque Savi, Seconda serie, b. 146, fasc. 26 (Aug. 9, 1553)).

licensed brokers. *Supranumerary*, the term used to refer collectively to this group of brokers by special privilege, bears witness to this relationship.

Converts: Christian Rhetoric, Civic Rhetoric

A good portion of the aspiring brokers were converts to Catholicism. Thanks to its commercial orientation, Venice had attracted in the course of the sixteenth century substantial numbers of Lutheran, Jewish, and Muslim merchants. Its fabled linguistic and religious heterogeneity appealed to many a heterodox, as well as to non-Catholics seeking to convert (see chap. 3).[47] Wishing to attract foreign business, Venetian authorities often acted on the principle of "don't ask, don't tell" when it came to matters of belief and ritual. Yet after 1557 Venice actively joined the conversionist frenzy that gripped Europeans in these years of Protestant and Catholic reform by establishing the Pia Casa dei Catecumeni (see chap. 4). True to its Roman Jesuit model, part of the mission of this Venetian institution was to secure material assistance for neophytes, either through private patronage or directly from the state, often in the form of guaranteed employment as commercial brokers.[48] Religious precepts and effective social control were thus articulated through civic patronage and charity.[49]

Whether converts highlighted in their petitions their command of Turkish and other languages, their extensive ties in the Ottoman Empire, or simply their abject poverty and fear of old acquaintances' ridicule, the expectation that the government should assume responsibility for their material well-being by providing employment as brokers was widespread. The expectation that converts should be provided for may have derived from the Ottoman custom of providing converts with money for new clothes and sometimes also with employment.[50] It also may have followed from the canon law concept that the convert must improve his or her material status upon conversion.[51] A link between many converts' Ottoman provenance and their presumed propensity to broker trade with fellow trans-imperial subjects further prompted converts to petition for employment as brokers.

---

47. Pullan (1983); Head (1990).

48. Extant work on other early modern Italian cities suggests that neophytes could get married to local Christians and settle in the city immediately following their baptism. For such evidence from Bologna, see Sarti (2001, 457).

49. On the importance of charity through networks of patronage and clientage to the maintenance of Venetian social hierarchies, see Romano (1987, 1993).

50. Minkov (2000, 179–80).

51. According to Kenneth Stow (1976, 179), sixteenth-century canon law conceived of the convert as a "new person," whose past is erased and who therefore must be treated on a par with Christians. From this followed the requirement that the convert's material status must improve as well.

Many convert supplicants framed their appeal in a Christian moral universe. Zuanne, a convert from Islam, appealed in 1611 to be appointed broker of "Turks, Armenians, Greeks, and Jews, and Christians."[52] It is significant that the residual category "Christians" does not encompass "Armenians" and "Greeks" because it suggests that for the author "Christian" was synonymous with "Catholic" and perhaps even "European."[53] Such a conflation of Christianity with Europeanness positioned the supplicant himself as somehow no longer Levantine by virtue of his conversion. The distinction between Greeks and Armenians, on the one hand, and Latin Catholics, on the other, had been established already under Byzantine rule. And it remained important in Ottoman officialdom's categorization of the "people of the book" (*dhimmi*) under its jurisdiction.[54] A similar differentiation among Christian religious communities under Ottoman rule became salient to the Venetian Board of Trade in the seventeenth century, suggesting, perhaps, the role of trans-imperial brokers of Ottoman provenance in transforming Venetian geopolitical categories and sensibilities (see chap. 7).

Other convert supplicants claimed to have been forced to apostatize as slaves and to have reembraced Christianity immediately on their release from captivity. Such supplicants often invoked the piety of the Venetian Republic to strengthen their appeal. So, for example, Michiel di Santo Summa, who petitioned for appointment as a commercial broker in 1560, recounted his mishaps as a mariner on a Venetian ship, on which he had been captured by Turks, forced to apostatize, and kept in captivity for nine and a half years. The opening lines of his petition read: "The faith of Our Lord Jesus Christ, founded on the Rock of St. Peter, can truthfully be said not to be defended by any Christian prince more than it is defended and conserved by the Venetian Republic."[55] By affirming the role of the Republic as the defender of the faith, Summa is simultaneously making a claim to the inherent Christian morality of Venice and to his own Christianity. The Christianity he refers to is Catholic: ecumenical and universalizing; centered in Rome (the Rock of St. Peter is the saint's tomb, on which, according to the Gospel of St. Matthew 16:18, God built his Church); and transcending

---

52. Collegio, Risposte di dentro, b. 13 (Aug. 25, 1611).
53. This is not the place to address early modern shifting notions of religious difference and the impact of reform, on the one hand, and missionary activity, on the other, on Catholic perceptions of the Christian communities of the Ottoman and Safavid empires. On the history of Jesuit, Carmelite, and other missionaries in the Levant, see Frazee (1983); Setton (1984). On the gradual severing of the Balkans from Venetian images of Europe, see Wolff (2001). For an analogous process in German lands, see Petkov (1997).
54. Goffman (1994, 144–46).
55. Collegio, Notatorio, reg. 33, c. 39r (March 12, 1561).

any political boundaries, so that Venice can become the defender of Rome.[56] As it turns out, Summa was a Venetian subject, perhaps even a citizen, if indeed his father was Venetian as he claimed. Moreover, he had served in the Venetian navy and had been taken captive in battle. Yet his appeal was primarily grounded not in the obligations of the state to its subjects and combatants but in Christian morality. Hence, he emphasizes his return from captivity—physical, but even more crucially, spiritual.

Summa's petition articulates a common expectation that the state should help redeemed slaves, especially ones forced to apostatize, by providing them with material assistance on their release. Thus, his narrative maintains a strong Christian sense of divine agency as it weaves together the story of his redemption from captivity: "[H]oping that the Divine Majesty would liberate me ... and also by His grace it occurred that I escaped from said places, and arrived in this blessed city, all by Divine miracle."[57]

Whereas in Summa's petition agency is entirely divine and it alone propels moral action, other petitioners invoked divine agency to make a claim not only to Christian charity but to civic duty as well.[58] In fact, the two often came together, especially in petitions by those Venetian-born Jews whose conversion to Christianity granted them entry both to the Christian moral community and, at least in theory, to formal citizenship. For example, in 1563 Zuan Giacomo, a convert formerly known as Jacob dalla Baldora, sought appointment as a broker by articulating a general rule:

> The immense goodness of Your Sublimity, which always helps all its loyal subjects, and the poor oppressed by adversity, and the travails of this world, and most of all, those poor ones who, being in the hands of the Devil wanting the true light of the faith in our Sweetest Lord Jesus Christ our redeemer illuminated by the light of the Holy Spirit humbly go to the water of the Holy Baptism relinquishing all their sustenance, and ascend in the blood of Jesus Christ, as I have done, poor Zuan Giacomo becoming from a Jew a Christian, and formerly called Jacob dalla Baldora, and having been baptized, and left without any sustenance, brought through God's grace

56. Presenting Venice as "Christianity's first line of defense" became part and parcel of Venetian propaganda in the early sixteenth century, when Venice abandoned the Holy League and concluded a separate peace treaty with the Ottomans in 1509 (Tenenti 1973, 28).

57. Collegio, Notatorio, reg. 33, c. 39r (March 12, 1561).

58. Not only was Summa appointed a commercial broker "with Turks only," but his case was cited a few months later by an Armenian named Simon to justify a similar request that would, he claimed, save him from having to beg for charity in order to feed his family. His request was similarly granted (Collegio, Notatorio, reg. 33, c. 62v (June 13, 1561)).

to the house of the Magnificent Master Andrea, and Girolamo Contarini and their brothers under the most eminent Mr. Dario for the love of God until some Christian help would provide for me, and although I was left without goods of any sort, grace has not left me, and hope in our highest redeemer, and the infinite clemency of Your Serenity. Therefore throwing myself humbly at your feet, as your most loyal slave, I ask for your Highness [celtitudine] to be content to grant me permission to exercise the office of broker in any place, as it has been conceded to others in such cases, until the occasion may come, to appoint ordinary brokers, so that with that favor, and thanks to Your Serenity, and to my Lord Jesus Christ, I can nourish my poor life, and pray the Highest God for the Felicity, and Exaltation of Your Serenity, and of Your Most Happy Dominion, and so I humbly beg your benignity and clemency.[59]

The state thus fits into a divine program when it supports those who are born in the blood of Christ. If God can provide spiritual sustenance, the state must do its share by providing material sustenance. Significantly, the transition in the text from the general to the particular, and from Jesus to the author's person, is immediately followed by the introduction of new actors, the Contarini brothers, members of the Venetian patrician class.[60] They too are part of a Godly plan. It is through them, as the providers of nourishment and shelter, that the convert finds his physical place after finding his new spiritual place in Jesus. In fact, their help is metonymical for the hoped-for governmental help in the form of the appointment as broker that Zuan Giacomo is ultimately seeking. Thus, by affirming the Christian charity of the state, the author also affirms his own worthiness as its intended recipient.

A call to the state to partake in a divine plan characterizes not only the petitions of former Jews but of former Muslims as well. Andrea, the son of Piero de Larta (Arta, in the Epirus), petitioned the government in 1595 and asked to be appointed a regular (i.e., guild-member) broker. He based his appeal on his poverty, "having left what little I had to come to the faith of Jesus Christ, and get out of the diabolical chains to live and die under the happy shadow of Your Serenity."[61] Here, although agency is "inspired by divine majesty," it also serves to highlight the intentional nature of the supplicant's own actions ("I left said place … in order to come to the faith of Lord our God, and make myself

59. Collegio, Risposte di dentro, b. 1, c. 7 (Sept. 27, 1563). See appendix 1.1 for a transcript of the original petition.
60. On Girolamo Contarini (1521–1577), who pursued a career in the Venetian merchant fleet, see Derosas (1983).
61. Collegio, Risposte di dentro, b. 33, c. 156 (April 13, 1569).

Christian ..."). Andrea argues that he should be given the job for "knowing the Turkish language, and other languages, and also for being very experienced in this affair." Interestingly, his petition was denied, suggesting that the granting of converts' requests for employment as brokers was not automatic.[62]

For some converts, the rhetoric of divine agency could serve to highlight both a continuity with their previous religious community and a new beginning. In 1618, a convert named Scipion Borghese, formerly known as Joel Ambasciadorino Hebreo, petitioned the government to grant him "2 brokerages in the Ghetto, so that they could be exercised by him or made to be exercised [by others] to support his family."[63] These brokerages had been previously granted to his father's maternal uncle, Dr. Salomon Ashkenazi, in recognition of his important role in negotiating a peace treaty with the Ottomans in 1573 and then extended to Salomon's nephew Samuel, Joel's father.[64]

Jews were not easily granted the privilege of brokerage in the ghetto. Yet this privilege was certainly understood as an acceptable token of recognition for special services rendered to the state by members of the Jewish community of the city.[65] What is significant about Borghese's petition is his expectation of having such a privilege renewed, but now based on his new status as a Christian. In fact, as a key argument in favor of his unusual request, Borghese suggested that such a privilege "would animate others to recognize the truth of our Holy faith, and abandon the errors of Judaism to the glory of God, and for the health of their souls."[66] A similar argument was put forth by another convert, Francesco Gritti, the son of Samuel Pichio, "an old Venetian Jew from the Ghetto." In his petition of 1620, Gritti claimed to have no other trade and urged the government to appoint him broker "to the glory of God who called me ... to the light of the Christian faith, and to the confusion of the obstinate Jews, who delight in seeing us, the baptized,

62. Collegio, Risposte di dentro, b. 33, c. 156 (April 13, 1569). See also Dal Borgo (1997).
63. Collegio, Risposte di dentro, b. 15, c. 2 (April 11, 1618). Evidently, he was named after Scipion Borghese Cafarelli (1576–1633), the Roman cardinal, suggesting a sojourn in Rome. Cafarelli later became the cardinal protector of the Roman Pia Casa dei Catecumeni, indicating a lasting relationship with converts (Rudt de Collenberg 1989, 19).
64. On Ashkenazi's exploits and for the family's genealogical tree, see Arbel (1991).
65. See, for example, the case of Orso and Cervo, Jewish brothers who sought, and received, perpetual appointment as brokers of carpets (*tapezzarie*) in the Ghetto Nuovo in 1577. In their petition the two emphasized their past services to the government, including the sale of carpets to the magistracy of the Rason Vecchie at cut-throat prices (Collegio, Risposte di dentro, b. 6, c. 197 (Nov. 13, 1577)). Two years later, Elia Francese of Famagusta (Cyprus), a Jew, asked to be appointed broker in the ghetto in recompense for his lost property in Cyprus. His request was similarly endorsed by the Board of Trade (Cinque Savi, Risposte, b. 136, cc. 129r–v (March 31, 1579); see also Arbel 2000a).
66. Collegio, Risposte di dentro, b. 15, c. 2 (April 11, 1618).

go wandering and dispersed."[67] In a prompt response only twelve days later, the Board of Trade recognized the custom of granting such requests by converted Jews and endorsed Gritti's appeal so that he could "continue [to live] in the holiest Catholic faith."[68]

Building on the ancient trope of conversion from Judaism to Christianity as a healing process of recognizing past error, Borghese and Gritti thus reminded the government of the political significance of providing for converts.[69] They also cast the state as a paternal figure responsible for converts' material well-being, recalling patricians understandings of themselves as the benevolent paternal custodians of a well-managed Republic.

By seeking appointment as brokers, converts articulated a sense of themselves as fully transformed into Christian moral persons yet also as potential links between the Christian universe of the Venetian metropole and the Jewish and Ottoman-Muslim merchant communities that made up its interior and exterior frontiers.

Jews: Usefulness and Loyalty

If a Christian frame was key to asserting a convert's newly found membership in Venetian society, what frames could Jewish supplicants employ? An interesting case is a petition submitted by four Jewish ghetto night guards in 1566 to renew their privilege to exercise brokerage in the ghetto as a supplement to their modest incomes of 2 ducats per month each.[70] To argue their case, the supplicants traced the Jews' long presence in Venice through reference to various government decrees of the previous fifty years.[71] By detailing the volatile nature of governmental Jewish policies, the petition makes evident the authors' own familiarity with Jews' historically changing juridical status in the city, suggesting to their patrician interlocutors their awareness of just how much this status depended on political exigency and was thus changeable.[72] More significantly, the petition characterized the Jewish community as morally upright and an integral part of Venetian urban society. According to the supplicants, their role as guards

---

67. Collegio, Risposte di dentro, b. 15, c. 231 (March 14, 1620). The same argument was brought up by another convert, Girolamo Valle, son of Samuel Abuaf, similarly a member of the Venetian community of the ghetto, in his petition in 1621 (Collegio, Risposte di dentro, b. 16, c. 41 (May 4, 1621)).

68. Cinque Savi, Risposte, b. 145, c. 58r (March 26, 1620).

69. On the continuities and discontinuities in converts' lives after baptism, see chapter 4.

70. Collegio, Risposte di dentro, b. 2, c. 76 (Sept. 6, 1566).

71. See Boccato (1974) for an overview of commercial activity in the ghetto since its establishment in 1516.

72. Indeed, their timing could hardly have been worse. The years 1565–1566 marked heightened anti-Jewish Venetian policies, which were only exacerbated with the outbreak of the Venetian-Ottoman War of Cyprus, for which Jews were blamed (Ravid 1982, 36–40).

was not only to prevent Jews from roaming outside the ghetto at night (the official argument) but also "to open the gates for the many [Jews] who continuously arrive from various parts of the world, and … for the physicians who get up and are very frequently called to cure the inhabitants in Your city."[73] Thus, the authors attempted to draw from a shared fund of "civic credit" that the Jews of Venice supposedly enjoyed with the authorities for their good services as international merchants and physicians.

The Jewish collectivity emerges from this description as taking care of the material—economic as well as physical—preservation of the city. This is particularly interesting in light of the petitioners' careful avoidance of references to ethnic and economic subdivisions within the ghetto. Distinctions among the Venetian Jewish populace were formally recognized and institutionalized both within the ghetto and by the government from the early sixteenth century on. In fact, it was the renewed enforcement of these divisions that prompted a change in regulations regarding the ghetto guards. Unlike most Jewish petitions to the Venetian government, which upheld the official distinction between "Levantine" and "German" (and sometimes "Venetian") Jews, each with its own privileges and duties, this one claimed to speak in the name of all of the ghetto residents. It is not inconceivable that the supplicants were actually "German" Jews (i.e., of Ashkenazi origin, even if their ancestors had lived in the Veneto for several generations), as these were the least privileged Jews in Venice and most likely to be employed in lowly occupations such as ghetto guards. Levantine (and later also Ponentine) Jews, descendents of exiles from Spain and Portugal, enjoyed for the most part extensive commercial privileges both in Venice and in the Ottoman Empire and frequently employed family ties in long-distance trade that stretched across the Mediterranean.[74] Unlike them, Ashkenazi Jews, who did not enjoy Ottoman protection, were formally banned from all commercial activities in Venice save for money-lending and trading in secondhand clothes. So, whereas Levantine Jews frequently exercised commercial brokerage with few governmental sanctions, both in the ghetto and outside it, Ashkenazi Jews faced much heavier policing of their mercantile activities and therefore had the most to gain from a formal permit to exercise brokerage, even if only within the ghetto.

73. "L'obligo grande che hanno ordinariamente, tutta la notte guardar esse porte, si per oviar che li Hebrei non vadino per la Città vagando per convenienti rispetti. come anchora per aprir molti di loro che vengono di continuo da diverse parti del mondo, et per aprire à medici, comare che arlievano, spessissimo chiamati alla cura, et bisogno delli habitanti, nella sua Città" (Collegio, Risposte di dentro, b. 2, c. 76 (Sept. 6, 1566)). On Venetian policing of the ghetto gates and the flow of people in and out during day- and nighttime, see Ravid (1999).
74. Arbel (2001).

Unlike brokerage within the ghetto, which was granted to Jews under certain conditions, Jewish brokerage in Rialto was met with fierce opposition. As early as 1520, the Board of Trade decreed that, given the existence of many Christian brokers, "Jews cannot be brokers" because "Justice does not suffer that Jews should take bread out of the mouth of Christians."[75]

As is often the case, however, practice proved much more dynamic than legislation might suggest. In 1641, on his return from Istanbul, bailo Alvise Contarini endorsed a request by Samuel Spiera, a Jew, and his four sons to be appointed brokers in Rialto "together with all the nations." The appointment was vigorously opposed by the Board of Trade, whose response is worth quoting in full:

Your Serenity, having recognized how important was the commerce in this marketplace, that the brokerage of trade in the market be contracted with the mediation of Civil and trustworthy persons, decreed in 1503 that these [brokerages] should be in the hands of born Venetians only, and instituted the corporation of 190 regular brokers of Rialto, to whom belongs this business of brokerage, obliging them to exercise no other trade, and prohibiting at the same time that anyone else should broker trade, and particularly the Jews, under the most severe punishments; although due to circumstances some other deserving individuals were granted permission to exercise [brokerage] as supranumerary; and the right to broker trade in the ghetto, and of secondhand clothes, which have nothing to do with the brokerages of Rialto, was conceded to some Jews; and on the last day of June 1532 it seems that the merits of Mr. Meir Maurogonato made the heads of the Council of Ten grant him and his descendents, among other privileges, also the right to broker trade in the ghetto, and outside the ghetto. Perhaps in these equivocal words Mr. Samuel Spiera grounded his case, asking Your Serenity by way of the excellent Mr. Bailo to agree to grant him and his four sons permission to broker trade in Rialto together with all the nations; this will be in our mind a contravention of all public decrees, and resolutions of the magistrates delegated in these matters; however there is no shortage of other means for the public munificence to console him who with his own fruitful efforts to public advantage has sought to make himself worthy of public favor, as has done the above-mentioned

---

75. Arti, b. 517, fasc. 1, c. 29r (Sept. 28, 1520). In many other cases, however, the Board of Trade represented a more pragmatic approach and emphasized Jewish merchants' contributions to the economy vis-à-vis the magistracy of Ufficiali al cattaver, who were placed in charge of the ghetto in 1516 and who tended to emphasize the need to curb Jewish infractions (Malkiel 1991, 100).

Spiera, particularly in the latest circumstances in Constantinople and for which our excellent Mr. Bailo Contarini provides ample evidence.[76]

This response sharply contrasts "Civil, trustworthy persons" with Jews, just as it juxtaposes the latter with Venetian citizens. It selectively recalls past legislation but glosses over concessions made to nonnative citizens to join the guild and the actual practice of admitting many non-Catholic Greeks and Armenians into its ranks. This erasure is meant to highlight the difference between Christian guild members and the specific Jewish supplicant, Spiera. Indeed, the board goes to great length to establish a history of legislation (and its careful enforcement) that has prevented Jews from brokering trade, save for trade within the ghetto. That the authors also mention trade in secondhand clothes,[77] the hallmark of Ashkenazi Jews' precarious legal status in the city, might be an attempt to add insult to injury, highlighting Spiera's Ashkenazi provenance as opposed to his connections in Istanbul.

Spiera, in all likelihood, was counting on a pattern of concessions of brokerage to Jews based on their services not only to the Venetian state but also to the sultan or to high-ranking Ottoman officials. For example, in 1583 bailo Maffeo Venier reminded the government of the request of Ibrahim Pasha to have Mordacai Graffini and his two sons Moise and Jacob appointed "regular brokers in the ghetto."[78] In such cases, official recognition of Jews as commercial brokers between Ottoman and Venetian mercantile elites also served to consolidate their already well-recognized role as power brokers between Ottoman and Venetian political elites.[79]

But Spiera's suggestion that the proverbial role of intermediary should place him in Rialto injured the sensibilities of Venetian authorities. By seeking appointment as a guild member, Spiera attempted to obtain official recognition of what in practice was quite common but always illicit and transgressive—Jews brokering trade outside the ghetto. The distinction "in the ghetto" and "outside the ghetto" was, as the Board of Trade must have recognized, nominal only. There were no

---

76. Cinque Savi, Risposte, b. 152, cc. 194r–v (July 12, 1641). See appendix 1.2 for a transcript of the original response.

77. On the trade in secondhand clothes in early modern Venice, see Allerston (1996).

78. Senato, Dispacci Costantinopoli, b. 17, cc. 213r–214r (May 17, 1583). I thank Benjamin Arbel for bringing the case to my attention and for providing me with a transcript.

79. Without entering into the important role of court Jews as political brokers in sixteenth-century Istanbul and elsewhere, it should be noted that international politics was clearly at stake in cases such as this. Interestingly, Graffini's case set a precedent later cited by the Board of Trade when it granted lifetime permission to another Jew, Gasparo di Cremonesi, and his two daughters Zanetta and Cecilia to exercise brokerage in the ghetto (Cinque Savi, Risposte, b. 137, c. 161 (Feb. 26, 1585 m.v.); b. 145, c. 24v (Dec. 4, 1629)).

restrictions on non-Jews' entry into the ghetto or on Jews' freedom to leave it during daytime.[80] In fact, court records of the brokers' guild list the names of dozens of Jews charged with illicit brokerage during this period. Their clientele were frequently non-Jewish merchants, and their minimal punishments, when convicted, clearly did not prohibit them from continuing to broker trade (see chap. 2). Yet, by attempting to formalize Jewish brokerage in Rialto and thus making the transgression explicit, Spiera and his Ottoman patrons exceeded what was permissible even for the pragmatically minded Board of Trade. Probably, the board was also responding here to complaints from the brokers' guild. In its repeated protests against the declining volume of Levantine trade in the 1630s and 1640s, the guild frequently decried Jewish competition, and it quite likely resented Spiera's request as well, especially given his demonstrated ties to Ottoman elites.[81]

Redeemed Slaves: From Willing Service to Forced Servitude and Back

In their petitions for jobs, supplicants did not rely solely on Christian morality and civic membership. We have already glimpsed other strategies, such as emphases on abject poverty, large deserving families, and past services rendered to the state (often in the military, which relied heavily on colonial conscripts). An emphasis on service to the state in petitions for brokerage was a particularly common strategy among colonial subjects, who invoked not only their own past service but also that of their ancestors, all the more so if they could claim relatives who had been killed, injured, or enslaved while fighting Ottoman incursions into Venetian territory. For example, Giovanni Babin, a "Cypriot nobleman," petitioned the government for employment as a broker in 1590, twenty years after Venice had lost Cyprus to the Ottomans. In his petition, Babin mentioned not only his five brothers, enslaved in Istanbul and Aleppo, but also other members of his long ancestry, all of whom were loyal servants to the Republic: his mother's brother Scipio Costanzo, his father Giofre Babin "who was viscount numerous times, and procurator of the corporation of Nicosia, general captain of the ram-

---

80. That Christians traded in the ghetto is well attested and was even part of official laments against Jewish brokers in the ghetto and attempts to limit their activity to brokering trade with Jewish merchants only (Senato, Terra, reg. 44, c. 127 (June 1, 1563)). See also Boccato (1974, 31).
81. For a sample of collective petitions submitted in the late 1630s by the brokers' guild that sought a reduction in mandatory payments on transactions involving Levantine merchants, see Collegio, Risposte di dentro, b. 27 (April 3, 1636 & June 20, 1636); b. 29 (Feb. 1, 1638 m.v.); b. 30 (June 22, 1639); Cinque Savi, Risposte, b. 151, cc. 37–38 (Dec. 30, 1636).

part of San Luca," and his paternal great-grandfathers "Cavalier Anibal Babin, and Pietro Gullo."[82]

Babin's Cypriot roots are worth dwelling on. Suppliants originating from Cyprus were far more likely than any other colonial subjects to invoke history in their appeals to the Venetian government. In particular, Cypriots sought to capitalize on memories of the lost Venetian colony, its riches, and the faithful services rendered by its feudatory class to the Republic. That Cyprus had been under (official or unofficial) Venetian rule for a particularly long time and that its strategic importance made its loss in 1571 especially painful may well have been important. How the well-established feudatory class of the island (from whose ranks many suppliants came) understood its Venetian-ness also calls for further study.[83]

The narration of family history was an effective means of both recalling illustrious ancestry and promoting offspring and agnates. At a deeper level, by invoking kin, redeemed slaves (whose whereabouts during their time of captivity were always suspect) indexed their rootedness in and continued commitment to a social order premised on kinship ties.[84] For example, in 1609 a commercial broker named Zorzi da Milo petitioned to have his guild membership transferred to his son-in-law, Pietro Francolin. Zorzi was a redeemed slave and an émigré from Venetian Cyprus, although his name suggests roots in Milos, another Venetian colony in the Aegean lost to the Ottomans in 1566. To justify his somewhat unusual request, Zorzi mentioned his own frailty and Pietro's command of Turkish and Slavic. He also directed attention to his own two illustrious uncles.[85] The Board of Trade opened its appraisal of the case by reminding the government that many Cypriots had been appointed brokers through special privilege in the past. It thus endorsed Zorzi's effort to achieve the status of a well-deserving colonial subject and place his request in the realm of "favors to Cypriots." The board then

82. Collegio, Risposte di dentro, b. 9, c. 130 (April 26, 1590) A second petition from 1601 deplores Babin's current poverty and reminds the government of his family's services and lost riches in Nicosia (Cinque Savi, Risposte, b. 140 (March 25, 1601)). His request to broker trade of "Turks, Jews, and Greeks" was endorsed the following year (Ufficio della Bolla Ducale, Grazie del Maggior Consiglio, reg. 7, cc. 43v–44r (Feb. 9, 1602 m.v.)). See also my discussion of the petition submitted in 1592 by Ambrosio Babino, who in all likelihood was Giovanni's brother.
83. Local Cypriot oligarchies were well-integrated into the Venetian system of rule on the island, not only as landowners but also as holders of key positions in the military and the civil service (Arbel 1996, 971). On the nobility of Venetian Cyprus in general, see Rudt de Collenberg (1983); Arbel (2000a; 2009, esp. 43–44). On Cypriot émigrés in Venice, see Kyrris (1968, 1969, 1970).
84. On the familial ideologies of the Venetian patriciate, see Grubb (1994); Sperling (1999a, 1999b); Sabbadini (1995). The rejection of a strictly descent-based social order was one of the aspects of Ottoman governmentality that epitomized its alterity in Venetian patricians' eyes (Wilson 2003, 39).
85. Cinque Savi, Risposte, b. 142, c. 119r–v (March 17, 1609); b. 144, c. 63r (n.d.).

verified the identity of Zorzi's two uncles, Agarico Zebeton and Zegno Procopi, and the fact of their deaths during the War of Cyprus (1570–1572). Finally, the board detailed Zorzi's long service as a ship captain in the service of various Venetian ship owners. Thus, the response established not only Zorzi's identity as a worthy subject but also the authority of the board as a body entrusted with appraising supplicants' merit and, indeed, identity.

Redeemed slaves often requested—and were granted—brokerage "of Turks only." The category *sensali di Turchi* ("brokers of Turks") included both guild brokers and non–guild brokers and, as should be evident by now, did not encompass all who brokered Ottoman trade. In fact, all brokers—regardless of their actual title—who transacted with Ottoman merchants were subjected to the same regulations and taxation. Yet the category "brokers of Turks" was acknowledged in many official documents, including privileges granted to redeemed slaves to exercise brokerage. By linking the brokerage of Ottoman merchants with meritorious ancestry and redemption from Ottoman slavery, the Venetian authorities recognized a kind of "poetic justice." In one case, a former slave's letter of appointment as broker stipulated specifically that the money earned was to be used to redeem his brother, who was still enslaved.[86] In another response from 1588 to a petition by Marco Bacco, an Albanian released from twenty years in Ottoman captivity, the Board of Trade mentioned services to the Republic rendered by the supplicant's grandfather Triffon, once the commander of Cattaro (Kotor, Montenegro). It ultimately recommended Bacco's appointment based on the precedent of brokerage "given to others in similar circumstances" and emphasized that his request was to broker trade "solely with Turks."[87] That such distinction was made only on paper does not seem to have mattered.[88] Symbolically, Bacco's appointment as the "broker of Turks" was a form of redress for his long Ottoman captivity.

Other redeemed slaves suggested in their petitions not only moral redress but certain useful skills acquired during their long captivity. Giulio Torquato had been captured by Maltese corsairs and had served as a slave in Istanbul for twelve years before he was finally released in 1564. A petition of 1567 requesting his appointment as a broker was written, quite unusually, in the third person.

86. In 1592, Ambrosio Babino was appointed broker of "Turks, Jews, Greeks, and Italians ... so that he could support himself, but also seek to recover from slavery Rimondo his brother" (Ufficio della Bolla Ducale, Grazie del Maggior Consiglio, reg. 6, c. 59r (June 16, 1592)).
87. Cinque Savi, Risposte, b. 138, c. 53 (Aug. 18, 1588).
88. After all, Ottoman merchants did not come to Venice to trade with other Ottoman merchants but primarily with Venetians and Germans. Evidence from trials for illicit brokerage similarly indicates that most transactions involving Ottoman merchants included other, non-Ottoman merchants as well.

Interestingly, impersonal terms (as opposed to the first person) were a required formula in all petitions addressed to the Ottoman sultan, including converts' petitions for financial assistance.[89] Torquato's petition emphasized "the great experience that he has among merchants of all nations and in addition to his fabled Italian, he also knows Greek, Turkish, Slavic, and other languages very well, so that he could be of universal use."[90] Torquato suggests that his knowledge of the languages of the Ottoman Empire lends him to "universal use." The Venetian universe, in this view, clearly encompasses the Ottoman Empire, although not transalpine Europe. Yet, as in the case of converts, redeemed slaves' connections in Ottoman lands were a sensitive issue. Given the suspicion with which they could be met (Had they apostatized? How true was their reconciliation with the Church?), emphasizing intimate ties with Ottoman subjects could clearly hurt their cause. Instead, redeemed slaves unfailingly mentioned another intercultural skill—their command of languages acquired while serving in Ottoman households.[91] Linguistic proficiency was often pointed out and capitalized on in official responses to petitions as well.[92] By invoking skill, supplicants and their official interlocutors were thus able to gloss over the potentially transgressive ties that bound petitioners to the Ottoman Empire.

Ottoman Christians as Trans-Imperial Subjects

As I have suggested, the status of converts, Jews, and redeemed slaves as trans-imperial subjects often cast some doubt on their loyalty to and, indeed, very belonging in Venice. For Ottoman subjects who sought to become Venetians, establishing and maintaining not only juridical but social membership in Venice

89. These petitions were known as *kisve bahası*, lit. "cash value of clothes" (Minkov 2000, 164).
90. Collegio, Risposte di dentro, b. 2, c. 224 (Jan. 9, 1567 m.v.). Evidence suggests that Torquato's request was granted, but for some reason he did not become broker. In 1573, he petitioned again, this time specifying his wish to be permitted to broker trade of "the Levantine Nation" (Collegio, Risposte di dentro, b. 5, c. 202 (Oct. 4, 1573)).
91. The category "slave" as used in these petitions derived from a much broader discourse about Christian captives in the hands of Muslims. Beyond the theological significance of the category, however, it should be emphasized that, whereas some Christians captured in the Balkans and the eastern Mediterranean served as oarsmen, many others were employed in domestic service under conditions that may not have differed substantially from those of servants and domestic slaves on the Italian peninsula and elsewhere during that period. The religious implications of such domestic arrangements are yet to be fully explored. On the ideological dimensions of the Mediterranean slave trade, see Rudt de Collenberg (1987); Bennassar and Bennassar (1989); Bono (1998, 1999); Davis (2003).
92. The extent to which supplicants' claims to know languages were substantiated remains unknown. So far, I have found no indications of governmental examinations of prospective brokers' linguistic skills.

entailed special (discursive or other) labor. The Ottoman Empire had inherited from its Byzantine predecessor a large array of Christian and Jewish communities whose religious, political, economic, and kinship structures might at times link them to other powers, including Venice.[93] These links were, of course, contingent and fluctuating, but they established a precedent for subsequent waves of émigrés, diasporic sojourners, and settlers in the expansive Venetian-Ottoman borderlands. The Venetian government was often sympathetic to Ottoman Christians' claims for a special affective tie to Venice, particularly when they could cite past services to the Republic.

An example of how Christian supplicants sought to capitalize on this supposed special bond to Venice is the following petition for a brokerage license, submitted by Lorenzo Capessich of Sebenico (Šibenik, Croatia) in 1621:

> While I, Lorenzo Capessich of Sebenico, sojourned in Turkey on the oc-
> casion of business for the entire course of twelve years, I have mastered
> perfectly the Turkish language, such that it adds to the Slavic and Italian
> that I know very well, making me fit to act for the public and private ben-
> efit in commerce, especially having acquired many friends in the country,
> which I have kept for the dependency that they have with our house in
> Sebenico, where I could make myself a fruitful subject and servant of Your
> Serenity in diverse affairs, in which I have been employed by Illustrious
> Public Representatives in the talks with the Lords Sancaks, and in the ne-
> gotiations with Turkish ministers; and since I have decided to settle and
> to be able to live with honest utility in this great [Alma] city which is
> Universal Fatherland to all the people and to me especially born of de-
> serving Parentage, and of a mother from the family of Vegici Spatafora
> of Nauplion, who with the loss of that most loyal city lost many riches; I
> petition reverently Your Serenity that it deign to grant me the favor that
> I be appointed Regular Broker, [so] that I will not stop laboring in that
> position to forever give preference with public service to the satisfaction of
> merchants for the growth of commerce.[94]

93. For studies of the historical transformations of the Ottoman system of ruling over Christian and Jewish communities, see Braude and Lewis (1982); Goffman (1994); Paraskevas (1999). I thank Tijana Krstić for introducing me to the debates about this issue and for suggesting these particular readings. See also Rodrigue (1996) for an insightful discussion of Ottoman conceptions of religious difference, albeit with a nineteenth-century focus.
94. Collegio, Risposte di dentro, b. 16, c. 135 (Nov. 13, 1621). See appendix 1.3 for a transcript of the original petition.

Capessich presents himself as the ultimate trans-imperial subject. First, he was the product of a colonial union between a Dalmatian father (as his name and place of provenance suggest) and a mother from Nauplion, a former Venetian colony in the Peloponnese, lost to the Ottomans in the Peace Treaty of 1540.[95] Moreover, his entire life trajectory seems to lead to Venice. Not only did he actively choose to become a Venetian by moving to the metropole, but he casts his long sojourn as a merchant in Ottoman lands as a "public service" to his beloved *patria*. Such a conflation of private interest and public service would have been a familiar trope to his patrician interlocutors because large Venetian merchant colonies had been established in major Byzantine trading hubs such as Smyrna (Izmir), Prusa (Bursa), and Trebizond (Trabzon) as early as the 1200s and had continued to thrive after these cities became Ottoman, often serving as centers for gathering military and political intelligence on behalf of the Republic.[96] Indeed, Capessich based his appeal neither solely on the merits of ancestry nor on his mercantile credentials and linguistic competence; rather, he emphasized his proven public service as an interpreter and a go-between. Most significantly, he made the case of being a child of Venice by virtue not only of parentage but of volition. Likewise, he suggested that his ongoing connections in Šibenik (where some of his family still resided) and among Ottoman friends would not hinder but rather advance his hoped-for new position as commercial broker. Finally, his petition suggests that his primary allegiance should be to the merchants he would service because this would guarantee "the growth of commerce"—appealing to the interest of the Board of Trade in renewing the commercial attractiveness of Venice in a period of sharp decline in the volume of international trade in the city. In short, Capessich aligned his life trajectory with the fortunes of the Republic in a move not unlike that of patrician self-representations, which "folded the individual family's claims to eminence into the overall glories of the ruling group."[97] Not surprisingly, Capessich's petition was enthusiastically endorsed by the authorities, which cited his mastery of language, his previous services as spokesperson for the Republic in border negotiations with an Ottoman Sancakbeyi (district governor), and his maternal pedigree.[98]

---

95. On Venetian Nauplion, see Wright (2000).

96. On the Venetian merchant colony of Istanbul, see Dursteler (2006). On merchant colonies in the Mediterranean more generally, see Jacoby (1997). On Venetian espionage in the Ottoman Empire, see Preto (1986, 1994). For a case study of a Venetian patrician who systematically conflated public service and private interests in his tenure as colonial administrator of Venetian Crete in the later sixteenth century, see Arbel (2008).

97. Grubb (1994, 377).

98. Ufficio della Bolla Ducale, Grazie del Maggior Consiglio, reg. 8, c. 153r (Nov. 15, 1622).

CITIZENSHIP RECONSIDERED

Historians have enumerated the immense diversity of purposes that led people to seek citizenship in late medieval and early modern city-states.[99] Far less attention has been paid to how civic membership was negotiated and practiced, beyond the legal act of naturalization.[100] We have seen that an appeal to civic membership was a powerful rhetorical tool that supplicants used to urge the Venetian government to appoint them as brokers. This suggests that formal citizenship was the purview of only a narrow segment of the Venetian population and that another form of membership in metropolitan society was elaborated by trans-imperial subjects. Indeed, their petitions to be appointed brokers articulate an ideal of membership in metropolitan Venetian society that shares some of the premises underwriting formal citizenship but extends such membership far beyond the citizen class. This expansive ideal of membership is significant not simply because it includes new constituencies but because it modifies the premises of citizenship. Rather than merely being incorporated into the city bureaucracy, the trans-imperial subject-turned-broker linked Venice with its colonies and frontiers, both juridical, religious, and ethnolinguistic.

This is not to suggest that legal citizenship did not matter. Indeed, trans-imperial subjects, particularly those engaged in long-distance trade, readily sought to become naturalized Venetians, given the economic advantages of that status. And even though metropolitan Jews were categorically denied Venetian citizenship, this did not always go unchallenged.[101] Mazo, the son of Gabriel, was born in Venice to a family of Jewish merchants and financiers. A highly inventive character, his petitions to the government, replete with suggestions for improvements of public administration, repeatedly crop up in the archives. In 1586, he and his brother-in-law Isac-dal-Ben from Casal di Monferà offered to reveal "a secret of great importance" in return for becoming Venetian citizens along with all their sons and daughters, current and future.[102] The same supplicants had petitioned

99. Kirshner (1973); Costa (1999).
100. For a notable exception, see Herzog (2003).
101. Venetian Jews were not granted citizenship until the city came under Napoleonic rule in 1797. But, as with many aspects of Venetian law, the situation differed in the Venetian Mediterranean colonies, where, at least in the fourteenth and fifteenth centuries, some Jews could enjoy the status of Venetian nationals, which granted them certain mercantile privileges such as tax and customs breaks. Such status, however, may have had more in common with the status of Venetian (and other Italian city-states) protégé enjoyed by many merchants in the Byzantine Empire (and later in the Ottoman Empire under the capitulation system) than with citizenship in the Venetian metropole. See Ashtor (1975); Jacoby (1987; 1997, esp. 1:549, 3:269). See also Cooperman (1987, 68) on the protected Jewish *Veneti albi* ("white Venetians") of Constantinople.
102. Collegio, Risposte di dentro, b. 8, c. 197 (Feb. 16, 1586 m.v.).

only four months earlier to become guild-member brokers. What they offered in exchange could itself be read as a token of their deep allegiance to the Venetian Republic—a new method for registering the population so that the authorities could "easily tell who comes and who goes in the entire state."[103]

To conclude, trans-imperial subjects employed myriad strategies in their quest to be appointed commercial brokers. Significantly, in the petitions they only rarely capitalized on some "radical alterity" of the Ottomans, a strategy that was more commonly employed by other supplicants and in other institutions, including by dragomans and some foreign merchants themselves (see chaps. 5–6). Rather, aspiring brokers grounded their appeals in a narrative that positioned the Venetian metropole as the telos of their life trajectory; at the same time, they emphasized their own embodiment of Venetian-Ottoman interconnectedness through kinship, patronage, and political exigency. Thus, they invoked the role of intermediary not only as their ultimate future but also as what they had been all along.

103. Collegio, Risposte di dentro, b. 8, c. 162 (Aug. 25, 1586).

2

Brokering Commerce or Making Friends?

I n 1594, Mano Gumeno, an unlicensed commercial broker of Greek descent
active in Venice, signed a partnership contract with two guild-member brokers, Manoli Gardichiotti and Piero Colona.[1] The partnership was ultimately
brought to the attention of the state magistracy in charge of supervising brokers, the Provveditori di Comun, which quickly annulled it.[2] In his hearing,
Colona, a Venetian citizen, argued that he had been coerced into the partnership
by Gardichiotti but that, once he learned it was illegal, he had kept the partnership inactive. He further urged the authorities to absolve him and condemn only
his partners. The magistrates agreed and fined his two Greek partners the rather
modest sum of 5 ducats each, "to be applied to the poor fund."[3] This brush with
the law clearly did not deter Colona from entering other questionable brokerage
partnerships. Only two months after denouncing his former partners Gumeno
and Gardichiotti, his name came up in the trial of two other Greek brokers, Niccolò Saccà and "Tarantà the Greek."[4] Although his exact relationship with the two
was never spelled out, he was mentioned as one of the people present at the "crime
scene" with the defendants, suggesting a similar arrangement to the one he had

---

1. Gumeno may have been related to the prominent Cypriot family of Goneme/Gomnene (Rudt
de Collenberg 1982a, 58).
2. Arti, b. 525, fasc. 1, c. 2v (Jan. 24, 1596).
3. Arti, b. 525, fasc. 1, cc. 32r–35v (March 14, 1597). The contract, which was included with the
trial records, had been signed in Greek by Gumeno and Gardichiotti, and in Italian by Colona.
4. Arti, b. 525, fasc. 1, c. 46 (May 16, 1597).

contracted with Gumeno and Gardichiotti. Four months later, Colona stood yet another trial for forming an illicit brokerage partnership with the same Niccolò Saccà.[5] Their fines, initially set at 60 lire di piccoli each, were later reduced to 50 lire (approximately 8 ducats) combined, suggesting that Colona's influence within the guild allowed him to continue in such shady deals relatively undeterred.

Another trial involving an alleged partnership between Giacomo di Suro, a Cypriot guild-member broker, and Zorzi, an unlicensed Albanian broker, Assan Beich "Sguerzo," a Muslim Indian merchant, and Zuanne della Nave, a Murano glassmaker, offers a further glimpse into the networks of friendship that linked trans-imperial and Venetian subjects and that remained largely undocumented. Such networks counteracted the potential anonymity of the marketplace and circumvented policing efforts by guilds, governments, and landlords. Their common structure suggests the central role of trans-imperial subjects as intermediaries between Muslims and Christians, foreigners and locals, Ottomans and Venetians.

As we will see, the gradual transformation of the Venetian commercial brokers' guild in the course of the sixteenth and seventeenth centuries is closely linked to efforts by certain trans-imperial subjects to cement and institutionalize their relationship with the Venetian state. This relationship was premised on the notion that indebtedness, loyalty, and mutual economic benefits forged affective ties between Christian Ottoman and Venetian colonial subjects, on the one hand, and the Venetian state, on the other. Yet such a relationship was further triangulated through wider networks, which included Safavid and Ottoman Muslims, Jewish brokers, and even members of other trading diasporas elsewhere on the Italian peninsula and beyond. Efforts to institutionalize this relationship were met with fierce opposition from the leadership of the guild of commercial brokers. On its part, this leadership used a variety of legal and commercial mechanisms in an effort to downplay and undermine the growing centrality of trans-imperial subjects to long-distance commercial networks, even as such subjects swelled the ranks of the guild itself.

In early 1597, a secret denunciation reached the brokers' guild. It claimed that a certain "Zorzi the Albanian" had helped an Indian merchant dubbed Sguerzo (lit. "squinter") to sell seven parcels of indigo to Zuanne della Nave (the Murano glassmaker) in exchange for "many glasses of different sorts" and then called Giacomo di Suro, a licensed broker and a Cypriot, to note down the transaction and "show that he was present in the said deal."[6] The first witness interrogated was Camilla Aclea, Sugerzo's landlady. She had learned about the deal

---

5. Arti, b. 525, fasc. 1, cc. 87r–88v (Sept. 3, 1597).
6. Arti, b. 525, fasc. 1, cc. 10v–12v (Feb. 6, 1596 m.v.).

from the Indian merchant himself, through the interpretation of a certain Pietro, a Muslim convert to Christianity. She believed that the broker in that deal had been Giacomo the Cypriot. Indeed, she had heard it from Giacomo himself. As for Zorzi the Albanian, he was also a familiar face in her house; he had gone with Sguerzo two or three times "to do what I do not know." To remove any doubt, she quickly added, "Zorzi told me I'm not a broker, Mr. Giacomo the Cypriot is a broker, and I didn't earn anything from that deal." And she conceded that "if Zorzi told me a lie, so am I telling it to you now." The day after her testimony, Camilla returned to the brokers' office, wishing to "unburden her soul" after a sleepless night. She now remembered having once seen Zorzi the Albanian in the house and having been told that he was there in the company of (or in partnership with) Giacomo the Cypriot. Another time, when she spotted Zorzi leaving the house, he told her he was going "to fetch ser Giacomo the Cypriot, so he could note down this deal of indigo." As a landlady, Camilla certainly kept a watchful eye on her Muslim tenant and his friends. Landladies and landlords, in this as in many other cases, could act as nodes of information serviceable to foreign merchants but also as crucial components in attempts by the authorities to regulate and contain trans-imperial networks that otherwise eluded the state.[7]

A few days later, the tribunal heard the testimony of Pietro, Sguerzo's convert friend. He too had seen Zorzi and Giacomo in the company of Sguerzo and had no doubt they were both brokers. Indeed, Sguerzo had told him so. But his testimony also suggested that Giacomo, the licensed broker, was not a mere "cover" for Zorzi: "I saw Giacomo show the indigo to the merchant, and another time I saw him bring money to the Muslim [Sguerzo], who said that he'd been in Murano to see the merchant."[8]

It is very plausible that Pietro coordinated his testimony with his friend Sguerzo because the latter's interrogation, performed through an interpreter named Nicola and under oath "all'uso di turchi," offered an interesting twist—he denied ever having discussed the deal with Zorzi and, when asked whether Zorzi had ever been present during negotiations, claimed that "Zorzi comes to my place often" but that he had never intervened in the deal. Against Sguerzo's ambiguous testimony, della Nave had little doubt about Zorzi's culpability: "I know him since he works there in Murano, he comes with Turks to the road outside [the church of] Paternostri." In fact, the first time Zorzi came "to ask if we wanted indigo in exchange for glass and money, I told him we didn't want to barter, and we let him go away."[9]

7. On the importance of oral networks in the circulation and control of politically sensitive information in early modern Venice, see Horodowich (2008).
8. Arti, b. 525, fasc. 1, c.11r (Feb. 19, 1596 m.v.).
9. Arti, b. 525, fasc. 1, c.12r (Feb. 27, 1596 m.v.).

Whereas Sguerzo and Zorzi met at home, della Nave knew the two only from the public space of the church square. What constituted for him an act of broker-age in the marketplace, for a foreign merchant may well have been a piece of friendly advice. This distinction proved crucial. A month later, formal charges were pressed against Zorzi and Giacomo, and the two were (separately) interro-gated. Both denied that Zorzi had anything to do with the deal between Sguerzo and della Nave, and both were acquitted shortly thereafter. This surprising ruling suggests that even when multiple witnesses testified to a person's close ties with merchants, and attested to his presence during the closing of a deal, the willingness of a licensed broker to take responsibility and a categorical denial by a merchant could counteract what may seem to us like fairly clear evidence of unlicensed brokerage.

This case, one of many in the archives of the brokers' guild, underscores the embeddedness of the Venetian marketplace in other institutions and modalities of sociability. Whereas all brokerage had the potential of being confused with acts of friendship, collegiality, or patronage, it was specifically outsiders—trans-imperial subjects and other non–guild members—who were singled out for engaging in it.[10] Consequently, I focus here on how the shifting understandings of foreignness in the marketplace were dialectically related to conceptions of space; to the eco-nomic fortunes of the city; and to the relationship among patricians, citizens, and trans-imperial subjects.

A GUILD AND ITS ARCHIVE

Venice was unique among early modern urban societies in requiring that eco-nomic guilds (*arti*) and their members operate religious charitable confraternities (*scuole*).[11] In 1497, when the Senate decreed the establishment of the brokers' guild, the Scuola di Sensali Ordinarii di Rialto, its charter was modeled on the confraternity of the silk workers at San Giovanni Crisostomo.[12] Like the silk workers (and, indeed, like most other Venetian tradespeople), brokers were thus incorporated in a double institution: a guild and a confraternity.[13] This duality was expressed in part by the use of the premises of the church of Ognissanti for

---

10. On early modern brokerage and patronage in general, see Kettering (1986).
11. Black (2000, 25).
12. Consoli dei mercanti, b. 58, fasc. "Magistrati a stampa," c. 8 (Sept. 19, 1503). On the silk workers' confraternity, see Molà (2000).
13. The difference between a simple *scuola artigiana* ("artisanal confraternity") and a composite *scuola artigiana e scuola di devozione* ("artisanal and devotional confraternity"), noted in passing by Lia Sbriziolo (1968, 414), is yet to be studied.

holding both confraternity and guild meetings, as well as daily mass celebrated by the membership.[14] But, despite this institutionalized display of piety, the confraternity operated for the sixty-two years of its existence as an extension of the guild, with little evidence of any pious fervor.

As scholars have argued, the relationship between Venetian trade guilds and their religious confraternities could be tenuous, with the two having rather discrete domains of activity.[15] In the case at hand, the Venetian brokers' confraternity had rather diminished religious, philanthropic, or convivial functions that can be clearly separated from the operation of the trade guild. In fact, until the members finally voted to replace their confraternity with an "office" in 1566, it was the confraternity, rather than the guild, that figured in all official deliberations regarding brokers as a corporate entity, but as such it reflected (and was ostensibly subjected to) the primarily organizational, economic, and legal agendas of the guild.

This is not to say that charitable activities are completely absent from the records of the confraternity. In 1524, the confraternity decided that every year, during Olive Week, the debts of its five poorest members should be reduced by 1 ducat each.[16] In 1595, it deliberated whether to contribute 50 ducats from its poor fund (Cassa de Poveri) toward redeeming Pasqua, the daughter of Piero Capello, a deceased broker. Pasqua, the membership noted, "finds herself a slave in Morocco with her 12-year-old daughter."[17] Two months later, Impolità, the wife of Zuan Francesco Pisani, a broker imprisoned by the guild, petitioned the confraternity for a monthly stipend of half a ducat and for her husband's release. Her request was granted.[18] In 1608, the guild waived its entry fee for Anzolo Bonaldi, a recent convert newly admitted as broker.[19] Given the very incomplete nature of the surviving treasury expenditure registers of the confraternity, it is hard to determine whether these cases of charity were the only ones for which the confraternity allocated funds or (more likely) whether the records of additional similar cases are now lost. Conversely, the replacement of the confraternity by an "office" in 1566

14. In early 1499, the Council of Ten approved a request by the brokers' guild to hold its confraternity meetings in that church. Once the first hundred guild members were elected in 1503, regular guild meetings were also held in the church, and by November of that year the membership deliberated whether to hold mass there every morning. The church, located in the *sestiere* of Dorsoduro, was demolished in 1820. The patron saint of the confraternity was the Holy Virgin Mary of the Ascension (BVM Assunta) (Arti, b. 517, fasc. 1, c. 2 (Jan. 17, 1498 m.v.); c. 7v (Nov. 13, 1503)).

15. Mackenney (1987, esp. 4).

16. Arti, b. 517, fasc. 1, c. 36r (Dec. 20, 1524).

17. Arti, b. 520, fasc. 1, unpaginated (Aug. 7, 1595). On the ransoming of captives from the Barbary regencies, see Davis 2003, esp. 151).

18. Arti, b. 520, fasc. 1, unpaginated (Oct. 10, 1595).

19. Arti, b. 520, fasc. 1, unpaginated (Sept. 16, 1608).

suggests that at least some of the more powerful guild members saw protecting corporate professional privileges as their main goal, not providing charity to their less fortunate brethren or fulfilling other religious functions.[20] This point merits further investigation, particularly in light of the growing social and religious heterogeneity of the profession.

Institutional definitions aside, the idiom of piety and the safeguarding of professional monopoly also coalesced in important ways. A copy prepared in 1687 of the guild bylaws had the following Latin "prayer in the guise of litany" on its frontispiece: "In the name of all saints, intercede on our behalf. Liberate us, Lord, from the insidious Jews and those who daily steal our bread. So we can live quietly and enjoy our industry with God's blessing, we ask you, hear us. Amen."[21] Although opening prayers were common to many confraternal statutes, this specific prayer deftly juxtaposed the Christian virtue of the guild with the insidiousness of its unlicensed competitors, cast as paradigmatically Jewish.

Decrying ungodly contraventions against guild laws and situating the industry and material well-being of brokers within a divine scheme were not the only measures the guild pursued during this period to guarantee its material survival. In fact, this 1687 copy was based on bylaws passed in 1670, part of guild officials' growing preoccupation with copying and archiving procedures. The guild took numerous new measures to preserve a record of its history for use in future litigation. It did so mostly by commissioning new copies of documents but also by periodically reorganizing existing files. Perhaps due to rapidly declining revenues and a palpable sense of economic crisis among the membership during this period, the guild governors lay ever greater stress on keeping an orderly archive and frequently referred to previous documents in their deliberations. On electing Francesco da Riva as the guild syndic in 1654, the membership mandated him "to save, and preserve, all the decisions, decrees, and similar materials ... which should be kept in an orderly fashion."[22]

Unfortunately, the consequent recopying and re-ordering of the guild archives has resulted in an incomplete and rather disorganized collection. Although the Provveditori di Comun instructed the guild as early as 1577 to keep records of all trials for illicit brokerage, up until 1670 a complete listing and transcripts of inter-

---

20. This change was voted into effect during a general membership meeting on February 1, 1565 m.v. (Arti, b. 520, fasc. 2, unpaginated).

21. "Omnes sancti et sancte Dei, intercedite pro nobis. Ab insidiis Iudeorum et ab illis qui panem nostrum quotidianum suffurantur libera nos, Domine. Ut quiete vivere et nostris industriis cum Dei benedictione gaudere possimus, te rogamus, exaudi nos. Amen" (Arti, b. 517, quoted in Tiepolo 1986, 28).

22. Arti, b. 530, fasc. 33, c. 23r (Feb. 16, 1653 m.v.).

rogations survive for only twelve years.[23] Many other transcripts of trials for illicit brokerage mentioned in the registers are now lost. The surviving materials for the period up to 1670 make up thirteen of the total thirty-three boxes in the guild archives and contain hundreds of indices, registers, and protocols.[24]

THE GUILD TRIBUNAL

Like many other Venetian trades, the brokers' guild was allowed from its inception to establish its own tribunal to adjudicate cases of violations of guild statutes, with the Ufficiali alla messetteria acting as an appellate court.[25] In practice, the tribunal focused exclusively on cases of illicit brokerage, whereas brokerage-related offenses by guild members were largely handled by the Board of Trade. Nevertheless, the authority of the tribunal to try and penalize unlicensed brokers, although confirmed in 1520 and reaffirmed periodically, was increasingly challenged from several directions, until in 1626 the Senate authorized the Board of Trade to use other courts to bring charges against unlicensed brokers.[26] This marked the growing tensions between the protectionist guild agenda and the tendency of the Board of Trade to uphold foreign merchants' interests.[27] Similarly, and despite fierce opposition by the guild to any infringements on its jurisdiction, defendants repeatedly tried to take their case to other magistracies, which, they hoped, would prove more sympathetic to their plight. In 1662, for instance, the guild pressed charges against the Armenian Ovanes, who operated as a commercial broker by special Senate privilege. Ovanes tried to move his trial to the Board of Trade,[28] but the guild opposed this, and the board

23. These are 1596–1598, 1608–1609, 1613–1614, and 1643–1647 (Consoli dei mercanti, b. 58, fasc. verde, c. 8r (Feb. 6, 1576 m.v.)).

24. Appendix 2.1 provides an inventory of the guild archives in their current form. Regrettably, most indices and registers refer to volumes no longer found in the archives. The extant twenty boxes span the period up to the disbanding of Venetian guilds under Napoleonic Law in 1806. See Tiepolo (1986, 118).

25. Consoli dei mercanti, b. 58, fasc. "Magistrati a stampa," c. 8 (Sept. 19, 1503).

26. Consoli dei mercanti, b. 58, fasc. verde, c. 14r (Feb. 7, 1625 m.v.).

27. Such tensions were evident in other cases as well. In 1615, despite petitions from Archduke Maximilian V and from Cardinal Marduzzo to reinstate Tomio Ottolino as a broker after he had been convicted of defrauding an Armenian merchant, the board refused to do so, recommending only that his prison sentence be shortened. The board argued that his sentence should "serve as example to others, and to avoid the danger of new frauds" ("così per essempio d'altri, come per non incorrer in pericolo di nuove fraudi") (Cinque Savi, Risposte, b. 144, cc. 27r–v (Jan. 21, 1614 m.v.)). I thank Giorgio Rota for bringing the case to my attention.

28. Due to the ongoing war with the Ottomans over Crete, the 1660s saw a lull in Levantine trade in Venice, which led the Board of Trade to repeatedly devise new policies sympathetic to Armenian merchants' interests in the hope of attracting them back to Venice and away from its emerging rivals, especially Livorno.

was eventually forced to return the file to the guild.[29] Ovanes then took his case to the powerful heads of the Criminal Court of Forty, only to fail again.[30]

The protectionist guild agenda vis-à-vis unlicensed brokers should not obscure its own internal power struggles. Like many other guilds, the brokers' guild was a two-tier institution in which a mass of relatively poor members were governed by more affluent and politically powerful officials. The names of the guild presidents, who also sat as judges on its tribunal, suggest that they were mostly citizens by birth, the second-highest-status group in Venice. The relative poverty and limited access to citizenship of many brokers thus contrasts sharply with the extensive judicial and administrative powers granted to the guild presidents, treasurers, syndics, and stewards. This raises important questions about the internal cleavages of the guild,[31] about unwritten requirements for election to the guild tribunal and other offices, and about guild officials' relationship to nonguild scribes and notaries who were key participants in the production of its massive archives. Quite possibly, the criteria for what constituted brokerage, perspectives on the marketplace, and involvement (often through kin) in larger mercantile networks differed markedly among guild judges, rank-and-file guild members, and unlicensed brokers.

Finally, a word is due on the legal procedure itself. Trials for illicit brokerage were usually prompted by secret denunciations (Venetian law stipulated a cash prize for denouncing unlicensed brokers). The court was presided over by investigative judges, who interrogated witnesses and then issued their ruling. Witnesses were summoned by the court, and defendants were allowed neither to present their own witnesses nor to cross-examine prosecution witnesses at the initial phase of the investigation. Nor did they normally use an attorney. In all these respects, trials by the tribunal of the brokers' guild resembled inquisitorial hearings more than other types of legal procedures.[32]

29. Arti, b. 520, fasc. 2, unpaginated (April 28, 1662–May 19, 1662).
30. Arti, b. 520, fasc. 2, unpaginated (May 31, 1662, July 16, 1662, July 21, 1662).
31. That conflict indeed arose periodically within the guild is suggested by a 1668 appeal by three Armenian brokers, Francesco Bartolazzo, Martin Valegian, and Ovanes (possibly the same Ovanes whose litigation with the guild I discussed previously), to the Provveditori di Comun against what they claimed was overtaxation by the heads of the brokers' guild "with most evident partiality and prejudice against us." The guild was instructed to present within three days all books of its treasury for the past twenty-five years. The Armenian brokers' claims were dismissed as "an attempt to evade a just tax" (Arti, b. 530, fasc. 54, c. 5r (Sept. 3, 1668)).
32. Yet, as Elizabeth Cohen notes with regards to the latter, "there were a lot of safeguards built into that system.... inquisitorial procedure was neither careless, nor unreasonable. E.g. the defendant did not bring witnesses in the initial phases of the 'trial for information,' but after the case had been assembled, the defendant was usually provided with a copy of the depositions (without the names of the speakers) and given a time to assemble a defense" (personal communication). On inquisitorial procedures and their role in early modern legal practice, see Langbein (1974); Tedeschi (1990); Buganza (1998); Ago (1999). I thank James E. Shaw and Laurie Nussdorfer for bringing these works to my attention.

TRIALS FOR ILLICIT BROKERAGE

Trans-imperial subjects figure prominently in the records of the tribunal of the guild of commercial brokers. Of the fifty-five names of those tried for illicit brokerage in the period up to 1670 listed in one nineteenth-century inventory of the guild archives (since reorganized), twenty-one (38 percent) can be definitively identified as Jewish, Greek, Armenian, or German.[33] More dramatically, of fifty-two trial records in one of the heftiest volumes of court records in the guild archives, only four cases (less than 8 percent) involved no defendants from these groups.[34] Early eighteenth-century copies of lists of brokers in the period up to 1670 marked with a red check the names of Jewish and Armenian violators of guild bylaws (but not Greek or German ones, suggesting gradations of foreignness within the city's trans-imperial population).[35] Even in the absence of conclusive statistics and with many of the original records now lost, trans-imperial subjects seem overrepresented—both as brokers and as clients—in trials for illicit brokerage. This holds true even given their predominance in the Venetian mercantile milieu. That said, they were by no means the only individuals targeted by the guild, which during this very period increasingly admitted to its ranks many Greeks, Armenians, and Germans—although not Jews.

As Sguerzo's case and Frangia's case (see chap. 1) suggest, many Greek-speaking émigrés from the Venetian-Ottoman borderlands operated as commercial brokers in Venice, some illicitly and others as guild members or through special privilege. In many cases, they formed partnerships with other brokers, Greek or otherwise.[36] Such brokerage partnerships were not necessarily illegal per se, as long as both partners were guild members.[37] As Antonella Astorri argues, such partnerships allowed participants to act as a true mercantile company and to benefit from commercial information to which some brokers had better access than others.[38] Nevertheless, a general ban on partnerships between guild and nonguild brokers was in place from the very inception of the guild in 1503 and was reiterated in a statute from 1533 decreeing "that from now on no broker of ours will collaborate

---

33. This is a partial list. By my count, at least 105 trials for illicit brokerage were held during this period.
34. Arti, b. 525.
35. Arti, b. 519, fasc. 2 (1705).
36. See, for example, the trial of Giacomo Greco and Baldissera Soeler ("Zotto"), a German broker, for facilitating the sale of twenty bags of Cypriot cotton by Donado Macarelli to Johannes ("Zuanne") Ernest (Arti, b. 525, fasc. 1, cc. 57r–58v (June 27, 1597)).
37. This is according to a ruling by the Board of Trade on July 4, 1553 (paraphrased in Arti, b. 525, fasc. 2). The situation was similar in early modern Rome, where the brokers' guild statutes specifically authorized partnerships between two (but not more) guild members (Colzi 1998, 407).
38. Astorri (1988, 395).

with any non-guild broker in concluding any business of any sort of merchandise either as partner or as interpreter or by any other name under penalty according to the law of 1503."[39]

The authorities often found out about the operation of unlicensed brokers when they were denounced by their licensed partners, possibly in an attempt to exculpate themselves from charges of illegal partnership. A guild resolution of 1595 denounced

> those who, having acquired some capital, or become incapable and unable to exercise anymore the trade [of broker], transact in partnership with an unlicensed broker in the presence of witnesses, and divide and share between them the profit of brokerage for that transaction which they have concluded. Then the unlicensed broker goes to denounce the licensed one to the office of brokers in virtue of the said law, and makes them grant him the prize of what he did, that is the place of the denounced broker, and he pays the pecuniary penalty, beyond what he gets from the agreement between them for the brokerage payment, and in this illicit and scandalous way the laws are vilified, a matter truly of little public dignity.[40]

This account underscores the extent of collaboration and often shared interests between unlicensed and licensed brokers. It is borne out by repeated evidence from trials for such illicit partnerships.

Few Jews were granted privilege to broker trade in the ghetto and none was ever admitted into the brokers' guild in Rialto. Repeated legislation threatened unlicensed Jewish brokers with harsh punishment.[41] Nonetheless, many Jewish

---

39. "Che de cetero niun senser n'ro non pratichi con alcun senser straordinario p[er] concluder mercadi di cadauna sorte si p[er] compagno come p[er] interprete overo p[er] qualunque altro nome caschi in pen'a giusto alla leze del 1503" (Arti, b. 520, fasc. 1, c. 2v (Oct. 9, 1533)).

40. "Loro si servono di quella per ministra delle sue cattive attioni in questa materia, che havendo alcuno di loro acquistando qualche capitale, ò essendo impotenti à non poter più esercitar tal'offitio fanno mercadi in compagnia con un'estraordinario alla presentia di testimonii, et dividono, et partiscono il vadagno della sansaria di quella tal mercantia, che hanno concluso, intendendosi trà di loro, poi quel tale estraordinario và a denontiar l'ordinario all' offitio de sanseri in virtù della detta legge, facendosi dar il beneficcio di quella, cioè il suo luoco dil sanser denonciado, et lui paga la penna pecuniaria, oltre il restar trà loro d'accordo dil precio della sansaria, et à questo modo illicito, et scandoloso, veghino à venderle in vilipendio delle leggi, cosa invero di pocca dignità publica." (Arti, b. 517, fasc. 1, c. 111r (March 3, 1595)).

41. For example, in 1553 it was decreed that "if indeed there shall be any Jew who will dare act as broker, he must be condemned to three years as a galley's oarsman in irons, and then be banned perpetually from the lands and towns of our Illustrious Signoria, in addition to paying

---

brokers did operate in Rialto, often in collaboration with licensed guild-member brokers as well as with Venetian merchants and factors.

The popularity of the broker's profession among seventeenth-century Sephardic Jews has been explained in another context by the decline in their traditional specialization in trade with Portugal and Brazil, their exclusion from other professions, and their commercial expertise and strong international trading links.[42] Similar reasons for engaging in brokerage obtained in Venice, which witnessed the transformation of its Ponentine and Levantine Jewish communities in the course of the seventeenth century. By 1670 the brokers' guild deemed the competition posed by Jews fierce enough to warrant an amendment to its statutes explicitly forbidding artisans from engaging in the sale of commodities unless through licensed brokers.[43] This amendment was probably inspired by several trials for illicit brokerage in which Jews had collaborated with Christian artisans, particularly jewelers, to bypass the brokers' guild. For example, in 1660 David Crespin, a Jew, was charged with the illicit brokerage of diamonds valued at 4,000 ducats. In his defense, Crespin claimed to have operated in partnership with Zuane Monte, a Christian diamond dealer. His version was corroborated by Monte as well as by several Jewish and Christian merchants and jewelers, who claimed to have known Crespin as a merchant rather than as a broker. Crespin was acquitted of all charges.[44]

This case was hardly unique. In most trials of Jews for illicit brokerage, the transaction involved at least one non-Jewish party, often a Venetian citizen.[45] Like their Greek and Armenian counterparts, many Jewish brokers were well positioned to serve Ottoman and Safavid merchants, who could benefit from a broker's bilingual skills and connections in Venice. Zuanne Battista Carminati, a

---

fifty ducats." ("Se veramente sarà alcun' Hebreo, che ardisca di far sansaria, debba per tre anni esser condennato al remo in Gallia, con i ferri a piedi et dipoi bandito di terre, et luochi dell'Ill.ma signoria imperpetuo, oltra il pagar di ducatti cinquanta.") (Arti, b. 517, fasc. 1, c. 63r (July 4, 1553)). See also Cinque Savi, Seconda serie, b. 146, fasc. 26 (May 3, 1562).

42. Israel (1990, 417); Ruspio (2007).

43. Manno (1995, 127).

44. Arti, b. 527, fasc. 13, cc. 1–10 (Jan. 1660). Already in 1637, Bernardo Bembo, Board of Trade member, lamented the Jews' takeover of the diamond trade and their purported advantage over jewelers and other artisans (Cinque Savi, Risposte, b. 151, cc. 126v–130v (Sept. 28, 1637)). I thank Federica Ruspio for bringing Bembo's report to my attention.

45. Santoph (Santo) Cohen was accused in 1597 of having acted as broker in the sale of seven rolls of woven felt by Beniamin de Lion to brothers Luzio and Leandro Patrini (Arti, b. 525, fasc. 1, cc. 77r–78v (Aug. 11, 1597)). In 1618, Giacon Sasso, "son of old Sasso," was convicted of illicit brokerage in the sale of satin by Gabriel de Zorzi to Ioseph Billanza (Abbolanza), a Jew (Arti, b. 538, fasc. 27, cc. 33ff (Sept. 11, 1618)).

Venetian merchant, was a key witness in the trial of a guild member, Zuanne dal Lauro, and an unnamed Jewish broker who had allegedly conspired together to sell to Carminati a Persian merchant's silk carpets in exchange for coral. Carminati consistently claimed that dal Lauro and the Jew both "negotiated and concluded the deal," but he could not remember any details about the Jew, other than his hat. Interestingly, the Persian merchant was never called to testify, and so, in the absence of other witnesses, Lauro was convicted and fined 10 lire, whereas his alleged Jewish accomplice remained unidentified.[46]

This case exemplifies another recurring aspect of illicit brokerage. Just like Greek brokers, many unlicensed Jewish brokers were prosecuted together with guild members, who may have operated as their long-standing partners. An explicit ban on brokerage partnerships between guild members and Jewish brokers was issued in 1580, threatening contraveners with severe fines of 200 ducats and galley sentences.[47] This ban was not enforced in practice, despite its periodic reiterations.[48] In fact, I could not find any evidence of brokers being required to pay such prohibitive fines. In 1597, Salomon Portogallo and Girolamo Griselli were denounced for illicit brokerage in the sale of 3,000 lire worth of grain by Aron de Menachem Cohen to a goldsmith named Zuanne. Both were convicted and fined 300 lire each, but shortly afterward Portogallo appealed the verdict and his fine was reduced to 60 lire, as was Griselli's.[49] Repeated legislation stipulated differential punishments for Jews and Christians, with much harsher maximum punishments for Jews, including banishment from the city. In practice, as Portogallo and Griselli's case illustrates, both Jewish and Christian brokerage partners, when convicted, were normally meted the same punishment. As a rule, fines for brokers' partnerships, as for illicit brokerage in general, were hardly prohibitive.

Indeed, fines clearly did not deter Portogallo from collaborating with guild-member brokers again. Only a few months after his conviction in 1597, he was tried once again, this time for collaborating with Zorzi Bergonzi. The two had allegedly helped Abram Cohen Na'ar sell Christoforo Rubi "gold and silver wool worth a good sum, and other silken cloth in exchange for many *zambellotti*."[50] In yet another case, Portogallo was accused of collaborating with Zuane dalli Quatro Todeschini, a broker, to help Abram de Ventura, a Jewish merchant, sell four rolls

---

46. Arti, b. 525, fasc. 2, cc. 106–10 (Sept. 1, 1609).

47. Consoli dei mercanti, b. 58, fasc. verde, c. 9r (March 4, 1580).

48. In 1595, the Great Council extended the ban to brokerage partnership with any foreigners ("estranei") (Consoli dei mercanti, b. 58, fasc. verde, c. 11v (March 3, 1595)).

49. Arti, b. 525, fasc. 1, cc. 20–22 (March 13, 1597).

50. Arti, b. 525, fasc. 1, cc. 54r–55v (Jan. 20, 1597 m.v.). *Zambellotti* was the Venetian term for an Anatolian woolen textile made of camel or goat hair.

of silk.[51] A month later, Portogallo and a fourth partner, a certain Lazari, were convicted as *incorregibili*. Yet, despite his proven incorrigibility, Portogallo's fine of 300 lire de piccoli was reduced to 160 lire shortly thereafter, suggesting he had some connections within the guild.[52]

A similar pattern of collaboration between guild members and unlicensed Jewish brokers emerges in the case of Menachem de Aron and Cecilio Albrin, tried for brokering the sale of two rolls of silk owned by Abram de Giuda to Zorzi Bergonzi (already mentioned as a broker).[53] That merchants sometimes acted as brokers (at least from the perspective of the guild) to friends, acquaintances, relatives, or business associates strengthens a point frequently raised by the defendants themselves, namely that to provide help and advice did not constitute brokerage but merely collegiality. A similar dual role as broker and merchant typified many Christian Venetians, including licensed brokers.[54] Zorzi Bergonzi himself, although a guild-member broker, also moonlighted as a merchant in clear violation of guild regulations.

Ultimately, the guild efforts to curb licensed brokers' collaboration with unlicensed Jewish partners failed, leading to harsher, but largely ineffective, measures. In January 1670, a new regulation required all guild members to take an annual oath before the guild presidents to not collaborate with any Jewish brokers.[55] An earlier statute of 1667, which promised denouncers of Jewish brokers a bonus of 25 ducats (50 ducats if the denouncer himself was a Jew), had apparently proved ineffective.[56]

Whereas some of those charged with illicit brokerage appear only once or twice in the guild records, others had a long career as litigants. Their repeated appearances in the records over an extended period of time allow us to consider more fully the competing claims invoked by the different parties as to the nature of their transgressions. A particularly visible case is that of brothers Jacob and Abram Cohen, and later their son and nephew Isach, whose litigations with the guild of commercial brokers span a half century, from the early 1560s to the 1610s. On September 26, 1562, the brokers' guild marked a small but significant

51. Arti, b. 525, fasc. 1, cc. 69r–70v (July 24, 1597).

52. Arti, b. 525, fasc. 1, c. 77v (Oct. 20, 1597).

53. Arti, b. 538, fasc. 27 (May 7, 1614). As for Menachem de Aron, the unlicensed Jewish broker, he may well have been the son of Aron de Menachem Cohen, whom we have seen figured as a merchant in a case from 1597. In the same year, Menachem Cohen, a merchant, sold two hundred *schiavine* (woolen blankets) to Alberto, a linen draper, through the brokerage of Abram Cohen and his brother Giacob (Arti, b. 525, fasc. 1, cc. 4v–5r (January 24, 1596 m.v.)).

54. See, for example, the trial of Bartolo Mascari, an oil seller (*travasador da oglio*) (Arti, b. 517, fasc. 1, cc. 108r–109v).

55. Arti, b. 517, fasc. 2, c. 4r (Jan. 15, 1669 m.v.).

56. Arti, b. 526, fasc. 50, c. 2r (Aug. 30, 1667).

victory in its legal battle with Jacob Cohen, obtaining a ruling by the Signoria that affirmed the sole jurisdiction of the guild tribunal over the case, against the New Civil Court of Forty where Cohen had sought to transfer his trial.[57] Cohen did not give up, however, and in 1566 he (unsuccessfully) appealed the tribunal verdict of a few months earlier, this time with the Provveditori di Comun.[58] Failure to convince the authorities to overturn the guild verdict did not deter Jacob and his kin from continuing in their commercial and brokerage activities in Venice.

Like other Levantine Jewish merchants, the Cohens enjoyed some clout in the Ottoman court, which they sought to convert into concrete commercial advantage in Venice.[59] Other members of the Cohen family engaged in a wide variety of commercial activities, ranging from international trade and brokerage to artisanal manufacture and the importation of technology from Ottoman lands.[60] This range of commercial activities and breadth of expertise informed the Cohens' actions when they periodically stood trial for what guild authorities perceived as infringements on their brokerage monopoly. In early 1598, Piero Ventura and Isach Cohen were charged with brokering the sale of indigo in exchange for quicksilver between Sebastian Balliani and Bartolomeo da Calese. In his interrogation, Cohen conceded that he knew the two from Calese's workshop and that, indeed, "I may have sometimes been there and sometimes not.... I am frequently in Calese's workshop, almost every day, because of some business that ser Calese and I have."[61] But, he argued, his interventions in the merchants' discussions were only as a colleague, not as a broker, "as one discusses among merchants," and in any case, the parties had not paid much heed to his advice.[62] Both Ventura and

---

57. Consoli dei mercanti, b. 58, fasc. verde, c. 6v (Sept. 25, 1562); Arti, b. 517, fasc. 1, c. 67r.

58. Arti, b. 517, fasc. 1, cc. 73r–75v.

59. In 1580, a certain "Giacob Coem" obtained a letter of recommendation from the Valide Sultan (sultan's mother) Nur Banu as a relative of the Ottoman court physician, Dr. Brodo, and a person "held in great esteem by Her Highness." The original Ottoman letter and an Italian translation were referred by the bailo to the heads of the State Inquisitors (Capi del Consiglio dei Dieci, Lettere di Ambasciatori, Costantinopoli, b. 5, cc. 193–95 (Dec. 10, 1580)). On Nur Banu's letters to Venice and her patronage of Levatine Jewish merchants, see Skilliter (1982).

60. In 1609, Isach petitioned the government for permission to bring goats to Venice to begin manufacturing high-quality, Angora-style *zambelotti* through a secret method he had developed (Collegio, Risposte di dentro, b. 12, c. 234 (March 8, 1609)).

61. "Poria esser qualche volta si qualche volta no, Dicens mi son spesso in bottega dal calese quasi ogni zorno p[er] alc[un]i negotii ha il S[igno]r Calese, & mi" (Arti, b. 525, fasc. 1, c. 74v (Jan. 9, 1597 m.v.)).

62. "Poria esser che loro mi havessero ditto qualche parola vegniando à proposito come se regiona tra mercanti, et che mi havesse messo qualche parola che no' mi racordo ma havendo ghene p[ar] lado ghene hanno p[ar]lado p[er] l'interesse che haveva come dalli ditti à lor sagrand.o interogando in tal material intenderesi no' dando vediso alle mie parole" (Arti, b. 525, fasc. 1, c. 80r).

Cohen were convicted as *incorregibili* and fined 300 lire di piccoli each. Eight years later, Cohen asked for pardon, and his fine was reduced to 80 lire.[63]

Unlicensed brokers were fully aware that the guild considered brokerage by non–guild members as illicit by definition, but this does not mean that the arguments they raised to counter accusations should be dismissed too quickly as mere opportunism. In fact, these arguments suggest, if not a multiplicity of understandings of the nature of mediation, at least a sense of what trans-imperial brokers and their clients considered to be convincing counterevidence, that is, what constitutes legitimate, nonbrokering intervention in a commercial interaction. Thus, defense arguments ranged from claiming not to have known the merchants in question at all[64] to having assisted a friend rather than having performed brokerage,[65] to having translated rather than brokered trade,[66] to having mediated without a commission, or to having simply been unjustly framed by a personal enemy.[67]

Merchants summoned to testify or charged with employing unlicensed brokers sometimes claimed not to remember very clearly whether any broker had been involved in the transaction or what the broker's name was,[68] or to have initiated business negotiations themselves, using the alleged broker merely as a proxy, an extension of one's will. Such was the strategy of Domenico Balduci, a wine merchant from the town of Monemvasia in the Peloponnese, who in 1609 was charged with employing the services of unlicensed broker Giacomo

---

63. Arti, b. 525, fasc. 1, c. 80v (May 1, 1606).

64. See Angelo Frani's testimony, in which he persistently claimed not to remember any of the people involved in a transaction he allegedly brokered (Arti, b. 525, fasc. 1, cc. 48r–50v (May 16, 1597)). Frani was convicted, but his punishment was reduced.

65. According to the testimony of Orfeo Gianucci, an apothecary, in the trial of Giovanni Domenico de Zorzi and Andrea Saraco, "it is indeed true that ser Zuanne Domenego said after we closed the deal ... I am here not as a broker, but only for service, and as a favor to ser Zuanne Uper." ("si è ben vero che esso sr Z. D[ome]nego disse doppo serado ... mi non son qua p[er] sanser, seno' p[er] servisio, e co m? gio dal s.r Zuanne uper.") (Arti, b. 525, fasc. 1, cc. 66r–67v (Aug. 19, 1597)).

66. A case in point is the testimony of Zacharia Cuchi, who was accused of having brokered the sale of four woolen cloths by Pietro Rezilion to Abram di Pietro, "a bald-headed Greek with a beret." Cuchi claimed to have "passed by Rezilion's shop, and so Mr. Rezilion called me to speak the language that the Greek couldn't speak [i.e., to translate from Greek to Italian], and then I left, and I don't know what they did." He was convicted, but his fine—7 lire—was rather minimal (Arti, b. 525, fasc. 1, cc. 17r–v (March 5, 1597)).

67. This was the strategy of Giacomo Raines, who claimed that Bartholomeo Polferin, an apothecary who allegedly had struck a deal with Lucillo Fossato through Raines's mediation, was his personal enemy. But Fossato, too, testified against him, and Raines was convicted and fined 10 lire (Arti, b. 525, fasc. 2, cc. 104–5 (Aug. 25, 1609)).

68. Cesare Amadio, an apothecary who in 1609 bought twenty-five parcels of wax from Jacob and Salomon Papo, persistently claimed in his testimony that he could not remember the names of the brokers or "the precise details of that deal." The two brokers allegedly involved in the case, David Farcas and Caliman Crassin, were acquitted (Arti, b. 525, fasc. 2, cc. 100–102 (June 11, 1609)).

Trenturi in the sale of sixty bottles of malmsey wine to Sebastian Soranzo, a patrician merchant. When asked who had told him about the potential deal, he responded, "I told said Giacomo to come with me, since I want[ed] to go and look for one [shop] of a nobleman, and so we went." Thus, Balduci suggests that the initiative was entirely his and that Trenturi came along only after being asked to. Later, Balduci described the negotiation itself: "I started negotiating with the gentleman, and not being able to easily conclude the deal, Giacomo, wishing to leave, asked me, what do you say? And he said many words and then addressed me again and closed [the deal] with the gentleman." In Balduci's account, then, agency was entirely his, even while conceding that Trenturi's intervention was crucial for closing the deal. In his version, Trenturi simply served as an agent who talked to Soranzo on Balduci's behalf. To remove any doubt of illicit brokerage, Balduci assured his interrogators that "Giacomo was not given brokerage fees, nor do I intend to give them to him, that's the whole story."[69] Unlike in similar cases in which merchants denied any illicit mediation to have occurred, Trenturi was convicted and fined 10 lire in addition to trial expenses.

Similar testimonies could lead to quite the opposite ruling. In 1597, Thodaro Memo, a Greek, was acquitted of charges of illicitly brokering a sale of twelve bales of Cordovan hides from the Morea by Spillioti Tapinò to Pietro Gozzi.[70] His trial offers another glimpse of the claims brokers and merchants made to justify unlicensed brokerage. The first attempt by the tribunal to interrogate Gozzi's nephew, Giovanni Battista, failed after he had refused to testify under oath. Threatened with a fine of 50 ducats, Gozzi reluctantly came back to testify the following week but insisted that the hides had been purchased "without a broker." Tapinò's testimony three months later yielded a different version altogether. Memo had indeed been present during the negotiations, and although not formally employed as a broker, he still had been paid 5 ducats by Tapinò's apprentice on at least one occasion and possibly more. Pietro Gozzi's interrogation produced even more specific evidence. Memo had not only been present at Tapinò's house when Gozzi had gone there to see the merchandise but he had been the one who "helped to transport the bales, and show the hides, and give me the merchandise."[71]

---

69. "Inter chi ne ha racorda detto mercato. risp mi ho ditto al ditto Jac[om]o vegni co' mi che vorio andar à cercar certi una da un zentil'homo, et cosi andassimo. inter. se detto Jacomo se ha adoperato de mezo tra lui, et detto Cl[arissi]mo Sorenzo nel trattar, e serar del mercato. risp mi cominciai à trattar co'l zentil'homo, e no' potenelo cosi facilm[en]te contremirsi, esso Jac[om]o poi volenndovi partir mi chiamò vi diciato? et disse tante parole e poi tornato vidriso se concluse con el zentil'homo; Dicens à detto Jac[om]o non dato sansaria, ne ho intentio' de sarghela, questo è tutto il fatto" (Arti, b. 525, fasc. 2, c. 52 (March 14, 1609)).

70. Arti, b. 525, fasc. 1, cc. 59r–60v (April 20, 1597).

71. "Aggiunto à averzer le balle, et mostrar li cordoani, et me batava li merzi" Arti, b. 525, fasc. 1, c. 60r.

Memo's own interrogation took place the following year.[72] According to his version, he had been dragged into the affair by Gozzi, who had called out to him and said, "do me a favor and … [help me] to mark one of these bales, and so I helped to mark a bale, and so I came back to account for [my actions] to said ser Piero Gozi."[73] But, Memo assured his interrogators, he had left the room immediately afterward and had no idea whether Tapinò and Gozzi had ever struck a deal. He further denied having received payment from Tapinò's apprentice. Despite his past convictions for similar offenses, cited by the court, Memo was acquitted the same day.

These cases reveal the inconsistency of rulings in cases of illicit brokerage. Why were some brokers acquitted while others were convicted based on similar, or even less, evidence? The records suggest interrogators' intense interest in the merchants' and brokers' intentions, not just in the evidence of fees paid or legal contracts signed. This is why the tribunal faced difficulty when confronted—quite frequently—with cases of friendship, family ties, and shared residence between brokers and merchants. Against a notion of brokers as impartial and disinterested intermediaries between two parties unfamiliar to one another, the magistracies encountered time and again brokers who were clearly affiliated with one of the parties and who, in fact, claimed to have acted precisely as friends rather than as brokers. That even the brokers' guild tribunal accepted their assertions suggests that the plausibility of social ties across political, religious, and ethnolinguistic boundaries was not completely eroded at that point.

OTHER FORMS OF (DOCUMENTING) STRUGGLE

Trials for illicit brokerage formed one of the main strategies employed by the brokers' guild in its effort to curb competition in the marketplace. But, although legal procedures allowed the guild to target individual contraveners and subject them to lengthy legal battles against a relatively well-oiled and well-funded corporate body, other forms of conflict pitted the guild against other corporate bodies that, at least in theory, could be just as well-organized and articulate.

In the course of the sixteenth and seventeenth centuries, the brokers' guild engaged in several massive (and costly) political battles against corporate bodies such as the brokers of the German Exchange House, Levantine Jewish merchants,

---

72. Such long turnaround times for investigations in matters of illicit brokerage were not unusual, highlighting their lack of prohibitive effect.
73. "De gratia feme sta cortena orideme gua a distigar una de ste balle et cosi aiudete à destigar una nalla, e cosi tognò à giustificar p[er] detto sr Piero Gozi" Arti, b. 525, fasc. 1, cc. 60r–v.

and other collectives of foreign merchants. Such campaigns involved the drafting of numerous petitions and counterpetitions to the Senate, the Board of Trade, and other magistracies and the hiring of lawyers in the hope of affecting legislation on matters such as taxation on brokerage, individual brokerage privileges, the size of the guild and its areas of monopoly, the jurisdiction of specific administrative organs over brokers, and, finally, the tense relationships with the Public Dragomans, the official interpreters of the Board of Trade and the tax imposed on brokers' commissions, ostensibly to finance the dragomans' (mandatory) services.

One such political battle opened in 1584, when a group of "Levantine merchants" (in this case, Jewish Ottoman subjects) lodged a seemingly procedural complaint with the Senate. Old guild statutes gave individuals convicted of illicit brokerage only one month to appeal their sentence; this, the merchants argued, put them at a serious disadvantage. But their complaint was more than procedural. They went on to challenge the very logic behind the guild legal procedures, suggesting that individuals charged with illicit brokerage were often not brokers at all:

> [I]f a merchant, although of great capital and reputation, is seen in the company of people buying silken cloth or another merchandise of the city, which requires intervention in Turkish and other Levantine trade, if people, often because they do not have the language, or fear being defrauded, bring along a friend to advise them on their purchase, these regular brokers, by virtue of some of their Statutes, immediately bring charges against these leading and honorable merchants as brokers, raising their malicious falsifications, which disturb the good faith and the freedom of the marketplace.[74]

The petition juxtaposes "merchant" and "broker" as two mutually exclusive social categories. As later became a common defense strategy in trials for illicit brokerage, the petition legitimizes a person's presence during a commercial transaction as a sign not of brokerage but rather of a personal favor to a friend, intended to provide commercial advice and assist with language interpretation rather than to mediate between the parties. To deny a person the right to be present, the petition argues, infringes on "good faith" and the "freedom of the marketplace." Harping

---

74. "S'uno mercante benche di Cavedale, e reputatione, è veduto in compagnia di persone, che compri panni di seda, ò altra merce della Città, come suole intervenire nè negotii di Turchi, è altri levantini, i quali ben spesso non havendo la lingua, ò temendo esser ingannati, conducono con essi loro uno qualche amico per Consiglio della sua compreda, subito essi sanseri ordinarii, in virtù di certi loro Capitoli querellano detti Principali, et honorati mercanti per sanseri, levando loro maliciose vanie." (Arti, b. 517, fasc. 1, c. 96v (Jan. 10, 1584)).

on the acute interest of the authorities in Levantine trade, one of the main sources of revenue for the Venetian state, the petition aligns the "merchant of good reputation" with the commercial interests of the Republic and against the brokers' guild. In another passage, the petition similarly juxtaposes virtuous merchants and deceitful brokers by claiming that brokers "(always excepting the honor of the good ones) are wicked men, who, like informers, set traps for this or that merchant, with secret denunciations, frequently naming themselves as witnesses, and the merchants are interrogated regarding these denunciations, against all law and religion, and although they are eventually absolved, they suffer innumerable worries, with little honor, and reputation in the marketplace."[75] Thus, the petition contrasts the honor of merchants operating in an open marketplace with the secret denunciations and abuses of brokers.

A few years later, in early 1593, a group of Jewish merchants petitioned the government again, claiming that "We can no longer find anyone who would dare walk with us, nor come in our direction, nor prevent us from being defrauded in the city; because as soon as anyone comes, he is sued by the brokers, for having committed brokerage, and harassed in a way that deprives us of our freedom, and counsel, and often defrauds us."[76] Here, emphasis is placed not only on the damage to the supplicants' reputation and freedom as merchants but also on their helplessness in the face of potential fraud. Indeed, the petition presents the supplicants' association with local "helpers" (the term *broker* is understandably avoided) as the only means of preventing (unnamed) malefactors from hurting them. The spatial dimensions of this passage is particularly telling; Jewish merchants are cast as coming from the outside (hence, their helpers should "come in [their] direction") and encounter potential fraud "in the city." By positioning themselves as foreigners (i.e., as spatially and socially distinct from city residents), the petitioners thus colluded in fundamental ways with the guild brokers' self-representation as the protectors of helpless foreign merchants and, at the same time, as Venetian citizens worthy of monopolistic privilege by virtue of being locals.

75. "(resservando sempre l'honor di buoni) sono de gli huomini re'i, i quali come spioni, stano insidiando questo, e quell'altro mercante, con secrete denoncie, spesse volte essi stessi nominando per testimonii, e sopra dette denonci' loro, contra ogni legge, et religione, essaminandosi [sopra linea: ondi] benche finalmente assoluti, i mercanti patiscono però inumerabili angustie, con puoco honore, e reputatione della piazza" (Arti, b. 517, fasc. 1, cc. 96v–97r).
76. "Non troviamo più alcuno, che ardisca caminar con noi, né venire alle nostre volte, né per la Città a disinganarne; perche subito, che viene alcuno, li vien dato querela da essi sanseri, di haver fatto sansaria, et sono travagliati in modo, che venimo à esser privi di libertà, et di Consiglio, et siamo spesso inganati." (Arti, b. 517, fasc. 1, cc. 114r–v (Jan. 25, 1592 m.v.)).

In a petition urging the government to establish harsher punishments against unlicensed Jewish brokers, submitted to the Senate in early 1587, members of the brokers' guild charged that "we are gravely injured by the said Jews, who daily devour the blood."[77] Overtones of blood libel apart, it was precisely the growing identification of Jews with unlicensed brokerage and the charge that they evaded taxation and competed with hard-working Venetian brokers that lay at the heart of several proposals to appoint Jewish brokers in Rialto submitted to the Senate by a Jew named Caliman Soncino in 1618–19. According to the proposals, fifty Jewish brokers would be licensed to operate freely in transactions involving Jewish merchants in the city.[78] Following the brokers' guild blood libel lament, Soncino asserted that much public revenue was being lost because the bulk of Jewish trade in Venice was concluded with the aid not of licensed brokers but rather of unlicensed Jewish ones: "Your Serenity does not extract any revenue [from Jewish commerce] due to the continuous, hidden and inevitable frauds, and transgressions, which are conducted by the Jewish traders." But, should his plan be accepted, Soncino expected that "from a great evil which is reputed incurable, a good of great profit for the public interest will come to be extracted."[79] Soncino's petitions thus made use of the familiar trope of Jewish tax evasion; but he also suggested that these violations were not "inevitable" and "incurable" but that, indeed, Jews could be transformed into productive members of Venetian society. To increase the appeal of his proposal, Soncino offered to pay the government 2,000 ducats annually, in addition to all other tax revenue that his brokers would be able to collect.[80] Finally, he suggested that Jewish brokers not be allowed to intervene in transactions "between Christian and Christian." This last caveat is significant for two reasons. First, Soncino employed religious, rather than civic, categories;

77. "Cosi gravemente dannificati da detti hebrei, quali quotidianamente ci devorano il sangue" (Collegio, Risposte di dentro, b. 8, c. 195 (Feb. 5, 1586 m.v.)).

78. Copies of both proposals, the first submitted anonymously on March 4, 1618, and the second submitted under Soncino's name exactly one year later on March 4, 1619, are preserved in the brokers' guild archive (Arti, b. 517, fasc. 1, cc. 131v–133r). Summaries of the proposals' contents are also included in a guild register prepared in 1682 (Arti, b. 520, fasc. 2, unpaginated). Soncino was probably a descendant of the celebrated printers' family of the same name, who operated Hebrew printing presses in Soncino (near Milan), Pesaro, Istanbul, Thessaloniki, and Egypt from 1483 to 1557.

79. "V'[ost]ra Ser.[eni]ta non cava alcun emulumento per le continue oculte, et inevitabille fraudi, et trasgressioni, che dalli hebrei negotianti sonno comesse di modo, che da un tanto malle che è riputato incurabile si venirà à cavare un bene di gran profitto per li publici interessi" (Arti, b. 517, fasc. 1, c. 132r (March 4, 1619)).

80. This was quite a substantial sum, comparable to the total annual revenue from the tax on brokerage of Muslim and Jewish merchants in those years. Whereas in 1602 the total annual revenue from the brokerage tax of "Turks" was 1,576 ducats, in the fifteenth century it averaged 60,000 ducats. See Chambers and Pullan (2001, 152); Lane and Mueller (1985, 189).

that is, he drew the line not between citizens and foreigners but, rather, between Christians and non-Christians. Second, his caveat did not limit brokers' domain of activity to transactions involving only Jewish merchants but, rather, to ones involving any non-Christians. At the same time that he drew religious boundaries, he also recognized their limited purchase in the marketplace.

The Board of Trade was unequivocal in opposing Soncino's proposal, citing as its main reason the need to protect local privilege. Rather than addressing the problem of tax evasion by Jewish merchants, it insisted that the existing 190 guild-member brokers were all "citizens by birth" and that there was no need for additional brokers, particularly in such times of lull in trade. Any competition from Jewish brokers, the board added, would hurt guild members, who were already subjected to high taxation.[81] Thus, its reinterpretation of Soncino's offer shifted the discussion from the problem of how to increase revenue to how to protect hard-working Venetian citizens from unfair competition. Whereas Soncino's petitions signaled an effort to incorporate Jews into Venetian society by making them pay taxes and gain more access to guild-regulated trades, the board redrew the line between citizens and Jews, reinforcing the latter's foreign status. Soncino's proposal was formally dismissed by the Provveditori sopra Danaro Pubblico on May 2, 1620.[82]

Soncino resubmitted his proposal in 1623, this time suggesting that Jewish brokers be limited to transactions in which at least one of the parties was a Jew. His revised petition also explicitly decried collaboration between Jewish merchants and brokers, who took their money but never reported the deal to the authorities, thus depleting the public coffers.[83] Yet, despite the alarming figures he cited for lost public revenue, the proposal never met with any success and was formally rejected by the Board of Trade in 1624. This time, however, the board did acknowledge irregularities in guild brokers' practices and urged them to register all transactions in their books.[84] The reluctance of the board to consider Soncino's proposal marks a political shift in its commitments—in this case, at least, maintaining legal and religious boundaries was deemed more important than the financial solvency of the Republic.[85]

Failure did not deter Soncino from claiming to have reached some understanding with the Board of Trade, whose implementation, he claimed, was delayed due only to "contradictions" and "objections" by the brokers' guild. When the guild

---

81. Cinque Savi, Risposte, b. 145, cc. 22v–23r (March 14, 1619).
82. Arti, b. 520, fasc. 2, unpaginated.
83. Collegio, Risposte di dentro, b. 16, c. 372 (Oct. 30, 1623).
84. Cinque Savi, Risposte, b. 146, cc. 100r–101v (March 30, 1624).
85. I thank Erika Gasser for highlighting this point.

followed up on a secret denunciation and sought to put Soncino on trial for illicit brokerage in 1635, he expressed concern that, although innocent, he might
be convicted if judged by "a passionate and angry person" and therefore asked
to have his trial heard by the Board of Trade or the Provveditori di Comun.[86]
The board endorsed his request and recommended that his trial be moved to the
Provveditori di Comun (all the while, remarkably enough, eliding the question
of whether his original proposal to appoint fifty Jewish brokers had ever been
accepted, as Soncino insisted, or not).[87] Unfortunately, the proceedings and outcome of Soncino's trial, if it ever took place, are now lost.

In 1693, the Londoner William Leybourn set out to define *brokers* in his *Panarithmologia or the Trader's Sure Guide*:

> *Brokers* are Persons generally, that have had Misfortunes in the World, and
> have been bred Merchants, (or else they are not capacitated to be *Brokers*)
> for they must be Men that have Experience in Goods, in Exchanges, in
> Seasons for buying and selling: They must be Men faithful, and of Repute;
> for the things they are entrusted with, are of great Consequence: And
> these Men are employed betwixt Merchant and Tradesman; and their
> Imployment is to find the Merchant a Shop keeper, or rather Chapman for
> his Goods.[88]

Despite the growing prominence of foreign merchants in late seventeenth-century
London, much like in Venice of a century earlier, Leybourn emphasized brokers'
role as intermediaries between merchants and artisans rather than between foreign and local merchants.[89] This is a reminder that the legal category of foreignness could have greater or lesser purchase in different contexts.[90] Leybourn also
alerts us to another important phenomenon—many brokers came from merchant
families, were trained as merchants, and were embedded in specific merchant networks. Evidence suggests that in Venice, too, many bankrupt merchants turned to
brokerage.[91] In fact, it was their commercial savvy that allowed them to perform
brokerage well. Yet it was precisely this inability to neatly distinguish brokers

86. Collegio, Risposte di dentro, b. 26 (April 24, 1635).
87. Cinque Savi, Risposte, b. 150, c. 54 (May 7, 1635).
88. Leybourn (1693, 55).
89. On foreigners in early modern London, see Selwood (2003).
90. See Herzog (2003).
91. According to Luca Molà (1994, 130), already in the first half of the fourteenth century many
silk merchants had taken up brokerage as a temporary solution to their financial woes.

from merchants that caused alarm among Venetian magistrates and guild officials alike because it undermined the basic legal fiction of the impartiality and anonymity of the marketplace. Finally, Leybourn's definition points to the importance of possessing specific social skills (such as trans-imperial ties or the reputation of being trustworthy) as much as proven commercial expertise in the making of successful brokers.

All three aspects of Leybourn's definition have important corollaries in Venetian brokerage practices and their representations by officials and modern scholars alike. Trust between merchants and middlemen has been the focus of much work in economic history, in which, all too often, it has been conflated with ethnic solidarity.[92] To be sure, foreign merchants stood to gain much from using unlicensed brokers. Not only did unlicensed brokers allow different commercial networks to intersect, but in fact they provided newly arrived merchants a relatively safe entry point into local markets by sharing their language, religious confession, or kinship ties. Nevertheless, we should be careful not to assume that such ties were necessarily ethnic or that they naturally produced trust. As I suggest here, at least in Venice, brokers and their clients were not always members of what might seem to modern readers to be a shared ethnicity. And even when they were, deep and institutionalized cleavages within the Jewish, Armenian, and Greek communities certainly should caution us against supposing that all members of these groups recognized a priori their fellow ethnics as trustworthy.[93] In fact, as we have seen, brokers and their clients often were united not as much by ethnicity as through networks predicated on kinship, previous commercial ties, or a shared working language. Linguistic skills in particular were perceived as crucial and thus gave bilingual brokers an advantage with a wide range of clients. By the seventeenth century brokers' real or imagined bilingualism was to stand at the heart of debates about what constitutes mediation, as well as foreignness (see chaps. 6–7).

We may speak of two contrasting views of brokerage that were articulated by different groups in early modern Venice. On one hand is a view shaped by the interaction between the juridical and financial institutions of a vigilant state and the protectionist agenda of the broker's guild. According to this view, brokers are semi-official bureaucrats, loyal Venetian citizens, intent on keeping a watchful eye on foreigners. Each group—Venetians versus foreigners, merchants versus brokers, and traders versus tradespeople—knew its place and kept separate. On the

---

92. Representative cases in point are Landa (1983, 1994). For a critique of middleman minority theories and their embeddedness in colonialist assumptions about social relations, see Rothman (2010) and the bibliography therein.

93. For one of many intriguing civil litigations among Armenian merchants in which *mistrust* prevailed, see AdC, Misc. Civil, b. 210, fasc. 2 (Jan. 29, 1664 m.v.).

other hand is a view of brokerage that is less explicitly articulated in statutes and other prescriptive documents but that emerges more clearly from the practices of guild members, unlicensed brokers, and their trans-imperial clients and interlocutors. According to this view, individuals could be Venetians and at the same time ally themselves with foreign kin or friends. They could be trans-imperial subjects *and* consider themselves upright members of Venetian society. They could be merchants in the morning and brokers in the afternoon, both guild members and the business partners of unlicensed brokers. Such a view made the policing of social boundaries much more difficult.

All this is not to say that legal categories were irrelevant to the activities of trans-imperial commercial brokers in early modern Venice. On the contrary, it is through an investigation of how various kinds of brokers invoked these categories differently and strategically that we can recognize conflict not simply in what brokers did but also in how they described what they did.

Finally, these conflicting conceptions of mediation must be studied within the larger processes through which trans-imperial brokers come to be seen as ethnic and new categories proliferated, which cast trans-imperial subjects from the Venetian-Ottoman borderlands as increasingly "foreign": the late-sixteenth-century requirement that an official interpreter be present during all transactions involving Ottoman merchants (and later also Jewish ones), the spatialization of foreignness through the highly contested effort to confine Ottoman and Safavid merchants to a separate residence in the Fondaco dei Turchi from 1621 onward, and the emergence of the category "Levantine" and the proliferation of other ethnolinguistic categories in Ottoman merchants' petitions to the Venetian government from the 1630s onward (I return to these developments in chaps. 6 and 7).

PART II

Conversion

3

Narrating Transition

For both the Church faithful and the Jews of Italy, the Casa dei Catecumeni, House of the Catechumens, was a place of the greatest significance. It straddled the border of the two worlds, and in its liminality lay its awesome power. A Jew could enter the Catechumens and come out a Catholic; in so doing he left one world and entered another. The convert was reborn, with a new identity and a new name.

—DAVID KERTZER (1997, 55)

Within the field of early modern studies, the religious domain in general and the phenomenon of religious conversion in particular have enjoyed renewed attention over the last decade.[1] For many scholars, the process by which people and groups moved from one confessional group to another seems to hold the key to the shifting nature of personhood, intentionality, and communal membership in the fateful years from the onset of the Reformations to the Enlightenment. The massive intervention of state and ecclesiastical institutions in projects of social disciplining, and the broad process that some historians have dubbed *confessionalization*, that is "the consolidation and advancement of the development of ... confessions ... in terms of religious doctrine, relationships with the state and developing religious identities" are still viewed by many as exclusively European (some would even say Northern European) phenomena.[2] Yet, more recently, scholars have pointed to parallel and intertwined processes spanning virtually all early modern Eurasian empires. What was seen, until recently, as a seamless continuation of the Christian reformations of the sixteenth century is emerging as a much broader process involving state-sponsored but highly contested proselytizing efforts, the recalibration of orthodoxies, and an uneasy alignment between confessional and ethnolinguistic

1. See, for example, Carlebach (2001); Stow (2001); Mills and Grafton (2003); Lazar (2004); Graizbord (2004); Luria (2005).
2. On this concept and its critics, see the 2005 H-German forum, www.h-net.org/~german/discuss/Confessionalization/Confess_index.htm.

identities in a rapidly globalizing early modern world. Such a perspective opens up new and exciting opportunities for a non-Eurocentric study of early modern empire-building by looking at the circulation of people, ideas, and objects both within and across political and confessional boundaries.[3]

This renewed interest in what Adnan Husain has dubbed "religious cultures" is of profound relevance to the history of the Mediterranean.[4] The study of religious conversion, in particular, can benefit from and contribute to this new historiographical moment, highlighting as it does the mobility of people and signifying practices across political and confessional boundaries. To understand this relationship, conversion should be studied as a set of historically shifting social practices rather than as individual spiritual choices.

Yet much work on religious conversion in the early modern Mediterranean has tended to focus precisely on the spiritual motivations and sincerity of converts, that is, whether people converted due to deep conviction or because of the material benefits that conversion promised.[5] As Talal Asad and Webb Keane argue, motivation and sincerity are not only extremely hard to gauge from the available documentation (often missionary) but also lack analytical rigor, embedded as they are in specifically modern Christian understandings of intentionality, interiority, and authenticity.[6] Scholars who have embraced these critiques are now emphasizing how converts and missionaries differentially understood the stakes involved in conversion, and they contextualize converts' transition from one moral community to another within wider imperial and colonial interests.[7]

In line with these historiographic shifts, in this chapter and the next I explore not so much *why* people converted but *how*. I ask what the assumptions were—

---

3. For a concise delineation of the challenges and possibilities of such an approach, see Subrahmanyam (2006). For specific studies of the Ottoman Empire see, García-Arenal (2001); Valensi (2001); Minkov (2004); Baer (2007); Krstić (2011). For the Safavid Empire, see Abisaab (2004); Babaie (2004). For the Mughal Empire, see Ramaswamy (2007). For South India, see Županov (2005). For Russia, Geraci and Khodarkovsky (2001). For China, Brockey (2007). Parallel processes, although shaped by different exigencies of empire, have been charted out by students of the Habsburg Empire. See especially Rafael (1988) on the Spanish Philippines and Hanks (2010) on New Spain.

4. Husain (2007), 23.

5. Bennassar (1988); Allegra (1996); Foa and Scaraffia (1996); Vanzan (1996); Bono (1998); Baer (2001); Scaraffia (2002). The renewed interest in Mediterranean slavery is no exception to this rule, and scholarship on the religious conversion of slaves is still very much informed by the same paradigm of sincere versus forced or induced conversion. See, for example, Bono (1999); Davis (2003).

6. Asad (1996); Keane (1997).

7. A partial list of works that address the imperial settings of early modern conversion includes Morrison (1985); Rafael (1988); Dorsey (1998); Geraci and Khodarkovsky (2001); Richter (2001); Mills and Grafton (2003); Abisaab (2004); Pardo (2004); Silverblatt (2004); Greer (2005); Metcalf (2005); Silverman (2005); Stephen (2008); Hanks (2010); Agmon (in progress).

in specific institutional contexts—about how to transform converts' subjecthood and what the consequences were for different kinds of converts and their social relations.

In 1608, a rather unusual petition reached the Venetian Senate. Teodoro Dandolo, born under the Safavids in the Uzbek city of Bukhara, asked to be appointed interpreter of Persian, Turkish, Arabic, and "Indian." About eight years prior, around 1600, Dandolo had migrated from Bukhara to Aleppo, where he had met Vicenzo Dandolo, the Venetian consul there (1598–1602). At the consul's behest, he traveled to Venice and was baptized. Shortly afterward, Dandolo relocated again, this time to Rome, where he spent the next four years in the household of Cardinal San Giorgio, Cinzio Aldobrandini (1551–1610).[8] Now, on returning to Venice, the convert Dandolo sought employment as a Public Dragoman (official interpreter for Ottoman merchants and dignitaries in Venice) so that he could support himself.[9] The members of the Board of Trade, to whom the case was referred for consultation, were divided. Two of them doubted Dandolo's skills as a translator and writer in Italian. But given his precociousness ("essendo lui de spirito vivo, et de ingegno pronto"), they recommended that he be placed under the tutelage of the acting Public Dragoman for training. A third member of the board was far less enthusiastic about employing Dandolo in the delicate position of dragoman:

> Having been born a Muslim, even though he has become Christian, he could always have some greater inclination towards his nation, and since he is not Your [i.e., Venetian] subject, and has lived for many years in the house of the Illustrious Signor Cardinal San Giorgio, it could be feared that he might continue to serve, and have affection for him, and from what can be understood from the outside he is not very stable in his actions.[10]

Although the board continuously struggled to find qualified dragomans, it could not agree on Dandolo's merit. Whereas some of its members challenged Dandolo's

8. Aldobrandini was the nephew of Pope Clement VIII, a Spanish sympathizer, and an influential courtier in Rome. See Rota (2004, esp. 2) for this and other details of Teodoro Dandolo's biography. I thank Giorgio Rota for sharing with me this unpublished paper and much information about Dandolo.

9. Cinque Savi, Risposte, b. 142, cc. 83v–84v (June 23, 1608 and Aug. 18, 1608).

10. "Essendo questo nato Turco, se ben fatto christiano, sempre potria haver qualche maggior inclinatione alla sua natione, no[n] essendo suddito suo, come anco p[er] esser vissuto molti anni nella casa dell'Ill.mo S[igno]r Gardenal S. Georgio, co'l quale si potria dubitare che potessi continuar nella servitu, et affettion sua poi che p[er] quanto esteriormente si può comprender lui no[n] è molto stabile nelle sue attioni" (Cinque Savi, Risposte, b. 142, c. 84v (Aug. 18, 1608)).

competence, others questioned his trustworthiness. Neither his conversion nor his linguistic promise sufficed to assuage the fears about his Muslim birth in a faraway country, foreign juridical status, and papal patron. Like many trans-imperial subjects, Dandolo was embedded in extra-Venetian networks of patronage that were essential for his new social persona but that also cast perennial doubt about his loyalty. Four months after its initial report, the composition of the Board of Trade changed and the new members decided to appoint Dandolo as interpreter, citing the frequent absence from the city of acting Public Dragoman Giacomo de Nores and a successful occasion on which Dandolo assisted the board to communicate with a group of Armenian merchants. Dandolo's appointment, however, does not appear to have ever materialized. His name does not show up again in the archives until 1615, when the Board of Trade approved his request to become commercial broker "of Turks and Levantines" and provided him with a booklet in which to keep a record of all his transactions with "the Turkish, Greek, and Jewish nations, and other Levantine merchants." The brevity of the response of the board on that date, which repeated almost verbatim its 1608 reply, suggests that Dandolo had not been in its service during the intervening period.[11]

Although Dandolo's case may seem exceptionally complicated, it reflects broader uncertainty about the juridicopolitical entailments of Muslim-Christian conversion in early modern Venice. The systemic distrust of Muslim converts to Christianity stemmed, in part at least, from Venetian efforts to understand contemporary Ottoman practices of conversion. Such practices came to typify Ottoman alterity in Venetian political thought. In a nutshell, Venetians began to view Ottoman subjects' supposed single-minded devotion to the sultan through the dual lens of confessionalization and Oriental despotism, thus translating converts' patronage by the Ottoman state into a conception of Ottoman subjectivity that obviated individual will in matters of religiopolitical affiliation.[12]

I address in this chapter the divergent narrative structures and presumed relationship between confessional identity and juridical subjecthood early modern Venetian notions of Muslim-to-Christian, Christian-to-Muslim, Jewish-to-Christian, and Protestant-to-Catholic conversion. I ask how conversions from Catholicism to Islam and from Islam, Judaism, and Protestantism to Catholicism were narrated in several genres in sixteenth- and seventeenth-century Venice. By looking at reports penned by Venetian representatives in Istanbul about renegades who had "turned Turk," inquisitorial depositions by Protestant subjects and by

11. Cinque Savi, Risposte, b. 142, cc. 95r–v (Dec. 6, 1608); b. 144, cc. 31r–v (Feb. 14, 1614 m.v.); Ufficio della Bolla Ducale, Grazie del Maggior Consiglio, reg. 8, c. 76 (Sept. 23, 1615); Cinque Savi, Seconda serie, b. 4, fasc. 47, unpaginated (Sept. 28, 1615).
12. On Venetian notions of Ottoman political order, servility, and volition, see Valensi (1990, esp. 182).

Muslims of presumed Christian background who sought reconciliation with the Church, converts' matrimonial examinations, and baptismal records, I suggest how the process of conversion and converts' subjectivity itself were articulated in different genres. Using Mikhail Bakhtin's concept of the chronotope (space-time frame), I identify two prototypical accounts of the spatiotemporal process of conversion prevalent in narratives of conversion to Catholicism from Ottoman Islam and Protestantism, respectively, and point to the key role of Venetian institutions and intermediaries in articulating both. In closing, I consider how divergent assumptions about continuity and discontinuity of the convert's intending self relate to contemporary notions of gendered and confessional subjecthood.

St. Augustine's *Confessions* envisioned two separate stages of conversion. The first, emphasized by many medieval Christian theologians, is a dramatic and singular moment of revelation, in which the self is radically transformed and created anew. According to historian Elisheva Carlebach, "Medieval religious usage borrowed the term *conversion* from the al/chemical sciences as a metaphor, in which one substance was changed into something utterly different by a mysterious process. Conceptions of transformation or rebirth had always informed the imagery of Christian conversion. In conversion to Christianity, divine grace transfigured the soul, created it anew, so that no residue of the earlier self remained."[13] Post-Tridentine conversion policies still featured many elements that both assumed and sought to reinforce this notion of radical transformation at the baptismal font through the convert's complete severance of previous social and kinship ties.[14]

Yet Augustine's *Confessions* also described conversion as a lifelong process of self-exercise, striving, and gradual modification. This second image of conversion links a journey that starts well before baptism and continues thereafter.[15] It is likely that this understanding of conversion as a lifelong process led Venetian administrators who dealt with converts to acknowledge tacitly converts' ongoing ties with their unconverted kin. Indeed, such ties were sometimes encouraged, seen as a key financial and emotional resource in safeguarding converts' wellbeing and as a first step toward converting additional family members.[16] Tolerance of such ties

13. Carlebach (2001, 1).
14. Stow (1976); Ravid (2001). But, as Elisheva Carlebach herself cogently shows, converts' claims to have completely severed their ties with family also stemmed from their "need to appeal to Christian charity. Orphaned from the community that had nurtured them, they appealed for financial support as well as social acceptance to their adoptive community" (2001, 24).
15. On the two meanings/stages of conversion in Augustine, see Outler (1955, esp. 19); Riley (2004, esp. 24–25).
16. On such lingering ties in Venice, see Pullan (1983, 275–93). In Rome, see Sermoneta (1993); Stow (1993, 2002).

could be interpreted as de facto recognition of converts' ongoing embeddedness in preexisting social relations, linking their presents with their pasts.

Ottoman Muslim notions of religious conversion also often took such continuity for granted. As in Venice, conversion to Islam in the early modern Ottoman Empire was not practiced as a moment of extreme rupture requiring the severance of the convert's former ties.[17] A host of practices that developed in Venice in the late sixteenth and early seventeenth centuries to integrate new converts into society—such as rapid baptism following only nominal catechization, and financial and material support for converts—bear striking similarities to Ottoman ones, in contrast to papal post-Tridentine dogma.

How are we to account for the many parallels and convergences between Ottoman Muslim and Venetian Catholic practices of conversion in the seventeenth century? As a partial answer to this complex question, we need to look at the specific institutional and intellectual contexts of conversion in these two polities as well as at the significant degree of overlap and interaction between them. At the outset, we should recognize that Venetian conversion practices were shaped not only by the awakened religious sentiments of the Age of Confessionalization but also by the political and economic exigencies of a changing Mediterranean. In particular, the need—recognized by many Venetian patricians—to maintain friendly relations with the Ottomans in the face of growing economic competition from Dutch, French, and English naval powers often produced less than enthusiastic responses to Muslims seeking Christian conversion. It also sometimes led to acquiescence in the face of Venetians who had converted to Islam. How, exactly, Catholic conversion was articulated in different Venetian institutional sites and what relationship the narratives produced in variegated contexts bore to emerging notions of Ottoman political and religious alterity are the subjects of this chapter.

CAPTURING RENEGADES

One of the dominant contexts of conversion to Islam in the early modern Venetian-Ottoman borderlands intimately linked the process of becoming Muslim with a radical shift in political subjectivity. The devşirme (child levy) system served to harness the loyalty of young recruits to the Ottoman imperial center. Ideally, if not always in practice, it made religious conversion part of a process of juridical transformation of subjects from free members of the Ottoman Christian provincial periphery to enslaved members of the military-administrative core of the empire.[18] We now know that the overwhelming ma-

---

17. Krstić (2004). See also, albeit for a later period, Deringil (2000, 554).
18. On the devşirme see Imber (2002, 140–42); Minkov (2004). On the broad significance of these processes for early modern Ottoman imperial identity, see Peirce (2010).

jority of converts to Islam in the early modern Ottoman Empire were not child recruits and that many subjects of neighboring polities entered the sultan's service and became Muslim under circumstances that had little to do with physical coercion. These subjects became known as "renegades." Significantly, the image of these "renegades"—just like that of the *devşirme* recruits—became a paradigmatic model of Ottoman religious conversion by fusing the notion of "becoming Muslim" with a transformation in juridical status and a new level of political submission to the sultan.

It is thus hardly surprising that early modern Venetian elites viewed subjects who had "turned Turk" with deep suspicion. Indeed, Venetian officials in Istanbul and throughout the eastern Mediterranean who reported on such cases took it for granted that Venetian subjects who had embraced Islam had thereby relinquished their ties of loyalty to the Venetian state, even if this was not always borne out in reality.[19] A variety of genres dramatized this transition, linking the profession of Muslim faith by non-Ottoman Christians—whether seen as instrumental and opportunistic or coerced—with rapid integration into an Ottoman (metropolitan) milieu. From ransomed slaves' reconciliation narratives in front of the Inquisition, through diplomatic reports from Istanbul, to rumors and folk songs about "renegades," the understanding of Muslim converts in early modern Venice coupled very clearly the transition from Christianity to Islam with political and juridical submission to the sultan. Gianfrancesco Morosini, who served as Venetian bailo in Istanbul from late summer 1582 to summer 1585 articulated this sentiment on his return to Venice: "The renegades are all slaves, and are proud to be able to say, 'I am a slave of the Grand Signor!' For it is known that it [the Ottoman Empire] is the dominion or the republic of slaves, where it is they who are in command. The other Turks, even though they are not slaves like these [the renegades], might as well be considered such, and they consider it an honor to be called by that name."[20] Several reversals are at work in this description: Ottoman subjects' supposed preference for servility over freedom is compounded by the travesty—

19. See, for example, Dursteler (2011, esp. 23).
20. "Li rinegati sono tutti schiavi, e tengono per grandezza il poter dire: Io sono schiavo del Gran Signore; poichè si sa che quello è il dominio o la repubblica de' schiavi, dove loro hanno da comandare; li altri Turchi, sebbene non sono schiavi come questi, nondimeno si possono essi ancora tener per tali, e si reputano ad onore di esser chiamati con questo nome, specialmente quelli che sono adoperati nel servizio del Gran Signore nelli carichi che ho detto di sopra" Albèri (1855, III. III.267), English translation adapted from Davis (1970, 139). Giovanni Botero was to repeat this argument almost verbatim in his *Relationi Universali* (1591–1601), when he wrote that the Sultan's slaves "thinke it as great an honour so be stiled, and so to live, as they do with us, who serve in the highest places of Princes Courts." Almost two centuries later, Montesquieu argued that the Ottoman state was an "empire of slaves" (quoted in Çirakman 2001, 52, 63).

particularly from a Venetian patrician's point of view—of a republic ruled by slaves.[21] These political aberrations, Morosini implies, are at least in part the result of two others: the Ottomans' perceived failure to distinguish between "original" and naturalized subjects, and their clear preference for parvenus at the expense of "old Muslims" from the heartland. Earlier, Morosini explains that

> There are two types of Turks. One consists of those who are native-born of Turkish parents, while the other is made up of renegades who are sons of Christian parents, taken by force in the raids which the fleets and the irregular troops customarily conduct on Christian lands, or else they are from among the Signor's subjects and tax-payers, removed by force from their own village. These, while still children, are circumcised and made Turks either by enticements or by force."[22]

I will come back to Morosini's definition of the *renegade* in a moment. First, a word is in order about the category "Turk." In early modern Italian, as in early modern English, *turco* could mean simultaneously an Ottoman subject, an ethnic Turk, a Muslim, or any combination of these. At first glance, this conflation seems like a European misrepresentation of what are now analytically distinct categories. It certainly speaks to a Venetian's (or a Briton's) inability to imagine Christian Ottoman subjects as truly Ottoman or foreign recruits as constituting the administrative core of the Ottoman Empire. But in light of Morosini's definition, this conflation of language, religion, and juridical subjecthood can also be understood as an attempt—misguided, to be sure—to come to terms with the perceived indifference of the Ottoman state to ethnicity, and with the Ottomans' own conflation of religious and political affiliation, at least as far as the making of bureaucratic-military elites was concerned. These conflations—in both their Ottoman and Venetian articulations—were productive forces in shaping early modern ideas about conversion and converthood.

To return to the figure of the "renegade," although Morosini had in mind the *devşirme* recruits, his explication of the category in fact mentions both the child levy in the Ottoman Christian villages and "the raids which the fleets and the

---

21. The trope of Ottoman subjects as essentially slaves was long-standing in Venetian political discourse. For additional examples from earlier and contemporary diplomatic reports from Istanbul, see Libby (1978, 117–20).

22. "Delli turchi se ne ritrovano di due sorte; l'una di quelli che sono naturali nati di padri turchi, e l'altra di rinegati, che sono figliuoli di padri cristiani, presi violentemente nelle depredazioni che sogliono fare le armate e li leventi in paesi cristiani, ovvero levati dal proprio paese per forza di mano de' sudditi e carzeri di quel Signor, li quali da fanciulli sono o per lusinghe o per forza ritagliati e fatti turchi" (Albèri 1855, 263–64).

irregular troops customarily conduct on Christian lands." In other words, "renegades" in this context include both Ottoman Christian subjects' children-made-conscripts and non-Ottoman subjects forced into slavery by corsairs. Significantly, this gloss excludes—or at least fails to mention—the numerous subjects who became Muslim not under conditions of slavery or physical coercion.[23] The figure of the "renegade" thus sidestepped volition and intentionality from the process of conversion, focusing instead on violence and coercion, and conflated the act of joining a new confession with juridical submission.

This conflation is evinced in references to "renegades" in Venetian diplomatic correspondence. A letter that the Venetian Senate dispatched to the bailo in Istanbul in May 1629 refers to the malevolent intentions and deeds of a renegade named Fontana, a youth sent from Venice to Istanbul to apprentice as a dragoman. According to the Venetians, Fontana's injuries were performed "not only against our Republic, but against our holiest Religion, with threats to the Church of St. Francis."[24] Fontana's disloyalty is cast first and foremost in political terms (treason) and only secondarily, and hence requiring more elaboration, in religious terms (threats ostensibly made toward a particular church in Pera). This case was hardly unusual. In commenting on individual converts in their weekly dispatches, Venetian diplomats in Istanbul often implied that such renegades were motivated by economic and social exigencies—debt, financial woes, frustration with limited prospects of social mobility, or personal envy.[25] The political damage they caused to the Venetian state, although a source of grave concern, was deemed inevitable.

This conception of renegades as motivated by this-worldly, contingent interests thus situated the process of becoming Muslim within a larger Ottoman project of imperial subject-making. In the case of both *devşirme* recruits and adult new Muslims, it implied that changing political affiliation was imposed by outside forces rather than accepted, let alone initiated, by intending purposive subjects.[26] This understanding came to color Venetian expectations about Muslim conversion to Catholicism as well. Such expectations obviated prolonged catechization and even the need to ascertain a Muslim catechumen's wishes prior to baptism, in con-

---

23. Throughout the sixteenth and seventeenth centuries, many non-Muslims in fact embraced Ottoman Islam in circumstances quite different from those of either the *devşirme* or of Mediterranean corsairing. Women in particular became Muslim in situations that are slowly becoming clearer thanks to recent scholarship. See Krstić (2004); Baer (2004); Dursteler (2006).

24. Senato, Deliberazioni Costantinopoli, Reg. 19, cc. 23r–v (May 26, 1629).

25. Dursteler (2006, 112–29).

26. The notion that intentionality was a precondition for naturalization was long-standing in Venetian political thought, dating back to Accursius (c. 1182–1263) and Baldus de Ubaldis (1327–1400), medieval Italian jurists (Riesenberg 1992, 131; Kirshner 1979).

trast to both post-Tridentine dogma and practice when it came to Protestant and Jewish baptismal candidates.

PEREGRINATIONS IN SPACE-TIME

One of the key early modern institutions prompting people to narrate the circumstances of their religious conversion to and from Catholicism was the Venetian Holy Office (see chap. 1). Whether through voluntary confessions or induced inquisitorial interrogations, deponents in front of the Inquisition had to explain or deny their alleged transition from one religious community to another. In some cases, they narrated their becoming Catholics; in others, their apostasy; and in yet others, their oscillation between the two. In all cases, however, deponents were faced with the need to fit their narratives into inquisitorial frames of reference, to make their narratives compelling, and, vitally, to prove their current sincerity and orthodoxy as good Catholics.[27] How did they achieve this? How did people of widely varied backgrounds negotiate the constraints of the inquisitorial genre, itself localized and prone to historical shifts?[28] How did they plot narratives deemed plausible and convincing?

A partial answer may come from scholars who have studied religious conversion in the societies from which these deponents hailed. As Tijana Krstić cogently argues, in the early modern Ottoman Empire the process of becoming Muslim often did not originate in deep spiritual transformation but in the acceptance of new ritual practices. Spiritual transformation may or may not have followed at a later stage, through participation in communal activities.[29] Such a conception of religious conversion contrasts with the Protestant Reformation emphasis on interiority, authenticity, and the subject's quest to find meaning in an unmediated relationship with God.[30] Yet, lest we essentialize a supposedly timeless prototype of Protestant conversion, it is helpful to heed the warnings of another historian, Keith Luria, who has studied Protestant-Catholic conversion in early modern France. According to Luria, it was precisely the seeming self-interestedness of converts and their frequent oscillation between confessions that encouraged both Catholic and Protestant clergy in the seventeenth century to develop "a model of

27. On the construction of plausible narratives within constraints imposed by genre and institutional setting, see Davis (1987). For an illuminating discussion of some specifically Venetian institutional genres, see Ferraro (2001).
28. On the differences between the Venetian Inquisition and its Roman counterpart, see Monter and Tedeschi (1986). See also Prosperi (1982) for a discussion of how inquisitors' perceptions of peasants on the periphery of Europe were shaped by missionary reports from the Indies.
29. Krstić (2004, 120–22). See also Krstić (2011).
30. On Protestant conceptions of conversion, see Keane (1997, 2002).

conversion that stressed the importance of conscience and deep interior motivation, as well as true doctrine and the role of intellect and emotion in adhering to it."[31] Thus, whereas for Muslim subjects of Christian origin seeking reconciliation with the Church the most readily available line of argument was one of contingency, for Protestants converting to Catholicism the expected driving force had to be interior and "pure." If Ottoman subjects could benefit from arguing implicitly for a distinction between their intentions and actions, it was precisely such a distinction that was increasingly problematized and suspected for confessants of Protestant background.

To elucidate this difference, I employ Mikhail Bakhtin's concept of the *chronotope* (literally, time-space), which he defines as "the intrinsic connectedness of temporal and spatial relationships that are artistically expressed in literature."[32] The differing chronotopic qualities of Ottoman-Muslim and Protestant inquisitorial depositions help to illuminate their underlying assumptions about the nature of the person undergoing conversion and, consequently, the nature of conversion itself. Building on Krstić's and Luria's insights, I identify two prototypical chronotopes of conversion in these inquisitorial depositions. The first, the chronotope of conjuncture, is especially prevalent in the depositions of Ottoman Muslim subjects who asserted their Christian background or parentage. This chronotope depicts the transition from one confession to another as the contingent outcome of deponents' entry into a spatially defined religious community at a particular historical moment. The second, the chronotope of purposive journeying, is especially prevalent in Protestant narratives. It describes deponents' journeys from non-Catholic to Catholic space as the outcome of a prior, inner, spiritual transformation. The journey is thus the result rather than the cause of conversion; it is a journey purposefully undertaken by an already converted subject.

The chronotope of conjuncture prevalent in conversion narratives produced by Ottoman subjects is well illustrated in the deposition of Abdone, son of the late Giovanni of Aleppo, who in 1616 confessed to the Venetian Holy Office his Christian birth, conversion to Islam, and desire to reembrace Christianity through a formal process of reconciliation with the Church.[33] In narrating his past, Abdone linked space, time, and ritual practice, suggesting that it was his movement

31. Luria (1996, 28).
32. Bakhtin (1981, 84). Put differently, it is "a unit of analysis for studying texts according to the ratio and nature of the temporal and spatial categories represented" (Emerson and Holquist 1981, 425). The concept avoids privileging either time or space but, rather, emphasizes their interdependence and inseparability.
33. Such reconciliation processes were authorized and supervised by the Holy Office, hence the need for a deposition. It should be noted that Venetian reconciliation procedures rarely involved more than some penitential exercises and/or religious instruction in the Pia Casa dei Catecumeni

in space, dictated by historical exigencies and life stages (pilgrimage, revolt, economic crisis, and war) that prompted him to identify himself at times as a Christian and at others as a Muslim:

> I was born a Christian in Aleppo, and baptized. After about 10 years I was made Muslim, and for that time I lived as a Muslim, and was circumcised. And now having arrived in Venice, and wishing to leave said sect of Muslims and to be a good Catholic I am in this place to do what I will be ordered to do.
>
> Asked on what occasion he had left the Catholic faith and became Muslim. He responded: I traveled from youth, and at a certain time when in Sidon in the territory of Tripoli some Muslims rebelled, I joined them [*lit.* went among them] and donned a turban on my head, and they accepted me and asked me who I was, and I told them that I was Muslim. And I told them that from a young age I had been away from my home, and that's why I wasn't circumcised, and so then they made me circumcise. But I [only] told them that because if I had told them I were Christian, they would have made me renege by force or they would have killed me, and that's why I told them I was Muslim. And then I also let them circumcise me for the same fear, so that they accept the fact that I wasn't circumcised.
> Asked why he went like that to Sidon among Muslims, and not among Christians.
>
> He responded: I was in Jerusalem to visit the Holy Sepulcher as a pilgrim, and on the way back I passed through Sidon and not knowing where to go, I joined them, because there was also a great need.
> [...]
> When they circumcised me and made me a Muslim they called me Ebraim. And I served as a soldier for a year under a captain who was called Magiar Mustaffa who was the head of the rebels. And after the year had passed I went to Cairo, and since no one knew that I had been a Muslim, I dressed as a Christian and stayed among Christians for seven years. After that I went in the direction of Constantinople, but in Bursa there was a Muslim who recognized me and knew I had been a Muslim, and in order that he does not uncover me, I ran away to the Hungarian border to come in these ways to Christendom, but a barber told me that the roads were not

---

and thus differed significantly from their Iberian counterpart, in which the reconciliation of *conversos* often also entailed a public abjuration of heresy and a potentially harsh inquisitorial sentence. On Iberian reconciliation procedures, see Graizbord (2004, esp. 105). On the Italian procedure, see Scaraffia (2002, 101).

safe, and that I would be captured as a spy, and so out of fear I came back and by other ways I then arrived in Sarajevo. And from there with some Muslim merchants I arrived in Venice, and while I was with them I acted as a Muslim, because they considered me to be a Muslim, and believed that I was one of those holy men [santoni] who go begging.

Asked, he responded: I didn't return to Aleppo because it was known there that I had become a Muslim, and it would not have been safe for long, although I was there for two months one time on my way, and went to Church like a Christian.[34]

In his deposition, Abdone presents an expedient understanding of religious adherence, premised on practice rather than belief. When being Christian was inconvenient, he practiced Islam; when it became convenient again, he reembraced Christianity.[35] By his own admission, he switched his allegiance at least five times, always due to contingent and pragmatic considerations. Abdone further invoked a popular trope of conversion to Islam at sword's edge, which dated back to the Crusades, and which morphed into an image of the Ottomans as barbarous people who violently converted their Christian slaves.[36] Yet, although he presented his conversion to Islam as coerced, Abdone himself seems to have sensed the inadequacy of such a line of argument in front of the Inquisition. To strengthen his case, he attempted to show a conscious plan to pursue a Christian life by prefacing his narrative with an explicit declaration of his wish "to leave said sect of Muslims and to be a good Catholic" and by framing his voyage to Venice as a purposive, active quest to reenter Christendom, presaged by his failed plan to reach Hungary and his boyhood pilgrimage to Jerusalem. Still, unlike many contemporary Protestant narratives of conversion, his is defined overall by exigency and serendipity rather than by purposive action.

Abdone was hardly unique in linking his shifting confessional affiliation to a set of ritual moments rooted in membership in particular communities and places. For him, as for many others appearing in front of the Venetian Inquisition,

34. Santo Uffizio, Processi, b. 71, fasc. "Abdone q. Giovanni Sensale d'Aleppo" (April 14, 1616). See appendix 3.1 for an excerpted transcript of the original.
35. The gloss "Muslim" for Abdone's self-reported conversion is somewhat misleading here. Abdone described himself as having "turned Turk" ("*turco*"). As I discuss in chapter 7, early modern Italian speakers rarely distinguished between Turks and Muslims and glossed both (as well as Ottomans and, less frequently, Ottoman subjects of whatever ethnoreligious affiliation) as "*turchi*." The complex of religious, juridical, and emotional identifications implied by having "turned Turk" is hard to disentangle in the absence of any other documents produced by or about Abdone.
36. Repeated conversions back and forth between Christianity and Islam have been documented in the Frankish kingdom of Jerusalem, as well as in Mamluk and Ottoman territories (Kedar 1997).

conversion entailed a journey from one geographical point to another, that is, from non-Christian to Christian space. The road offers the opportunity for both religious indeterminacy and for a smooth(er) transition from one confession to another. Moreover, journeys in space are linked to specific time periods and are segmented by rituals such as baptism, pilgrimage, and confession or, alternatively, circumcision and the donning of the turban.

Abdone's effort to link conversion to specific chronotopic moments should be understood within the constraints of the genre of reconciliation depositions. It also speaks to the difference between the narratives of Ottoman deponents, on the one hand, and of Protestant ones, on the other. Comparing these two groups is facilitated by the survival of two dozen reconciliation narratives in three files in the archives of the Venetian Holy Office, dating from 1616, 1630–32, and 1647, respectively.[37] The first and last files contain a total of seven depositions by Ottoman subjects who all claimed to have been born Christians and to wish to return to Christianity after having lived as Muslims for years, sometimes decades. The middle file, dating from 1630–32, contains thirteen depositions, three by Ottoman subjects in circumstances similar to the ones just described and ten by German- and French-speaking subjects who were raised as Lutherans or Calvinists and who wished to become Catholic. Of these twenty depositions, five are by women (four Muslims and one Protestant) and fifteen are by men (six Muslims and nine Protestants). Most depositions were facilitated through the active intervention and mediation (linguistic and, most probably, also theological) of clergymen: the prior of the House of Catechumens in the case of Ottoman deponents and the preacher-confessor of the German "nation" in the Fondaco dei Tedeschi (German Exchange House) and other Venetian clergymen in the case of Protestant deponents.

Two striking differences stand out between the depositions of Muslim-Ottoman and of Protestant deponents. First, most Ottoman deponents emphasized their changing family circumstances and spatial location as being key to their shifting religious affiliation and rarely dwelt on personal motivations for such shifts. According to Ottoman deponents, they were Christian while living in a Christian household/community and became Muslim once they moved into a Muslim one. They often accounted for such transition by referring to a parent's death or conversion to Islam, enslavement, marriage to a Muslim, or migration in search of economic betterment. In these accounts, as in Abdone's, conversion followed spatial transition and change in personal status. Conversely, Protestant deponents, while acknowledging their birth into Protestant families as the source

37. Santo Uffizio, Processi, bb. 71, 88, 103.

of their heretical upbringing and former beliefs, consistently highlighted their individual choice to become Catholics, often linking this temporally defined act of choice to key transformative moments—a dream, a vision, a vow taken during severe illness, or a chance encounter with a Catholic preacher—that led to a spiritual awakening. In their accounts, the formal outward assumption of a Catholic identity followed inner persuasion and was followed by a journey in space from Protestant to Catholic territory. Spatial mobility, in other words, was the outcome, rather than the cause, of their inner religious transformation, which takes center stage.[38] Protestant depositions are also more detailed than those of Ottoman subjects with regards to articles of faith, highlighting both deponents' past errors and current belief in Catholic truths. Theological issues are almost entirely absent from Ottoman depositions.

To illustrate these differences, let us compare two depositions. One was produced by a Calvinist, Pierre Blanche, in 1631; the other was produced by a Muslim, Maddalena (formerly Rachima) in 1647. Here is the deposition of eighteen-year-old surgeon Pierre Blanche ("Pietro Blanco"), native of Lyon, who was the son of a Calvinist father and a Catholic mother:

> I have followed the life of my father, nourished and raised in the sect and heresies of Calvin ... and having left my country last year in the month of October I stayed in Piedmont for several months, practicing medicine according to my profession and finally five months ago I came to Venice, and stayed in the old Lazaretto for about three months, and then in Venice, and after I left France, I have always thought of leaving that heretical sect of Calvin, and becoming Catholic because in France I saw some miracles and even more elsewhere in Italy, performed by the Blessed Virgin. Therefore I resolved with determination to become Catholic, and actually made a vow to go to Rome, and I went to Genoa to be quarantined and in the past days I went to [the church of] St. Francis of Paola to the Father Confessor who is present here ... because knowing to have been in a most grave error having held, observed, and believed all that which the Calvinist sect holds, sees, and observes, and recognizing the Catholic and Apostolic Roman Catholic faith to be true I ask now this most holy tribunal to be reconciled with the Holy Catholic and Apostolic Roman Catholic Church.[39]

38. On the geographical mobility of Lutheran converts to Catholicism in the early modern Holy Roman Empire, see Corpis (2001, 112). On the journeys of early modern Jewish converts in the Holy Roman Empire and in England, respectively, see Carlebach (2001, 112, 120); Dureau (2001, 34).
39. Santo Uffizio, Processi, b. 88 (Oct. 16, 1631). See appendix 3.2 for a transcript of the original deposition.

In contrast to Pierre, here is the deposition of Maddalena:

I was born in the countryside of the city of Clini [Koljane], three days from Sebenico, to Christian father and mother. My father was called Melin, he was a peasant and a soldier, my mother was called Chiarana; both died. I don't know the name they gave me when I was baptized, and my sister Maddalena, who may be alive or dead, told me I had been baptized. And I lived with my father until I was about ten. [Scribe's note:] Correcting herself, she said: I had lived with my father until I was five, when I was taken by Turkish relatives of my father's, who took me to Zemonico [Zemunik Donji, Croatia], where I was raised and was given the name Rachima, and they made me live according to Turkish law, and married me to a Turk called Fasula, who may be alive or dead, but we did not have any children. I am about 50 years old and all this time I have lived as a Turk, and conformed to the Mohammedan rites. Now having arrived in this Catholic City and having been instructed for about 40 days in the House of the Catechumens in the articles of the Catholic holy faith I see that Our Lord Jesus Christ is God, born of the Virgin Mary, that there are three divine persons, that the Church has seven sages.[40] And I hold and believe universally all that the Holy Mother Church holds and believes. And therefore I am ready to abjure, and live and die in this holy Christian faith.[41]

Whereas Maddalena-Rachima dwells on her childhood vagaries and the circumstances that turned her into a Muslim, Pierre sums up his childhood in one sentence. And whereas for Maddalena her life story is one of changing family attachments over which she has no control (and narrated, accordingly, mostly in the passive voice), Pierre narrates his life as one of active, solitary traveling and career development. His geographical journeys—his departure from heretical France and entry into Catholic space via the territories of Piedmont and Genoa—are presaged (and presumably prompted) by the experience of miracles in his native country and are closely interlinked with his spiritual journeys. Pierre emphasizes this spiritual transformation by defining his former beliefs as "sectar-

40. This reference could not be confirmed with certainty, but it is probably an oblique reference to the widely circulating *Book of the Seven Sages of Rome*, popular around the Mediterranean basin from the late Middle Ages on, according to which people were encouraged to turn to the seven sages to profess their faith. I thank Father Juan Flores for his assistance on this issue.
41. Santo Uffizio, Processi, b. 103, fasc. "Madalena q. Melin Turca" (June 4, 1647). See appendix 3.3 for a transcript of the original deposition.

ian" and "heretical" right from the start.[42] Conversely, Maddalena describes the forty-odd years she had lived as a Muslim in a factual manner, suggesting no contrition or spiritual transformation until the very last sentence. She presents her current embrace of Christianity as the result of learning—the forty days of catechetical instruction she had received in the House of the Catechumens. Yet she does not claim to have had any intentions to return to Christianity prior to her arrival in Venice, which she casts as happenstance, not as a purposive journey. Furthermore, she does not attest to any deep spiritual transformation in the wake of her travels. Whereas Pierre's narrative implies that he had waited all his life to become Catholic and to arrive in Catholic lands, Maddalena's narrative does not dwell on intentions. Here, religion is determined by kinship networks. She had been a Christian when raised by her Christian parents, but became a Muslim once her Muslim relatives took her to Zemunik and married her off to a Muslim husband. Now that she is in a Catholic land, her return to Christianity follows. For Pierre, intentions are the driving force of his life story. He is a willing individual, who shakes off the shackles of heretical kin to pursue his own desires, namely to reach Rome and embrace Catholicism. He actively pursues this goal, first by embarking on a journey, then by seeking out a Catholic clergyman to assist him. Whereas Maddalena's arrival in the House of the Catechumens is left unaccounted for in her narrative, Pierre presents his encounter with the confessor at the church of St. Francis of Paola as the direct result of his endeavors, and his alone.

What might account for these stark differences between Maddalena's and Pierre's narratives? We may look for an explanation in gendered notions of the self and its transformative capacity. Certainly, even these brief narratives already suggest the important role that gender played in shaping conceptions of the self for these two deponents. This, however, does not mean that kinship alliances determined women's conversion more than men's or that spatial mobility characterized men more than women. Nor should conversion narratives be read as unmediated reflections of the protagonists' predicament.[43] Rather, at work here are highly gendered narrative frames. The propensity of women converts from Christianity to Islam to justify their apostasy in front of the Holy Office as resulting from their master's or husband's wishes has also been attested to in other contexts.[44] Women converts often suggested that the continuity of their social role as caregivers (wives, mothers, concubines, or domestic slaves) justified the discontinuity

---

42. On the concept of spiritual journey as a hallmark of early modern Venetian evangelism, see Martin (1996).
43. Anna Vanzan has gone so far as to conclude that Muslim women converts' narratives reflect their "passivity and resignation" (1996, 332).
44. Bennassar (1996, 106).

of their religious affiliation or, perhaps, that such discontinuity was not as total as their inquisitors imagined because conversion helped them retain their overall social position. These tropes are clearly at work in Maddalena's narrative, which, unlike Pierre's, emphasizes rootedness in family and place as defining the protagonist's membership in a particular religious community. Men, on the other hand, rarely argued for continuity in social role as a justification for their conversion. Rather, they emphasized time and again the coercive dimension of their conversion, the fact that they had no choice but to convert or become martyrs.

Along with widespread gendered representations of the converting self, converts' depositions were also shaped fundamentally by specific intermediaries and institutions. Maddalena's narrative, like most other reconciliation depositions, is delivered to us through the mediation not only of a specific genre—the inquisitorial dialogue, of which the reconciliation deposition was a highly structured component—and specific (if sometimes anonymous) judges and scribes but also of a particular clergyman (named in the preambles to several of the depositions), Girolamo Pastriccio, the prior of the House of Catechumens.[45] Although the extant record casts Pastriccio's mediation as strictly linguistic, stemming from deponents' ignorance of Italian, it was also, perforce, theological and cultural as well. Pastriccio's considerable role in shaping deponents' narratives is further suggested by the strikingly similar structure and contents of several other reconciliation depositions in which he was involved. Among them are the narratives of two other Ottoman Muslim women professing to have been born to Christian parents and seeking reconciliation with the Catholic Church, the fifty-year-old Catterina Odorelavich, whose story was almost identical to Maddalena's, and Anastasia Viggenich, who arrived in Venice with her Muslim husband and two sons, all of whom converted to Christianity.[46] The three testimonies were recorded within a few days of one another. Of particular interest is Anastasia's deposition, which presents not only her early childhood adhesion to Islam but also her very recent reembrace of Christianity as determined by her kinfolk. Her first conversion was brought about by her father's decision to sell her to Muslims. Now, "I find myself married to a Turk [Muslim] named Mustafâ, who came to Venice with [our] two sons to become Christian."

Pastriccio's understanding of the genre of inquisitorial reconciliation and his theological imagination no doubt played a decisive role in the construction of these narratives. His mediation was essential not only during the depositions but

45. Pastriccio was born in Split (Croatia) and became prior of the House of Catechumens in 1645 (ASPV, Curia Patriarcale di Venezia. Sezione Antica, Catecumeni, Registri battesimi (henceforth: ASPV, CRb), reg. 2, c. 19r (July 22, 1645)).
46. Both files are in Santo Uffizio, Processi, b. 103 (June 4 and 7, 1647).

in deponents' prior socialization in the House of Catechumens, which lasted anywhere from days to months. As I show in greater detail in the next chapter, while in the House, catechumens were guided by Venetian patrician patrons and by Jesuit friars and Catholic clergy who themselves often possessed, like Pastriccio, roots or rich past experiences working in the Ottoman-Venetian borderlands.

Deponents emphasized contingent ritual practice rather than deep spiritual conviction as what defined their membership in a religious community. This emphasis was predicated not only on deponents' sojourn in the House of Catechumens, their acquaintance with Pastriccio, and their gendered experience of kinship and mobility.[47] Crucially, it was also shaped by their Ottoman provenance. Both Ottoman women's emphasis on kinship and Ottoman men's emphasis on fear of violence as the determinant factor in changing their religious allegiance share an important characteristic—they place the locus of agency outside the speaking subject. The twenty-one-year-old Giovanni Romolo of Thessaloniki became Muslim when he was taken to Istanbul at age eleven, "forced to renege, circumcised, and made to trample on the cross." He subsequently lived as a Muslim for nine years until his arrival in Venice eight days prior to appearing in front of the Holy Office in 1630.[48] The eighteen-year-old Christoforo Sansona Sinope of Crete was recruited at age six to be a "zamora"[49] and "was always a Muslim by force, and externally and [in] exterior life but in my heart I was always a Christian. And I was a Muslim only outwardly, because I couldn't do otherwise."[50] These cases do not suggest that Ottoman deponents did not have a notion of intentionality. On the contrary, as I note earlier, Abdone framed his narrative by an abiding intention to reach Christian territory. Similarly, Christoforo Sansona Sinope distinguished between his "exterior life," in which he practiced Islam, and his inner locus of perduring Christian belief. But unlike Protestants, Ottoman deponents did not ascribe to interiority and intentionality the force to change the course of their lives; that is, they did not account for their religious transformation by way of their will.

---

47. Marc Baer (2004) addresses the gendered nature of conversion by examining the strategic use of conversion by women appearing before Sha'ria courts to dissolve their marriages in sixteenth-century Istanbul. Unfortunately, the article does not consider how our notions of agency, subjecthood, and conversion may be at odds with early modern Ottoman ones.

48. Santo Uffizio, Processi, b. 88 (Oct. 3, 1630).

49. Perhaps the word *zamora* refers to a player of the Dzamare flute, common in the southern Balkans.

50. "Sempre son stato turco per forza, et quanto all'estrinsero et al vivere esteriorm[en]te ma nel mio core son sempre stato christiano. Et solam[en]te Turco di fuora, perche non poteva far di manco" (Santo Uffizio, Processi, b. 71 (June 7, 1616)). The surname Sinope may indicate family roots on the Black Sea coast.

Indeed, the one deposition in the collection by a female Protestant, a twenty-four-year-old Swiss woman named Anna Frais, bears greater similarity to those of her male Protestant fellows than to any deposition by a Muslim woman. According to Anna,

> having been born, nourished, and raised by a father and a mother in the lands of Lutherans, I have always held and believed all that the sect of Luther teaches, except that I have believed that there is purgatory, and also in the intercession of saints. Finally I have come to recognize my errors through the preaching and exhortations of the above-mentioned Father Fra Giacomo [and] have resolved to bring myself to the bosom if the Holy Catholic Church, totally detesting everything that contradicts said Church, [and] I confirm to believe in the future and observe that which the Holy Mother Catholic Church holds, believes, and teaches. Therefore I humbly appeal to this holy tribunal wishing to reconcile myself with said holy mother Church.[51]

As in Pierre Blanche's narrative, and in striking contrast to those of Muslim women, Anna has scant little to say about her past kinship ties, other than to confirm her spiritual transformation and thus to exculpate herself in part by suggesting her early skepticism about the basic Lutheran critiques of purgatory and intercession.

I must insert here a word of caution against treating Ottoman and Protestant chronotopes of conversion as the products of internally cohesive and self-contained cultures. Rather, they may serve as prototypes that congealed in specific (in this case, Venetian) institutions and genres through the active mediation of identifiable social actors. As an illustration, let us examine a conversion narrative produced by a Venetian nobleman that articulates an intermediate chronotope of conversion. In his reconciliation deposition of 1632, Marco Lombardo, a twenty-seven-year-old Venetian patrician, described how, six years earlier, he had been on board a Venetian ship near Alexandria, Egypt, from which he had been captured by Muslims and taken to a castle where

> I stayed for four months and observed there the Mohammedan ceremonies, and had violence used against me by getting me drunk with brandy, and was violently circumcised and forced to speak Turkish, and I confessed

---

51. Santo Uffizio, Processi, b. 88 (June 4, 1630). See appendix 3.4 for a transcript of the original deposition.

to them to be Muslim for the fear of death with which they threatened me. But in my heart I had God, the Virgin, and the saints, which I always honored with my orations day and night. And I did not perform any other ceremonies, and that which I did, I did only with the exterior and never with the heart. Then when I saw an opportune time, I moved to Nazareth, and here I found a Franciscan friar who reconciled me [with the Church] in the manner that can be observed from the certificate he gave me, which I now present to the Holy Office. Now sorrowful and repentant I ask God for forgiveness and this holy tribunal to be reconciled to the holy faith, promising to live from now on as a good and true Catholic, and it is only a few days since I came back to Venice, that is about 5 days, and after I escaped from the Muslims [Turks] I have always lived in the Catholic manner and I confessed and communicated in Nazareth three times during the eight days I stayed there, and another time when I was in Zante.[52]

This dramatic narrative exploits the common tropes of Muslim barbarity and forced conversion at sword's edge to appeal to the inquisitors' mercy and to exculpate the speaker from charges of apostasy. Unlike most Ottoman subjects who sought reconciliation with the Catholic Church, Marco identifies himself as an actor and an intentional subject. After narrating an initial episode of captivity and forced conversion in which he is a passive victim ("had violence used against me," "was violently circumcised and forced to speak Turkish"), the remainder of his deposition narrates his own purposive actions ("I saw an opportune time, I moved to Nazareth, and here I found a Franciscan friar," "I ask God for forgiveness," "I confessed and communicated"). Yet, like most other deponents in front of the Venetian Holy Office discussing their conversion to Islam, Marco says little about matters of belief and presents the locus of religious affiliation in ritual practices (e.g., circumcision and "speaking Turkish"; in other narratives: trampling on the cross or eating meat indiscriminately on Fridays and holidays) rather than in theological or spiritual transformation. This calls for a further examination of other narrative genres, both Venetian and Ottoman, that were available to deponents and their spiritual counselors and that no doubt shaped their accounts.

In a few other cases, however, personal will *is* referred to a posteriori to justify Muslims' conversion to Christianity—particularly that of women and girls—against the wishes of their kinfolk. For example, in 1586 the Venetian authorities had to decide on the case of a daughter of an Ottoman çavuş (messenger), who

---

52. Santo Uffizio, Processi, b. 88 (Nov. 8, 1632). See appendix 3.5 for a transcript of the original deposition.

had been wedded to a renegade from Puglia, in southern Italy. After the two arrived in Budua (Budva, Montenegro) in early 1586, perhaps because of her husband's attempt to return to Christianity, the young woman, now named Dorotea, was transferred to a Venetian charitable institution, the Casa delle Convertite, where, on interrogation, she declared—in Turkish writing—her wish to remain Christian.[53] In another case, in 1627 an Ottoman Bosnian provincial governor, who suspected that his daughter had been kidnapped and forcibly converted five years earlier, was taken on a well-orchestrated tour of the premise of the Casa delle Zitelle (another Venetian institution for girls), where his daughter insisted she was free and "did not wish to leave Heaven for the earth" nor "depart from the salvation of the soul."[54] In 1642, a Bosnian woman named Lucia, who had escaped her husband and relatives several months earlier and was now tracked down in Venice by her brother, stated that she had been "carried to a ship against her will" and that "her wish was to stay in Venice as a Christian, since she feared being killed by her own relatives if she returned to her homeland."[55] Yet all these professions of intentionality, willfulness, and, indeed, individual agency were made after the fact, by "model converts" who were already well-versed in Venetian genres of narrating conversion. They cannot be taken as evidence about the nature of the interactions that led up to their baptism.

FIXING ITINERARIES, ASCERTAINING INTENTIONS

Another genre in which the competing chronotopes of conjuncture and purposive journeying can be traced is the *examinum matrimoniorum* (matrimonial examination). In an effort to eliminate irregular forms of cohabitation, concubinage, secret marriages, and other matrimonies concluded without a priest officiating, the Council of Trent decreed that, if an intended bride or groom had lived away from their place of origin for a substantial period after puberty, their free (unwedded) status had to be verified prior to marriage.[56] The process of verification took different forms and applied to different categories of people in different Catholic societies.[57] In seventeenth-century Venice, all Christians who

53. Senato, Deliberazioni Costantinopoli, Reg. 7, cc. 32r–33r, 40v, 46r (March 14, 1586).
54. Senato, Deliberazioni Costantinopoli, reg. 18, cc. 40r–v (June 5, 1627). For a fuller analysis of this case, see Rothman (2011).
55. "portata in vassello contro sua voglia … esser sua volontà di star a Ven[ezi]a christiana dubitando di esser morta da proprij parenti se ritornasse alla sua Patria" (Avogadori di Comun, Misc. Penale, b. 343, fasc. 15, c. 3v (Aug. 7, 1642)).
56. Franco (1995, 86).
57. For example, in one of very few studies of *examinum matrimoniorum* to date, Luis Martínez-Fernández has shown that in nineteenth-century Puerto Rico, for example, "certificates of *soltería*

sought a marriage license and whose baptismal records were unavailable, namely foreign-born Christians, as well as converts from Judaism and Islam, had to produce two witnesses who had known them their entire adult life. These witness testimonies, now preserved in the archives of the Venetian Patriarchal Curia, attest to the social networks that foreigners forged within and outside the city, and that were mobilized to weave plausible biographical narratives.[58] In particular, the testimonies suggest how foreigners and locals understood intimacy, localness, and embeddedness in specific social roles.

Of course, we should not read these testimonies as reliable sketches of actual life trajectories. As will become clearer soon, the testimonies rarely contradicted one another openly and the remarkable level of detail that witnesses were ready to provide about neighbors' and mere acquaintances' lives suggests careful prior briefing. To be granted a marriage license, applicants had to recruit witnesses who could claim familiarity with their whereabouts not only in Venice but, if possible, throughout their adult lives. This was highly unlikely in the case of Muslim converts and other Christian subjects of Ottoman background, who often had traveled a fair amount or who had experienced uprooting due to war. Such individuals had to either forge life histories that omitted inconvenient sojourns outside Venice or summon witnesses of similar background who could claim to have known them for their entire adult life.

Like the reconciliation depositions, testimonies on behalf of converts often linked their spatiotemporal movement with key ritual moments and religious transformation. The striking differences between the testimonies on behalf of three Jewish and Muslim women converts, discussed here, allow us to pose an initial hypothesis about the chronotopic features of such narratives. All three

---

(bachelorhood or spinsterhood) were required of foreigners, so-called *vagos*, people without a fixed domicile, widows and widowers, and all those who had absented themselves from their parishes for more than a year" (2000, 267).

58. The archives of the Patriarchal Curia in Venice contain a large corpus of *examinum matrimoniorum* from the period 1506–1807, collated in 338 volumes of hundreds of pages each. For the first seventy-five years alone (that is, the period up to 1670) roughly eighty volumes of these examinations survive, including contemporary indices and summaries. To the best of my knowledge, this corpus has not yet been studied in detail. To be sure, the vast majority of petitioners for marriage licenses who were subjected to the *examinum matrimoniorum* procedure were not converts but, rather, foreign-born Christians, mostly journeymen and servants from the Terraferma (the Venetian colonies on the Italian mainland) and from transalpine Europe and, much less frequently, merchants and mariners from the Stato da Mar (the Venetian Adriatic and Mediterranean colonies). Of the dozen or so converts who underwent this process to verify their celibate status before 1670, all but one were former Muslims (I discuss the one Jewish case later). Men and women were more or less equally represented, but their typical witnesses and the resulting narratives differed markedly. Whereas women's witnesses were mostly neighbors and masters, men's were as often work associates.

cases are premised on the interlacing of spatiotemporal movement with women's changes of status, both religious and familial. But whereas conversion enabled, if it did not determine, the Jewish convert's transformations of status and geographical journeys thereafter, the conversion of the two Muslim women followed their transformation of status and geographical journeys and was implicitly presented as their effect.

Felice, daughter of Benetto and Dolcetta Cesana, was born in the Venetian ghetto and was baptized in 1651 at age thirteen.[59] In 1667, at age twenty-nine, she approached the Venetian patriarch for permission to marry. Felice's two witnesses were long-time immigrants to Venice: a fifty-year-old gondolier named Alvise, son of Daniele de Blanchis of Pinzano in Aquilea, who had lived in Venice for thirty years, and the sixty-year-old Maddalena, daughter of Giovanni Facini of Feltre, who had lived in Venice for thirty-seven years.[60] According to their testimonies, both witnesses came to know Felice as neighbors shortly after her baptism, but had kept in touch with her over a sixteen-year period, despite her several changes of residence.

The most striking aspect of Alvise's and Maddalena's testimonies on Felice's behalf is their contrived nature. Both witnesses provided the exact same chronology and geography for Felice's whereabouts over a sixteen-year period, including a sojourn in Ferrara fifteen years earlier and a list of all the parishes in Venice where Felice had lived since leaving the ghetto at age thirteen. It is unlikely that the two would have been able to date Felice's move to Ferrara (1652) and state its exact length (ten months) unless briefed by her. Yet, despite their fabricated nature, and potential suspicions that her ten-month sojourn with Francesco Colombo in Ferrara might have raised about her celibacy and eligibility for marriage, the testimonies went unchallenged and Felice's request to marry was granted.[61]

Felice's witnesses have little to say about her conversion and make no explicit links between that event and her spatiotemporal transitions thereafter. Her con-

59. Felice's baptismal record does not survive in the registers of converts' baptisms in either the Pia Casa dei Catecumeni or the Patriarchal Curia.

60. It is noteworthy that Felice did not summon any Venetian natives as witnesses. Perhaps she did not know any well enough, or perhaps she considered her witnesses localized enough to produce convincing testimonies on her behalf.

61. This was not always the case. Three years after Felice, Pier'Antonio, son of the late Bechir, a Muslim convert from the Šibenik area, had to summon no fewer than ten witnesses (including two who submitted their testimonies in writing) before the Venetian patriarch granted him permission to marry. Perhaps the fact that his baptism had taken place far away, in the town of Bisceglie in Spanish-controlled Puglia, and his lengthy sojourns away from Venice as a mariner warranted greater scrutiny. For Felice's case, see ASPV, Sezione Antica, Examinum Matrimoniorum (henceforth: EM), reg. 81, cc. 1574r–v (Aug. 27, 1667). For Pier'Antonio's, see ASPV, EM, reg. 68, cc. 375r–379r (Aug. 20, 1670).

version is clearly delimited in time (a past event that took place at the moment of transition from childhood to adulthood) and place (the convert left the ghetto and entered Catholic Venetian space). It is independent of Felice's later peregrinations.

In sharp contrast, another matrimonial examination, that of Maria, a widowed convert of Muslim background from the Aegean Island of Skyros, articulates a chronotope of conjuncture much akin to that characteristic of Ottoman women's reconciliation depositions to the Inquisition previously discussed. Indeed, all of Maria's witnesses make explicit the connection among her shifting kinship and household position, geographical and social mobility, and religious affiliation.

According to Maria's three witnesses, she was captured as a youth by the Venetians on Skyros in 1652, was brought to Crete by Count Sabeni, her captor and the commander of the operation, who promptly had her baptized, placed in a monastery, and then married off to one of his lieutenant captains, a German Lutheran ensign named Stefan, who died a few months later. When Sabeni decided to move to Venice he took Maria along, possibly at her request, and put her to work as a maidservant in his and in other, patrician households. But when her plans to return to her *patria* were uncovered two years later, in December 1654, Maria was sent to the Casa del Soccorso, where she remained for a year and a half until May 1656, when she was allowed to resume employment as a maidservant in the house of Girolamo Avogadro, a Venetian patrician. Now, in 1659, a possible matrimony prompted her to approach the patriarch with her witnesses.[62]

The biography outlined, based on Maria's three witnesses, systematically links her conversion to her social and geographical mobility. Not only was her baptism a direct consequence of her capture and transfer to the Venetian colony of Crete, but her marriage to a Christian (although "heretical," i.e., Lutheran, as one of her witnesses obliquely remarked) was made possible by these moves. Her widowhood, which followed shortly afterward, occasioned another journey—this time to the metropole and a new state of servility. Whereas marrying an officer gained her freedom from formal slavery, becoming a widow forced her to go back under the direct patronage and patriarchal control, first of Count Sabeni, then of Girolamo Avogadro, and now, possibly, of a second husband. Indeed, as she discovered once in Venice, her desire to go back to Skyros became the pretext for her removal from Avogadro's household and enclosure in a charitable institution. Only after her religious orthodoxy was confirmed (i.e., once she was sufficiently dissuaded from leaving Christian Venice to reembrace her Muslim past) was she released from confinement. Now, perhaps at Sabeni's and Avogadro's behest, she was to be wedded again.

---

62. ASPV, EM, reg. 63, cc. 371r–372v (March 20, 1659). On the Casa del Soccorso, a Venetian charitable institution for women, see Chojnacka (2001, esp. 125).

As I discuss in the next chapter, the conflation of patronage, patriarchal authority, and religious discipline typified the relationships of female converts of Muslim background with their Venetian masters. Such complex relationships could involve additional members of a master's household and an extended network of friends and kin. It is these complex ties of authority and patronage that may account for the occasional contradictions found in matrimonial examination records. For example, Maria's three witnesses diverged in important ways on the question of her relationship to Sabeni. Her first two witnesses, a thirty-seven-year-old ex-soldier named Emanuel Machergiotti and the twenty-nine-year-old coppersmith named Giacomo, son of the late Raffaele Arneri, were both under Sergeant Major Sabeni's command in 1652 and had remained his protégés after moving to Venice. Both claimed to have been present at Maria's first wedding and plainly stated that Maria could not have remarried after her first husband's death "because she has always stayed by the said Count." These two testimonies apparently did not satisfy the patriarch because a month later another witness was summoned, Girolamo Avogadro, the fifty-three-year-old Venetian native who by his own account was an old acquaintance of Sabeni and who had employed Maria in his household "for the past three or four years." His testimony told a rather different story. At the urging of the Venetian authorities, he had taken Maria into his household in 1654, shortly after she had been "prompted by the chaplains of S. Zaccaria to turn to the Tribunals" against Sabeni. Avogadro was not interrogated as to the nature of Maria's allegations against her patron and did not divulge any further details. But Sabeni's efforts to have Maria sent to the Casa del Soccorso only a few months later, under the pretext of her alleged desire to return to Skyros ("with evident danger of reneging the faith"), may suggest an effort to silence a potential scandal. Significantly, Avogadro's insistence at the closing of his testimony that it was Maria who had prompted Sabeni to take her to Venice with him—unconfirmed by the other witnesses—may have also served to emphasize Maria's agency in a chain of events over which she exercised very little control and to assuage any concerns about her interests in the prospective marriage.

Maria's tangled relationship with Sabeni is only obliquely hinted at by the three witnesses (and, to be sure, was quite likely understood differently by each). Was she Sabeni's beloved daughter-like protégé? Concubine? Sexual slave? In sending her first to a Cretan monastery, then to marry a German mercenary, then to Venice, then to Avogadro's household, then to the Casa del Soccorso, and finally to a new marriage, was Sabeni covering up or trying to guarantee Maria's well-being? These questions are impossible to address given the patriarchal tribunal's glaring lack of interest in them and in the absence of any additional archival traces.

Similar ambiguities emerge from the matrimonial examinations of other converted women slaves of Ottoman background, raising similar questions about the interdependence of religious conversion and social and geographical mobility. Take, for example, the testimonies produced the same year, 1659, on behalf of Cattarina, purchased in 1649 as a child of ten or twelve by Gabriele Gozzi, a Venetian, from a merchant on Zante (Zakynthos), a long standing Venetian island colony in the Ionian. According to her two witnesses, thirty-seven-year-old Girolamo, son of the late Aurelio Pruni, and twenty-nine-year-old Domenico, son of the late Bartolomeo Furello, both members of the Gozzi household, Cattarina had always been under Gozzi's "protection." Gozzi, they claimed, had kept Cattarina in his house in Venice under lock and key until shortly before his death, when he had her transferred to the Casa del Soccorso of Vicenza, from whence she was returned to Venice by Gabriele's father, Alberto, only a few weeks before the testimonies were produced.[63] Whether Cattarina was Gabriele's concubine or not (the witnesses claimed she had been a child of ten or twelve when captured in 1649, yet her baptismal certificate of 1654 defined her as "of adult age"), some of the dates in the narrative raise questions. Why was Cattarina baptized in the small village of Bevadoro (now part of the city of Vicenza) rather than in Venice, in which case she would have been eligible for support from the House of Catechumens but also subjected—along with her master—to much closer scrutiny? And why was her baptism held only in 1654, approximately five years after her arrival in Venice? More interestingly, how was she admitted into the Casa del Soccorso prior to her baptism (the governors of the Soccorso claimed in 1659 she had lived there for seven years)? And what prompted Alberto Gozzi to retrieve Cattarina from Vicenza and seek a husband for her now?

Here again, the extant documentation does not allow us to answer these questions conclusively. Yet, when read serially, the testimonies on behalf of converts repeatedly suggest the oversimplification of complicated itineraries, the glossing over of inconvenient details, and the irreconcilable contradictions between the testimonies of witnesses attached to converts and their masters in dense ties of patronage and outright dependence. These narratives both attest to the link between conversion and the vagaries of colonial and domestic subordination, and seek to erase their traces.

63. ASPV, EM, reg. 63, cc. 647v–648v (Oct. 29, 1659). Alberto Gozzi was a Venetian merchant with some Ottoman trading partners. He was the master of at least one other converted slave girl, thirteen-year-old Antonia Margarita (formerly Sala), who was baptized in the House of Catechumens on Oct. 13, 1655 (ASPV, CRb, reg. 2, c. 45v). For Gozzi's commercial activities, see Cinque Savi, Risposte, b. 154, cc. 26v–27v (June 6, 1646).

CATEGORIZING PEOPLE

A brief discussion is in order here of the differing images of conversion and converthood as they emerge from the documents produced by the House of Catechumens. This House (the subject of chap. 4) was established in 1557 to shelter, instruct, and ultimately baptize its Muslim and Jewish charges. The main genres of documentation in the House archives were records of neophytes' baptism and departure, on the one hand, and notes from meetings of the House Board of Governors on the other. Both types of documentation were produced under very similar circumstances: in short proximity to the events they describe; by individuals who were House priors or clerks; and for consumption by the same milieu of priors, members of the institutional gubernatorial board, and Venetian government and ecclesiastical officials. Yet they were organized around quite distinct logics. These genres are highly significant for reconstructing converts' life trajectories and for suggesting the ways in which such trajectories did or did not fit preexisting patterns and the governors' expectations. Beyond that, these genres, when read against one another, allow us to ask how their authors and readers understood the institution of which they were part and how they imagined the process of conversion and the making of converted subjects.

The House of Catechumens baptismal records and departure registers allocated to each entry only a limited, fixed, and clearly demarcated space on the page—not more than a few lines in most cases—concretizing materially the tendency to fit catechumens into one of few, preestablished categories: "Jew," "Turk," "Moor," "child," "slave," "soldier," and so on. The registers noted only the barest milestones in a convert's life prior to baptism, and even less of his or her whereabouts thereafter (see figs. 3.1 and 3.2). For the most part, they specified only when individuals left the House and where to, dates on which they received disbursements from a special fund for long-time converts, and the sum given. This stands in stark contrast to the elaborate attention paid to converts' conduct for decades after their baptism, characteristic of the House meeting notes, and the range of disciplinary practices devised by the House personnel (see chap. 4).

The allocation of only limited space for each entry in the baptismal and departure registers, and the division of each entry into two columns to mark two discrete stages, a "before" and an "after" in a neophyte's life, were hardly accidental or inevitable. That these techniques were carefully observed over a long period suggests that for the purposes of the registers' compilers, neophytes' whereabouts after baptism mattered less than the need to count souls, prevent repeated baptisms, and ascertain the facts of baptism and departure themselves. Thus, the moments of baptism and departure represent in these genres the legal fiction of a radical break

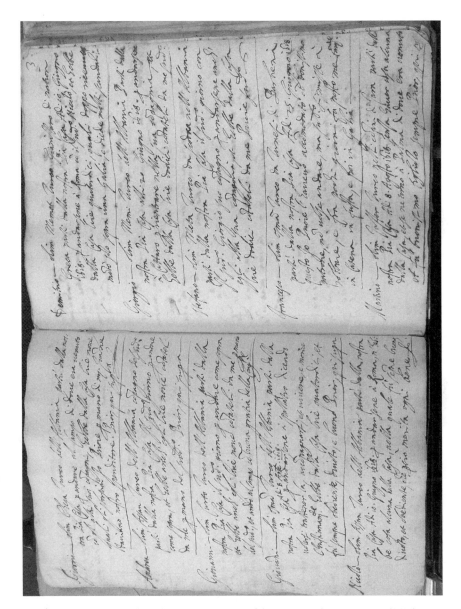

Figure 3.1 *Sample page from the departure register of the Pia Casa dei Catecumeni (1616). ASPV Curia Patriarcale di Venezia. Sezione Antica, Catecumeni, Registri battesimi, reg. 2, cc. 2v–3r. Reproduction: author, by permission of Ministero per i Beni e le Attività Culturali.*

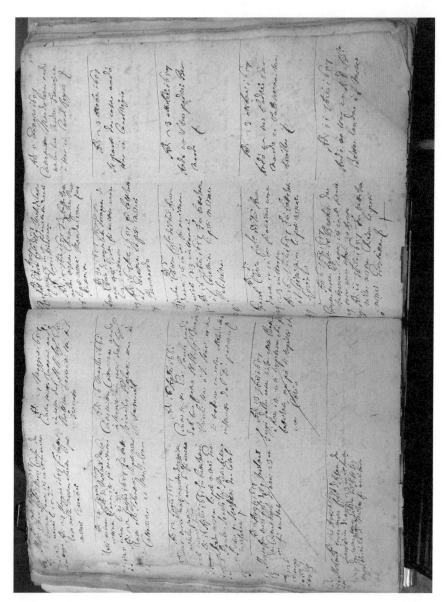

Figure 3.2 *Sample page from the baptismal register of the Pia Casa dei Catecumeni (1657). ASPV Curia Patriarcale di Venezia. Sezione Antica, Catecumeni, Registri battesimi, reg. 2, cc. 47v–48r. Reproduction: author, by permission of Ministero per i Beni e le Attività Culturali.*

with the past and the beginning of a new life. This legal fiction was worlds apart from the actual trajectories of Venetian converts upon baptism.

While often missing much vital data, the vast majority of baptismal and departure records did not fail to register catechumens' previous, non-Christian names. As Duane Corpis notes in the context of Protestant conversion to Catholicism in early modern Augsburg, the meticulous registration of converts' previous names suggests that they "were not perceived as vagabonds or rootless foreigners" who could not be integrated into the Catholic community.[64] A similar logic guided the governors of the Venetian House of Catechumens in noting down converts' names and places of origin. Rather than being transitory sojourners who passed through the city on their way to another locale, converts were strongly encouraged to grow roots in Venice, and such roots were themselves often seen as indices of successful conversion. In fact, an individual's entry in the baptismal register marked only the beginning of a process of localization that was expected to last a lifetime. Whereas neophytes were subjected to a host of disciplinary techniques that forever marked them as "baptized infidels," they were also, crucially, to become part of the Venetian moral community. In a sense, as David Nirenberg argues in relation to religious communities in late medieval Aragon, it was precisely such indelible marks of difference that made their bearers vital members of a community, holding an important lesson for everyone to see about God's grace and the possibility of salvation.[65]

Beyond fixing the identities and trajectories of catechumens and neophytes through the use of a predetermined grid, the records of the House of Catechumens are also significant in suggesting differential expectations about catechumens' intentions (and, indeed, the very possibility of an intending subject) along lines of religion and gender. Dozens of documents in the House registers vouch for Jewish male catechumens' intentions as a precondition for baptism, in phrases such as "wishing to become Christian"; "strong will to become Christian"; "came," "went," "requested," or "presented himself to become Christian"; "intentions to become Christian"; "not wishing to become Christian"; "wants to be baptized"; "tell the prior if he wants baptism"; and "hear the wish to be baptized."[66]

64. Corpis (2001, 119).
65. On difference as being what binds various groups together in a moral community, see Nirenberg (1996).
66. See, for example, Archivio delle Istituzioni di Ricovero e di Educazione (henceforth: AIRE), CAT B 4, c. 50r (June 8, 1595). See also "voler farsi cristiano" (AIRE, CAT B 4, c. 19v (May 28, 1593); c. 74r (Jan. 2, 1596 m.v.); 77v (July 25, 1597)); "volersi far cristiano con bonissima volonta" (ASPV, Sezione antica, Catecumeni, Documenti diversi (henceforth: CDd), b. 2, reg. 2, c. 14v (May 11, 1664)); "vene/andò/si presenta per farsi cristiano" (ASPV, CRb, reg. 1, c. 6v (March 31, 1592); c. 8v (April 25, 1592); c. 9v (Sept. 8, 1592 and Nov. 17, 1592); AIRE, CAT B 4, c. 47v (April 13,

Far less frequently do the same records ascribe individual wishes to Muslim catechumens. Of over seven hundred Muslim men baptized by the House of Catechumens from 1590 to 1670, the vast majority were noted in the records simply as "admitted" or, sometimes, "admitted for baptism." In only six cases were individual wishes explicitly recorded.[67] Instead, the scribes used a range of different phrases: "came/admitted in order to be baptized,"[68] "admitted in order to be converted,"[69] and "sent" or "admitted in order to become Christian."[70] Such phrases either skirt the question of agency and motivation or ascribe it to someone other than the catechumen himself—a patron, a master, a colonial clergyman, or, indeed, the governors of the House. Typical cases are those of "Assaim turco," who was presented to the governors by the archbishop of Corfu, and of Alia of Cetina in Dalmatia, recommended by Mons. Simon de Floris, vicar of nearby Traù (Trogir). Both were admitted without any reference in the records as to their own volition.[71] In numerous other cases, Muslim candidates for admission were interrogated as to their names and places of provenance, yet the records are completely silent about their wishes to be admitted, catechized, or baptized. This seeming lack of interest in gauging Muslim catechumens' intentions and volition prior to baptism may be connected to how Venetians interpreted the presumed sociopolitical ramifications of becoming Muslim in an Ottoman context, that is, slavish submission to the sultan. Whether this was the case or not, the marked dif-

---

1595)); "intenzioni di farsi cristiano" (AIRE, CAT B 4, c. 30r (Feb. 16, 1593)); "non vuole farsi cristiano" (AIRE, CAT B 4, c. 73r (Nov. 26, 1596)); "scegliere di farsi battezzare" (AIRE, CAT B 4, c. 89r (Oct. 7, 1598)); "domanda di farsi cristiano" (AIRE, CAT B 6, c. 29v (Aug. 25, 1611)); "dica al priore se vuole il battesimo" (AIRE, CAT B 4, c. 72v (Nov. 7, 1596)); "vuole battezzarsi" (AIRE, CAT B 6, c. 21v (June 9, 1611); c. 108v (Nov. 23, 1617)); and "per sentire la volontà di battezzarsi" (AIRE, CAT B 4, c. 61r (March 28, 1596)).

67. One document refers to a Muslim man brought to the house by an interpreter who claimed that the man said he "volersi far cristiano" (ASPV, rb, reg. 1, c. 11v (Nov. 24, 1592)). A second records a slave who "desidera battezzarsi" (AIRE, CAT B 4, c. 28r (Jan. 7, 1593 m.v.)). A third documents a Turk who "desidera andar a Roma per batezzarsi" (AIRE, CAT B 4, c. 80v (Oct. 2, 1597)). A fourth mentions a slave who "chiede di essere battezzato" (AIRE, CAT B 4, c. 86v (June 4, 1598)). A fifth describes a black slave "che vuol battezzarsi" (AIRE, CAT B 6, c. 22v (June 16, 1611)). A sixth describes a slave who "volersi ... battezare" (ASPV, CRb, reg. 2, c. 52v (June 6, 1660)).

68. "venuto" or "accolto ... per farsi battezare" (AIRE, CAT B 4, c. 14v (March 11, 1593); c. 20v (June 10, 1593)); "venuto per battezzarsi" (AIRE, CAT B 4, c. 86v (June 4, 1598)); and "accolto per battezzarsi" (AIRE, CAT B 6, c. 164r (Jan. 30, 1619, m.v.)). These phrases could obviously also be used in the case of Jews, for example, AIRE, CAT B 4, c. 18r (June 5, 1593); c. 54r (Aug. 17, 1595); c. 61v (April 4, 1596); AIRE, CAT B 6, c. 23r (June 23, 1611); c. 29v (Aug. 25, 1611); ASPV, CRb, reg. 1, c. 14v (May 23, 1593); AIRE, CAT B 4, c. 19v (May 28, 1593).

69. "accolto per esser convertito" (AIRE, CAT B 4, c. 94r (May 27, 1599)).

70. "mandato per farsi cristiano" (AIRE, CAT B 4, c. 63r (May 2, 1596)); "accolto ... per farsi cristiano" (AIRE, CAT B 4, c. 93v (May 14, 1599)).

71. AIRE, CAT B 6, c. 19v (May 19, 1611); 50v (June 1, 1612).

ferences between the commonsense narrative frames of Muslim-Catholic versus Jewish-Catholic and Protestant-Catholic conversion in the early modern period point once again to the need to understand the process of becoming Catholic as an articulation of a space of encounter in which expectations about the other side clearly informed practices of conversion and subject-making.

In the case of female catechumens too, the records often located agency outside the subject. One girl (of unknown religious background) is mentioned as "sent in order to be baptized";[72] another Muslim woman is recorded as "accepted in order to become Christian."[73] A black slave woman is noted down as having been baptized "as her protector wished."[74] A fourth, a Jewish convert's wife, was simply "made to come to the House to become Christian."[75] A fifth, also Jewish, "declares not wishing to be baptized because a certain Christian does not wish to marry her."[76] Of roughly 340 female catechumens recorded by the Pia Casa throughout this period, only one, a slave in the ghetto, is explicitly described as "wishing to become Christian."[77] In one other case, the governors decide to send a Turkish or Slavic interpreter "to learn about a woman's will and wish."[78]

The character of individual baptism rituals and/or the convert's new Christian name were also ascribed to personal wishes much more often in the case of Jewish than of Muslim converts. In 1594, Leon of Mantua was baptized by the patriarch of Venice "as he himself wished."[79] In 1595, Mazo Colombo of the ghetto "presents himself in order to become Christian ... and wants to be called Andrea."[80] In 1618, twenty-seven-year-old Livia, wife of Lazzaro del Baffo, "asks to prepare herself for baptism in an honourable place, but not at the Institute, and at her own expense."[81] I have not found equivalent descriptions of ritual details ascribed to catechumens' wishes in any of the records of the nearly 1,000 Muslim men and women catechized in the House up to 1670. In fact, in the case of Muslim

72. "mandata a battezzarsi" (AIRE, CAT B 4, c. 78v (Aug. 27, 1597)).
73. "accolta per farsi Cristiana" (AIRE, CAT B 6, c. 158v (Oct. 17, 1619)). See also the case of an unidentified woman who "came in order to be baptized" ("venuta per battezzarsi") (AIRE, CAT B 4, c. 27v (Dec. 30, 1593)).
74. "come vuole il suo protettore" (AIRE, CAT B 4, c. 89v (Oct. 7, 1598)).
75. "far venire la moglie di Anzolo per farsi cristiana" (AIRE, CAT B 4, c. 62v (April 18, 1596)).
76. "dichiarita di non volersi battizare p[er]ch'un tal Christian non volia sposarla" (ASPV, CRb, reg. 2, c. 27r (May 28, 1649)).
77. "vuol farsi cristiana" (AIRE, CAT B 6, c. 31r (Sept. 15, 1611)).
78. "per intendere il voler et desiderio di una donna" (AIRE, CAT B 4, c. 50r (June 8, 1595)).
79. "come vuole egli stesso" (AIRE, CAT B 4, c. 41v (Nov. 24, 1594)).
80. "si presenta per farsi cristiano Mazo Colombo ebreo del ghetto e vuole esser chiamato Andrea" (AIRE, CAT B 4, c. 47v (April 13, 1595)).
81. "chiede di prepararsi al battesimo in luogo onorato ma non nell'istituto e a sue spese" (AIRE, CAT B 6, c. 121v (June 12, 1618)).

catechumens and neophytes, personal will is mentioned almost exclusively as a negative force that makes them "wish to leave" the House without awaiting help from the governors or "not wish" to behave like good Christians.[82]

The various genres through which conversion was documented and regimented in early modern Venice illustrate how spatiotemporal conceptions were key to the differing articulations of the process of religious conversion and its presumed product, the converted subject. The chronotope of conjuncture, which characterizes narratives by or about Ottoman converts, conceived of religious conversion as the possibly unintended consequence of spatiotemporal transition from one spatially defined religious community to another and from the former's ritual time to the latter's. Conversely, the chronotope of purposive journeying, which characterizes narratives by or about converts from Protestantism, conceived of religious conversion as the intentional ur-cause (rather than a consequence) of a convert's peregrinations and possible change of status. These differences parallel the frequent reference to volition as a precondition for baptism in the cases of male Jewish catechumens and the almost complete lack of such references in the cases of women and Muslim men.

Identifying the paradigmatic chronotopes at work in different genres alerts us to a tension between how converts' itineraries were narrated in reconciliation depositions to the Holy Office and in matrimonial examinations by the Venetian patriarch, on the one hand, and in baptismal and departure records of the House of Catechumens, on the other. Inquisitorial depositions often linked the transition from one religious community to another with geographical mobility and with significant ritual moments in deponents' life cycle. They envisioned the (re)turn to Christianity as a journey, with the Venetian metropole as an end point, both physical and spiritual. Matrimonial examinations also frequently linked conversion with geographical journeys, although in this genre mobility was sometimes reduced to "plausible" itineraries from "there" to "here." This tendency to simplify complex itineraries is even more tangible in records produced by the House of Catechumens. Rather than as journeys with multiple stops, potential complications, detours, and delays, these institutional archives crystallized con-

---

82. See, for example, "no' volse andare" (ASPV, CRb, reg. 2, c. 3r (June 25, 1618)); "non volse aspettar" and "senza voler aspettar la Cong[regazio]ne" (ASPV, CRb, reg. 2, c. 4r (March 17 and 23, 1619)); "no' vuole vivere sotto la disciplina Christiana" (ASPV, CRb, reg. 2, c. 15v (March 8, 1631)); "non volendo inparar" (ASPV, CRb, reg. 2, c. 26r (April 8, 1649)). A galley slave named Ahmed was dismissed from the house "per che voleva battezarsi con patto che resti libero dalla Caena" (ASPV, CRb, reg. 2, c. 51v (March 6, 1659)).

verts' biographies into three crucial dates—arrival at the House, baptism, and departure—mediated via a limited set of pregiven categories of vital data, such as place of provenance, age, and former name and confessional affiliation. Perhaps the fiction of the fixity of identity was particularly important to maintain in the face of the alchemical transformation envisioned to take place at the baptismal font—to bring closure to a previous life sequence, its contours had to be established first. Indeed, baptismal registers visually and textually divide converts' lives into two radically separate phases: a "before" and an "after." Yet, as I demonstrate in the next chapter, a radical break with their previous life was rarely achieved by early modern Venetian converts. Instead, converts' preexisting social networks repeatedly shaped their itineraries after baptism.

4

Practicing Conversion

Ln a pathbreaking study of conversion in the Victorian British Empire, Gauri Viswanathan urges us to see conversion "as an act akin to the forces of modernity in its appeal to personal (rather than collective) choice, will, and action... Conversion posits a severe challenge to the demarcation of identities set by the laws that govern everyday life and practice."[1] In a similar vein, Lucetta Scaraffia defines early modern Mediterranean "renegades" as the paradigmatic articulators of modern individual identity. Because of their exterior status in both Christian and Muslim communities, she argues, "renegades" had to "produce their own values and norms, based on their individual choice."[2] A different view emerges in Venice. Rather than as the epitomes of individual free choice, converts and their local patrons operated within specific institutional constraints that shaped their social relations, subjectivities, and, indeed, the very category "convert" according to strictly enforced and differentially defined standards of morality and productivity. Converts' ability to renegotiate the boundaries of social inclusion and exclusion in early modern Venice was therefore heavily mediated by localized assumptions about juridical subjecthood and its transformative potential. Rather than being the heralds of modern identity politics, converts were both paradigmatic products of post-Tridentine charitable institutions and

1. Viswanathan (1998, 75).
2. Scaraffia (2002, 169); my translation. The extant literature on the integration of "renegades" into the Ottoman Empire seems to contradict this argument and to suggest, instead, the centrality of such recruits to Ottoman governance (Isom-Verhaaren 2004; Ágoston 2007; Brummett 2007b; Krstić 2009).

elements of Venetian imperial policy, even as they ultimately played a constitutive role in reshaping both.

Our understanding of the long process through which Muslim and Jewish subjects became Catholics in seventeenth-century Venice is greatly enhanced by the archives of the Pia Casa dei Catecumeni (Holy House of Catechumens). These archives contain over 1,000 converts' baptismal records, as well as account books and other documents for the period 1590–1670, the first eighty years for which substantial serial documentation by and about the House survives. In studying the archives of the House of Catechumens in this chapter, I offer neither institutional nor Church history per se. Rather, I underscore how religious conversion formed a web of social practices that were deeply embedded in processes of subject-making and imperial consolidation. The House of Catechumens was instrumental not only in mediating the ongoing relationship among converts, their patrons, and the early modern Venetian state but, more broadly, in articulating categories of religious and juridical difference. As such, it is best understood as a trans-imperial, rather than a strictly local, Venetian institution.

Religious conversion in early modern Venice was inseparable from two other projects critical to the early modern state: (1) the encouragement of migrants from the neighboring Ottoman Empire to permanently settle the borderlands and (2) the attempt to subject the entire populace to parish-based forms of social discipline and supervision through Church activities, such as regular confession and communion.[3] While focusing on how conversion related to immigration and social discipline in Venice proper, I place these projects squarely within their trans-imperial context. I explore how both Venetian administrators and converts themselves exercised conversion not as a miraculous moment of rebirth but as a lifelong process intended to transform foreigners into loyal juridical subjects of metropolitan state and society.

CHARITY, DISCIPLINE, AND IMPERIAL SUBJECT-MAKING

As I show in chapter 1, converts figured prominently among the trans-imperial subjects who petitioned the Venetian government for employment as commercial brokers. Converts' petitions repeatedly articulated the notion that subjects and rulers were mutually linked through moral and civic obligations. Although

3. On vagrancy in the Ottoman-Venetian borderlands, see Pedani (2002). For a sample of legislation by the Senate intended to curb emigration from and the depopulation of the Venetian countryside by penalizing emigrants, see Compilazione delle leggi, b. 203. On parish-based social discipline in the Venetian state, see Montanari (1987); Bizzocchi (1995).

they cast the Church as the guarantor of their spiritual well-being, converts also exhorted the state to assume its own, material duties by providing them with employment.[4] Such an understanding of the state as converts' ultimate patron was articulated through other practices as well, in addition to petitioning and brokerage. Chief among those were the charitable activities coordinated by the House of Catechumens. In particular, the House helped shape distinct forms of charity that allowed two groups of Venetian elites, patricians and citizens, to bring together their corporate spiritual and civic claims, and at the same time to further their individual and family interests by weaving dense vertical and horizontal networks of patronage. Through the negotiation of converts' adoption contracts, dowries, apprenticeships, and employment opportunities and the periodic disbursement of alms, the institution also served as a laboratory for the elaboration of practices of social discipline and community-building that were key to Venetian elites' mythic self-representations as the benevolent custodians of a well-run republic.

Established in 1557, the Pia Casa dei Catecumeni was the fruit of a collaboration among Venetian ecclesiastical authorities, Jesuit friars, lay patricians, and colonial administrators.[5] Its model was a similar house established by the Jesuits in Rome in 1543 in response to calls for apostolic rejuvenation of the Church.[6] It was also deeply rooted in a long and thriving tradition of semi-autonomous charitable institutions in Venice and elsewhere on the Italian peninsula, predating the Catholic Reformation. Such institutions provided an opportunity for patricians and nonpatrician well-to-do citizens alike to exercise patriarchal modes of authority by distributing charity to socially inferior members of the congregation, be

4. The practice of converts' petitioning to the sovereign (or to lesser patrons) for financial assistance is not unique to Venice; it is well documented in the seventeenth century in both the Ottoman Empire (Minkov 2004) and the Holy Roman Empire (Corpis 2001, 109–10, 114).

5. Ellero (1987); Vanzan (1997). The founders were Dr. Giovanni Battista Trescolini, theologian, and Giacomo Foscarini, Giovanni Battista Contarini, Alfonso Maravessi, Girolamo di Cavalli, Giusto Morosini, and Francesco Marcolini, all patrician laymen. Contarini and the Jesuit sympathizers, Cavalli and Foscarini, were among the founders and governors of another Venetian charitable institution, the Ospedale dei Derelitti (AIRE, CAT A 1, cc. 4–5; Aikema and Meijers 1989, 215–23). The Jesuits enjoyed great success among Venetian political elites in the second half of the sixteenth century, which had far-reaching consequences given the tight control exerted by the Venetian patriciate over ecclesiastical benefices throughout the empire (Cozzi 1994; Del Torre 1992).

6. Following Rome and Venice, institutions for catechizing and baptizing converts were established in several other cities on the Italian Peninsula during this period, including Bologna (1568), Ferrara (1584), Naples (1601), and Reggio (1630). For Rome, see Milano (1970); Rudt de Collenberg (1986, 1989); Rocciolo (1998); Caffiero (2003), Lazar (2005). For Bologna, see Campanini (1996); Sarti (2001). For Ferrara, Lattes (1999). For Naples, Nardi (1967).

they poorer men, youths, or women.[7] In the case of the House of Catechumens, a general injunction to engage in charitable works was reinforced by the specific Church teaching that "a person who helped save the soul of an unbeliever earned divine blessing, performing a deed that would be remembered at heaven's gate."[8] In 1687, Pope Innocent XI issued a plenary indulgence and a perpetual remission of sins to all governors of the Venetian House of Catechumens. Thus, in addition to concrete social advantages, serving as a governor of the House also brought a spiritual return. On a governor's death, five masses were to be celebrated in his honor in the House chapel, the remaining governors were to recite *De Profundis*, and the catechumens were to recite the Rosary.[9]

Although the Venetian House of Catechumens has not been studied in detail until recently, several historians have given it some attention.[10] Some, notably Brian Pullan and Benjamin Ravid have emphasized its coercive mechanisms, particularly vis-à-vis Jews, in the context of Tridentine reform. Others, such as Monica Chojnacka and Anna Vanzan, have pointed to its charitable activities and role in facilitating patronage across geographical, gendered, and economic divides.[11] The analysis here seeks not only to combine these two perspectives, and to treat the conversion of Jews and Muslims as one analytical field, but to identify how, as a nexus of benevolence and discipline, the House of Catechumens functioned as an imperial state institution. Rather than viewing the House as distinct from its charges, this perspective calls attention to the transformative quality of institutional practices to define and redefine the institution itself and all of those who were involved in its operations, including its citizen and patrician patrons.

Indeed, although part of the mission of the House was to integrate converts and governors into preexisting local networks of patronage, in fundamental ways it was also an imperial institution, linking the Venetian metropole with its colonies and frontier regions. Frequently, House governors bore personal ties to the Adriatic and Mediterranean through years of service as Venetian colonial officials or as merchants in the Ottoman Empire. High-ranking Venetian clergymen serving in the colonies were also part of the extended patronage network of the

---

7. Of the vast literature on early modern charitable institutions, see especially Pullan (1971); Grendi (1983); Cavallo (1995); Eisenbichler (1997); Gentilcore (1999); Terpstra (2000); Black (2004). For an illuminating discussion of the role of confraternal charity in shaping early modern civic elites' ideas about welfare reform, see especially Terpstra (1994). On charity from a cross-cultural and comparative perspective, see the collected essays in Cohen (2005).

8. Kertzer (1997, 56).

9. AIRE, CAT A 1, cc. 16, 73–74 (Jan. 10, 1687 m.v.).

10. Ioly Zorattini (2008) devotes two chapters to the House of Catecumens. In chapter 4 he sketches out the history of the institution, while in chapter 5 he provides a largely statistical analysis of converts based on its baptismal records.

11. Pullan (1983); Ravid (2001); Vanzan (1997); Chojnacka (2001).

House. They participated in the House gubernatorial board meetings while in Venice, sent donations to the House, facilitated the transfer of potential catechumens to Venice, and hired neophytes upon baptism to serve in their households. For example, the archbishop of Split was invited to participate in the interrogation of Chiarina, a prospective convert from the town of Dubar in the Sarajevo region of Bosnia in 1595. The following month, he was asked to chastise two recalcitrant converts and then to intervene on behalf of one of them with a prospective patrician patron. Three years later, the archbishop was involved in an attempt to secure a spot for a young Jewish convert, Pietro Angelo Zen, in a seminary and ultimately took him into his own house until another arrangement could be found. In exchange for employing another convert, Marco, the archbishop promised to buy him clothes. Another clergyman, the archbishop of Corfu, penned a letter that secured the entrance of a Muslim catechumen by the name of Assaim to the House in 1611. A letter by the House governors in 1619 asked the bishop of Treviso to recommend a recently baptized neophyte, Orsetta, to one of the local convents. The same year, a letter by Marco, the bishop of Padua, urged the governors to admit Ibrahim, a Muslim in need of a catechist who knew his language. In 1654, the general meeting of the governors was attended by the Bishop of Kotor Vicenzo Buchia and his nephew, who asked to take into their care the eighteen-month-old baby Paolin (formerly Giosef, son of Rachel) and promised to raise him and prepare him for the priesthood in due course. Finally, one of the major bequests left to the House during this period was from Bernardo Florio, the archbishop of Zara (Zadar, Croatia), in 1657.[12]

Links with the Ottoman borderlands were also forged by hiring colonial subjects to serve in a variety of positions in the House administration. For example, in choosing priors for the House, preference was given to candidates who commanded Greek, Hebrew, or Turkish, "so they could understand, and instruct, similar infidels."[13] Not surprisingly, many priors and prioresses were émigrés from Venetian colonies in the Adriatic and eastern Mediterranean, and some were converts themselves.[14] Their trans-imperial connections were often capitalized on.

---

12. AIRE, CAT A 1, c. 15; AIRE, CAT B 4, c. 50r (June 8, 1595); c. 52r (July 20, 1595); c. 53v (Aug. 10, 1595); c. 90v (Dec. 10, 1598); c. 92r (Feb. 25, 1598); c. 94v (June 11, 1599); c. 95v (July 1, 1599); AIRE, CAT B 6, c. 19v (May 19, 1611); c. 147v (June 6, 1619); c. 159v (Nov. 7, 1619); AIRE, CAT E 8, c. 44v (Sept. 24, 1654); Degli Avogadro (1857, xxv).

13. AIRE, CAT A 1, c. 29.

14. Girolamo Pastriccio from Split became House prior in 1645. Nicolò Nepusa, from Kotor (Montenegro), became House prior on March 26, 1654. A year later, on March 4, 1655, he was replaced by Michel Cozunovich, also from Split. Cozunovich served as prior for the next two decades. For a (partial) list of the House priors, see AIRE, CAT G 3, f. 1 ("Serie dei Priori del Pio Logo de Catecumeni").

Permission to return to the frontier was almost invariably granted to neophytes who sought it, especially if they went there to serve in Venetian colonial households or in the military. In 1591, Bastian, a slave who ran away from his Ottoman Muslim master while sojourning in Venice, was able to prove he had been born a Christian. He was reconciled with the Church, confessed and communicated, and then was allowed to leave for Kotor (Montenegro) to serve there in the household of the Venetian governor, Domenico da Revera.[15] Another case concerned Antonio (formerly Amer) from Klimno (Croatia), who had been baptized in 1653 at age seven. After serving for six years in the household of Andrea Contarini, who was the House governor and a procurator of St. Mark, Antonio was sent to the colony of Zakynthos to work for William Vit, the English consul. On his return to Venice in 1670, and after a short sojourn in Bergamo, his old master and patron, Contarini, procured for him a captaincy in a cavalry regiment in Dalmatia.[16]

Converts and their patrons thus extended the Venetian moral community to the frontier and sometimes beyond it.[17] This process of network-building operated in multiple directions. Occasional references to catechumens sent to the House by colonial Venetian magistracies suggest that the prospect of conversion could help consolidate ties with colonized populations and perhaps elicit consent in places where Venetian rule was premised primarily on military and economic might.[18] For example, in 1663 the governors admitted into the House an unnamed renegade, sent at the explicit request of the Camera dell'armar (Defense Ministry) to be catechized and sent back to his place of residence, Šibenik in Dalmatia.

Fund-raising was another mechanism through which the House fostered horizontal and vertical ties across estates in Venetian society and throughout the empire. Most funding for neophytes was secured from bequests left to the House by lay patricians and citizens, both men and women, and, significantly, also by leading clergymen from the Terraferma and the Stato da Mar.[19] Additional funds were procured through fund-raising campaigns undertaken by patented convert alms-collectors in various Venetian territories, including campaigns dedicated to

---

15. ASPV, CRb, reg. 1, c. 6r (July 15, 1591 and Oct. 30, 1591). For other similar cases see also ASPV, CRb, reg. 1, c. 3r (Nov. 13, 1590); c. 8v (July 12, 1592); ASPV, CRb, reg. 2, c. 2v (April 8, 1618); c. 3r (June 20, 1618); c. 16v (March 3, 1633); c. 19r (Sept. 1, 1645); c. 40r (Feb. 27, 1652 m.v.); c. 60v (July 22, 1665).
16. ASPV, EM, reg. 63, cc. 151r–152r (Jan. 29, 1670 m.v.).
17. Evidence suggests that Orthodox Christian clergy in Mt. Athos and elsewhere in the Ottoman Empire periodically assisted converts to cross the border and reach Venice (Krstić 2004, 290–91).
18. AIRE, CAT C 2, c. 427r (Sept. 6, 1663).
19. For a list of the bequests, see Degli Avogadro (1857, xxv).

De ordine dell'Illuftriffimo, & Reuerendiffimo Vefcouo.

Si commette à voi Reuerendi capi di Monafterij, cofi di Religiofi, come di Religiofe, & à tutti li Vicarij, Forani, Arcipreti, Curati, della Città, Caftelli, & Ville della giuridirione noftra, che effendo ftare fufpefe, & annullate dalla Pia Cafa di Cathecumeni di Venetia tutte le Patenti, ò mandati per innãzi conceffi a diuerfi infedeli venuti alla S. Fôte di poter cercare elemofine in ogni luoco, Che de ce tero in neffun modo permettiate, che nelle Ville, & luochi al detto Territorio foggetti pofsino più cercare in virtù delle predette Patenti, ma folamente lo pofsi fare, & far fare Antonio Giuftiniano già Hebreo fatto Chriftiano lattore del prefente noftro mandato, come eletto dalli Sig. Gouernatori della predetta Pia Cafa di poter vna fola volta all'anno da principiare li 15 di Agofto giorno della B. Vergine far fare (conforme al fuo ordine) vna cerca generale per tutte le Città, Terre, & luochi del Serenifs. Dominio, per foftegno di tutti quelli, che concorrono ogni giorno al fanto Battefimo, alquale ui cõ mettemo, che preftiate con carità ogni fauore accompagnandolo a tutte le Cafe, & Maffarie, perche riceua da tutti li deuoti di Chrifto Signor noftro grani, vini, danari, & altro per poter fupplire alle necefsità di quella Pia Cafa, & perche puo effere, che quelli che fin' hora hanno cercato in virtù delle predette Patenti, fi pofsino aggrauare per tal prohitione, li perfuaderete di ricorrere alla predetta Pia Ca fa loro madre, afsicurandoli che gli farà dalli predetti Sig. Gouernatori prouifto, come è mente, & loro penfiero.

Effendo tenuti far publicare nelle loro Chiefe otto giorni auanti la fudetta fefta della Beata Vergine il prefente mandato accio tutti li fedeli fi preparino di fare quella fanta Elemofina.

Figure 4.1 *Antonio Giustiniano's alms-collecting patent (1619). ASPV Curia Patriarcale di Venezia. Sezione Antica, Catecumeni, Documenti diversi, busta 2, reg. 1, c. 95. Reproduction: author, by permission of Ministero per i Beni e le Attività Culturali.*

specific converts.[20] The administration of alms-collecting patents was also one of the mechanisms through which the House sought to establish its jurisdiction over all converts of the Venetian state. Rather than allowing converts to beg for charity on their own, the House sent authorized converts on annual alms-collecting campaigns throughout all the churches of a given territory, the proceeds of which were then to be distributed among eligible converts.[21] For example, a contract and alms-collecting patent issued in 1619 to Antonio Giustiniano, a Jewish convert (fig. 4.1) forbade any other converts from independently collecting alms on the Terraferma. Instead, they were to be "persuaded to return to the said Pia Casa their mother, assuring them that they will be provided for by the Governors, as is their intention and thought."[22] The patent conceived of Venetian territory as a

20. In 1595, the Venetian House of Catechumens raised money as far away as the Church of Val de Reder in the diocese of Trent for the dowry of a convert named Antonia, who was to marry Zuane, a Venetian scale-maker (AIRE, CAT B 4, c. 50r (June 14, 1595)). See also, AIRE, CAT B 4, c. 55v (Oct. 13, 1595).
21. The practice seems to have originated in Rome, where converts were patented as almscollectors as early as 1551 (Simonsohn 1989, 34).
22. ASPV, CDd, b. 2, reg. 1, c. 95 (July 1, 1619). See appendix 4.1 for the translation.

unified Christian space, where the moral authority of the House and, hence, its ability to raise funds for its cause would go unchallenged. Yet its careful attention to the need to collaborate with and appease both local clergy and Venetian colonial administrators suggests a de facto recognition of the limited reach of the House outside the city proper. The governors' repeated correspondence with colonial administrators and clergy pledging them to assist its alms-collectors confirms this sense.

BECOMING CATECHUMENS

In the period 1590–1670, the House of Catechumens hosted five to fifty baptismal candidates per year, for a total of approximately 1,300. Most stayed for a month or two prior to baptism and shortly thereafter, but some sojourned in the House for significantly shorter or longer periods.[23] Before they could be baptized, candidates underwent a period of catechetical instruction by the House prior, during which they were taught to recite their prayers and attended mass and confession regularly.[24] The House employed a variety of techniques intended to produce disciplined, docile subjects. Catechumens were subjected to monastic-style time discipline, with clear limits on their hours of sleep and with activities carefully regulated and scheduled for specific times of day.[25] Male and female catechumens were socialized into normative gender roles, with carefully enforced segregation between the sexes. Female catechumens were restricted to the premises and employed in cooking, spinning, and washing laundry (see fig. 4.2).[26]

Jewish catechumens, many of whom came to the House with or following relatives, made up approximately one-quarter of the House population during this period. A large percentage of them, 43 percent of men and 64 percent of

23. The regulations required at least eight months to elapse before a catechumen was baptized, to make sure of his or her true intentions. In reality, the period was often much shorter (AIRE, CAT A 1, c. 43).

24. Catechumens could also receive instruction from mendicant friars fluent in their languages. The regulations stipulated that if the prior did not command the language of a prospective catechumen, he was to find a mendicant friar or another Christian to serve as interpreter and then locate a clergyperson to provide religious instruction (AIRE, CAT A 1, cc. 42–43).

25. AIRE, CAT A 1, c. 52.

26. The first extant regulations of the House, which date from 1737, suggest the limitations of earlier efforts to shape catechumens' daily life. Much attention was devoted to the physical separation of female catechumens from the outside world. Any unmediated contact with men was strictly prohibited. Visits to the female wing by the governors were to be infrequent and conducted only by pairs of older governors past their fiftieth year while accompanied by the prioress. The prioress was likewise required to accompany the confessor during his weekly visits to the female wing and to stay close by for the entire duration of his visit (AIRE, CAT A 1, cc. 19, 33).

Figure 4.2 *Frontispiece of the* Regulations for the Governance of the Pia Casa *(1802). Venezia, Archivio Storico IRE, CAT A1, c. 1. Reproduction: author, by permission of the Ufficio Conservatori IRE.*

women, were Venetian. The now extensive scholarship on Venetian Jewry has alerted us to important socioeconomic and cultural differences within the ghetto population—among Levantines and Ponentines with roots and lingering contacts in the Ottoman Empire and Iberia, "German" (Ashkenazi) Jews, and Italian Jews. Still, all Venetian Jewish converts shared some important features. Almost all spoke some variety of Italian, and many wrote and read it as well. Long before their conversion, many Jewish converts formed part of kinship, social, intellectual, and commercial networks that extended beyond the ghetto and indeed beyond Venice and the Mediterranean. Such networks and skills proved decisive in shaping converts' future residential and professional paths. It also made the risk of relapse following a chance encounter with former coreligionists, especially un-converted relatives, more palpable in the governors' eyes, warranting prolonged seclusion in the House prior to baptism.[27]

Perhaps even more than other conversionist institutions of its era, the Venetian House of Catechumens did not cater only to local Jews. Quite a few Jewish cat-echumens came from other parts of the Italian peninsula (26 percent); the rest of Europe (8 percent); Ottoman commercial centers such as Istanbul, Izmir, and Thessaloniki (8.6 percent); Venetian and other Mediterranean colonies (3.4 per-cent); and North Africa (2.3 percent). But the majority of catechumens, about three-quarters, were Muslims, mostly from the Ottoman Balkans (58 percent), North Africa (13.5 percent), the Greek islands (12 percent), and Anatolia (6.7 per-cent). Only 6.3 percent came from the Black Sea, Ottoman Syria and Palestine, and the Safavid and Mughal empires combined.[28] In other words, most converts came from the Ottoman-Venetian borderlands and from Mediterranean regions with a long history as trading hubs with large foreign mercantile colonies and, thus, may have had some prior contact with the Venetian world; quite a few may have been first-generation Muslims.[29]

Some Muslim catechumens were soldiers in the Venetian army on the main-land or oarsmen and mariners in the Venetian fleet. They were sent to the House by or with the consent of their commanders and usually returned to their posts shortly after baptism. Others came on their own or were sent specifically for bap-tism from the Venetian Adriatic and Mediterranean colonies.[30] But the large ma-jority of Muslim converts were domestic slaves in Venetian patrician and citizen

27. On Venetian Jewry in general, see Malkiel (1991); Arbel (1995b); Davis and Ravid (2001); Favero and Trivellato (2004). On Jewish commercial networks, see Arbel (2001). On Jewish converts' professional skills, see Segre (1975). On converts' relapse, see Pullan (1983, 255–71); Head (1990, 180). See also the testimony of Giulio Morosini, a Jewish convert, in a 1651 Holy Office investigation into the suspected marranism of Agostino Fonseca, reproduced in Ioly Zorattini (1972, 337–41) and the 1634 trial of Francesco Maria de Giacinti, a Modenese Jewish convert turned Dominican friar, and his unconverted father, who had persuaded him to run away to Venice and return to Judaism, discussed in Zanardo (1996).

28. These figures, as well as the ones regarding the provenance of Jewish catechumens and of Muslim women elsewhere in this chapter, are based on the 651 catechumens whose place of provenance was registered and identifiable (exactly one-half of all catechumens registered by the House for the period 1590–1670).

29. This was especially true of Muslim women, 84 percent of whom came from the Balkans and the Greek islands, compared with 65 percent of Muslim men. Only 3 percent of Muslim women came from Anatolia, Arabic-speaking regions of the Ottoman Empire, and the Black Sea region combined. None came from central Asia.

30. On Ottoman subjects in the Venetian army and navy, see Petta (1996); Pilidis (1999); Lo Basso (2001a, 2001b). On Ottoman merchants in Venice, see Vercellin (1979, 1980); Kafadar (1986). On Venetian colonial officials sending catechumens to the House, see Vanzan (1996).

households, where they sometimes served for years prior to their conversion.[31] Although they were immigrants, and thus "poor in relational resources," as Simona Cerutti puts it, the long sojourn in Venice made at least some of them less poor in such resources than is sometimes assumed.[32] Still, because slaves often arrived in Venice alone, they were already separated from natal kin and community, obviating the need to confine them to the House for long periods, as in the case of Jewish catechumens.[33] From the 1640s on, rather than being secluded in the House, many Muslim catechumens, especially children and women who had already been employed as domestic slaves around the city, remained in their masters' homes while receiving catechetical instruction. Nominally registered with the House, they came in only for their baptism ceremony, which could take place at any time between a day and over a year from the date of their admittance as "children of the House."[34] Some were even registered with the House ex post facto, after their catechization and baptism elsewhere. These procedures did not supplant catechization in the House but, rather, reflect the growing reach of the institution in its effort to exert authority over all convert baptisms in Venice.[35]

This demographic sketch should not obscure the fact that the majority of catechumens ranged from newborns to teenagers.[36] This is significant in that the

31. On domestic slavery, see Romano (1991). On Bolognese slave converts, see Sarti (1991).

32. Cerutti (1995, 452). For evidence of Balkan immigrant servants' networks in Venice, see Romano (1996, 99, 100, 121, 133, 156).

33. Archival traces in the wake of attempts by Ottoman Muslims to claim their relatives converted in Venice, especially young women, confirm the governors' fears. See, for example, the case of a Muslim convert who, after twelve years in Venice, attempted to return to the Ottoman Empire but was captured in the Fondaco dei Turchi (Senato, Deliberazioni Costantinopoli, reg. 14, cc. 89v–90v (Oct. 9, 1622)). See also the case of the converted daughter of a high-ranking Muslim Ottoman official from Klis who moved to Venice, and whose father's attempts to persuade her to return home were met with counterattempts to convert him to Catholicism, analyzed in Rothman (2011). Finally, see the case of a Bosnian convert who claimed to have run away from her husband and to have been consequently kidnapped by her Muslim relatives with the help of Venetian collaborators (Avogaria di Comun, Misc. Penale, b. 343, fasc. 15 (Aug. 7, 1642)). This and similar cases are briefly discussed in Vanzan (1996), and more extensively in Dursteler (2011).

34. Such arrangements clearly benefited the masters, who did not wish to part with their domestic laborers for extended periods of time. It also offered the House an effective way to claim authority over more neophytes without shouldering all the responsibility for their future. For a sample of cases, see ASPV, CRb, reg. 2, cc. 19v, 20r, 21v, 22r; ASPV, CRb, reg. 3, cc. 12r–v.

35. This hypothesis is supported by the unusually high number of baptisms registered by the House in 1647–1649—thirty-seven, forty-five, and thirty-seven, respectively—compared with the annual average of ten in the previous quarter century.

36. In the period 1640–1670, during which the age at baptism was registered in over 95 percent of the cases, children and youths under sixteen constituted over 37 percent of all converts, with additional 20 percent in the 17–20 age group. Because other parameters of the convert population (gender ratio, prior religious affiliation, and place of provenance) did not change much between

younger the converts, the more their future depended on governors' efforts to place them in domestic service (for both girls and boys), negotiate an apprenticeship or military post (for boys), or marry them off honorably by financing their dowries or facilitate their monachization (for girls). Efforts to secure neophytes' future took different paths, depending on how governors perceived the moral, intellectual, and physical aptitudes of different kinds of converts. Future paths were also shaped by Jewish and Muslim converts' uneven access to local social networks.

Of the roughly 1,300 catechumens who entered the House from 1590 to 1670, over 160 (12 percent) did so with or following relatives. In several cases, nuclear families from the Ottoman Empire arrived in the House together and, significantly, always departed en bloc shortly after baptism to resettle outside Venice, often in the borderlands. For example, on August 1, 1619, the "well deserving" Paolo Armano (formerly Regeb) from Scutari (either Üsküdar in Anatolia or Shkodër in Albania); his renegade wife Maria, who had been baptized as an infant; and their five sons all arrived in the House. Paolo had served on board a Venetian armored vessel and on baptism was persuaded to resume his post, along with three of his sons. The governors promised to assist Maria and their remaining children, and both spouses received money and new clothes as they departed from the House. In early 1624, another converted couple, Paolo and Rosetta Marina, left the House with their daughter and moved into their own place in "a village in the region of Parenzo" (Piran, Istria). Later that same year, Giovanni Pietro de Piccolo, a renegade Christian from Udine, now reconciled with the Church; his still Muslim wife; and their five baptized children left the House with the governors' permission to go to the town of Loreto, where the wife was to be baptized.[37]

In these examples, conversion fitted not only into a familial quest for social or spatial mobility but also within an imperial logic that sought to repopulate the Venetian-Ottoman borderlands and extend the metropolitan moral community to it. More frequently, a parent wishing to convert arrived at the House and brought his or her children along.[38] The records rarely reveal the motivations behind such

---

1590 and 1670, it is safe to assume that children and youths constituted an actual majority of converts even before 1640. These figures diverge quite dramatically from the corresponding figures for Rome, where many more Jewish converts seem to have been adults between nineteen and thirty, with children and youths constituting a much smaller portion of the total convert population. For a table of Jewish converts by age in early modern Rome, see Milano (1970, 144–45).

37. AIRE, CAT B 6, c. 154r (Aug. 1, 1619); c. 156v (Sept. 12, 1619); c. 159r (Sept. 26 and Oct. 24, 1619); c. 159v (Nov. 14, 1619); ASPV, CRb, reg. 2, c. 8v (Feb. 13, 1623 m.v.); c. 10r (July 23, 1624).

38. In the case of local Jewish converts, this could often lead to acrimonious legal battles. See, for example, the failed appeal to the Venetian Senate by Abram Caneiani and the Venetian Jewish community in an effort to retrieve Abram's son, taken to the House of Catechumens in 1616 by his

moves, but it is safe to assume that the arrival of free Muslim Ottoman women and children in the House was part of a broader quest for new prospects, either upon a spouse's death or in an attempt to break free from an unhappy marriage.[39] A case in point is that of the thirty-year-old widow Salige from Corquiza (Korce in Albania), who arrived in the House with her two children, a twenty-five-year-old fellow townswoman, and two other children on July 1, 1665. All six, along with another Muslim convert and her two children, were baptized in a single public ceremony in the church of the Jesuits two months later. With the governors' blessing, a few weeks after baptism the three women went to live together on their own in a house in Corte Morosina in the parish of San Martin, and their children dispersed: one became an apprentice to a local weaver, and the other five were placed as domestic servants in Venice, Padua, and Cremona.[40] The children's divergent paths proved key to their future. In 1670, all five children who had remained in the Veneto region received funds from a bequest left to the House, whereas the girl who had been sent to Cremona never showed up in the records again, perhaps suggesting that her tracks were lost.[41]

In considering how conversion could facilitate family mobility, we should be wary of assuming that the family acted as the agent of purposive action. This is well illustrated by the de Castro family, whose five adult siblings passed through the House at considerable intervals: Salamon, Mosè, Sara, Rachel, and Abram, children of Bianca and the late Isach de Castro, a well-respected Venetian Jewish family of Iberian descent, were all baptized between 1650 and 1665.[42] Significant are both the timing and order of their arrival at the House and their respective ages at the time. First to convert were the two younger sons, followed by their two youngest sisters. All four were between eighteen and twenty at the time of their baptism. In 1657, when the youngest sister Rachel arrived at the House, she was accompanied by her widowed mother, Bianca, who was sixty at the time. Perhaps Bianca preferred baptism over severing ties with four of her five children; perhaps the prospect of staying by herself in old age without even her youngest

---

mother, Altadonna (Compilazione delle leggi, b. 294, c. 278 (March 14, 1616)). On child baptism in Venice, see Ravid (2001). On contemporary theological debates regarding child baptism, see Roth (1936); Rowan (1975); Bernos (2003). For an extensive treatment of two nineteenth-century cases of children baptized against parental wishes in the Papal States, see Kertzer (1997, 2002).

39. On conversion as an Ottoman women's strategy for escaping marriages, see Baer (2004).

40. ASPV, CRb, reg. 2, c. 62r (Oct. 25, 1665); c. 62v (Sept. 8 and Oct. 5, 1665); c. 63r (Nov. 17 and Jan. 22, 1665, 1665 m.v.).

41. ASPV, CRb, reg. 3, c. 31v (Sept. 7, 1670–Feb. 25, 1670 m.v.)

42. By the mid-seventeenth century, the Iberian de Castro family was scattered throughout Europe. On some of the highly learned and prolific branches of this family, many of whom were physicians and academics in Hamburg and Amsterdam, see Kayserling et al. (1971, esp. xiv).

daughter to assist her seemed bleak enough to warrant such a move. Finally, when the last sibling to convert, Abram, set foot in the House in 1665 at age forty, he brought along his wife Stella and their five children.[43] Abram was the eldest and, unlike his siblings, had already established a family of his own at the time of conversion. Like his mother, his ultimate baptism—years after his four siblings— suggests a reluctant surrender to a move that was probably not of his own making but that would reunite the family. Indeed, on baptism Abram, Stella, and their children joined Abram's siblings in the family house in the parish of San Maurizio.

Unlike the de Castros, the vast majority of converts arrived in the House alone and left it alone. Even when parents arrived with their children, they were likely to be separated and set on different tracks, sometimes for good, with the children sent to work or given in adoption to Venetian families. For example, in 1592 the governors decided that the convert Gerolamo, recently employed by the Venetian Salt Office, could visit his daughter, who was still living in the House, only every fifteen days, and then only in the presence of female guardians. In 1616, the two school-age sons of a Muslim convert from Antivari (Bar, Montenegro) were taken from her and placed first in the prioress's quarters and then outside the House with an older convert and her husband. Five months later, in an unusual move, one of the boys was consigned to his mother for a week only "because otherwise he suffers."[44]

To understand the logic of this separation of convert parents from their children, let us look at the long-term patronage that the House claimed over neophytes. Perhaps the key principle organizing the relationship of the House with neophytes was the reconfiguration and sometimes severing of former kinship ties. These processes were mediated by a patriarchal vocabulary, which defined the different positions of authority within the institution. Catechumens were referred to as "children of the House" in all official documentation, a designation that stuck, regardless of age, for years after baptism. Governors, on the other hand, were "brothers," following the official egalitarian ideology (if quite tenuous practice) of confraternities. They also figured as "fathers" to the catechumens, over whose destinies they exerted enormous control. The two patrician or citizen women appointed to counsel the prioress on the management of the female wing were similarly to show converts "charity, and maternal love."[45]

---

43. ASPV, CRb, reg. 2, cc. 63v–64r (Sept. 27, 1665).
44. AIRE, CAT B 4, c. 4r (June 25, 1592); AIRE, CAT B 6, c. 99r (March 3, 1616); c. 103r (June 16, 1616); c. 105v (Aug. 25, 1616); c. 107v (Nov. 10, 1616); c. 108v (Nov. 23, 1617).
45. "Carità, ed amore Materno" (AIRE, CAT A 1, c. 20). The incorporation of women in the House management dates to 1613, when a group of patrician and citizen ladies were prompted to provide "useful observations" on the proper running of the female wing in the wake of an unnamed scandal.

This patriarchal logic was articulated in myriad charitable and disciplinary practices that cemented the bond between neophytes and the House, and which defined converthood for years after baptism. The House extended its paternal care not only to converts but to their well-behaved children as well. In some cases, the governors stepped in to support converts' children on a parent's death. At least as frequently, convert parents themselves sought the governors' intervention. For example, in 1615, the governors were asked to help provide a dowry for a convert's daughter, who was soon to get married. They approved the request because "the mother has always behaved herself well." Later, they also gave the daughter a straw mattress.[46] By scaling charity to match converts' moral conduct, the governors not only encouraged their former charges to meet their standards of good behavior but on occasion acted as surrogate parents, with lifelong ties to and claims over converts and their families.

Baptism and Beyond

The form and meaning of the sacrament of baptism was the subject of much debate among medieval and early modern theologians. Thomas Aquinas emphasized in his *Summa Theologica* that the validity and efficacy of baptism depended on the intentions of the recipient, not on the officiate. He therefore demanded prior catechism and evidence that the catechumen would be able to lead a Christian life on baptism. Late medieval missionaries in the field, on the other hand, were often willing to confer baptism on anyone expressing the wish to receive it, regardless of prior instruction or future prospects.[47]

The House governors were less eager to baptize at all costs, and on several occasions they denied baptism (or even admittance to the House) to people deemed insufficiently prepared or willing. In 1615, Alegra of Corfu was admitted to the House "after having been denied entry once for not being well-instructed in the matters of faith." Permission to baptize her was sought only a week later, suggesting that, in this case at least, her arrival at the Pia Casa marked the end of catechetical instruction rather than its beginning.[48] In most other cases, however, on admission candidates underwent a period of catechization. This could last from a day to a year or more and took place either on the premises or, in the case of slaves, on galleys, in prison, or in a master's home. Only after an "examination of conscience" by at least two governors could catechumens be led to the font to be baptized.

---

46. AIRE, CAT B 6, c. 91r (May 14, 1615); c. 96r (Nov. 19, 1615).
47. Ryan (1997, 149–51).
48. AIRE, CAT B 6, c. 95v (Nov. 12 and 19, 1615).

As I show in chapter 3, contemporary Christian theology considered baptism to encapsulate and enact a radical break with the convert's past and the beginning of a new life. Yet House governors often conceived of the ritual itself and its attendant privileges in terms of the convert's previous, non-Christian trajectories. For example, although regulations required that all baptisms be held in the small chapel of the House itself, such baptisms account for only 44 percent of the total for which location is documented. When the convert was a slave sponsored by his or her master, the ceremony was sometimes held in the master's parish church.[49] These public ceremonies, attended by numerous acquaintances and neighbors, and with the convert's old master or his immediate kin often acting as godparents, served not only to ritually enact spiritual transformation but to reaffirm a preexisting social order that the ceremony itself did little to alter.

In addition to baptism in a master's parish church, public baptisms were also held periodically in various churches around the city, especially when a large group of converts could be gathered for the occasion, as in the case of the conversion of an entire family. Such ceremonies were ideological victories. They celebrated not only the transformation of an individual convert but his or her removal from an enemy community, whether "Jews" or "Turks."[50] Baptism, which crystallized the moment of transition from one community to another, thus also served as a reminder of the convert's indelible past.

That the public aspect of conversion necessitated the repetitive recalling of a convert's previous identity is well attested to in the frequent designation of converts in the House archives as either *infedeli convertiti* ("converted infidels") or as former Muslims or Jews, even decades after their baptism. For example, Isabetta of Oderzo (near Treviso), baptized sometime before 1592, was still referred to in the House's account books as "formerly Muslim" as late as 1619, after becoming first an Ursuline nun, then a wife, and finally a widow.[51] A certain Zuan Battista, who was baptized (possibly as a child) in 1594, and who later became a commercial

---

49. Of the 512 baptisms whose location is documented, only 227 (44 percent) were held in the House chapel. Another 163 (32 percent) were celebrated in one of seven churches: the Tolentini, Frari, Gesuiti, Santa Maria Formosa, Umiltà, Santi Apostoli, and Santi Giovanni e Paolo. The remaining 122 (24 percent) took place in any of fifty other churches, which hosted up to five convert baptisms each.

50. On the long-standing Christian trope of baptizing the enemy and thereby achieving a political victory, prevalent already in early Crusading rhetoric, see (Tolan 2008, esp. 66–68).

51. AIRE, CAT B 6, c. 116r (March 29, 1618); c. 143v (May 2, 1619). The references to Isabetta as "formerly Muslim" ("*olim turca*"; "*già turca*") appear in two contexts: first, her return to live in the House after a long sojourn in Oderzo, near Treviso and the death of her first husband, Zuane Comin; and, second, a proposed employment contract for her with Giulio Rossi, a Venetian silk merchant, later to become her second husband. On other occasions in the same period, archival documents referred to her by her deceased husband's name and by her place of provenance.

broker, was similarly referred to as "formerly Muslim" seventeen years later, in 1611.[52]

As far as I know, no surviving records describe baptismal ceremonies sponsored by the House of Catechumens before the eighteenth century. But some of the paraphernalia used was documented in the House meeting notes, from which a picture emerges of differential treatment of converts predicated not only on gender but also on age and, most tellingly, social status prior to and after conversion. For example, the baptism ceremony of a Jewish boy renamed Pietro Angelo Zen warranted the presence of two trumpeters and some pipers, perhaps due to the fact that the child was destined to be trained by the Dominican friars at the monastery of San Giovanni e Paolo. The special celebration may have been prompted also by his status as heir to a substantial inheritance from his paternal grandfather.[53] Soon after Zen's baptism, however, House regulations sought to limit musical accompaniment during ceremonies.[54] They also decreed that the clothing given catechumens to wear at the font should be "proportional to their merit."[55] (Unfortunately, the governors did not indicate how merit was to be calculated.) Later revisions decried the excessive jewelry worn to the font by some women catechumens and stated that "the Sacrament should regenerate the Spirit, not the Body."[56] Obviously, converts had quite different ideas of what was proper dress on their baptism day. In at least one case, a convert refused to don a garment of "low-grade cloth" (*panno basso*) assigned for his baptism and was temporarily banished from the House.[57]

The actual nature of baptismal ceremonies, although never described in the documents, was informed at least in part by the suggestions of converts them-

52. AIRE, CAT B 6, c. 18v (May 8, 1611).

53. AIRE, CAT B 4, c. 85v (May 14, 1598); c. 86r (May 21, 1598); c. 87r (June 18, 1598); c. 88r (July 9 and 23, 1598); c. 89v (Oct. 15, 1598); c. 90v (Dec. 10, 1598); c. 92v (March 1599).

54. "Si ribadisce quanto deliberato nel 1611, che nei battesimi si chiami a suonare un solo complesso di suonatori, o i piffari o i cornetti" (AIRE, CAT B 6, c. 158r (Oct. 10, 1619)).

55. "La spesa del vestito ai nuovi battezzati sarà proporzionata al merito dei neofiti" (AIRE, CAT B 6, c. 118r (April 21, 1618)). An effort to correlate the quality of a convert's new set of clothes to his or her social status prior to conversion was common in early modern Ottoman Islam as well (Minkov 2000, 233–34).

56. "Siano nella funzione d'esso Battesimo rigorosamente proibite tutte le gale, ed ornamenti secolareschi ... nè le Donne possano usare vestimenta preziose, Gioje, Oro, ed Argento, ma compariscano tutte modestia, ed umiltà al Sacramento rigenerante lo Spirito, e non il Corpo" (AIRE, CAT A 1, c. 98).

57. AIRE, CAT B 6, c. 4v (Nov. 12, 1610). The same convert was the cause of much trouble to the governors due to his rowdy behavior before and after baptism. The decision to dress him in simple cloth may have been in retaliation. Ultimately, a year later when he asked for a new coat, the governors not only denied his request but issued orders prohibiting him from ever again knocking on the House doors and ordering the prior and porter not to let him in (AIRE, CAT B 6, c. 33r (Oct. 6, 1611)).

selves. In 1611, a record was made of the special preparations undertaken on the occasion of the baptism of a young Jewish woman named Ricca "as recommended by Enrigo, baptized in Mantua."[58] And although the regulations stipulated that expenditure on baptismal clothes should not exceed 15 ducats, the baptism of at least one other Jew, Raffael of Mantua, warranted spending the substantial sum of 20 ducats and 2 lire.[59] Similarly, in several cases, the Christian name given a convert was his own choice. For example, in early 1597 Moise Abrananel (Abravanel), a Tripolitan Jew, arrived in Venice by sea and declared his wish to become Christian and to be named Costantino. His wish was granted.[60] Male Jewish converts' greater leverage in shaping the terms of their conversion—of which the baptism ceremony and a new Christian name were two important aspects—suggests once again the different ways in which conversion practices were embedded in larger power structures. It seems hardly accidental that all these examples refer to the baptismal paraphernalia of Jewish men and not of women or Muslims (whether men or women). Volition and intention played little role, if any, in how governors conceptualized the ultimate baptism of most women and Muslim catechumens (see chap. 3).

GODPARENTHOOD AND CO-PARENTHOOD

The institution of godparenthood has been the subject of much anthropological inquiry, beginning with a pathbreaking essay by Sidney Mintz and Eric Wolf in 1950. In that essay, the authors suggest that vertical godparenthood across classes is instrumental in furthering social solidarity, especially by establishing a strong bond between parents and godparents, known as co-parenthood. They also emphasize the importance of godparenthood and co-parenthood across ethnic boundaries.[61]

Although the sponsorship of converts in early modern Venice was premised on specifically Christian notions of what constituted a moral community, it was clearly familiar to Balkan Muslim converts as well. Baptismal sponsorship and its

---

58. AIRE, CAT B 6, c. 23r (June 23, 1611).
59. AIRE, CAT B 6, c. 67v (March 21, 1613); c. 68v (March 28, 1613). For a reference to the bylaws, see the case of Sara, a foreign Jew, for whose baptismal garment the governors were especially reminded not to exceed the 15 ducats stipulated (AIRE, CAT B 6, c. 85v (Sept. 4, 1614)).
60. AIRE, CAT B 4, c. 74r (Jan. 2, 1596, m.v.); c. 74bis. (March 6, 1597).
61. Mintz and Wolf (1950, 342). Mintz and Wolf productively emphasize godparenthood's "functional relationships to other aspects of culture" and warn against treating kinship as a separate domain. My investigation of the baptismal sponsorship of converts is greatly indebted to Mintz and Wolf's insights, as well as to more recent studies they inspired on baptismal sponsorship of indigenous converts to Christianity in colonial New Spain, such as Charney (1991); Cline (1993).

ensuing relations of ritual kinship were widely practiced in Christian Orthodox communities in late Byzantium.[62] These institutions did not disappear with the establishment of the Ottoman Empire but found new forms and meanings in both Muslim and Christian ritual practice. For example, scholars have long noted the strong structural-conceptual linkage of civic and spiritual mutual obligation between the Ottoman sultan and the subject-convert. As caliph of all Muslims, the sultan could make spiritual claims to universal dominion over believers and non-believers alike.[63] This dominion was often articulated through practices such as the patronage and sponsorship of converts.[64] Moreover, in regions of the Ottoman Empire with substantial Christian populations, such as the Balkans, Muslim members of the community could often serve as baptismal godparents of their Christian neighbors' children. The Bosnian Catholic practice of including Muslim sponsors on special occasions was prevalent enough to warrant a papal decree in 1676 forbidding "the admission of heretics as sponsors, even though the strongest reasons of friendship and familiarity prompted the choice of such a person."[65] The secularized uses of godparenthood were thus a potentially shared idiom for catechumens from Ottoman lands and their Venetian patrons.

In contrast to the prevalence of direct sultanic patronage in the Ottoman Empire, the Venetian church-state compact was mediated through charitable institutions such as the House of Catechumens, which allowed a broad swath of the patrician and citizen ranks to further their civic as well as spiritual claims.[66] What makes the godparenthood of converts particularly interesting in this case is that the parental figure with whom godparents were to establish co-parenthood relationships was not a person but an institution—the House of Catechumens itself, which, as we have seen, claimed paternal guardianship over all "children of the House." Thus, just as the baptism ceremony helped forge spiritual kinship and further patronage ties between godparent and convert, it also consolidated claims by the House to be the convert's true parent.

How, then, was the godparenthood of converts organized? Of 304 "children of the House" whose godparents are known, 277 had one godparent, 23 had two, and only 4—all women and girls—had three or four godparents. The overwhelming majority of godparents were men, and the eighteen godmothers on record sponsored mostly female converts (and two very young boys). Although Jews make up only one-quarter of converts with known godparents, they constitute

---

62. Macrides (1987, 1990).
63. Necipoğlu (1989); Fleischer (1992).
64. Minkov (2004).
65. Quoted in Mintz and Wolf (1950, 349–50).
66. On civic patronage through charitable institutions, see Mueller (1972, 76).

over half of those with multiple godparents, suggesting their greater insertion into local networks of patronage. In contrast, Muslim women were especially unlikely to receive multiple godparents; only two such cases are registered.[67]

The majority of godparents of both Jewish and Muslim, female and male, converts were patrician Venetians, but quite a few were citizens and artisans, and occasionally foreign dignitaries and even servants. When two or more godparents were assigned, one was often patrician, the other citizen or artisan. This reflects the collaboration of patrician and citizen elites on the House Board of Governors as well as the claim of the institution to supervisory power over all convert baptisms in Venice. It also alerts us that not all godparents assumed actual responsibility for their godchildren but were sometimes selected primarily for their social prominence, especially when multiple godparents were assigned.

In general, the practice of godparenthood in Venice, as in many other societies, strongly prohibited parents from serving as their children's baptismal sponsors.[68] This rule was repeatedly broken in the case of converts, however, for whom the House governors often took the place of birth parents. Here, many, although by no means all, godparents were House priors, governors, or their immediate kin and, not infrequently, the converts' past or future masters and legal guardians.[69] Thus, baptismal sponsorship also strengthened the authority of individual governors and priors over neophytes, who became their godchildren or employees. In 1591, forty-seven-year-old Sabatai, son of Isach of Ferrara, was introduced to the House by one of the governors, Eusebio Renati, himself a Jewish convert, who eventually served as Sabatai's baptismal godfather four months later.[70] Renati was not the only governor to sponsor converts. In the two decades from 1647 to 1665, Paolo Cremona, citizen, long-time governor of the House, and one of two commissioners in charge of an enormous bequest distributed to converts, served as either godfather or master to at least six converts.[71] Thirty-year-old Zanbattista

67. One was Anna (formerly Fattime from Alexandria), a moor who went to serve in the household of Francesco Contarini, a patrician. The other was Marina (formerly Sabba), a fourteen-year-old Russian slave of the Marini family who went back into their service after baptism (ASPV, CRb, reg. 2, c. 42r (April 26, 1654); c. 60r (Dec. 29, 1664)).
68. On this prohibition in general, see Gudeman (1975); Pitt-Rivers (1977). For Venice, see Grubb (1996, 48–49).
69. This phenomenon requires further discussion because it raises crucial questions about the relationship between spiritual kinship (particularly adoption by patrons) and Venetian patrimonial state formation. For suggestive comments about this relationship in general, see Parkes (2003, esp. 762). On Venetian patrimonialism and its attendant forms of genealogical consciousness, see Raines (2006, 454–551).
70. ASPV, CRb, reg. 1, c. 4v (March 20, 1591); c. 5r (July 7, 1591). On Eusebio Renati, see also Pullan (1983, 127, 245, 289).
71. In 1647, he became master to twelve-year-old Niccolò (formerly Husaim) from Strana, and a year later to eight-year-old Pietro (formerly Xafer) from Klis (Croatia). In following years, he

(formerly a Turkish slave by the name Jesup) had as one of his godfathers the House prior, Gerolamo de Roca, himself a convert of unknown background. Zanbattista's second godfather, Serafin Serafinelli, a long-time House governor, was a commercial broker who later became president of the commercial brokers' guild.[72] Zanbattista's long career as a broker may have been facilitated by Serafinelli's own ties.[73] The conflation of duties demonstrated in Cremona's and Serafinelli's cases must have been quite common because later regulations specifically forbade governors from serving as converts' godparents to prevent them from favoring their godchildren over other neophytes and to encourage them to keep to their role as "communal fathers" of the entire House.[74]

Baptismal sponsorship also brought new godparents into the House orbit, allowing the institution to further its patronage networks into new milieus. Unlike Rome, where a large percentage of Muslim converts' godfathers were clergymen and foreign dignitaries, in Venice both the godfathers and godmothers of Jewish and Muslim converts were primarily local lay patricians, usually not of the first rank of the political elite but, rather, members of the patriciate's minor branches or the children or younger siblings of important state officials, as well as quite a few well-to-do citizens.[75] Even with less illustrious godparents, not only convert godchildren but the House itself stood to gain powerful patrons. In the mercantile and artisanal milieus in which many converts aspired to find employment, a merchant godfather could prove at least as useful as a diplomat or a high-ranking civil servant.

In addition to weaving new patronage ties or strengthening existing ones between converts, their godparents, and the House, baptismal sponsorship could also reinforce ties between older converts and the institution itself. By inviting older converts to sponsor the baptism of more recent catechumens, the House not only

godfathered twenty-two-year-old Giovanni (formerly Assan) from Edirne; thirty-year-old Paolo (formerly Mehmet), an Istanbulite foot soldier, twenty-year-old Paolo (formerly Michiel) from Asistat (Hungary); and twenty-seven-year-old Lorenzo (formerly Michiel Francese), a Venetian Jew (ASPV, CRb, reg. 2, c. 21r (Aug. 15, 1647); c. 23v (Sept. 13, 1648); c. 30v (June 25, 1650); c. 34r (June 4, 1651); c. 54r (May 8, 1661); 64v (Jan. 24, 1665 m.v.)).

72. ASPV, CRb, reg. 1, c. 12r (Feb. 7, 1592 m.v.).

73. Serafinelli godfathered at least three other converts: twenty-two-year-old Giulio (formerly Samuel) from Ferrara; eighty-six-year-old Giacomo (formerly Ali Moro), an oarsman from Alexandria; and fifty-eight-year-old Zuanne (formerly Ali), an oarsman from Gallipoli (ASPV, CRb, reg. 1, cc. 16v–17r (Jan. 6, 1593 m.v.); c. 17v (June 5, 1594); cc. 17v–18r (June 24, 1594)).

74. AIRE, CAT A 1, c. 43.

75. Unfortunately, the surviving documentation does not allow a clear identification (and hence prosopographical and genealogical study) of most patrician godparents. A preliminary search for the names of several dozen converts' patrician godparents in the *Dizionario Biografico degli Italiani*, however, yielded almost no entries, suggesting the godparents' secondary political and cultural prominence as a group. For a discussion of Roman converts' godparents, see Rudt de Collenberg (1989, 50–71).

consolidated its ongoing ties with its former charges but also cashed on their value as living proof of the efficacy of its work. To be worthy godparents, converts had to first prove themselves as good Christians over a lengthy period of time. Serving as godparents was thus evidence of success as converts and, indeed, as upstanding members of a locally based Christian community.[76]

Another practice that suggests how converts were localized is their renaming at baptism. Whereas some converts were recorded simply as "the moor of X" (a slave or servant of African descent) or "the Turk of Y," the majority were referred to by Christian names, sometimes even prior to their baptism. Unlike the Muslim and Jewish traditions, in which converts were often given names that singled them out as converts, the names given to converts in Venice were mostly common in the population at large.[77] Despite their generic nature, or precisely because of it, such names both signaled and solidified the convert's newfound membership in Venetian society. At the same time, unlike other Venetians, whose personal names were "above all a statement of the natal family" and hardly ever based on a godparent's name, converts' names not infrequently followed those of masters, godparents, or their relatives. Converts' names thus also reinforced their embeddedness in patronage systems and spiritual, rather than natal, kinship networks.[78]

In other cases, converts' new names actually recalled their pre-Christian lives. Converts might be given Christian names that sounded similar to their original names, as in the case of Samaria, a Jew who was baptized as Zamaria in 1626, or the twelve-year-old Fumia, a Muslim girl who was baptized as Euffemia in 1665.[79] Some converts kept their previous names.[80] Even when a new Christian name was

76. In 1592, Nicolò, a Jewish convert, godfathered another Jewish convert, thirty-eight-year-old Andrea Stefano (formerly Jacob Cain) from Frankfurt. Perhaps the neophyte's foreign provenance warranted his godfathering by a more established convert. Andrea Stefano ran away from the House only nine days after his baptism, taking away some clothes, to the governors' great dismay (ASPV, CRb, reg. 1, c. 9v (Nov. 17, 1592); c. 10r (Dec. 26, 1592)).
77. Giovanni/Giovanni Battista was by far the most popular convert's name, given to over 30 percent of male converts; the most popular female convert name was, not surprisingly, Maria, given to almost 20 percent of female converts. For both men and women, the five most popular names appeared in over 50 percent of the cases. For men, these were, in descending order of popularity, Giovanni, Francesco, Giovanni Battista, Antonio, and Pietro. For women, the names were Maria, Caterina, Anzola (Angela), Anna, and Maddalena. Approximately 80 percent of converts, both women and men, received a single Christian name; only a tiny fraction received more than two.
78. On Venetian naming practices, see Grubb (1996, 42–47).
79. ASPV, CRb, reg. 3, c. 1v (Oct. 10, 1626); BdC, 2, c. 62v (Sept. 8, 1665). The governors' creativity stopped short of following the same naming practice with Fumia's mother and five-year-old brother. The former, Salige, was renamed Francesca; the latter, Mustafa, was renamed Francesco.
80. For example, in 1617 the governors decided to buy a used cloak for "Matine, ex turco," now a servant in the house of Leonardo Priuli in the parish of San Stae (AIRE, CAT B 6, c. 109r (Dec. 1, 1617)).

registered at baptism, the old name sometimes stuck. Sultana, a Muslim convert-turned-nun who was a frequent recipient of charity from the House, was referred to by her prebaptismal name far more frequently than either by her Christian name, Lucia, or by her monastic name, Zuanna, and this for several years after her baptism.[81] Cases such as this suggest continuity rather than a radical break with the past.

BECOMING LOCAL?

In theory, if not always in practice, conversion in the House of Catechumens served as an act of becoming simultaneously a Catholic and a juridical subject of the Venetian state. Contemporary legislators often linked converts' new civic membership to concrete economic benefits and opportunities for social mobility by offering them artisanal patents. From the mid-seventeenth century on, papal bulls and Venetian Senate decrees alike repeatedly sought to guarantee converts' economic advancement by allowing them to exercise any trade or profession of their choosing without paying guild entrance fees.[82]

Another path of insertion into Venetian Christian society was the pursuit of education. University or seminary fees for promising young converts were occasionally paid for by the House. Soon after his baptism in 1592, Zanetto, son of Tomasina, was sent to the seminary of San Cipriano in Murano, all expenses covered by the House. Five years later, notices about the cost of his books, writing materials, and clothes, as well as general reminders to "take care of the needs of Zanetto in the seminary," still figured prominently in the House records, as they did throughout the register (which ends in 1599).[83] A similar pattern of heavy

81. Of the forty-odd references to her in the House meeting notes, she is named "Sultana" twenty-three times, "Lucia-Sultana" eleven times, and "Lucia" only once (AIRE, CAT B 6, c. 13r (Feb. 13, 1610 m.v.); c. 13v (Feb. 25, 1610 m.v.); c. 17r (April 21, 1611); c. 19r (May 13, 1611); c. 29r (Aug. 18, 1611); c. 33r (Oct. 6 and 13, 1611); c. 38r (Dec. 22, 1611); c. 45r (March 15, 1612); c. 54r (Aug. 23, 1612); c. 55v (Sept. 20, 1612); c. 56r (Sept. 27, 1612); c. 58v (Nov. 8, 1612); c. 63v (Jan. 18, 1612 m.v.); c. 66r (Feb. 28, 1612 m.v.); c. 71r (May 23, 1613); c. 76r (Oct. 31, 1613); c. 77v (Dec. 19, 1613); c. 78r (Jan. 2, 1613 m.v.); c. 89r (Feb. 19, 1614 m.v.); c. 89v (April 9, 1615); c. 91r (May 29, 1615); c. 96v (Nov. 26, 1615); c. 97r (Dec. 17, 1615); c. 97v (Jan. 7, 1615 m.v.); c. 98v (Feb. 4, 1615 m.v.); c. 102r (June 3, 1616); c. 116v (March 29, 1618); c. 129r (Oct. 16, 1618); c. 134r (Dec. 20, 1618); c. 135r (Jan. 18, 1618 m.v.); c. 141v (March 21, 1619); c. 144v (May 16, 1619); c. 163r (Jan. 23, 1619)).
82. The Senate issued decrees in this matter on January 2, 1676 m.v., and on June 30, 1688. Both are reproduced in AIRE, CAT A 1, cc. 68–70.
83. AIRE, Cat B 4, c. 61r (March 7, 1596). See also, c. 4r (June 18, 1592); c. 11r (Jan. 13, 1592, m.v.); c. 13r (Feb. 18, 1592 m.v.); c. 15r (March 18, 1593); c. 16r (April 8, 1593); cc. 20r–v (June 10, 1593); c. 21v (July 15, 1593); c. 22r (July 29, 1593); c. 23r (Aug. 16, 1593); c. 25r (Oct. 14, 1593); c. 26r (Nov. 10, 1593); c. 27r (Dec. 2, 1593); c. 33v (March 31, 1594); c. 34v (May 5, 1594); c. 35r (May 17, 1594); c. 36v (June 16 and July 7, 1594); c. 37v (Aug. 4, 1594); c. 38r (Aug. 11, 1594); c. 39r (Sept. 15, 1594); c. 40r (Sept. 22, 1594); c. 40v (Sept. 27, 1594); c. 44v (Feb. 9, 1594 m.v.); c. 47v (May 9, 1595); c. 62r (April 4, 1596); c. 70r (Aug. 13, 1596).

financial investment in a particular child convert destined for an ecclesiastical career emerged in 1610, when Giovanni-Iseppo Strassoldo, a Jewish convert, asked for his son Paolo to be sent to the seminary of Castello. Three years later, on completing his course of studies, Paolo was first assigned to serve as an assistant to the patriarch of Aquileia and then sent to the seminary of the Somascan order. His annual tuition of 30 ducats, a new set of clothes, and a bed were all paid for by the House. Long after he had left the Somascans to attend the Neophytes' College in Rome, and after his stipend from Venice was officially terminated, the House still paid for Paolo's books.[84]

That neophytes placed in seminaries clearly mattered more than others is signaled by the level of detail of the entries about them in the House register, as well as by their sheer volume. Beyond their individual merits, perhaps the special treatment of these children was warranted by their families' long-term pattern of "exemplary" relationship with the House. Paolo's two sisters, Maria and Giulia, both became nuns in the monastery of Saints Mark and Andrea in Murano, whereas their father, Iseppo, later became the House solicitor and envoy to Rome.[85]

A few other Jewish converts, especially if baptized as adults and of elite background, could cash in on their claim to prior expertise in Hebrew, Talmud, or Kabbala, all highly valued commodities in the world of humanistic learning.[86] The bulk of neophytes, however, especially of Muslim background, could not build on their intellectual assets in staking out a future as converts. Only rarely, if ever, could converts with knowledge of Arabic, Ottoman Turkish, the Qur'an, or Shari'a law find scholarly employment in Venice. The reasons for this are multiple, including social competition and differing perceived levels of literacy, given

84. AIRE, CAT B 6, cc. 2r–v (Oct. 12, 1610); 4r (Nov. 9, 1610); 8r (Dec. 16, 1610); 9v (Jan. 7, 1610 m.v.); 20v (May 26, 1611); 21v (June 9, 1611); 27v (Aug. 11, 1611); 37v (Dec. 15, 1611); 66r (Feb. 28, 1611 m.v.); 71r ((May 23, 1613); 72r (June 20, 1613); c. 85v (Sept. 4, 1614); c. 86r (Sept. 18, 1614); c. 107v (Nov. 3, 1616). On the Roman Neophytes' College, established by Pope Gregory XIII in 1577 with the intention to train young catechumens for eventual church service, see Bono (1998, 434).
85. AIRE, CAT B 6, c. 1v (Oct. 1, 1610); c. 22v (June 16, 1611); c. 37v (Dec. 15, 1611); c. 77v (Dec. 19, 1613); c. 89v (April 9, 1615); c. 94v (Oct. 15, 1615); AIRE, CAT C 2, c. 430r (July 3, 1608); 430v (Sept. 1, 1610).
86. Simonsohn (1989). Two cases stand out: (1) the Jerusalemite Domenico Gerosolimitano (formerly Rabbi Samuel Vivas), who became censor of Hebrew books after his baptism in 1593, and (2) the Venetian Giulio Morosini (formerly Samuel ben David Nahmias), who enjoyed a long career in papal service in Rome following his baptism in 1649. In both cases, exceptional education in their youth enabled these converts to become serviceable in ecclesiastical circles and to secure not only their own future but, in the case of Morosini, that of his brother and nephew as well. For Gerosolimitano's baptism, see ASPV, CRb, reg. 1, c. 14v (Aug. 6, 1593); Ioly Zorattini (1998). For Morosini, see ASPV, CRb, reg. 2, c. 29r (Dec. 22, 1649); Simonsehn (1903); Ravid (1983); Ioly Zorattini (2000).

Muslim converts' limited command of Italian, in contrast to Jewish converts, who were often fluent Italian speakers. They also have to do, in part, with humanists' general lower level of interest in Islam and Turkish and Arabic letters, compared with Judaism and Hebrew, and the availability of Christian native Arabic and Turkish speakers.[87] Finally, they may have stemmed also from a wide perception of enemy subjects as mostly fit for menial work as slaves, servants, or soldiers, rather than as scholars and educators.

Not surprisingly, most converts eventually found themselves occupying the same status and trade they had held prior to their conversion. Many also remained dependent on charity from the House of Catechumens for years after their baptism, if not for life. This situation forced many to tighten their local networks of patronage and eventually inserted some Muslim converts more permanently into Venetian society, compared to Jewish converts-turned-friars, priests, preachers, and scholars; as slaves and servants, soldiers and journeymen, Muslim converts could and did get adopted by or marry into local families.

The overall dependence of converts' career paths on access to local social networks is further illustrated by the rarity of Jewish converts in the military. Out of a population of approximately two hundred teenage and adult male Jewish converts, only six are documented as having become soldiers. None of them originated from Venetian territories, although Venetians constituted over one-half of Jewish converts in the House of Catechumens.[88] This suggests that it was not so much that Jews were deemed unfit for military service in the eyes of the House governors but, rather, that local converts had more career paths available to them than foreign-born converts, either Jewish or Muslim.

Like other members of early modern Venetian society, converts faced a highly gendered occupational structure. If most young male converts could expect placement as either apprentices with local artisans or as soldiers and mariners, the overwhelming majority of young female converts became maidservants in Venetian households. But it was neither gender nor prior confessional affiliation alone that determined neophytes' trajectories but their intersection. Thus, only half a dozen Jewish women converts are documented as having become maidservants compared with over one hundred Muslim women. Similarly, although monachization was often women converts' only viable alternative to marriage or domestic service, of the sixteen documented monachized women converts none seems to have been a moor.

---

87. On Arabic in the humanist curriculum, see Dannenfeldt (1955). For studies of specific Christian Arab scholars in early modern Italy, see Rietbergen (1989); Hamilton (1994).

88. Of the six, three came from Istanbul, one from Avignon, and one from Poland (the sixth was of unknown provenance).

Of course, career paths were determined not only by the governors' wishes and perceptions of the transformative potential of different types of converts but also by converts' own inclinations and resources. Yet the paucity of cases of neophytes who completely severed their ties with the House on baptism suggests that the ability of the governors to keep converts under their watchful eye remained strong throughout the period.

From a convert's point of view, one powerful incentive for keeping in touch with the House was the distribution of charity. This practice too mirrored, and at times enhanced, the strikingly uneven trajectories of different kinds of converts. This is well illustrated by the list of recipients of a major bequest of 4,000 ducats left to the House of Catechumens in 1626 by the patrician Tommaso, son of Andrea Mocenigo. For a quarter century, the governors engaged in constant litigation with various magistracies that administered the funds, and in those years its moneys were distributed only sparingly and for specific ends.[89] But starting in 1652, the House began distributing interest revenue from the bequest annually to between fifteen and thirty converts, who received 30 ducats each. Technically, all converts baptized through the House after 1626 were eligible, by order of their baptism date, as long as they registered on designated dates with their baptismal certificate in hand (see fig. 4.3).[90] The recipients' profile, however, diverges considerably from that of the overall convert population. Of the twenty-eight Jewish children baptized from 1630 to 1670, twenty-one (75 percent) became beneficiaries. Four out of the seven who did not were foreign born or the children of newly arrived foreigners.[91] In comparison, of 140 Muslim children baptized in those years, only 59 (42 percent) became beneficiaries. This suggests that local-born Jewish children converts stood a much greater chance than did foreign-born Muslim ones of staying in Venice through adulthood and thus benefiting from the magnanimity of the House. Similarly, although women constituted only 28 percent of those baptized in the House during this period, they account for 46 percent of beneficiaries of the Mocenigo bequest.

A similar pattern emerges for another major bequest, left to the House by the patrician Vincenzo Garzoni in 1592, which provided a life-long stipend of 50 ducats per year to twenty converts, with new recipients added as older ones passed away. Of thirty-four recipients documented up to 1670, eighteen (53 percent) were Jews; nineteen (56 percent) were women, of whom eleven (one-third)

89. AIRE, CAT E, F. 8, c. 3v.
90. These requirements clearly advantaged children over adult converts because the wait period for the Mocenigo bequest could be as much as a couple of decades after baptism.
91. They hailed from Split, Amsterdam, Parga in the Epirus, and North Africa.

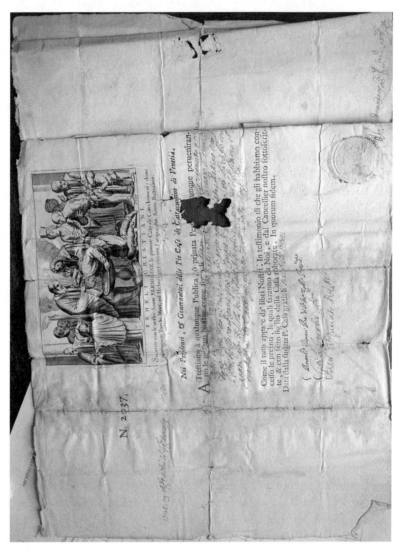

Figure 4.3 *Baptismal certificate issued by the governors of the House of Catechumens (1730). The certificate attests that Elisabetta, formerly Fatè Turca, was baptized in 1697, at the age of twelve, and was sponsored by her godfather, the patrician Marco Pisani. A marginal note confirms that she received 30 ducats from the Mocenigo bequest in 1735. The print shows a young Jewish woman and a turbaned old man watching in the background as two men and a child await their turn at the baptismal font. ASPV Curia Patriarcale di Venezia. Sezione Antica, Catecumeni, Documenti diversi, busta 2, reg. 1, c. 9r. Reproduction: author, by permission of Ministero per i Beni e le Attività Culturali.*

were Jewish—compared with only 6 percent Jewish women in the overall convert population.

Another strong incentive for women converts to stay in Venice was the prospect of marriage negotiated and funded by the House. Because non-Christian marriages were automatically dissolved if only one of the spouses converted, the House governors did not shy away from seeking to match formerly married converts with new spouses. In particular, governors actively sought out eligible husbands for female converts of childbearing age. Although the surviving records do not give a complete picture of convert marriages, they do indicate that the bulk of converts who got married in Venice did so with either fellow converts or local artisans. For example, in 1593, the governors sought to contract the marriage of two converts, a former Jew named Girolamo, and a former Muslim named Isabetta, as long as the dowry could be limited to 90 ducats.[92] I found no records of Venetian converts during this period who married citizens, hardly surprising in light of the self-conscious endogamy of this estate. Nor is there any evidence that converts obtained even the lesser status of naturalized Venetian citizens (de intus), despite the bull Cupientes iudaeos issued by Pope Paul III in 1542, which guaranteed converts from Judaism citizenship in their place of baptism.[93] Without the economic privileges granted by citizenship, marriage to a fellow convert or to an artisan could only rarely guarantee financial independence and thus furthered the couple's reliance on the House for continued support. For example, despite a substantial dowry of 600 ducats provided by her adoptive parents and by her godfather, Father Francesco dell'Orio, on her marriage in 1597 to Francesco ai Servi, a Venetian tailor, the convert Marina still relied on the House for charity for over twenty years, during her entire marriage and into her widowhood. Christmas Charity for her is noted in the House records as late as 1620. Marina's case was hardly unique; several other women converts made repeated appearances in the House records as regular recipients of charity.[94]

92. The wedding did not materialize due to the groom's illness and eventual death (AIRE, CAT B 4, c. 18v (May 13, 1593)).
93. On the papal bull, see Pullan (1983, 251–52). A late-eighteenth-century decree by the Venetian Senate mentions only converts' eligibility for Venetian subjecthood (sudditanza) (Compliazione delle Leggi, b. 294, c. 263v ("Sulla capacità de Neofiti agli Ecclesiastici Benefici," April 8, 1785)).
94. AIRE, CAT B 4, c. 69v (June 27, 1597); c. 79r (Sept. 4, 1597); c. 86r (May 28, 1598); c. 86v (June 4, 1598); c. 87v (July 9, 1598); AIRE, CAT B 6, c. 37v (Dec. 15, 1611); c. 45r (March 15, 1611); c. 56r (Sept. 27, 1612); c. 57v (Oct. 25, 1612); c. 77v (Dec. 19, 1613); c. 83v (June 5, 1614); c. 88r (Jan. 15, 1614 m.v.); c. 89r (March 5, 1615); c. 89v (April 9, 1615); c. 97r (Dec. 12, 1615); c. 100r (March 24, 1616); c. 110r (Dec. 22, 1617); c. 124r (July 19, 1618); c. 141v (March 21, 1619); c. 158v (Oct. 17, 1619); c. 163r (Jan. 23, 1619 m.v.).

As scholars of early modern conversion policies have noted, the provision of dowries for young female converts was of crucial importance in facilitating their transition from one community to another.[95] Here, godparents' vital role is visible once again; they not only offered employment opportunities but also vouched for their godchildren's merit and interceded on their behalf when appealing to patrons to finance their dowry. Indeed, the distribution of dowries was shaped by and made manifest the divergent types of patronage available to Jewish and Muslim converts. Many formerly enslaved Muslim converts depended on a master's support to secure the House endorsement of their marriage and provision of a dowry. For example, in 1639, the patrician Paolo Capello approached the House on behalf of his maidservant, Zaneta, who had been baptized a decade earlier and whose marriage he was negotiating at the time. Thanks to his efforts, the governors decided to increase the House contribution toward Zaneta's dowry from 20 to 40 ducats.[96] Jewish converts, on the other hand, sometimes had previously converted relatives who could contract their marriage and turn to the governors for assistance in financing a dowry. In 1654, Fra Angelico, a Jewish convert turned monk, asked the governors for assistance in securing a dowry for his relative, Angelica (formerly Bona), who had been baptized and adopted by a Venetian shoemaker at age four in 1639. Her prospective husband, a goldsmith, an only child and "a person of means and good customs" from Ancona, was himself a Jewish convert. The governors stepped in and allocated 160 ducats from the House treasury toward the substantial dowry of 300 ducats asked for.[97] Although the governors endorsed the marriages and contributed toward the dowries of both Zaneta and Angelica, the scale of their contributions, the marriage alliances themselves, and the patronage networks they cemented differed significantly.

95. For Turin, see Allegra (1991). For Rome, see Van Boxel (1998). For Florence, see Siegmund (2006, esp. 332–85).

96. Zaneta's ties to the House did not end there. Three years later, widowed and with a baby daughter, she approached the House again to have her child sent to a nursemaid so she could take up a position in the household of Tommaso Morosini. The governors approved her request and decreed a monthly stipend of 6 lire for her daughter's upkeep for as long as Zaneta held her job with the Morosinis. Finally, in 1661, Zaneta was among the lucky converts to receive a lifetime stipend of 50 ducats per year from the bequest of Vincenzo Garzoni (ASPV, CRb, reg. 3, c. 2v (March 4, 1629); AIRE, CAT E 8, cc. 17r–v (June 9, 1639); c. 21r (Oct. 18, 1642); ASPV, CDd, b. 2, reg. 2, cc. 1r and 5r (Dec. 1, 1661)). On Garzoni's bequest, see Degli Avogadro 1857, xxvii).

97. The sum was to be paid in part by Angelica's and her brother Iseppo's 30-ducat shares each of the Mocenigo bequest and in part by the House general treasury, which had provided dowries of 100 ducats in other similar cases. The union, however, did not materialize, and a year later Fra Angelico approached the congregation again and received their approval to use the funds as dowry for Angelica's marriage to another eligible subject, Antonio f. Luca, a Friulian (AIRE, CAT E 8, c. 44v–45r (Sept. 24, 1654); c. 47r (May 11, 1655)).

ADOPTION AND OTHER TIES

Whereas the provision of dowries on the occasion of young female neophytes' marriage positioned the House governors rather unambiguously in a paternal role, their familial relationship to converts in other contexts was more complicated. In both Western and Byzantine patristic and liturgical writings, strong conceptual links obtain between adoption and baptism.[98] Whereas baptism provided converts with a set of spiritual kin and matrimony with a set of affinal kin, adoption was to supplant, rather than supplement, converts' birth kin. In the case of converts' adoption, it formed part and parcel of the efforts to sever former family ties and place the House governors in key roles in converts' reconfigured kinship networks. Adoption also provided an important venue for the placement of young converts. Yet converts' adoptions, as mediated and recorded by the House of Catechumens, hardly formed a unified practice. The sixteen cases of adoption documented in the House archives for 1570–1670 concern eight girls and eight boys, both Jewish and Muslim, ranging from newborns to young men and women. The records themselves vary, from brief references to a child having been taken by so-and-so as "soul son" or "soul daughter" to elaborate notarized contracts detailing parents' obligations toward their adoptive child, as well as sanctions to be taken by the House should parents default on their promises.[99] Some contracts focus on the commitment to nurture an adopted child and provide for her. Others highlight, instead, the future inheritance that awaited the child once the adoptive parents died. Some only stipulate that the child was to love and honor her parents, whereas others clearly require that the child serve her parents and nurse them in their old age. Some pledge to provide dowries on an adopted daughter's marriage and others when she joined a monastery. Several contracts include additional contributions to the House itself.

The variety of assumptions about financial and affective obligations between adoptive parents and children manifest in the documents is equaled by the wide range of social status and wealth of adoptive parents and their presumed motivations in adopting a convert child. Although none explicitly pledged to make their adopted child a legal heir, it may help to qualify Christiane Klapisch-Zuber's conclusion that adoption became "impossible" in early modern Italy.[100] As the examples discussed next show, actual affective ties between adoptive parents and children did not depend solely on legal endorsement.

98. On the relationship between baptism and adoption, see Macrides (1999, 309–10).
99. For examples of the latter, see AIRE, CAT C 1, cc. 33v–34r (Oct. 16, 1572); cc. 34v–35r (Jan. 26, 1576 m.v.); cc. 35v–36r (March 2, 1577); cc. 69v–70v (Nov. 16, 1591).
100. Klapisch-Zuber (1999).

Some adoptive parents were artisans and professionals, such as Zordan Prosdocimo, a Greek tailor, and his wife Margarita, who in 1577 adopted Marina, an eleven-year-old Muslim convert, or Pietro Cazzi, a physician who in 1632 adopted his godchild Paolo Ignazio (formerly David Cohen), born to a Jewish Venetian family.[101] Some explicitly mentioned as their motivation for adoption their wish to pass on their trade. Dr. Mattio Suriano, physician to the grand duke of Tuscany, adopted nine-year-old Carlo Francesco in 1616 "so that he can instruct him in medicine." Stefano Pironi, a merchant, adopted fourteen-year-old Giovanni Battista Pironi (formerly Çavuş) as his godchild in 1633 "so that he learns the trade of silk weaver." According to the entry in the House register, Stefano was to keep Giovanni Battista "as a son, and according to his behavior so will he be well kept, and treated, [and] no mention of a salary was made."[102] In 1654, the bishop of Kotor, Vicenzo Buchia, and his nephew, Abbot Marco Buchia, received at their request twelve-year-old Paolin (formerly Giosef), promising to "raise and educate him to lead him to become a priest at the time God pleases." Up to that point, Paolin, who had been baptized as a toddler, had been raised in the House and "educated to become a monk." Both he and his mother were consulted and agreed to the bishop's offer.[103]

The wish to raise convert children to follow an adoptive parent's trade, as well as contracts that specified the parent's material obligations to the child, suggest that adoption and apprenticeship were sometimes conflated. A different type of adoption involved wealthy patrician women, such as the widow Leonarda Cumena, owner of extensive fields in the Este region, who in 1591 adopted Nicolosa, a teenage convert from Lepanto.[104] Cumena followed a pattern documented elsewhere in early modern Europe—a childless widow who exerted control over her own lineal property and who sought to continue her family line by passing on that property to her adoptive child.[105] Perhaps she also sought to secure nursing in her old age.

Clearly, both boys and girls could be adopted to fulfill a host of affective, spiritual, and nurturance needs, providing an important mechanism of social reproduction in the absence of natural progeny.[106] Given the scant documentation

101. AIRE, CAT C 1, cc. 35v–36r (March 2, 1577); ASPV, CRb, reg. 2, c. 16v (April 18, 1632).
102. For Carlo Francesco's adoption, see AIRE, CAT B 6, c. 98r (Jan. 28, 1615 m.v.). For Giovanni Battista's, see ASPV, CRb, reg. 2, c. 17r (May 10, 1633).
103. AIRE, CAT E 8, c. 44v (Sept. 24, 1654); ASPV, CDd, b. 2, reg. 2, cc. 13v–14r. Paolin had received 30 ducats from the Mocenigo bequest two months prior to his "adoption" by the bishop (ASPV, CRb, reg. 3, c. 9r (July 18, 1654)).
104. AIRE, CAT C 1, cc. 69v–70v (Nov. 16, 1591).
105. Gager (1997). Adoption contracts that referred specifically to services to be rendered by the adoptee have been documented elsewhere in early modern Europe, for example in Florence (Fubini Leuzzi 1994, 883–84).
106. For a survey of these functions from a cross-cultural perspective, see Goody (1969).

of convert adoptions, it is hard to gauge the extent to which parents' expectations in such adoptions were gender-specific. Here I can only provide some preliminary observations, based on the limited sample of surviving adoption records. The adoption of convert boys more often than that of convert girls served as a kind of apprenticeship, with the adoptive father passing a trade on to his son. Conversely, girls' adoptive parents more often expressed a commitment to their moral Christian upbringing and promised to provide a suitable dowry or other forms of sponsorship.[107] Yet social reproduction and the preservation of artisanal identity were not entirely absent from girls' adoptions either. This is illustrated by the previously mentioned case of Marina, who was adopted by a tailor and his wife and who eventually married another tailor, Francesco ai Servi, two decades later. On Francesco's death, Marina became known as "the seamstress" ("*la sartora*") herself, clearly having picked up the trade.[108]

The adoption of both girls and boys could also be cast as intended to fulfill primarily affective, rather than practical or financial, ends. In 1577, an elderly childless couple, a cobbler named Bortolo and his wife Maddalena, approached the House with the explicit request to adopt a child "for consolation and solace in their old age." They were given Catterina, a seven-year-old Muslim convert, whom Bortolo immediately "took in [his] arms and kissed paternally, and promised to keep by him in his house as an adopted daughter, and treat her as such, educate her in good customs, and in the holy Christian religion, in the same manner they would have treated her if she were conceived and born to the couple."[109] Catterina's adoption followed a path familiar to us, in which a childless couple approaches a welfare institution and adopts a relatively young child previously unknown to them. Other adoptions were quite different. In 1572, Matteo, son of the late Andrea Dragacich, a Bosnian clerk in the Venetian Arsenale, and his wife Franceschina brought to the House a nine-year-old Muslim slave girl named Stana, whom they had acquired in the region of Zadar. A few months later, on Stana's baptism in the parish church of San Salvatore, the couple professed to be childless and offered to adopt her "as their true daughter ... and treat her and

107. On the cross-cultural significance of apprenticeship and sponsorship in adoption, see Goody (1982). On the nexus of adoption and apprenticeship for foundling boys and adoption and domestic service for foundling girls, see Gavitt (1990, 243).
108. For Marina's marriage to Francesco ai Servi and the dowry provided by her parents and by her godfather, Father Francesco dell'Orio, see AIRE, CAT B 4, c. 69v (June 27, 1597); c. 77r (July 10, 1597).
109. "Pigliata quella nelle braccia, et basiata paternamente, et promettono quella tenir appresso di se in casa sua come figliola adottiva, et come talle trattarla, educarla in bonj costumi, et nella s[an]ta religione cristiana in quel modo istesso che la trarebbono se fusse concetta et natta de loro Jugali" (AIRE, CAT C 1, cc. 34v–35v (Jan. 26, 1576 m.v.)).

marry her as such."[110] In 1634, Pietro (formerly Osman of Bosnia) was adopted by his eponymous godfather Pietro Garofalo. The adoption took place after Garofalo had expressed his wish to keep the godchild "in his house, next to him, and take care of him as his own son." The adoptee was twenty-two years old at the time.[111] As these cases suggest, legal adoption was only occasionally contracted between strangers, with the House serving as both legal guardian and broker. In most cases, it was the culmination of long periods of cohabitation between adoptive parent(s) and child, often under a different header, such as domestic service.

Indeed, the line not only between adoption and apprenticeship but also between adoption and domestic service was sometimes blurred. Nicolosa, although adopted by a wealthy patrician widow, was not to become heir to the bulk of her adoptive mother's possessions.[112] Her case, more than others, resembles an employment contract between a lady and her waiting maid. But the stipulation of services to be rendered in exchange for future inheritance was not entirely absent from other cases as well.

Although governors were attentive to adoptive parents' needs, on occasion they did put the child's interests (as they understood them) first. In 1612, a hat maker named Chiara, who had served as a baptismal godmother to a young Muslim convert, sought to adopt him. After much deliberation, and with several governors expressing concern that such a move will be "contrary to [the child's] wellbeing," Chiara was granted her wish, only to have the child taken away the following week and, eventually, placed with a haberdasher in the parish of San Moisè.[113]

Chiara's wish to adopt her godchild should be understood within a larger context in which the line between kinship, guardianship, and ownership was often crossed regardless of conversion, especially in the case of slaves and servants. Affective ties between masters and servants were channeled to a variety of practices, ranging from the provision of dowry and various types of financial assistance to concubinage and adoption. Thus, we should not assume that affective

110. "Atteso che non si attrovando loro figlioli, detto Mathio si offeriva, come si offeriße di accettarla in propria figliola, insieme con detta sua Consorte, et come tale trattarla, et maritarla" (AIRE, CAT C 1, cc. 33v–34r (Oct. 16, 1572)).
111. ASPV, CRb, reg. 2, c. 17v (Feb. 15, 1633 m.v.).
112. Instead, she was guaranteed only 200 ducats in inheritance, and her use of the funds was severely restricted. Specifically, on her adoptive mother's death, Nicolosa was to receive 50 ducats to dispense as she pleased and additional 50 ducats to pass on to her blood relations. In the absence of such relations, the money would go to the House. Another 100 ducats would become available to Nicolosa only as a supplement for her religious dower, should she choose to join a monastery. In exchange, the girl was obligated to accompany her adoptive mother if and when she decided to pursue her plan of joining a Jesuit monastery (AIRE, CAT C 1, cc. 69v–70v (Nov. 16, 1591)).
113. AIRE, CAT B 6, c. 57r (Oct. 19, 1612); c. 57v (Oct. 25, 1612); c. 58r (Nov. 2, 1612); c. 67r (March 14, 1613).

ties across ranks necessarily undermined the power structures in which they were embedded. Rather, as Dennis Romano has shown, such ties often helped cement power relations and were part and parcel of the patriarchal logic of Venetian housecraft and statecraft.[114] A case in point, and illustrating masters' lingering attachments to their convert slaves as godparents and as patrons, is the relationship between Zamaria Schietti and his slave Fumia. In 1619, Schietti committed in writing to give a 50-ducat dowry to Fumia, his fourteen-year-old slave whom he had purchased in Istanbul, on the condition that she be accepted as "daughter of the House." A week later, Fumia was introduced and accepted as a catechumen. Despite rumors of her "falling down" with a mariner the following month, she was eventually baptized, with Schietti serving as her godfather.[115] Schietti's relationship with Fumia presented, at least to the governors, a model of Christian charity. After purchasing her from infidels, Schietti brought Fumia to Venice, where he guaranteed the salvation of her soul by admitting her to the House to be catechized and baptized. Moreover, by agreeing to pay for her dowry, he offered her the prospect of respectable, if humble, marriage.

As these records suggest, the dyadic relationship between masters and their convert slaves was complicated by the unequivocal claim of the House to guardianship over converts. The governors exercised this guardianship by watching over converts' masters and, in some cases, removing children from households when suspicion of maltreatment arose. Indeed, the House's custodial claims over converts did not terminate even after their legal adoption. All adoption contracts in the House archives contain clauses specifying the governors' right to intervene and retrieve children from their adoptive parents in cases of maltreatment or failure to provide appropriate dowries. For example, in April 1618 a child convert named Orsola was placed with a Venetian jeweler named Lorenzo, with the prospect of legal adoption. Several weeks later, the House governors called the parish priest of San Polo to intervene on Orsola's behalf and protect her from the jeweler. The following week, the governors decided to visit Orsola themselves, accompanied by the women governors "to make sure she is treated well by the jeweler." A few weeks later, the parish priest again was instructed to "visit the child consigned to the jeweler ... see how she is treated, and, if necessary, remove her." Apparently, the visitors were satisfied with what they had found because they ultimately decided to sign a formal contract with Lorenzo for Orsola's adoption.[116]

---

114. Romano (1991, 1996). For a broader discussion of intimacy as a space for the articulation of social boundaries and hierarchies in imperial settings, see Stoler (2004).
115. AIRE, CAT B 6, c. 138v (Feb. 21, 1618 m.v.); c. 139r (Feb. 28, 1618 m.v.); c. 141r (March 21, 1619); c. 142v (April 11, 1619).
116. AIRE, CAT B 6, c. 117r (April 9, 1618); c. 118v (April 24, 1618); c. 123v (July 12, 1618); c. 125v (Aug. 9, 1618); c. 127v (Sept. 21, 1618).

[*155*]

Many other convert children placed with masters or adoptive parents outside the House were visited periodically by the governors. Even after adoption had been cemented contractually, the governors still treated adoptees as "children of the House." The bond between a convert and the House thus was believed to take precedence over other kinship ties forged throughout a convert's life, whether prior to baptism or after.

Fear of concubinage may have led the governors to remove young female converts from patrician households where they had been placed as servants and where they might also cohabit with unmarried men. Yet the governors' ability to control and prevent such cases was clearly limited because repeated allusions to scandals do crop up in the archives. The prevalence of concubinage between female slaves and their Venetian masters is also suggested by a number of cases of young children brought to the House to be baptized and promptly returned to their masters' homes. For instance, in 1580 the baby son of Mariana, a "Moorish" converted slave, was consigned on baptism to his father—Sempronio Maltempo, Mariana's master and a physician. The latter promised to "educate [the baby] out of charity, and return him [to the House] at the request of the Governors, without asking for any expenses, and with no exceptions."[117] How widespread concubinage really was between Venetian masters and their slaves is difficult to determine. Some cases do suggest that conversion became a channel for legitimizing and supervising otherwise problematic intimate ties between Venetian patricians and citizens and the Muslim slave children and women in their households.[118]

Finally, governors' concern for converts' sexual morality was highly gendered. Whereas the cohabitation of female converts with men to whom they were not legally married was strictly forbidden, when it came to male converts, governors seem to have been less troubled. On November 11, 1629, the House departure register notes that "Signor Zacomo Martin, formerly Lazaro the Jew from Padua, left the House on the day he was baptized, and went to live in the street of Santa Sofia, in the house of the Venetian Signora Alba, whom he wants as a wife."[119] No mention is made of chastisement or any attempt to prevent Zacomo from moving in with his lover.

117. AIRE, CAT C 1, c. 41v (Aug. 4, 1580).
118. Sally McKee's study (2007) of sex slaves in premodern Italy is an important contribution to this field. On concubinage in Venice specifically, see also Cowan (1999, 2003); Byars (2005).
119. "Il sig[no]re Zacomo, et Martin, olim Lazaro hebreo da padua l'isteso giorno fu battizato se parti di casa, et andò ad habitare in casa della sig[no]ra Alba Venetiana in strada di santa Sofia, quale la volse per sua mogliere" (ASPV, CRb, reg. 2, c. 14r (Nov. 11, 1629)).

SURVEILLANCE

As previously noted, financial assistance provided a strong incentive for neophytes to settle permanently in Venice and meet governors' moral standards. Indeed, as a precondition for any assistance from the House, converts were asked to present not only their baptismal certificate but also a letter from their parish priest to ascertain *vita & moribus* (good Christian behavior and periodic confession).[120] After 1623, all neophytes departing from the House were, in addition, required to report their whereabouts every three months.[121] In 1613, the governors threatened to discontinue the stipend of Lucia-Sultana, a convert and a long-time recipient of House charity, unless she moved out of her current residence and refrained from visiting homes that were "scandalous and contrary to the Catholic faith." Earlier inquiries concerning Sultana's morality and poverty seem to have satisfied the governors. She was even given a small regular stipend throughout 1611–12. Ultimately, in 1615 Lucia-Sultana joined the pizzochere tertiary laywomen of San Stefano. The House provided her with a stipend for rent, clothing, and food for the first year, later extended for a second year "or until some other funding source came up."[122] In another case in 1615, the governors gave 12 lire and 12 soldi in charity to a convert turned commercial broker "upon proof of confession and communion." The man had been baptized twenty years earlier, in May 1595.[123]

How effective the supervision by parish priests and the periodic head counts were in inducing converts' proper behavior is hard to gauge. Yet the very notion that governors should keep track of neophytes for decades after their baptism suggests the extent to which the relationship of the institution with its former charges was understood to be lifelong rather than limited to the period of catechization in preparation for baptism. Conversely, the attempt itself to exercise lasting disciplinary control over neophytes was hardly unique. The Tridentine reform was a project of comprehensive social discipline, a reorganization of parishioners' daily life and its subjection to close supervision by parish clergy.[124] In that sense, neophytes seemed particularly suitable subjects for ecclesiastical injunctions, applied in this period to other groups as well.

120. AIRE, CAT A 1, c. 23.
121. ASPV, CRb, reg. 2, c. 7r (Feb. 16, 1622 m.v.).
122. AIRE, CAT B 6, c. 71r (May 23, 1613); c. 91r (May 29, 1615); c. 102r (June 3, 1616). See also AIRE, CAT B 6, cc. 13r–v, 17r, 19r, 29r, 33r, 38r, 45r, 54r, 55v, 56r, 58v, 63v, 66r, 76r.
123. AIRE, CAT B 4, c. 47v (April 12, 1595); c. 48r (May 12, 1595); AIRE, CAT B 6, c. 87r (Jan. 8, 1614 m.v.).
124. On Tridentine emphasis on parochial conformity, and on social discipline in early modern Italy more broadly, see Bossy (1970); Prodi and Penuti (1994); Prodi and Reinhard (1996); de Boer (2003).

Another way for the governors to keep in close touch with neophytes was to employ them within the House, even in positions requiring a high level of trust. In 1613, the governors elected a Jewish convert, Giovanni Battista Malipiero, as the House bookkeeper, pledging to pay him 10 ducats per year in return for his keeping the register and arriving in the House periodically to note down the governors' decisions.[125] In 1615, they appointed as solicitor Iseppo Strassoldo, who had converted with his son and two daughters some years earlier. His task was to collect money owed the House from credits and legacies. On other occasions, Strassoldo was entrusted with keeping the keys to the House archives and sent on a fund-raising mission to Rome—both responsible and sensitive assignments.[126] As previously noted, converts were regularly sent as alms-collectors for the House to various parts of the Venetian state, with a percentage of the money collected to be kept by the collector as a means of supporting himself and his family.

Hiring poorer members of a congregation to perform tasks previously undertaken by volunteers from among the membership was a typical development of late-sixteenth-century Venetian confraternities.[127] For the House governors, in addition to minimizing expenses, such arrangements allowed the use of funds as an extra carrot for inducing converts' good behavior. In 1612, the convert Geronima took into her care the young neophyte Orsetta and another convert's two newborn babies, who remained in her custody for the next decade. The monthly stipend paid her for keeping these neophytes in her household supported both her and her convert husband Francesco, a builder. Francesco himself, like other converts who had already established themselves as artisans, was assigned a young neophyte apprentice with a contract, after the latter had quit an earlier assignment to a vocational school for dealers in secondhand clothes.[128]

Although the governors clearly considered it their duty to secure neophytes' shelter and employment upon baptism, not all their charges appreciated such efforts. The records, brief as they are, allow us a glimpse of at least some dissenting converts who did not welcome these governors' paternalistic disciplinary interventions. In 1595, two Jewish neophytes, accused of leading a "bad lifestyle" and consorting with a "malicious sort of women" were threatened with being removed from House protection and having their stipends revoked. When these admonitions did not meet with any results, the governors asked the archbishop of Split to strongly

125. AIRE, CAT B 6, c. 64v (Jan. 24, 1612 m.v.).
126. AIRE, CAT B 6, c. 90r (April 23, 1615); c. 90v (April 30, 1615); c. 94v (Oct. 15, 1615).
127. Glixon (2003, 2).
128. AIRE, CAT B 6, c. 61v (Dec. 14, 1612); c. 63v (Jan. 18, 1612 m.v.); c. 84r (June 12, 1613); c. 85v (Sept. 4, 1614). References to young neophytes kept by Geronima appear in the register up to its end in 1619.

chastise the two and further decreed that, until they behaved like good Christians, the wayward neophytes were to fast on Wednesdays and Fridays, confess to the Jesuit friars at the church of Umiltà, and be prevented from leaving the House unless accompanied by the prior. If all failed, they were to also be denied bread and milk. Only after being threatened with removal from the House altogether did the disobedient neophytes come to meet the governors' demands. They were then unceremoniously led to the patriarch for their reconciliation ceremony.[129]

Some converts were more resolute in rejecting the governors' efforts to intervene in their future. In March 1619, a neophyte named Antonio (formerly Assan), from a village near Skopje (Macedonia), left the House to join his friend Michiele, another convert baptized twelve days earlier. Both had decided to go to Mestre to join a cavalry company. As the House prior noted, Antonio left

> without wishing to wait for the Congregation to procure accommodation, and said he wanted to go … nor did he wish to heed my admonitions as Prior, in which I begged him and begged him again to stay, attend confession and communion for Easter, and let the Venerable Congregation provide for him. I also showed him that his [actions] were a temptation and a clear sign of wishing to be a bad Christian; to which he did not respond other than [by saying:] give me my proof [of baptism], for I want to go away, and so he left, or rather he went to Ca' da Mula in the parish of San Vio, where the aforementioned Michiele lived, and they left together.[130]

Much to the House prior's chagrin, Antonio and Michiele rejected the spiritual and financial security offered to those who stayed in Venice and under the governors' watchful eyes. The governors intended to place Antonio in the service of Ottavio dall'Oglio, who later employed several other converts, whereas Michiele had already been placed in the house of the patrician Alvise da Mula.[131] Instead, the two opted for employment away from the city, among fellow converts. This

---

129. AIRE, CAT B 4, c. 48v (May 18, 1595); c. 52r (July 20, 1595); c. 52v (July 24, 1595); c. 53r (Aug. 3, 1595); c. 53v (Aug. 10, 1595).

130. "Senza voler aspettar la Cong[regazio]ne la quale procurava accomodarlo, disse voler andar à Mestre p[er] entrar in una Compagnia di Cavalli, ne volse accettare le amonitioni fatteli da me Priore, q[ua]le lo pregai, e ripregai à voler fermarsi, co[n]fessarsi, e co[m]municarsi p[er] Pasqua e lasciarsi provedere dalla Venerabil Cong[regazio]ne mostrandoli esser la sua una Tentatione, e segno manifesto di voler esser poco buon christiano; alche altro no[n] rispose seno' datemi la mia fede, che voglio andar via, e così se n'andò, anzi andò à cha da Mula à San Vio dove si era accommodato il retroscritto Michiele, lo sviò, e se n'andorono insieme" (ASPV, CRb, reg. 2, cc. 4r–v (March 23, 1619); AIRE, CAT B 6, c. 134v (Dec. 20, 1618)).

131. ASPV, CRb, reg. 2, c. 3v (March 11, 1619); AIRE, CAT B 6, c. 140r (March 14, 1619).

case may have inspired others. Only three days later, Francesco (formerly Suliman) similarly set out to try his luck as a soldier in Padua rather than wait for the House "to provide for him, even though his godfather and the scribe of the ship Mascherina, who had brought him to the House, wished to place him in a trade," as the prior lamented.[132]

As these records suggest, the governors understood the role of the institution as not merely to catechize its charges and then set them up with means of supporting themselves but also to socialize them as morally upright and economically productive members of Venetian metropolitan society. Sometimes this warranted disciplinary action. In 1631, Giovanni Giacomo (formerly Mustafâ from Izmir), who had been baptized the previous year and posted onboard ship, was sent away. When he returned less than a month later, the governors declared him a "scurrilous person," foulmouthed and obstinate, and banished him "so that he does not harm the other children of the House."[133] Conversely, only rarely were disciplinary measures taken against neophytes simply for holding unorthodox beliefs. In May 1598, a neophyte named Marco, a catechumen for the previous six months, was removed from the House for eight days with a small stipend "in order to see if he can be cured from his contempt for the Holy Mass and for the veneration of sacred images."[134] I could not find indications of similar measures taken against any neophytes already baptized. The overall laxity in enforcing converts' doctrinal conformity (as opposed to the careful attention to their socially normative behavior) fits a larger pattern in Venice, where, as a rule, authorities tended to curb theological heterodoxy primarily when it might lead to public scandal. This further suggests how the House of Catechumens functioned as a trans-imperial institution, geared to producing loyal juridical and social subjects rather than merely saving souls.

For both (primarily local) Jews and (primarily émigré) Muslims, becoming Catholic in early modern Venice entailed a prolonged process of social transformation and insertion into new social relations of patronage and surrogate kinship. In this sense, baptism marked the beginning, rather than the end, of a transformative process. Because aptitude for self-transformation was understood to be heavily dependent on a convert's moral, physical, and intellectual quali-

---

132. "Non volse aspettar, che la Venerabil Congregatione gli provedesse, et se ben Il suo santolo, et lo scrivano della Nave Mascherina, che lo condusse alla Casa lo volevano mettere à un'arte no' volse acco[n]sentire, ma disse voler andar à Padoa p[er] soldato, e cosi se n'andò senza haver cosa alcuna dalla Casa" (ASPV, CRb, reg. 2, c. 44 (March 17, 1619)).

133. ASPV, CRb, reg. 2, c. 15r (Aug. 5, 1630); c. 15v (March 8, 1631).

134. "Per veder se si corregge dal disprezzo per la messa e per la devozione alle sacre immagini" (AIRE, CAT B 4, c. 86r (May 28, 1598)).

ties, a radical break with his or her previous life was only seldom attempted, and even more rarely achieved. Instead, converts' preexisting social networks were crucial in determining their itineraries after baptism. Local Jewish converts, especially those male adults who commanded Italian and who had a trade, valued intellectual skills, or some prior contacts among Venetian elites, were less dependent on the House to provide them with employment and thereby define the terms of their insertion into society. Muslim converts, whose only available career paths were often domestic service (especially for women) or the military (for men), frequently with their prebaptismal masters, depended much more on House patronage in the long run. Strong incentives to maintain good ties with the House were further provided by the prospects of marriage with local artisans or fellow converts, financial support, and employment opportunities facilitated by the governors and by the convert's godparents. These potential resources, and the hierarchical relations they helped cement, were rooted in many converts' original status as immigrant servants and slaves.

More broadly, conversion in early modern Venice operated as a mechanism for the transformation of Muslims and Jews, two prototypical others of the Venetian state, into properly constituted Catholic subjects, capable of filling normative kinship and institutional roles in metropolitan Venetian society. In addition to producing such subjects, leading non-Christians to the font also brought moral prestige to converts' patrons, who thus participated in a more general, imperial enterprise of projecting the self-image of Venice as a Christian republic beyond its frontiers.

Following Simmel's famous definition of *strangers* as full-fledged organic members of the groups to which they come to attach (see the introduction), I consider Muslim and Jewish converts to Catholicism as essential members of early modern Venetian metropolitan society. Not only was the position of the converts determined by the multiplicity of shifting social relations in that society, but their very insertion therein shaped Venetian social relations, as well as boundaries of inclusion and exclusion. Indeed, conversion through the House of Catechumens operated not only to transform non-Christians into loyal subjects of the Venetian state but also to define the mutual obligations of different kinds of subjects within metropolitan society and between metropolitan and colonial subjects. Through the guardianship and spiritual kinship of converts, the House articulated an important self-understanding of Venetian patrician and citizen elites as disinterested guarantors of the common good of the Republic. At the same time, through the administration of bequests and the negotiation of dowries, adoption, and employment and apprenticeship contracts, the House governors wove dense horizontal and vertical networks of patronage and clientage, with both the converts and governors themselves as nodal points for the distribution of money, power, and affect. In other words, individual patricians and citizens could thus further their private interests while exercising forms of charity that constituted them as moral individuals and as political subjects. By partaking in a ritualized ideological victory over the Ottomans, the House governors and benefactors became the executors of the common good of the Republic. At the same time, by casting this ideological victory in terms of religious conversion, and by collaborating with both Jesuits and locally appointed patrician clergy, the House championed Venetian claims to Catholic orthodoxy in the face of pervasive criticism from Rome. Finally, through practices such as alms-collecting campaigns throughout the Venetian Terraferma and the resettlement of converts in various colonial outposts, the House also participated in the process of empire-building.

PART III

Translation

5

Making Venetian Dragomans

W hether due to the growing presence of Ottoman merchants in Venice or to the standardization of diplomatic protocol between the two empires, by the early sixteenth century official interpreters to and from Turkish became ubiquitous in the official dealings of Venice with Ottoman subjects. Early documents make little distinction between the services that bilingual secretaries rendered as translators, either in Venice proper or in its maritime colonies, and their occasional work for the Board of Trade as face-to-face interpreters accompanying sojourning merchants and dignitaries. But by the mid-sixteenth century, a distinction had emerged—in practice although not always in terminology—between interpreter and dragoman, with important consequences for how Ottoman linguistic difference was conceptualized and managed in Venice and for the presumed nature of mediation itself. In this chapter, I trace the emergence of specialized Public Dragomans, official interpreters employed by the Venetian Board of Trade to assist Ottoman subjects while sojourning in Venice. I follow the trans-imperial trajectories of virtually all holders of this office over the first 150 years of its existence and consider how they merged the practices of self-representation and engaging officialdom that typified metropolitan Venetian elites with ones developed by dragomans in Istanbul at around the same time.

Long before the office of Public Dragoman was institutionalized in Venice, interpreters were employed throughout the Venetian maritime empire, where they facilitated communication with non-Italian-speaking populations.[1] Interpreters for Greek and Slavic especially were in great demand in the Venetian Adriatic, Mediterranean, and Aegean colonial chancelleries. Some of the interpreters employed there, although themselves Venetian colonial subjects, were newcomers to the locales in which they served.[2] This was in line with general Venetian colonial policy, which, in an effort to prevent the consolidation of potentially rebellious local bureaucratic elites, discouraged the employment of immigrant settlers in the colonial administration.[3] Indeed, the (often handsomely salaried) office of interpreter was one of the benefices through which the Venetian central government sought to maintain the goodwill of powerful colonial families while allowing them a certain degree of physical and social mobility.[4]

Unlike these colonial interpreters, the Venetian institution of dragoman, whether as a diplomatic interpreter aiding the bailo in Istanbul or as a chancellery secretary seconded to the Board of Trade in Venice, was clearly an adaptation of the Ottoman office of Grand Dragoman (*divanı hümayun tercümānı*). Holders of this office enjoyed a prominent position in negotiations with foreign powers

1. On the limited Italianization of Venetian colonies, see Cortelazzo (1989a); Eufe (2003; 2005). At the same time, throughout the first half of the seventeenth century, returning *provveditori* (governors) of Zakynthos repeatedly urged the Venetian Senate to abolish the position of "interpreter of Greek letters." In their *relazioni*, Maffio Michiel (1605), Agostino Sagredo (1625), Zuan Bondumier (1633), Stefano Capello (1637), and Antonio Molino (1644) all suggested that the position was superfluous because very few Greek letters were ever in need of translation and because many other bilingual chancellery employees were available for the task. That the position was maintained despite these repeated suggestions perhaps speaks more to the need to keep worthy individuals on the payroll than to the overall linguistic limitations of colonial administration. See Arvanitakis (2000, 172, 231, 247, 269, 315).
2. See, for instance, references to Zuan Madachi, interpreter to the Venetian Capitan General in 1532; the replacement of the "interpreter and chancellor of Greek Letters" on Nauplion, friar Anzino Spiera alias Hadriano, by one Zaneto Aliprando in 1533; the election of Giovanni Aggiondrito of Methoni by the Provveditor General in Kefalonia as "interprete della lingua greca" in 1553; the election of Giovanni Britanico by the *Rettori* of Zadar as "interprete della lingua schiava" in 1567; and, a century later, the election of Silvio Dragazza by the captain of Trogir as "interprete della lingua illirica" (Sanuto 1969, 57:230 (Oct. 19, 1532), 476 (Jan. 31, 1532 m.v.); Cinque Savi, Risposte, 137, cc. 95v–96r (Nov. 12, 1553); b. 154, c. 104r (Jan. 24, 1648 m.v.); Senato Mar, reg. 38, c. 39 (Sept. 1, 1567). On Corfu in 1571, the post of dragoman was one of only four to which local subjects could not qualify (Miller 1908, 533). On the importance of interpreters to colonial administration throughout the Venetian maritime state, see Thiriet (1959, 217–19). On the duties of colonial secretaries/interpreters in sixteenth-century Venetian Corfu, see Karapidakis (1992, 191–92, 204, 207). For a brief discussion of the duties of interpreters in Venetian service in Dalmatia, see Pederin (1990, 324). On the practice of recruiting local interpreters in Cyprus after the Ottoman conquest, see Çiçek (2002).
3. Instead, Venetian citizens and patricians who were sent on short-term assignments to the colonies reported directly to the Senate (McKee 2000, 21). See also Arbel 1995b.
4. On the attenuation of direct rule through the flexible distribution of offices on Venetian Crete, see O'Connell (2001).

as de facto ambassadors, and a diplomatic mission to Venice was part and parcel of the process of confirmation of all Ottoman Grand Dragomans up to the War of Cyprus (1571).[5] Many sixteenth-century Ottoman Grand Dragomans came from the ranks of converts and captives, including Yunus Bey (d. 1551, son of Giorgio Taroniti of the town of Methoni, which the Ottomans conquered from the Venetians in 1500), Ahmed (the Viennese Heinz Tulman), İbrahim Bey (the Pole Joachim Strasz), and the Hungarian Murad bin Abdullah.[6] In other words, these dragomans were themselves trans-imperial subjects whose familiarity with foreign languages, speech styles, and courtly etiquette was essential for their success in this powerful office. Several holders of this position, including Yunus Bey and İbrahim Bey, maintained lifelong ties with relatives across the border, as well as professional and personal ties with members of the Venetian elite.[7] By the mid-seventeenth century, such trans-imperial recruits were replaced by members of prominent Greek families of the Istanbul quarter of Phanar (hence their collective name, Phanariots). Their metropolitan birth, however, did not mean they lacked trans-imperial ties; many of them were educated in Padua or Rome, were competent in numerous languages, and possessed strong political and intellectual ties across various capitals.[8]

The term *turchimanus* (also spelled *torcimano, turcimano, terzimano, dragumano, drogumano*, or *drogomanus*) appears in Latin notarial records from the Genoese colonies of Pera (across the Golden Horn from Constantinople) and Caffa (Feodosiya, on the Crimean Black Sea coast) as early as the 1280s.[9] Its Italian cognates, *dragoman/dragomano* appear in Venetian and other Italian diplomatic records starting

---

5. Pedani (1994, 41).
6. Matuz (1975); Pedani (1994); Krstić (2009).
7. For example, during his embassies to Venice, Yunus Bey repeatedly asked for favors for his relatives on the island of Zakynthos. In the 1530s, he also collaborated with Alvise Gritti, the illegitimate son of Venetian doge Andrea Gritti and himself an Istanbul-based courtier, in the publication of a treatise on Ottoman government in Venetian dialect. Yunus maintained business ties and personal friendships with several Venetian patricians who hosted him in their homes during his numerous visits to the city. İbrahim Bey corresponded with Michiel Membré. On Yunus, see Lybyer (1913, 314:16); Pedani (1994, 144–53). On İbrahim, see Bombaci (1948); Conley (2002).
8. On the Phanariot dragomans, see Janos (2006). On the institution of Ottoman Grand Dragoman in general, see Balcı (2006).
9. See, for example, notarial records no. XXXVI, CLXX, CLXXXII, CXC, CCXCVIII, CCCXVIII, CCCXIX in Brâtianu (1927, 95, 185, 194, 199, 272, 289, 290), dated July 10, 1281; May 5, 1289; May 14, 1289; May 26, 1289; April 27, 1290; May 12, 1290; and May 13, 1290, respectively. Many of these records refer to the same person, Pietro "dragoman of the Genoese" (*torcimano pro Januensis*), suggesting that the office was already institutionalized to some degree. At the same time, the variations in orthography, although common in documents of this period, may indicate the relative newness of the term itself. Of the various spellings, *torcimano* is by far the most common in this sample. The Latin translation of a letter by the Mongol il-khan Arghun to Pope Honorius IV (1285) similarly refers to certain "Ise turciman" and "Ugeto turciman." See Howorth (1880, 348).

in the late fifteenth century. For example, the statutes of the Florentine nation (i.e., resident merchant community) in Istanbul in 1488 mention the consul's right to hire one dragoman, pending approval by a majority of the merchants.[10] A contemporary list of expenses for a Venetian embassy to the Porte refers, inter alia, to payments to a dragoman in Gallipoli.[11] By that time, the term *dragoman* appears in numerous other Venetian documents without a gloss, suggesting a certain level of familiarity with the institution among political elites. In these documents, the term denotes either an Ottoman government official (whether in Istanbul or on a diplomatic mission abroad); an interpreter employed by foreign embassies to the Porte or to the Mamluk court in Cairo; or, indeed, one aiding foreign merchants in other eastern Mediterranean ports.[12]

By the early sixteenth century, Venetian diplomatic missions to the Porte usually included a dragoman who accompanied the ambassador on his trip from Venice. Daily interactions between the bailo and Ottoman officials were initially carried out mostly via the Ottoman Grand Dragoman. For example, a letter by bailo Leonardo Bembo in 1518 mentions that the Ottoman Grand Dragoman "Ali Bey wished to speak in our defense, [but] he was rebuffed by the Pasha, and kept silent." A few paragraphs later, however, the letter mentions that "dragoman Zuan Spinola provides good service and is commended."[13] This arrangement did not last long. A few weeks later in a ciphered letter, the bailo urged the government to "send another dragoman, who would be our subject, and would have the spirit to speak [up]."[14] A third letter shortly thereafter confirmed that a new

10. "Capitoli della colonia dei fiorentini in Costantinopoli (1488, dicembre 15). Copia autentica sincrona" (Archivio di Stato di Firenze, Consoli del Mare, reg. XII, cc. 243–59 (Classe XI, distinzione IV, n. 88), item XI; available in a modern edition in Masi (1941), 47.

11. "Per contati al ofitial del sobassi che accompagno el turziman de notte aspri 8" (March 18, 1488, quoted in Bertolini 1881, 134)).

12. Venetian documents relating to commercial and diplomatic dealings with the Mamluks in the last two decades of the fifteenth century regularly mention Grand Dragoman Tangravardi, a Mamluk of Circassian origin stationed in Damascus (Sanuto 1969, 7:596 (Nov. 1507)). A guide to pilgrims penned by Venetian patrician Francesco Suriano in 1484 mentions a 1-ducat obligatory payment to the Mamluk Soldan's dragoman for anyone traveling to the Holy Land, whether a merchant, a mariner, or a pilgrim (Suriano 1900, 17). Giacomo Contarini's *relazione* from his mission to Istanbul in 1507 refers to the Florentines' "valentissimo dragoman . . . che si chiama Baptista Salvaressa, il quale fu altra fiata dragoman salariato de vostra celsitudine" (Sanuto 1969, 7:19 (1507)). On Salvaressa/Salvarese/Sarvarosa, who was born in Caffa (Feodosiya), see also the Florentine documents reproduced in Müller (1966, 258–59, 266). A letter from Ragusa in 1521 mentions "the son of our dragoman to the Porte" (Sanuto 1969, 32:21 (Oct. 10, 1521)).

13. "Alibei dragoman volse parlar in justification nostra; il Bassà li fe' uno rebufo; li convene tacer" (Sanuto 1969, 26:263 (Oct. 12, 1518)). "Zuan Spinola dragoman fa bon oficio et lo ricomanda" (Sanuto 1969, 26:265 (Oct. 12, 1518)).

14. "Voria si provedesse di uno altro dragoman fusse subdito nostro e li bastasse l'animo di parlar" (Sanuto 1969, 26:302 (Nov. 14, 1518)).

dragoman was needed because Ali Bey, who used to render good services to the bailo, could no longer be trusted to do so.[15]

Simultaneous employment as both Ottoman and Venetian dragoman in Istanbul was not limited to Ali Bey's case. During his embassy to Venice in 1533, Yunus Bey, the Ottoman Grand Dragoman, "spoke through the interpreter Girolamo Civran, but understood everything that the Doge said to him, as he was the dragoman of the [Venetian] nation at the Porte."[16] This reliance on Ottoman state officials as occasional interpreters for the bailo was short-lived, however. Already by the first decade of the sixteenth century, a dragoman was retained as a member of the bailo's household and eventually became a fixture in all communication between the bailo and the Porte.[17] The bailo's dragomans were initially hired locally, from the Latin (Roman-Catholic) community of Pera, a suburb of Istanbul. By the mid-sixteenth century, additional dragomans were recruited from Venetian colonial nobilities throughout the Adriatic and Mediterranean, as well as from prominent families of citizens by birth in Venice itself. Regardless of their diverse provenance, most dragomans were apprenticed in the bailo's house from their early teens and often served in various colonial outposts before assuming more prestigious appointments in either Istanbul or Venice. Thanks to a high degree of intermarriage among dragoman families, by the early seventeenth century the Venetian dragomans in Istanbul formed a highly unified and endogamous cadre.[18] This endogamy had important consequences for how dragomans understood their office and, as a result, for how they engaged both Ottoman and Venetian officialdom.

Alongside the institutionalization of the office of dragoman attached to the Venetian bailo's house in Istanbul and the office of chancellery interpreter in the maritime colonies, by the early sixteenth century we see the emergence of

15. "Ali beì turziman, qual prima li deva ogni favor, adesso non lo serve ben, *imo* non si vol impazar e dise vilania al suo dragoman" (Sanuto 1969, 26:417 (Dec. 6, 1518)).
16. "parlava per Hironimo Zivran interpetre, ma intendeva tuto quelo li diceva il Serenissimo per esser dragoman de la nation a la Porta" (Sanuto 1969, 57:413 (Jan. 9, 1532 m.v.)).
17. Sanuto's summary of bailo Agostin Bernardo's letter of 1511 mentions the ambassador's audience with the sultan, at which only a few members of the bailo's house were honored with gifts, including the carver, a servant, and the dragoman "that is, mister Jacomo da Rimano" (Sanuto 1969, 12:173 (April 22, 1511)). Rimano, born c. 1473 and taken captive by the Ottomans in Negroponte, apparently became the bailo's dragoman in 1503. He certainly appears as such in Andrea Gritti's *Relazione* of 1503, where the returning bailo relates how, during a border dispute, Ali Bey, Grand Dragoman for the Porte, suggested that the two of them should prepare a joint translation of a letter and a treaty, to be signed by both parties. A few months later, he was in Venice and served as interpreter to a party of dignitaries who received an Ottoman ambassador (Sanuto 1969, 5:26 (April 26, 1503), 450 (Dec. 29, 1503), 746 (Jan. 17, 1503 m.v.), 802 (February 4, 1503 m.v.), 835 (Feb. 10, 1503 m.v.), 1022 (March 21, 1504))).
18. For a detailed discussion of Venetian dragomans' recruitment, training, and employment in the Ottoman capital, see Rothman (2009a).

the office of Public Dragoman in Venice proper, a position unparalleled in other Italian states. This institution combined the diplomatic functions of the Ottoman Grand Dragoman with the mercantile duties of the bailo's dragomans (who, in addition to their involvement in diplomatic negotiations were charged with assisting Venetian merchants in Istanbul in their dealings with local merchants and Ottoman magistracies). Unlike the interpreters employed in the Venetian colonial administration, Public Dragomans mediated not between the rulers and the ruled but between government officials and Ottoman and Safavid sojourners, both diplomatic envoys and merchants. Thus, whereas in the Ottoman context dragomans dealt with both subject populations and foreign dignitaries of all provenances, in Venice they dealt primarily with foreigners. Moreover, their position was unique in Venice as well because the only specialized full-time interpreters on record in the Venetian chancellery during this period were for Turkish and Greek.[19] The very association of the presumed foreignness of Ottoman sojourners with special linguistic needs thus became institutionalized in Venice in ways that the foreignness of the subjects of other neighboring states was not.[20]

The duties of the Public Dragoman in Venice were multiple: to translate official letters sent to the doge by the sultan, as well as internal Ottoman correspondence intercepted by the Venetians; to accompany Ottoman dignitaries on official audiences and produce authoritative reports on such occasions; to travel to the Venetian-Ottoman borderlands to negotiate in border disputes; and, most frequently, to assist Ottoman and Safavid merchants in Venice in their interactions with often less-than-scrupulous merchants and commercial brokers. The Public Dragoman's position can thus be summarized as two-pronged; he was a civil servant, expected to keep tabs on Ottoman and Safavid foreigners and report on their whereabouts to his patrician employers, the Senate and the Board of Trade; at the same time, he was charged with safeguarding Ottoman merchants' interests under the assumption that they were vulnerable and in need of special protection due to their lack of connections in the city.[21]

---

19. Neff (1985, 60).
20. With Latin and Italian the dominant languages of European diplomacy well into the seventeenth century, the Venetian government had only limited use for translation and interpretation to and from most other vernacular languages. Sanuto's rare references to a chancellery secretary providing translations for German documents sent by the emperor or offering simultaneous interpretation to Russian or Hungarian emissaries confirm the sense that, by and large, Venetian use of interpreters for languages other than Turkish was unusual. On the dominance of Latin and Italian in the linguistic training of Renaissance diplomats, see Roland (1999, 44).
21. On the early modern legal doctrine of foreigners' "lack of relational resources," see Cerutti (1995).

This two-pronged position is well illustrated by the career trajectories of the first Venetian interpreters for Turkish, Teodoro Paleologo and Girolamo Civran. Paleologo, born in 1452, had initially served as Ottoman tax collector in the Peloponnese. In 1478, he left the Ottoman Empire to become the commander of a Venetian stradiot cavalry company, a career that took him all across the Venetian maritime and mainland empire. In 1500, his knowledge of Turkish prompted the Venetian government to send him along with Ambassador Alvise Manenti, secretary of the Council of Ten, to negotiate with Ottoman officials in Edirne. On retiring from military service in 1517, Paleologo settled in Venice and became a prominent member of the local Greek Orthodox community. That same year, Paleologo translated into Italian the newly signed Venetian-Ottoman peace treaty.[22] On numerous occasions, he appeared in front of the government as a spokesperson for the Orthodox community and was among those who purchased a plot of land to build an Orthodox church in the city in 1526, the future church of San Giorgio. He is recorded as interpreting the speeches of Ottoman ambassadors in the Venetian Senate and assisting them throughout their Venetian sojourns in 1518 and 1530, as well as partaking in three diplomatic missions to Istanbul in 1517, 1527, and 1530. In 1524, Paleologo traveled to Dalmatia to aid Venetian ambassador Pietro Zen during border negotiations with the governor of Bosnia. He died in 1532.[23]

Girolamo Civran was born in the late fifteenth century in the small port town of Methoni, at the western tip of the Peloponnese peninsula, to a Venetian citizen family sent there to found a Venetian colony.[24] When the Ottomans occupied Methoni in 1500, Civran fell into captivity, whereupon he learned Turkish. On his release and arrival in Venice, he pursued a career as a chancellery secretary, and from 1515 on, he is recorded as serving as interpreter of Greek and Turkish during Ottoman officials' visits. From 1524 to 1531, he was sent to Dalmatia on numerous occasions, where he interpreted in border negotiations between Venetian and Ottoman provincial governors. Despite these trans-imperial trajectories, and the breadth of the Civran family commercial network spanning various parts of the Venetian Empire, Civran's will of 1548 listed only one person of colonial background, Paolo de Signa, a priest from Koroni who served as the chaplain of the

---

22. Theunissen (1999, 10).
23. Sanuto (1969, 25:53 (Oct. 28, 1517); 31:382 (Sept. 9, 1521); 37:50–51 (Oct. 16, 1524); 41:616 (June 16, 1526); 43:51 (Oct. 9, 1526), 127 (Oct. 25, 1526); 46:177 (Oct. 8, 1527), 381 (Dec. 18, 1527); 47:210 (April 9, 1528); 49:249 (Dec. 17, 1528); 52:435 (Jan. 1, 1529 m.v.); 54:93 (Oct. 31, 1530)). See also www.condottieridiventura.it/condottieri/p/1358%20%20%20%20%20%20 TEODORO%20PALEOLOGO%20%20Greco.htm.
24. Scarcia (1969, lxiii). Other members of Civran's family settled in various parts of the empire to attend to their commercial affairs.

church of San Zaccharia.[25] As we will see, a similar pattern of Veneto-centric patronage emerges from the extant wills of other Venetian Public Dragomans, despite—or perhaps because of—their extended sojourns abroad.

Although it was only retroactively that Paleologo's and Civran's position was entitled Public Dragoman, their two-pronged diplomatic and commercial duties, and, in Civran's case, his strong affiliation with the newly established Board of Trade, were to characterize the careers of all their successors in that office throughout the sixteenth and seventeenth centuries. Moreover, with the exception of one Public Dragoman, Francesco Scaramelli, all others throughout this period came from colonial and/or trans-imperial backgrounds, whether in Cyprus, Dalmatia, or in Ottoman lands (see table 5.1, later in the chapter).

What made trans-imperial subjects warrant such powerful appointments, against the otherwise clear Venetian tendency to elect only its own citizens by birth to key positions in the administration? In part, this was a matter of exigency, given the rarity of Turkish speakers among Venetian citizens. But another part of the answer may lie in the ways in which specific trans-imperial subjects fashioned themselves as loyal and useful to the state beyond their mere linguistic competence. After Civran's death in 1550, the Board of Trade appointed in his stead Michiel Membré, a powerful and well-traveled Cypriot, whose long tenure as Public Dragoman for almost half a century, from 1550 to 1594, decisively shaped the office.[26] By looking at how Membré came to monopolize a special tax levied on Ottoman merchants' brokerage fees and how others sought to undermine his power, it is possible to see how commercial activity became a central node in defining the role of Public Dragomans as essential intermediaries between Ottoman subjects and the Venetian state.

Membré was born c. 1509 on Cyprus, then still in Venetian hands, and was initially employed in the Venetian island chancellery. He soon caught the attention and patronage of the noble merchant Bernardo Benedetti, to whom he was related through his maternal grandmother.[27] Membré traveled as Benedetti's representative on numerous business trips in the Levant, and on the latter's recommendation, in 1538 he was sent as the Republic envoy to the court of Shah

---

25. Notarile, Testamenti, b. 1209, fasc. 539 (Jan. 8, 1547). Other people mentioned in the will were Civran's wife Semaritana and their children (including an illegitimate son, Michele), a fellow chancellery secretary, and a friar from the church of Santi Giovanni e Paolo. For Civran's employment in the chancellery, see Sanuto (1969, 25:52 (26) (Oct. 28, 1517); 26:249 (133) (Dec. 10, 1518); 29:425 (257) (Nov. 28, 1520)). On the war and its captives and refugees, see Doumerc (2002). For an outline of Civran's career, see Neff (1985, 595); Scarcia (1969, lxiii).
26. On Membré's biography, see Arbel (To appear).
27. On the Benedettis, see Rudt de Collenberg (1982a, 27).

Tahmasp I (1514–1576) in Isfahan.[28] Back in Venice in 1542, he was soon sent to Istanbul to accompany, as a dragoman, Venetian Ambassador Stefano Tiepolo on a special mission.[29] His appointment as Public Dragoman in 1550 was thus in recognition not only of proven linguistic skills but also of previous diplomatic services to the state and strong connections among Ottoman and Safavid elites.[30]

Membré's contacts, knowledge, and business savvy served him in his private enterprises as well as in his work as Public Dragoman. In 1550, he collaborated with Giovanni Battista Ramusio, Venetian cosmographer, and Giacomo Gastaldi, Piemontese printer, in producing a map of Asia and the eastern Mediterranean. In 1559, he helped translate into Turkish the text of a world map, following a 1553 Senate order to print such a map for Ottoman Prince Selim. It was possibly the same printable woodcut heart-shaped map that in 1568 Marc'Antonio Giustinian, governor of the island of Kefalonia, tried to produce for the Ottoman market, again with Membré's assistance.[31] These cartographic enterprises combined commercial and political interests. By harnessing the specialized linguistic skills he had acquired in Istanbul and Persia to the service of Venetian commercial, scholarly, and diplomatic milieus, Membré, a seasoned entrepreneur, benefitted handsomely. His three surviving wills all left generous bequests to relatives and charities around the city.[32]

INHERITANCE BATTLES

The position of Public Dragoman and its attendant assumptions about dragomans' skill and loyalty were shaped during not only Michiel Membré's long tenure but during also that of his two assistants and soon-to-become successors, Giacomo de Nores and Andrea Negroni. Their 1594 petitions for employment offer a glimpse into the shifting nature of mediation between Venetian and Ottoman subjects as articulated in the presumed prerequisites for service as Public

---

28. A *relazione* of that trip was delivered to the Senate on his return in 1542 (Membré 1969).

29. Capi del Consiglio dei Dieci, Lettere di Ambasciatori, Costantinopoli, b. 1, c. 182a (Sept. 15, 1545); Compilazione Leggi, b. 146, c. 786 (June 29,1547). See also Scarcia (1969, lxii). In his petition for Venetian citizenship in 1565, Membré claimed to have been living in Venice continuously since 1542. Remarkably enough, the Board of Trade denied his request for citizenship *de intus et extra* because he was a year and a half short of the twenty-five-year residency requirement and approved only his citizenship *de intus tantu* (Collegio, Risposte di dentro, b. 1, c. 188 (Oct. 23, 1565); Cinque Savi, Risposte, b. 135, cc. 127v–128r (Nov. 19, 1565)).

30. Among his numerous contacts, Membré maintained friendly correspondence with İbrahim, an Ottoman Grand Dragoman of Polish extraction, who in letters from Ragusa in 1567 informed him of the latest Ottoman victories in Hungary and of various commercial enterprises of Ottoman merchants in Venice (Conley 2002, 265). See also Bombaci (1948).

31. Arbel (2002a). See also Ménage (1958); Fabris (1989); Casale (2005).

32. Notarile, Testamenti, b. 394, fasc. 625 (July 14, 1591); b. 1245, fasc. 561 (Oct 25, 1594); Ospedali e luoghi pii diversi, b. 86, fasc. GG (Nov. 21, 1594).

Dragoman.[33] They further suggest how trans-imperial trajectories came to be seen as essential for becoming a Venetian Public Dragoman. De Nores and Negroni had both served as Membré's assistants since 1589, monitoring transactions between brokers and Ottoman merchants.[34] Both had been involved in repeated litigations with Membré during the last five years of his life for his failure to pay their salary in a timely manner.[35] And, upon his death, both produced lengthy petitions in an effort to convince the Senate of their suitability as his replacement (and superiority over one another). They were both appointed Public Dragomans in 1594. Their arguments, however, were strikingly different.

Born c. 1569 in Nicosia, the capital of the then-Venetian colony of Cyprus, de Nores was the descendant of two of the oldest and most distinguished local noble families, the de Nores and the Podocataros, whose roots on Cyprus extended back to the Crusades.[36] Shortly after Giacomo's birth, his eponymous paternal grandfather, the count of Tripoli, was killed while defending Nicosia from the besieging Ottomans (July–September 1570). The following year, Giacomo's maternal grandfather, Viscount of Nicosia Livio Podocataro, lost all his possessions with the Ottoman conquest of the remainder of the island. Consequently, several dozen members of both the de Nores and the Podocataro families, including toddler Giacomo himself, were taken captive and sent to Istanbul, Chios, Rhodes, Algiers, and elsewhere in the Ottoman Empire. Most of them were eventually ransomed and relocated to Venice, Spain, Rome, or other parts of Christendom. But a few, including one of Giacomo's aunts, converted to Islam and stayed in Ottoman territory. Her two daughters later became sultanas to Mehmet III.[37]

Giacomo spent his childhood and youth as a slave in the household of an Ottoman bombardier by the name of Turan Bali of Scutari (Üsküdar, the Anatolian part of Istanbul). In 1581, he traveled with his master to the Safavid frontier, where in all probability he learned some Persian. Six years later, he was ransomed by a Cypriot merchant, Dimitri Gonneme, who paid Turan Bali 260 ducats on behalf of de Nores's mother, Maria Podocataro.[38] At the time of his

33. See appendices 5.1 and 5.2 for transcripts and translations of the two petitions.
34. Their annual salaries of 150 ducats each were paid by Membré out of the revenue he derived from the *terzo* tax (see chap. 7) (Senato Terra, filza 105, unpaginated (Jan. 29, 1587 m.v.)). I thank Maartje van Gelder for the reference.
35. AdC, Misc. Civil, b. 260, fasc. 20, cc. 17–24 (March 31–June 10, 1594).
36. The de Nores were among the Frankish feudatories of the islands, whereas the Podocataros were Greek-Cypriot Catholics. On the Cypriot nobility under Venetian rule, see Arbel (1995a).
37. Rudt de Collenberg (1982a, 52, 60–61). On the de Nores family, see also Nicolaou-Konnari (2006).
38. Notarile, Atti, b. 32, cc. 41r–42v (Feb. 17, 1591 m.v.). The deed for the ransom and power of attorney signed by Maria Podocataro and Dimitri Gonneme are discussed in Corazzol (1994, 776). The author does not identify de Nores as a future dragoman.

release and arrival in Venice in 1587, de Nores was thus a young man of seventeen or eighteen, with no experience in Venetian service and with limited—if any—command of Italian.[39]

De Nores opens his petition by focusing on loyalty stemming from juridical subjecthood, which implicitly sets him apart from Negroni. He dwells at length on his noble lineage and the blood spilled by his ancestors in defense of the lost colony of Cyprus. By emphasizing his noble status and distinguished ancestry—and thus reaffirming his ties to Venice—de Nores might have hoped to overcome concerns about his loyalty, given his many years in Ottoman service. Such emphasis also reminded his patrician interlocutors of their commitment to his well-being as a noble but dispossessed colonial subject.

At the same time, de Nores does not shy away from capitalizing on his Ottoman sojourn. References to his long captivity might have not only induced sympathy for his plight but also lent credibility to his claim to deep knowledge of Ottoman language and society. After discussing his personal merits, de Nores reverts to the first person plural to juxtapose "our" customs with "theirs" (i.e., the Turks'), thus emphasizing his role as an intermediary:

> since it is no less useful for that task to be familiar with the customs of the Turks, their inclinations and their manner of negotiation, *which are very different from ours*, Your Serenity can easily be convinced, that being, I might say, born among these people, and to my bad fortune raised and educated [there], having been involved in their affairs for many years, and traveled in many and diverse provinces and lands here and there.[40]

By using the inclusive first person *our* while narrating his tale of a youth spent in enemy lands, de Nores emphasizes his own distance from the Ottomans (treated in the third person). By positioning himself squarely within a Venetian moral community, de Nores's long sojourn in Ottoman territory becomes an asset rather than a liability; it foregrounds, rather than undermines, Ottoman alterity. His disenfranchisement by the Ottomans comes in this way to strengthen his claim to special sensibilities and helps underscore his antipathy to his former captors.

Andrea Negroni, unlike de Nores (who in 1594 had little actual experience as intermediary to speak of), was by then already an accomplished interpreter, with some twenty years work experience.[41] It is not surprising, therefore, that

---

39. I thank Maria-Pia Pedani (personal communication) for emphasizing these issues.
40. Emphasis added.
41. In the mid-1570s, Negroni served as imperial representative to the Ottoman court. See the travel narrative composed by Johann Jacob Amman, Negroni's physician during a trip through eastern Hungary and the Balkans, *Reisz in das Gelobte Land* (1677–1678).

he begins his petition by narrating at length his diplomatic role in settling border disputes between Venetians and Ottomans, highlighting his interpersonal, military, and political mediation. In that narrative, he invokes specialized diplomatic vocabulary, refers to the Ottoman genre of 'arz, or sultanic decree, and lists his numerous engagements with Ottoman provincial rulers, including the powerful Sinan pasha. The lengthy narrative of his accomplishments takes up two-thirds of the petition and is strewn with a series of active verbs that celebrate his singular agency ("I petitioned . . . went . . . handled . . . wrote down . . . noted . . . put an end . . . stopped . . . went . . . did . . . stated . . . ordered . . ."). He continues with a brief reference to his proficiency in Turkish and (quite hyperbolically, no doubt) his knowledge of "12 Oriental languages." Next, he offers the following general observations about the intermediary's skills, in which he shifts from the first to the third person singular:

> it is not enough to speak it and write it, but to do so prudently, which is that with which those [persons] who possess the greatest understanding and utmost discretion are able to maintain the dignity of their Prince and avoid offending the pride, as it happens, of another great potentate with whom they negotiate. And in explaining in writing it may end up being useful to demonstrate vigor, and boldness, and at the same time good attention and respect, in the ambit of which alone consists the perfection of affairs.[42]

These observations about prudence, vigor, and respect—all central tropes of contemporary humanist understandings of diplomacy—are generalized and abstract, pertinent to any negotiations rather than specific to Venetian-Ottoman relations. Here Negroni reminds the readers of his extensive diplomatic career prior to becoming a Venetian interpreter, without explicitly referring to his non-Venetian patrons and potentially casting doubts about his loyalty. These general observations are followed by only a brief reference to the petitioner's neediness (e.g., his dependent parents, wife, and children). Negroni does not mention his ancestors, presumably because they were, like him, Ottoman subjects (of possible Greek provenance), with no Venetian pedigree to speak of. Unlike de Nores, Negroni's kin are a liability rather than an asset.

---

42. "non bastando il parlare, et lo scrivere mà il prudentemente fare questo, et quello con il quale i più intendenti eversati con singulare discretione possino conservare il decoro del suo Principe, e non offender l'orgoglio per aventura d'altro grande Sig[no]re con cui occora negotiare, et nello spiegare in scrittura po occorer che torni à bene mostrare vigoria, et ardimento, et congiontamente bona mente, et rispetto nella quale sola distrezza consiste la perfetione di negotij") Senato Mar, filza 128, unpaginated (Dec. 9, 1594); another copy is available in Risposte di dentro, b. 10, c. 50).

Negroni's petition thus incorporates both a personal, highly specific account of his involvement in Venetian-Ottoman diplomatic and military negotiations, and some broad observations of an impersonal nature. Combined, these elements serve to emphasize his accomplishments, his skills at conflict resolution, and his deep familiarity with Ottoman bureaucratic hierarchy and diplomatic protocol, gained through extensive practical experience.

The comparison of Giacomo de Nores's and Andrea Negroni's petitions reveals two competing articulations of accomplishments and loyalty in dragomans' understandings of their intermediary work at the end of the sixteenth century. For Negroni, skills were for hire and accumulated from one employment to the next. It was precisely his unattached ability to know both sides that he cast as his greatest merit. Indeed, three years after becoming Venetian Public Dragoman Negroni left Venice to assume another position in the service of the Habsburg emperor.[43] De Nores, who emphasized an emotional and familial attachment to Venice as what allowed him to "see like a Venetian" so shortly after his ransom, stayed on as a Public Dragoman in Venice until his death in 1617. Evidence suggests that at least some of his children remained in Venice. One of his daughters, Elena, married the patrician Francesco Trevisan, and two others, Tadea and Cecilia, became nuns in the convent of Santa Marta.[44] Other family members, including Giacomo's sisters Fiorenza and Lucia, his aunt Elena, and his nephew Livio, also settled in Venice.[45]

Both dragomans instantiated enduring models of trans-imperial subjecthood in the early modern Mediterranean. The de Nores clan, after establishing themselves as potentate local nobility on Cyprus, insinuated themselves into Catholic ecclesiastical and scholarly networks that extended to Rome, Venice, and Padua. Whereas Giacomo settled in Venice, some of his relatives pursued careers elsewhere, including Ottoman Cyprus.[46] Like them, Andrea Negroni placed his skills

43. Spuler (1935, 330); Neck (1950).
44. Notarile, Atti, b. 8454 (April 18, 1645), b. 8460, c. 163r (Feb. 4, 1652 m.v.); b. 8465, cc. 87v–88r (Sept. 18, 1657); b. 8470, c. 39v (May 12, 1662).
45. See Elena de Nores Bustrona's will, taken down by her nephew Livio in Giacomo de Nores' house in early 1605 (Notarile, Testamenti, b. 1177, fasc. 141 (Feb. 23, 1604 m.v.)). On his sisters, including a genealogical tree, see Rudt de Collenberg (1983, 46–57; 1993, 182).
46. In 1647, a certain Calimeris de Nores was active in Larnaca, where he befriended the Venetian consul there, a member of the Cypriot Soderini family. Other branches of the de Nores clan maintained close ties to Venice. Giacomo's great-uncle, the scholar Jason de Nores (1530–1590), left Nicosia in the wake of the Ottoman conquest and moved to Padua, where he was given the chair of moral philosophy at the university. He published astronomical, philosophical, and literary works. His son Pietro, after a duel with a Venetian patrician in 1589, was forced to flee to Rome, where he served as secretary to several cardinals and published historical and literary works. Jason's grandson, Giorgio, born in 1619 in the Venetian colony of Pula in Istria, published a guidebook for secretaries, in which he advocated adherence in writing to "the rule of good Tuscan language." Giorgio de Nores also published a historical discourse on the kingdom of Cyprus, which included

in the service of several patrons, first foreign diplomats and scholars in Istanbul, then the Venetian state, and finally the Habsburg emperor. Viewed over several generations, both the de Nores and the Negroni families "hedged their bets" by weaving dense networks of patronage across empires. That de Nores emphasized his pedigree more than his skills is particularly noteworthy in light of the preponderance of scholars and secretaries among his kin, as well as their dispersion across empires. It was thus not so much his objective difference from Negroni by way of skill or career path as the opportunity to harp on Venetian imperial sentiments over the loss of Cyprus that prompted him to fashion himself first as a worthy and loyal subject and only then as a qualified intermediary.

SERIAL PETITIONING AND TRANS-IMPERIAL SUBJECTHOOD

Whereas de Nores and Negroni highlighted two components of the Public Dragoman's desired profile—accomplishments and loyalty—other crucial elements, such as connections among the Venetian elite and the establishment of dragoman dynastic continuity, were perfected by their two successors. The Venetian-born, Istanbul-trained Francesco Scaramelli (in office 1626–1643) relied on his extensive ties among the Venetian patriciate and on his command of both Venetian and Ottoman semiotics of honor for his performance of mediation. Scaramelli was born in the last decade of the sixteenth century to a family of Venetian citizens by birth. During their long careers as secretaries in the Venetian diplomatic service, Scaramelli's own father, Giovanni Carlo, and brother Moderante sojourned in various capitals, including Milan, London, and Istanbul.[47] Following in their

---

genealogies of the leading families of the island. Giacomo's uncle, Cesare de Nores, was the bishop of the Venetian colony of Piran (Istria) from 1573 to 1597. Several Podocataro family members were prominent clergy. Bishop of Cyprus and later Cardinal Lodovico Podocataro (d. 1504) was buried in Rome. Archbishop Livio Podocataro was buried in the church of San Sebastian in Venice, where a funerary monument was erected for him by Jacopo Sansovino (Arbel 1989a, 187, 189; personal communication; Scarabelli 1847, xx–xxv; Rudt de Collenberg 1982b, 456–57). On the extensive ties of members of the de Nores clan to the intellectual and ecclesiastical elites of Venice, Padua, and Rome, see also Rudt de Collenberg (1983, 1990); Nicolaou-Konnari (2006).

47. Brown (1900, lxii–lxix). Giovanni Carlo served as a high-level Venetian civil servant and diplomat for forty-seven years. His pride in his professional identity can be gleaned already from an early memoir, which he composed in 1569 at age twenty. In it, he criticized Sansovino's ideas about secretaries' inferiority, as articulated in his tract *Del segretario*. Based on his practical experience, Scaramelli recorded the great esteem with which the patrician members of the Council of Ten held their secretaries and the secretaries' de facto authority and influence. Giovanni Carlo's own elevated position enabled him both to secure the status of citizen for his apparently illegitimate eldest son, Moderante, and to guarantee Moderante's and Francesco's entrance into public service (although the latter's election as apprentice dragoman occurred after Giovanni Carlo's death). It also allowed him to marry his daughter Chiara to a Venetian patrician, Bartolomeo Barbaro (Trebbi 1986, 55–56).

footsteps, Francesco trained to be a secretary and a diplomat, and even apprenticed for a decade (1611–1621) as a diplomatic interpreter in the house of the Venetian bailo in Istanbul. On returning from the Ottoman capital, he entered the Venetian ducal chancellery and in 1626 was appointed Public Dragoman.[48] He was the first and only Venetian-born citizen to occupy this position in the seventeenth century. During his long career, Scaramelli was involved in several high-profile and sensitive negotiations with Ottoman officials regarding Ottoman subjects who had converted to Catholicism on Venetian soil. In these negotiations, his assertive stance relied on his status both as a Venetian citizen by birth and as a long-time resident of the Ottoman capital, versant in Ottoman elite culture.[49]

Whereas Scaramelli's career as a Public Dragoman was an extension of his family's typical specialization as civil servants, notaries, and secretaries in the Venetian Chancellery, Pietro Fortis, his successor, was much more of a parvenu. Unlike previous holders of the position, this Istanbul-born subject created a trans-imperial dragoman dynasty that bridged Venetian understandings of the patrimonial state with Ottoman dragomans' expectations about patrilineal succession in office. Fortis, his brother Giacomo, and sons Giacomo and Alvise not only resettled in Venice after two generations in Istanbul but trained in languages from a young age, specifically in anticipation of their entry into Venetian service as dragomans. This model of familial career development prevailed among dragoman families in Istanbul, but the Fortis were the first to import it to Venice. One way to explore their strategy, and the vision of Venetian-Ottoman mediation it implies, is by looking at the trajectories and petitioning practices of Pietro Fortis, the founder of the dynasty, over three and a half decades, from shortly before his appointment as Public Dragoman in Venice in 1643 to the Senate approval of a monthly stipend to support one of his daughters in 1678.

Pietro Fortis was born in the Istanbul suburb of Pera in the late 1610s. He moved into the bailo's house as a young child in 1627 and in 1634 began his formal dragoman apprenticeship there.[50] In 1643, while sojourning in Venice, he was appointed Public Dragoman in place of the recently deceased Francesco Scaramelli.[51] Fortis's meteoric transformation from a young apprentice in Istanbul into a Public Dragoman in Venice shocked his fellow dragomans and apprentices

48. Bailo a Costantinopoli, b. 277, reg. 397, cc. 1v–2r; Dursteler (2000, 173–74).

49. Senato, Deliberazioni Costantinopoli, reg. 18, cc. 38r–48v (June 3–11, 1627); Cinque Savi, Risposte, b. 151, cc. 1–6 (Oct. 6, 1636); Senato, Deliberazioni Costantinopoli, reg. 23, fasc. 2, cc. 64r–66v (Oct. 8, 1636).

50. Collegio, Risposte di dentro, b. 34, unpaginated (May 29, 1643). His status during the previous seven years, while living as a child in the bailo's house, is unknown.

51. Cinque Savi, Risposte, b. 153 (Feb. 17, 1643 m.v.); cc. 172v–173v (May 10, 1645).

in the bailo's house. Many of them aspired to the position themselves. In fact, as bailo Giovanni Soranzo intimated in a dispatch to the Senate, many of them had withdrawn their candidacy only because their most senior member, the aging dragoman Giovanni Battista Salvago, had coveted it and was considered by his fellows to be the most qualified. When, instead of Salvago, the Senate elected Fortis, his colleagues in Istanbul were outraged. Had they known that he had clandestinely submitted his candidacy, they would have done the same![52]

But Fortis had several things going for him. First, he happened to be in Venice when the Board of Trade made its recommendations for the position.[53] Second, his father and grandfather had been Venetian citizens, making him technically eligible for citizenship (which he eventually received in 1651).[54] Third, as was mentioned, he had been raised from infancy in the bailo's house in Istanbul. His Venetian ancestry, coupled with familiarity with Ottoman society and long apprenticeship in various aspects of the dragoman's craft, made him an ideal candidate. Finally, his youthfulness, especially when compared with the aging and ailing Salvago, might have been considered another clear advantage—unlike Salvago, twenty-something Fortis had many more years of service ahead of him. Indeed, relatively young appointees seem to have been the norm in this office, in contrast to the prevailing gerontocracy of Venetian officialdom as a whole. With the exception of Andrea Negroni, all Public Dragomans in the period 1517–1682 served for over thirty years (or longer, if their apprenticeship or other services in Istanbul are also taken into account).

Young Fortis's ability to convince the Venetian Senate to appoint him as a Public Dragoman set the terms for a long and successful career, during which he proved himself a gifted petitioner. In 1651, he was recognized as Venetian citizen by birth, making him eligible for privileges and revenue reserved for that class and distinguishing him as the second dragoman after Michiel Membré to gain Venetian citizenship while in service (although Membré was a naturalized citizen). Fortis was clearly aware of the advantages of his newly acquired status. In 1655, he petitioned to receive, along with his sons, the sinecure of captain on Zakynthos, reserved for citizens, citing the fabled magnanimity of the Serenissima toward its citizens by birth.[55] Through other petitions, Fortis eventually increased both his

52. Senato, Dispacci Costantinopoli, b. 124, cc. 598r–v (Nov. 9, 1643).
53. Earlier in 1643, Fortis took a leave of absence in Venice to attend to family matters (Senato, Deliberazioni Costantinopoli, reg. 27, c. 5r (March 21, 1642); Senato, Dispacci Costantinopoli, b. 123, cc. 35v, 38r (May 19, 1642); b. 124, c. 293r (July 6, 1643); Cinque Savi, Risposte, b. 153, cc. 104v–105r (Feb. 17, 1643 m.v.)).
54. Ufficio della Bolla Ducale, Grazie del Maggior Consiglio, reg. 10, c. 106r (April, 1651).
55. Collegio, Risposte di dentro, b. 46, unpaginated (May 7, 1655).

base salary and, more important, his cut from commercial brokers' commissions from an initial 5 to 15 percent.[56] He soon arranged for his brother Giacomo, already fluent in "Greek, Turkish and Armenian" to work as a dragoman.[57] Where and when the Fortis brothers had learned Armenian remains unknown, but both Pietro and Giacomo had extensive ties to the Armenian merchant community in Venice. In 1644, Pietro helped interpret testimonies in a trial involving an Armenian merchant named Zorzi and a Jewish merchant named Isaia son of Isac Camis. In 1652, he served as an interpreter for the will of Cozà Mezadur son of the late Baldassar, an Armenian on whose inheritance he later became a creditor. A notarial deed of 1659 grants one Armenian merchant, Pietro de Battista, power of attorney to represent another, Baina Calili, in litigation against Fortis. This and his other numerous litigations with Armenian merchants in Venice over the years were connected perhaps with their rejected petition of 1650 for exemption from the dragoman's tax on brokers' commission on the grounds of not using Fortis's services. In 1658, Giacomo too became involved in litigation with an Armenian merchant, Antonio Bagos, who owed him a great sum of money. This, however, did not end his relations with the Armenian community, and in 1670 he appeared as a witness and interpreter in another notarial deed signed by a group of Armenian merchants.

This litigious record notwithstanding, Pietro was apparently held in high esteem by his employers on the Board of Trade, enough to secure employment as dragomans for two of his sons. In 1666, he offered to send Alvise and Giacomo to Istanbul to be apprenticed under his brother's guidance, clearly with the expectation that they would inherit his position after him. Repeating his offer to send his sons to be apprenticed in Istanbul in 1667, Pietro also sought Senate commitment to have the sons inherit his cut of 15 percent of brokers' commissions. His request was granted, and in 1667 his son Giacomo was appointed notary in the ducal chancellery (a position reserved for citizens by birth). Three years later, he was sent to serve as interpreter in Dalmatia. In 1676, the Board of Trade noted

---

56. Starting in 1652, Fortis petitioned to bring his cut of the brokers' commissions in line with that enjoyed by his predecessor Scaramelli. The Board of Trade endorsed his requests, but Fortis did not actually enjoy this increase until the 1670s. Similar delays were common in other cases (Collegio, Risposte di dentro, b. 36, unpaginated (April 20, 1645); b. 43, unpaginated (Sept. 12, 1652); b. 50, unpaginated (Aug. 8, 1658); b. 60, unpaginated (July 11, 1663); b. 62, unpaginated (June 5 and Aug. 8, 1664); Cinque Savi, Risposte, b. 155, c. 78r (June 21, 1656); cc. 135v–136r (Aug. 22, 1658); cc. 195v–196r (Feb. 14, 1661 m.v.)).

57. AdC, Misto, b. 3015, fasc. 7, unpaginated (1644); Notarile, Testamenti, b. 402, fasc. 201 (Dec. 6, 1652); AdC, Misc. Civil, b. 235, fasc. 2 (April 16, 1654); Notarile, Atti, b. 7467, c. 73r (July 1, 1659); b. 8846 cc. 52r–v (July 30, 1670); Collegio, Risposte di dentro, b. 41, unpaginated (March 9, 1650); Cinque Savi, Risposte, b. 154, cc. 155v–156r (Sept. 28, 1650); b. 155, cc. 144v–145r (Jan. 21, 1658 m.v.).

that Fortis's two sons had reached "perfect knowledge of the Turkish and Greek languages" and recommended appointing one of them as dragoman in Dalmatia. Alvise Fortis appears in the records as a dragoman as late as 1695. His brother Giacomo was employed as a Venetian dragoman at least until 1701, when he translated the Treaty of Karlowitz. Their uncle, Giacomo, also enjoyed a long career in Venetian service. In 1670–71, he even replaced his brother while the latter was sent on mission to Dalmatia, and in 1682, he succeeded him as Public Dragoman.[58]

Fortis's efforts to pass on his office (and financial privileges) to his sons and brother were rooted, no doubt, in his earlier experiences in the bailo's house in Istanbul, where dragomans' sons customarily inherited their fathers' office. It was, however, quite a novelty in Venice, where Fortis was the first dragoman to secure similar employment for his kin. In contrast, not a single one of Giacomo de Nores's nine children became a dragoman. This was despite explicit prompts by the Board of Trade, which in 1620, on the occasion of securing additional revenue for the dragoman and his heirs, suggested that "we consider it also public service to grant it in order to encourage his sons to follow in the footsteps of the father, and set out with great willingness towards the service of Your Serenity in imitation of their predecessors."[59]

Other aspects of Fortis's life also conjoined practices common among Venetian citizen families with those of the Latin community of Pera. Like other Venetian citizens by birth, Fortis engaged in charitable activities, including, in 1650, serving as godfather and eponym to a Turkish convert, the twenty-year-old Istanbul-born Pietro (formerly Ali).[60] Like other Latins of Pera, he produced a large family, which by the end of his career included eight children, who depended on the government for support. In 1676, with two sons placed as apprentices in the bailo's house in Istanbul, Fortis petitioned to receive some financial aid toward the dowry of one of his daughters, citing the custom of helping other dragomans in similar situation, including an unnamed dragoman who had received assistance for "four or six" of his daughters. Here, again, Fortis was relying on precedence

58. Collegio, Risposte di dentro, b. 66, unpaginated (April 15, 1666); b. 68, unpaginated (March 4, 1667); b. 75, unpaginated (Jan. 5, 1570 m.v.); Cinque Savi, Risposte, b. 156, cc. 51v–52r (Oct. 29, 1670); cc. 73v–74r (March 2, 1671); c. 94r (Sept. 22, 1671); cc. 99r–v (Sept. 28, 1671); Cinque Savi, seconda serie, b. 61, fasc. 1, unpaginated (March 2, 1671, July 22, 1671, Sept. 28, 1671, Feb. 6, 1675 m.v., Feb. 23, 1689 m.v., July 5, 1690, Nov. 5, 1690, June 6, 1693, and Sept. 20, 1695); Documenti Turchi, b. 15, fasc. 1612 (April 1701).
59. "stimamo ancora publico serv[izi]o il concedergliela per dar a'io à suoi fig[liuo]li di seguire le vestigie del Padre, et incaminarsi con tanto maggior prontezza nel serv[izi]o di V. Ser.tà ad imitate[ion]e de' suoi antenati" (Cinque Savi, Risposte, b. 145, unpaginated (Sept. 1, 1620)).
60. ACPV, BdC, 2, c. 31r (Aug. 21, 1650).

TABLE 5.1 VENETIAN PUBLIC DRAGOMANS, 1534–1682

Name	Provenance	Years in service	Year appointed Public Dragoman in Venice
Girolamo Civran	Cyprus, Ottoman captivity	1515–1549	1534
Michiel Membré	Cyprus	1538–1594	1550
Andrea Negroni	Istanbul	1587–1597	1594
Giacomo de Nores	Cyprus, Ottoman captivity	1587–1627	1594
Francesco Scaramelli	Venice	1611–1643	1627
Pietro Fortis	Istanbul, Venetian father	1627–1682	1643
Giacomo Fortis	Istanbul, Venetian father	1670–after 1701	1682

in the bailo's patronage of dragomans employed in his household in Istanbul, part of a broader system of classic early modern patronage that conflated public service and informal social networking. His request was approved in 1678 when the Board of Trade authorized a monthly stipend of 10 ducats for his daughter.[61]

That Fortis's sons carried on in their father's profession was standard practice among Venetian colonial interpreters and dragomans in Istanbul.[62] More noteworthy was the transfer of the position of Public Dragoman in Venice to Pietro's brother Giacomo. As I have shown, although other chancellery positions certainly circulated within citizen families, the position of Public Dragoman was, until then, reserved for trans-imperial subjects, either Ottoman or Venetian colonial émigrés (see table 5.1).[63] At least in theory, their appointment was based on their individual qualifications and merit rather than on their father's service as dragomans. That the two Fortis brothers were able to keep the position in their hands for over half a century suggests the power of the combination of recognized Venetian ancestry with long residence in Istanbul.

How did Fortis's trans-imperial trajectories shape the horizons of his expectations for remuneration from the Venetian state? How did he articulate his own

61. Cinque Savi, seconda serie, b. 61, fasc. 1, unpaginated (Feb. 6, 1675 m.v., and Aug. 3, 1678).
62. In addition to the Borisi, Bruti, Grillo, Navon, Parada, Piron, Salvago, and Tarsia families in Istanbul, other father-son dragoman chains in Venetian service include Giovanni and Andrea Aggiondrito in Kefalonia c. 1553, Simon and Giovanni Britanico in Zadar c. 1565, Christoforo and Giovanni Maria Bonà in Aleppo c. 1600, and Girolamo and Marco Pace in Split c. 1640.
63. Only in one previous case was a Venetian *cittadino originario* appointed to the position: Francesco Scaramelli, Fortis's immediate predecessor.

position vis-à-vis Venetian officialdom? His first petition (in 1643) was fairly modest. He submitted it shortly before his appointment as Public Dragoman, while on leave in Venice from his position in the bailo's house in Istanbul to attend to family business, following the death by plague of two of his siblings.[64] Fortis used the petition to underscore his loyal service of nine years, the fact he had been raised from infancy in the bailo's house, and his loyal and arduous effort to learn Turkish so that he could be of greater service to the Republic. He requested a raise that would make his condition equal with that of the other apprentices of his rank, Tarsia, Pace, and Agapito.[65] Significantly, Fortis chose to mention only these three apprentices, who were all colonial Venetian subjects from Dalmatia and Cyprus, and to ignore other contemporary apprentices, members of the Latin community of Pera (and therefore Ottoman juridical subjects). In this early petition, Fortis implied that he left his "mother's arms in tender age" and entered the bailo's house specifically to become a civil servant. The private interests that no doubt prompted his ancestors to settle in Istanbul are here seamlessly merged with public service. Yet, in another petition two years later, Fortis reversed his argument, emphasizing his constant service "far from my house and relatives" (i.e., away from Istanbul) as grounds for a salary increase.[66] It was precisely his unquestionable Venetian ancestry that allowed Fortis more leeway in invoking his Ottoman connections and trans-imperial trajectories without casting doubt on his loyalty. His request was endorsed by the Board of Trade.[67] Fortis's later petitions were even more florid in their invocation of loyalty, as in this passage from 1664: "As my native fervor toward my Prince in the avidity of my loyal service harnessed all my spirit to the only end of public satisfaction, so must I confess to not have so far provided for the needs of my eight children with anything but the constant, hereditary devotion towards Your Serenity."[68] Like other serial petitioners, Fortis used this medium to constantly remind his employers of his merit. His rhetorical skills and his unique life trajectory, which combined Venetian citizenship with birth and long apprenticeship in Istanbul, enabled him to strategically and simultaneously fashion himself as both local and foreign.

64. Senato, Dispacci Costantinopoli, b. 123, cc. 35v, 38r (May 19, 1642).
65. Collegio, Risposte di dentro, b. 34, unpaginated (May 29, 1643).
66. "Presto incessante, assidua, devota, e fedele servitù; lontana dalla mia casa, e parenti." (Collegio, Risposte di dentro, b. 36, unpaginated (April 20, 1645)).
67. Cinque Savi, Risposte, b. 153, cc. 172v–173v (May 10, 1645).
68. "[S]icome il nativo fervore della siusserattezza verso il mio P[rinci]pe nell'avidità di questo mio fed[elissi]mo ministerio attrasse tutto il mio spirito al solo fine del Pub[lic]o agradim[en]to, così devo pure confessare di non haver sin quì proveduto alla neccessità di otto miei fig[liuo]li d'altro che d'una costante hereditaria devotionne verso alla S.tà V.a" (Collegio, Risposte di dentro, b. 62, unpaginated (June 5, 1664)).

P ublic Dragomans not only embodied the tension between foreign and local. They also played an active role in developing a set of metrics by which the boundary between the two could be established in individual cases. On April 30, 1624, a Persian Jewish merchant named Giosef arrived in Venice on board ship. The same night, he was apprehended by the Ufficiali al Cattaver, the magistracy in charge of enforcing Catholic religious orthodoxy and supervising Jews in the ghetto. The magistracy accused him of violating required Venetian dress code for Jews by sporting a striped hat. Soon, however, the Board of Trade intervened, protesting that all Levantine and Ponentine Jews, and especially foreigners who arrived in the city on business, were under its jurisdiction rather than that of the Cattaver. Moreover, such Jews, the Board intimated, should wear "a yellow hat or beret, to distinguish them from the Christians. It is not specified, whether this hat should be striped or not, as this makes no difference, for these hats keep them distinct and recognized by the Christians."[69] In passing, the Board also reminded the Senate of the hefty revenue that Jewish merchants brought to the city, making it prudent to treat "that nation" favorably and protect its members from harassment. Most important, to substantiate its claims, the Board marshaled evidence culled from Public Dragoman Giacomo de Nores, and from other Persian merchants in the city, to the effect that "Persian Jews in their country sport on their heads striped hats, and it seems that last year ten Persian Jews who arrived in this city with their merchandise always sported on their heads striped hats: so it seems to us, that this arrest is without offense."[70] Significantly, de Nores's expert opinion was deemed authoritative enough to be explicitly named in the Board's response. Moreover, it was used specifically to foreground the arrested merchant's trans-imperial status, as not only Levantine but a newly arrived sojourner, ignorant of local custom and hence falling under the jurisdiction of the Board of Trade rather than the Ufficiali al Cattaver. It is irrelevant whether de Nores derived the information about Persian Jews' sartorial customs from first-hand observations in his youth in Istanbul or on the Safavid frontier (at least thirty-seven years earlier) or, more likely, from conversations with Persian merchants in Venice. In either case, it was his pronouncement that lent authority to the Board's claim to substantiated, factual knowledge of customs in a foreign land.

69. "portare la cessa, ò bareta Giala p[er] distinguerli dalli Christiani, ne viene specificato, che detta cessa debba esser più vegata, o non vengata, non facendo questo effetto alcuno, ò alteraz[io] ne mà restano con dette cesse distinti et conosciuti dalli Christiani" (Cinque Savi, Risposte, b. 146, cc. 11v–112v (May 10, 1624)).
70. "Hebrei persiani nel loro paese portano le cesse vergate in capo, et pare l'anno pass[at]o sono capitati in questa Città hebrei persiani al n[ume]ro di x.ci con loro m[ercan]tie, che hanno sempre portato in capo le cese vergate: si che parendo à noi, che questa ritentione sia senza delitto." (Cinque Savi, Risposte, b. 146, cc. 11v–112v (May 10, 1624)).

In another case, in 1603, de Nores was entrusted by the Board of Trade with paying a visit to a Persian merchant recently arrived in Venice. Within an hour, he appeared in front of the magistrates with a detailed report. Significantly, his narrative was recorded in the first person in the Board registers so as to lend greater authority to the information it conveyed. It was later copied into a forty-four-page court record heard by the Quarantia Criminal in the matter of Anthony Sherley, an English charlatan.[71]

These brief anecdotes suggest the privileged position of trans-imperial subjects as Public Dragomans. Claiming specialized knowledge by virtue of their trans-imperial life trajectories and having immediate access to the highest echelons of the Venetian political elite in the Board of Trade and Senate, dragomans came to play a powerful role in defining who and what could be deemed properly foreign in Venice.

The next two chapters address the process by which this powerful role was attained, its consequences, and the numerous trans-imperial interlocutors that engaged dragomans in its wake.

71. Quarantia Criminal, b. 114, f. 142 (March 3, 1603, "Antonio Scerles Inglese"). For de Nores's assistance in translating and authenticating several notarial documents in the merchant's possession, see Cinque Savi, Risposte, b. 141, cc. 35r–v (March 14, 1603).

PART IV

Articulation

6

Articulating Difference

In chapter 3, I introduce Teodoro Dandolo, the Bukhara-born convert-turned-commercial broker who in 1608 failed to secure an appointment as official interpreter of Persian, Turkish, Arabic, and "Indian." His case raises fundamental questions about the nexus of ethnoreligious and juridical transformation in the trajectories of trans-imperial subjects in early modern Venice. Why was the Board of Trade hesitant to appoint Dandolo as dragoman but quite willing to make him a commercial broker? What differing assumptions about skill and embeddedness in local and inter-imperial networks of patronage and affect characterized the two professions? And how did the two interrelated professions and their trans-imperial practitioners come to shape Venetian notions of Ottoman otherness in the course of the sixteenth and seventeenth centuries?

So far, I have described the emergence of three specific cadres of trans-imperial subjects between the Venetian and Ottoman empires—commercial brokers, religious converts, and dragomans. It is now time to look at the multiple interactions among the three. Such interactions bring to the fore both the varied nature of practices of boundary-making in the early modern Mediterranean and their embeddedness in specific institutions and genres. In particular, by revisiting two key genres discussed throughout the book, the *supplica* (petition) and *risposta* (official response), I explore in these two final chapters the role of trans-imperial subjects in articulating ethnolinguistic taxonomies in the Venetian-Ottoman borderlands. I begin by charting the emergence of a highly powerful office of Public Dragoman in charge of mediating and (in principle) translating between Ottoman sojourning merchants and their Venetian brokers and trade partners. I then outline how a tax called the *terzo* came about in 1534, ostensibly to fund the activities of the Public Dragoman, and how it was gradually applied to all Ottoman and Safavid merchants in Venice, with important consequences for the notion of linguistic (in)competence as a marker of foreignness. Next, I consider the establishment in 1621 of the Fondaco dei Turchi, the "Turkish" exchange house and the consequent arguments over the signs of difference that mark those who properly belong there. Through these episodes I explore the important roles of trans-imperial commercial brokers, converts, dragomans, and merchants in articulating the relationship among the Venetian, Ottoman, and Safavid states. The categories of inclusion and exclusion that were negotiated in these distinct moments of institutionalization were premised in part on trans-imperial subjects' own interpretations of Venetian, as well as Ottoman and Safavid, legal regimes and practices of governance. The ability of specific trans-imperial subjects to claim familiarity with multiple state institutions was often pegged on both their foreign provenance and their long sojourns in a host country (spatial ambiguity was clearly of the essence in such pronouncements of familiarity).

BROKERS, DRAGOMANS, AND THE STRUGGLE OVER THE *TERZO*

In the previous chapter, I note the simultaneously diplomatic and commercial functions of Venetian Public Dragomans. A similar duality was also at the heart of endless struggles between brokers and dragomans revolving around the tax of *terzo* ("a third"). This tax of literally one-third of brokers' commissions was established in 1534 to fund the services of Girolamo Civran, the first Public Dragoman. It was initially levied on all brokerage fees in transactions involving "Turkish merchants" (a term that requires some explication and that is discussed later). The Public Dragoman, in return, was required to attend all the commercial transactions of such merchants in Venice. In addition to being present at the conclusion of a deal, he was to help translate between the parties, guarantee the fairness of the transaction, and register its details in a special log to be kept by the Board of Trade. The tax was therefore ostensibly instituted to offset the cost of keeping the dragoman away from his other assignments at the chancellery. The institution of the *terzo* tax came in the wake of growing efforts by the newly established Board of Trade to exert control over all commercial operations in the city and specifically to regulate the activities of a somewhat unruly guild of commercial brokers. This guild itself was a relatively new development. As discussed in Part I, it had emerged only three decades earlier and included, contrary to its bylaws, a fair number of brokers who did not meet Venetian citizenship requirements, who hailed from the Ottoman Empire and the Venetian Mediterranean colonies, and who maintained close contacts on the other side of the Venetian-Ottoman frontier.[1] Their proverbial ability to evade taxes was, no doubt, part of the reason why the Board of Trade wished to supervise brokers' activities in the first place.

Technically, then, the *terzo* was a commission for services rendered. But the services were mandatory regardless of merchants' actual needs or wishes and implied brokers' inadequacy in assisting their clients and safeguarding their interests. Litigations soon ensued, revolving around several issues: Did all Ottoman merchants really need the Public Dragoman's linguistic assistance and protection in their dealings with brokers and Venetian merchants? Were all brokers as fraudulent as the legislation implied? Were all dragomans as efficient and conscientious in providing services as they claimed to be? Were there no other people more qualified to assist foreigners than the Public Dragoman? Were there no other ways of replenishing the dwindling coffers of the Venetian state?

With time, the groups whose commercial transactions were subject to the *terzo* grew to include Safavid (both Muslim and Armenian) and Jewish merchants as well, casting ever greater doubts about the rationale of the tax. At the same time, the struggle over the *terzo* was colored by the experiences and aims of specific dragomans and their adversaries within the guild of commercial brokers. Because both dragomans and brokers were overwhelmingly trans-imperial subjects from Dalmatia and the eastern Mediterranean, their specific trajectories and lingering ties in the Venetian-Ottoman borderlands and beyond shaped their competing ideas about foreignness, linguistic skill, merit, and loyalty, all of which were at play in these struggles. By tracing how dragomans came to dominate the institution of the *terzo* for long periods and how others in the same trans-imperial commercial milieu sought to undermine their power, we begin to see the important role played by the Venetian Board of Trade in defining the relation between the Venetian state and Ottoman and Safavid merchants.

Struggles over the *terzo* tax came to a head during Michiel Membré's long tenure as Public Dragoman (1550–1594). The same business savvy that characterized his entrepreneurial endeavors (see chap. 5) also served Membré well throughout his lengthy career as a civil servant. As a Public Dragoman with the Board of

---

1. The establishment of the commercial brokers' guild and its subjection to the jurisdiction of the Board of Trade were part of a concerted effort to centralize Venetian commercial policies, to facilitate long-distance trade, and to attract foreign merchants to the city. For centuries up to that point, individual brokers were required to report to different government agencies, including the Consoli dei mercanti, the Ufficiali alla messetteria, or the Visdomini al Fondaco dei Tedeschi. All these magistracies saw their jurisdiction substantially reduced with the establishment of the Board of Trade in the sixteenth century (Da Mosto 1937, 189, 198; Fusaro 2000, esp. 145). On the Board of Trade, see chapters 1–2.

Trade, Membré enjoyed, in addition to an annual salary of 220 ducats, one-third of the brokerage commissions of all transactions involving Ottoman merchants, just like his predecessor Civran. This commission was substantial indeed. In 1587, the Board of Trade estimated the annual *terzo* revenue at 5,000–6,000 ducats, a true fortune.[2] Although Membré did not collect the entire sum, he did become quite a wealthy man. His legendary revenue from the *terzo* became the target of many brokers' envy. Not only were they forced to put up with his presence and surveillance (and, some suggested, corruption) but also to pay him one-third of their own fees!

Brokers were not the only ones dismayed by Membré's growing fortunes. Many merchants were equally disgruntled because the burden of the *terzo* was often passed on to them, even if officially it was levied on brokers alone. Repeated decrees forbidding brokers from making their clients shoulder the tax in any way merely confirm the prevalence of the practice. Some merchants sought to avoid the extra burden by convincing the government that they did not require the Public Dragoman's services because they all spoke perfect Italian.[3] Others tried to appoint a separate dragoman specifically for their needs. This was the case of the "Armenian nation," which in 1582 petitioned collectively to appoint a certain Armenian named Zorzi as its authorized dragoman, to whom the commission of *terzo* would be paid. The Board of Trade warned that conceding to the Armenians' request would open the door to much trouble and complaints by the brokers' guild. Instead, they recognized Zorzi's past services in Istanbul and recommended that he be appointed commercial broker. As in other cases, rather than disrupt Membré's monopoly and set a dangerous precedent for particularistic collective rights, the board sought to maintain the status quo and extend its patronage network to a worthy individual.[4]

This was the context in which, in 1587, Giulio Torquato, an old commercial broker and a former mariner who had sojourned in the Ottoman Empire for over a decade in his youth, petitioned the Senate to have the *terzo* abolished

---

2. Three years later, it was estimated at "only" 2,000 ducats. After Membré's death in 1594, the collection of the *terzo* was farmed out for an annuity of 2,650 ducats, increased by 1617 to 2,720 ducats. That year, Giacomo de Nores enjoyed, in addition to an annual salary of 800 ducats (an impressive increase from his original 200), one-third of the commissions of the trade transacted by "Greeks, Armenians, and other Levantines, excepting those of Turks and Jews." In 1634, Francesco Scaramelli received, for the same position, only 312 ducats per year and 13 percent of the *terzo* commission. On appointing Pietro Fortis in 1643, the Board of Trade recommended that he be given the same salary but only 5 percent of the *terzo* (Cinque Savi, Risposte, b. 138, cc. 17–19 (Sept. 28, 1587); b. 144, cc. 148r–v (Jan. 12, 1617 m.v.); b. 153, cc. 104v–105r (Feb. 17, 1643 m.v.); Collegio, Risposte di dentro, b. 43, unpaginated (Sept. 12, 1652)).
3. See, for example, Collegio, Risposte di dentro, b. 41, unpaginated (March 9, 1650).
4. Cinque Savi, Risposte, b. 137, cc. 71v–72r (Aug. 18, 1582).

altogether. Claiming to speak on behalf of "other brokers of Turks," Torquato accused Membré not only of greediness but of embezzlement. Membré, he alleged, often turned a blind eye to corrupt brokers prone to cheat their clients and the state to receive his fat commission.[5] The Board of Trade concurred with Torquato on the shortcomings of Membré's service, although it suggested the dragoman's less-than-perfect performance was due, rather, to his old age and failing health. A few months later, instead of abolishing the *terzo*, the Senate recommended that two more interpreters be appointed to assist Membré.[6] I return to these two interpreters shortly.

Another effort to abolish the *terzo* took place on Membré's death in 1594. That year, two brokers petitioned the government on behalf of twenty-four of their colleagues who dealt with Ottoman clients and asked that, instead of the *terzo*, they be required to contribute to the government every year 1,500 ducats collectively.[7] Within a few weeks, another anonymous petition promised the government a sure method of curbing "the many frauds, and deceits, which Turks suffer" in the hands of cunning brokers. In return, the authors, who later identified themselves as Zuan Domenico di Zorzi and Antonio Cigoto, asked to receive the *terzo* revenue for twenty-five years, from which they would give the government an annual commission of 1,500 ducats. They also offered to employ a dragoman and an accountant, to whom they would pay out of pocket an annual salary of 500 and 120 ducats, respectively.[8]

Not surprisingly, the Board of Trade rejected this proposition to completely abolish the *terzo*. According to the board, once new regulations had been instituted in 1587 requiring brokers to register with the Board of Trade all transactions involving merchants subject to the tax, no complaints were filed, although merchants were otherwise "quick and ready to complain about trifles."[9] At the same time, the majority opinion on the board endorsed the brokers' request to pay a reduced collective tax, citing their large and needy families (and thus emphasizing, not for the first time, the merit of the petitioners rather than the merit of their cause). The minority opinion, drafted by Andrea Gussoni and Girolamo Giustinian, board members, suggested that, in fact, many frauds were still committed against Ottoman merchants and that it might thus make sense to endorse Zorzi

5. Cinque Savi, Risposte, b. 138, cc. 17–19 (Sept. 28, 1587).
6. Compilazione Leggi, b. 146, c. 786 (Jan. 29, 1587 m.v.). The two were finally elected a few months later, on August 28, 1588, with a combined annual salary of 300 ducats (Cinque Savi, Risposte, b. 138, cc. 98r–v (Jan. 13, 1589 m.v.); 110v–111r (March 31, 1590)).
7. Senato Mar, filza 128, unpaginated (Dec. 9, 1594).
8. Senato Mar, filza 128, unpaginated (on or before Jan. 7, 1594, and Jan. 11, 1594 m.v.).
9. "Ne sentitoli alcuna loro lamentatione con tutto che siino pur troppo facili, et pronti p[er] ogni minima cosa à co[n]dolersi." (Senato Mar, filza 128, unpaginated (Dec. 9, 1594)).

and Cigoto's proposal and entrust them with supervising the brokers. Curiously, neither the majority nor the minority opinions addressed explicitly the relationship between the appointment of dragoman assistants in 1587 and the alleged decline in brokers' fraud. Yet the board did combine its response to the *terzo*-related petitions with its assessment of the two petitions by Membré's assistants who sought to inherit his position as Public Dragoman (see chap. 5). Thus it seems that for board members the Public Dragoman's identity and his ability to curb brokers' infractions were closely interlinked and premised not only on linguistic skill but on loyalty and character as well.

If specific groups' efforts to rid themselves of the *terzo* sometimes failed, the general logic of linguistic difference as the basis for collective privileges was to have a long trajectory in the Venetian commercial sphere. In 1582, two Bosnian merchants, Hassan and Risuan, heads of "la Nation Turcha Bossinese" (the Turkish Bosnian nation), petitioned the Venetian Board of Trade to appoint additional commercial brokers who spoke "our language."[10] According to their petition, only three licensed brokers spoke their language and, because the three acted in concert, they practically counted as one. Public Dragoman Michiel Membré also failed to help them, although his task, according to the petitioners, was precisely to protect foreign merchants' interests and prevent them from being defrauded by brokers "of bad quality." By claiming to speak a distinct language and to constitute a separate nation, the petitioners distinguished themselves from other kinds of Ottoman subjects trading in Venice and implied they were a collective body entitled to its own institutionalized protections.

The Board of Trade, on its part, interpreted the request as seeking brokers who spoke "the Slavic language." The petitioners had used neither "Slavic" nor "Bosnian" as linguistic descriptors and, indeed, had left the identification of "their language" entirely vague. Yet in its response the board collapsed any dialectal distinctions to suggest that the petitioners' language was simply Slavic, spoken by many other merchants in Venice. Moreover, it countered the petitioners' claims by presenting its own hard figures, according to which Venice boasted no fewer than twenty Turkish-speaking brokers, of whom four even spoke Slavic as well.[11] Those brokers, the board concluded, "are sufficient and good to serve that nation, for although it is said that these Bosnian Turks use the Slavic language, and that they need brokers who know it, we view this as of no consideration, since all those Turks, who know the Slavic language, likewise use, and speak the Turkish

10. Collegio, Risposte di dentro, b. 7, c. 127 (June 21, 1582).
11. The figures, according to the board, were based on a survey conducted by interviewing the heads of the brokers' guild as well as select Turkish merchants (i.e., representing both parties) and based on concrete evidence.

language."[12] Against the merchants' claim of linguistic distinctiveness, the board thus responded with not only the view that all Slavic languages were essentially the same but with specific observations about the Turkish-Slavic bilingualism of Balkan Muslims, thus suggesting that there was no need to further accommodate the petitioners' linguistic differences. Notice also that the response implicitly subsumed the petitioners under the category "Turks." Similar linguistic arguments were to figure time and again in merchants' petitions for collective privileges. In a petition by Marcantonio degli Eletti, a commercial broker, and other members of the brokers' guild, put forward in 1584, the suppliants claimed that Turkish merchants' ignorance of the Italian language occasioned many opportunities for unscrupulous brokers to defraud, overcharge, and force them into illegal transactions involving installment payments. Furthermore, the suppliants repeated the claim that Public Dragoman Membré had failed to protect merchants' interests by neglecting to be present during the conclusion of deals and that, moreover, he accepted bribes from unlicensed brokers to turn a blind eye to their operations. Here it was not foreign merchants who voiced concerns about their linguistic competence but, rather, brokers, whose own interests clearly prompted their emphasis of Ottoman merchants' foreignness and special needs.[13]

The portrayal of certain groups as linguistically incompetent could be used in an effort to secure other collective privileges as well. A petition from 1596 by the "nation of Levantine Jews" called on the government to allow them to purchase bread and redistribute it within the ghetto so that "the poor Jewish foreigner, who knows neither the Italian language, nor anything about the customs of the city, is not forced, with notable and evident danger, to leave the ghetto to get bread."[14] Here the same group that on many other occasions was quick to note its rootedness in Venice by virtue of de facto long residence, proclaimed, rather, its juridical status as *viandanti* (transient sojourners), made evident by its supposed linguistic difference.[15] The point, of course, is not whether some long-term Jewish residents in the ghetto *really* could not speak Italian or find their way outside the ghetto but that such arguments became plausible in the first place.

12. "Siano sufficienti et buoni per servitio di detta nattione, che se bene vien detto, che loro Turchi bossinesi si serveno della lingua schiava, et ch'habbino bisogno di sanseri che sapino q[ue]lla, questo noi reputamo de niuna co[n]sideratione, percioche tutti essi Turchi, che sano la lingua schiava, usano, et parlano medesim[amen]te in lingua Turca" (Cinque Savi, Risposte, b. 137, cc. 68r–v (July 31, 1582)).

13. Collegio, Risposte di dentro, b. 7, c. 255 (April 26, 1584).

14. "Accio che il povero heb[re]o forast[ier]o che non ha la lingua Italiana, nè sà alcun uso della Città non sij con suo notabile, et evidente pericolo astretto ad'uscir di Ghetto, per haver pane" (Collegio, Risposte di dentro, b. 10, c. 91 (March 31,1596)).

15. On the Levantini's tendency to disregard legal restrictions on period of residence in Venice, see Ravid (1976, 190–91); Arbel (1995b, esp. 6). See also Genot-Bismuth (1993, 30n. 17, 32n. 28).

Even more significant is that the Board of Trade itself began using foreign merchants' alleged linguistic incompetence as an occasional argument for special concessions. In 1586, it endorsed a request by Manusso Cresci, a merchant from Monemvasia, to be appointed consul of the "Athenian nation" in Venice on the grounds that the few Athenian merchants in the city were "ignorant both of the Italian language and of the orders and laws of this city" and thus needed a person to protect their interests.[16] Conversely, in 1588 it rejected a request by the papacy to establish a consul in Venice who would represent merchants from the Papal States trading in the city. In its response, the board conceded that such consulates were established for Spain and France but that, at least in the latter case, "subjects of that Crown arrived from the farthermost parts and were most inexperienced in the business and customs of this city, and [spoke] a different language."[17] These arguments seem to have been meant to keep the papacy from stationing in Venice another official representative who would send sensitive news from the Serenissima. A later concession of a consulate to the merchants of Hamburg made no reference to language as a reason to grant their request.[18]

Thus, even though the *terzo* was initially introduced to facilitate surveillance over unruly brokers, it ultimately authorized claims about linguistic particularity as a basis for difference and preferential treatment by the state. This was the context in which, in 1587, several petitions were submitted to the board seeking to either abolish the *terzo* or replace the current Public Dragoman, Michiel Membré. Two aspects of these petitions are worth pointing out. First, they were both initiated by trans-imperial subjects, merchants or brokers, who in articulating collective demands contributed to an emergent taxonomy of Ottoman and Safavid groups in Venice. Second, it is significant that the Board of Trade chose to combine its response to these *terzo*-related petitions with its assessment of two applicants to become Membré's assistants and eventual heirs as Public Dragomans. This underscores how for the board members, and Venetian officialdom more broadly, the Public Dragoman's identity and his ability to curb brokers' infractions became closely interlinked and premised not only on linguistic skill but on a particular kind of loyalty and set of affective attachments as well. This is borne out by another, somewhat later example. In 1650, the "Armenian nation" supplicated the Venetian Senate for exemption from the *terzo* tax, which by then was

16. "Li qual pochi come ignazi, et della lingua Italiana, et delle ordeni et leggi di questa citta hanno p[er] il vero bisogno di persona, che difenda, et aiuti loro in q[ue]lle cose, che li occorressero à beneficio di detta nattione"(Cinque Savi, Risposte, b.137, cc. 161v (March 26, 1586)).

17. "P[er]che capitando qui sudditi di q[ue]lla corona da lontanissime parti inespertissimi di negotij, et usi di q[ue]sta città, et di lingua differente" (Cinque Savi, Risposte, b. 138, cc. 57–59 (Sept. 1588)).

18. Cinque Savi, Risposte, b. 144, cc. 74v–75r (April 30, 1616).

used to finance the activities of dragoman Pietro Fortis. Fortis himself was deeply involved in the business transactions of Armenian merchants in Venice (see chap. 5). Why, then, were the petitioners reluctant to pay him? The petitioners suggested they would have been more than happy to shoulder the tax had they had any use for Fortis's services. But because all Armenian merchants spoke Italian and used their own Armenian commercial brokers, they claimed, they had no need for the dragoman.[19] Similarly, in 1658, the "ambassadors of the people of Niscichi" (Nikšić, Montenegro) expressed their concern about the difficulties their merchants encountered in Venice due to their ignorance of the Italian language and petitioned to have a specific broker, Nicolò Scura, appointed to assist them.[20]

Linguistic arguments served sojourning merchants in Venice to request other concessions in addition to the appointment of brokers and interpreters. In 1654, "the Greek nation" requested that the Venetian government allow Anzolo Cozzi, a lawyer, to represent their cases in front of the magistracy of the Syndic, even though he was Athenian-born rather than Venetian. The petitioners explained that many of them did not command any language but their native Greek and thus needed the services of someone who "understands their language."[21]

Although "Bosnians," "Athenians," or "Spaniards" were not recognized by the Venetian Board of Trade as separate categories for tax purposes, their very recognition as linguistic groups might have served as a first step toward greater economic privileges. Certainly, Levantine Jews, who repeatedly harped on their foreignness in Venice, enjoyed extensive protections, both commercial and otherwise, that no other Jews in Venice (perceived as more localized), much less any other foreign merchants, could ever achieve.[22] Similarly, "Bosnian" became a familiar category in Venetian governmental discourses about Ottoman merchants in Venice, as evidenced in part by their special mention in the 1621 regulations for the Fondaco dei Turchi, where Bosnians and Albanians were to live separately from "Asiatics."

The *terzo* underwent important permutations in later decades. I return to this shortly, but first, let us look at another important conjuncture in the process of establishing criteria of difference and foreignness.

---

19. Collegio, Risposte di dentro, b. 41, unpaginated (March 9, 1650).
20. Collegio, Risposte di dentro, b. 50, unpaginated (April 1, 1658).
21. Collegio, Risposte di dentro, b. 45, unpaginated (March 23, 1654). A decade later, Cozzi was involved in a major civil litigation that ripped apart the Armenian community in Venice (AdC, Misc. Civil, b. 210, fasc. 2, unpaginated (Jan. 29, 1664 m.v.)).
22. On differences among various Venetian Jewish communities, see Davis and Ravid (2001); Favero and Trivellato (2004). On the emergence of the category of "Levantine Jews" in the 1540s, see chapter 7.

FONDACO

In chapter 1, I describe how Francesco Lettino, alias Frangia, a Greek commercial broker, found himself at the center of an inquisitorial inquiry into his complicity in hiding a runaway slave in his attic. In the wake of his trial, he proposed opening a fondaco for Turkish merchants. He likened the proposed establishment to a "particular hotel like the ones that many other nations and peoples have in this city and that the Turks have provided in their countries of the Levant for the Christian Nation."[23] He further suggested taxing the future residents of the fondaco to finance custodial services, "as is customary in Syria in the fondacos of the Christians."[24] Frangia's petitions of 1574 and 1575 not only set in motion discussions about the merits of such a fondaco, but articulated many of the fundamental presuppositions of the debate for years to come, including the inherent danger of residential mixing and commensality, the presumed helplessness of foreign merchants, and their need for special protections. Among the alleged evils inflicted by Turkish merchants in Venice, Frangia listed robberies, kidnappings of Christian boys, and Muslims' sexual relations with Christian women. The source of these evils was supposedly the Turkish merchants' freedom to live where they pleased. In approving Frangia's petition the following year, the Senate referred to the danger of Turks' nocturnal wandering around the city and socializing in Christian homes.[25] Thus, we see how Frangia, an unscrupulous but well-positioned broker, was instrumental in establishing the conjunction between a general culture of prejudice and state policy, and how his rhetorical flourishes gained authority as they were repeatedly picked up and given new moral force in the discourse of officialdom.

At the same time, both Frangia's petition and all subsequent official pronouncements on the matter sought to present the establishment of the fondaco as a protective measure serving merchants' own interests, premised on the supposed analogy with other institutions for hosting foreign merchants in the city, such as the German Exchange House and the Jewish ghettos. According to Frangia, under the previous conditions, Turkish merchants had sometimes been robbed and even murdered while staying in Christian households. He further emphasized their peculiar cleansing, eating, and sleeping habits as grounds for a separate lodging.[26] Later legislation on the matter repeatedly invoked similar ethnographic

23. "Albergo particolar, come hanno molte altre Nationi, et genti in questa Città, et come anco lor Turchi nelli loro paesi di Levante han provisto alla Nation Christiana" (Cinque Savi, Seconda serie, b. 187, fasc. 1, unpaginated (Oct. 28, 1574, and Aug. 16, 1575)).
24. Cinque Savi, Seconda serie, b. 187, fasc. 1, unpaginated (Aug. 16, 1575).
25. Cinque Savi, Seconda serie, b. 187, fasc. 1, unpaginated (Oct. 28, 1574, and Aug. 16, 1575).
26. Cinque Savi, Seconda serie, b. 187, fasc. 1, unpaginated (Aug. 16, 1575).

claims about the distinctiveness of "Turkish" customs and rituals, and insisted that foreign merchants were disadvantaged by their dispersal around the city, which supposedly subjected them to fraudulent landlords. The legislation specifically highlighted the many advantages that the new fondaco would offer its tenants. This suggests how claims to experience and knowledge produced through sustained close contact with clients/tenants allowed Frangia—himself a trans-imperial subject—to elaborate taxonomies of Turkish difference that were then taken up by officialdom, through the Board of Trade and its authorized agents, the Public Dragomans.

The following decades saw a continued debate over residential segregation, already underlying the establishment of the German Exchange House and the Jewish ghettos much earlier, although in widely different contexts.[27] In 1588, the Senate ordered commercial brokers, on pain of losing their brokerage license, "to direct the Turks who come to this city from time to time" to a makeshift hostel operated by Frangia's wife Giulia and his nephew, Pietro.[28] Despite these decrees, the following year the Senate conceded that the plan to open a fondaco had not materialized and instructed the Board of Trade to locate a new house suitable for hosting a large number of merchants.[29] Two reports by the Board of Trade in 1601 and 1608 referred back to the mandate it had been given years earlier to locate such a house. When an actual site for the fondaco was finally identified, the appointed custodian was none other than Giovanni Battista Lettino, Frangia's grandson.[30] Other members of the Lettino family continued to operate the fondaco for decades thereafter, leading fierce battles (and often invoking Christian morality) against any efforts by Ottoman merchants to extricate themselves from their establishment.

Religious rhetoric and ethnographic observations therefore legitimated and naturalized the economic protectionist measures of instituting the fondaco, thus localizing a shared circum-Mediterranean practice of hosting foreign merchants in

27. On the Fondaco dei Tedeschi, which was established in 1225 but became the subject of increased government regulation from the late fifteenth century on, see Constable (2003, 320–23); Simonsfeld (1968); Lupprian (1978). On the Jewish ghettos, see Malkiel (1991); Davis and Ravid (2001); Ravid (2003). Significantly, Venice imposed Jewish residential segregation in its maritime colonies from around 1325, almost two centuries before it did so in the Lagoon (Jacoby 1987, 37). 28. "Et siano obligati tutti li sanseri sotto privatione del carico loro à condur li Turchi, che veniranno in questa Città di tempo in tempo in d[ett]a Casa" (Cinque Savi, Seconda serie, b. 187, fasc. 1, unpaginated (June 4, 1588)). 29. Cinque Savi, Seconda serie, b. 187, fasc. 1, unpaginated (March 28, 1589). 30. Cinque Savi, Seconda serie, b. 187, fasc. 1, unpaginated (Jan. 4, 1600 m.v., and March 20, 1608). For brief overviews of the history of the establishment of the fondaco, see Sagredo and Berchet (1860); Preto (1975, 126–36); Tucci (1985, 51–55). For the much longer history of the building, see Schulz (2004, 133–63).

special *funduqs* and calibrating it with Venetian reason of state.[31] Yet what came to be seen as natural in the 1620s had been rather contentious only a few decades earlier. Indeed, the author of an anonymous petition against the opening of such a fondaco in 1602 presented the confinement of Jews, Germans, and Turks to special lodging places as concessions to the groups themselves rather than as serving the policing objectives of a vigilant state. Separate residence, the motion suggested, should be rewarded for services rendered by worthy and "safe" groups, such as the Jews. Unlike the Turks, the petitioner argued, Jews were dispersed among the nations, lacking either a powerful emperor or a strong navy. Moreover, Jews provided useful services, such as pawning and the sale of drugs, which kept the populace content, whereas Turks did nothing but export merchandise from Venice for the benefit of Ottoman subjects. Although Jews did not use the same name, they did worship the same God as did Christians and considered Him as their father. Muslims, on the other hand, worshipped a wicked man, Muhammad. The Protestants in the German Exchange House, although no doubt heretics, performed their heretical rituals only clandestinely. The German Exchange House, moreover, had been established well before its residents became heretics, and thus the authorities had no way of predicting what would become of it, whereas the Fondaco dei Turchi was to house the pronounced enemies of Christ. The author finally warned that designating a separate residence for Turks might set a bad example, as other nations might soon seek the same privileges for their merchants in Venice.[32]

Despite the anonymous petitioner's selective interpretation, a comparison of the Fondaco dei Turchi with the Fondaco dei Tedeschi and the Jewish ghettos is, in fact, pertinent. In both these earlier cases, Venetian authorities were much more inclined to accommodate non-Catholic religious practices. Although Catholic preachers were regularly sent to proselytize in the Fondaco dei Tedeschi, many of its residents were self-professed Lutherans, on whose rituals in the compound the authorities may have turned a blind eye.[33] More openly, Jews enjoyed ritual and administrative autonomy within the ghettos. The government even made special provisions to accommodate Jewish ritual needs outside the ghettos, for example by allowing representatives to observe the preparation of bread in Christian bakeries. No such explicit autonomy was ever granted to Muslim merchants,

31. On the medieval genealogy of the institution and its attendant practices of hosting, see (Constable 2001, 2003).
32. Correr, Cod. Cicogna 978, f. 17 ("Attione fatta Adi 13 April 1602 che in Caso che il Turco ricercasse dalla Sig[no]ria che fosse fatto un Fontego per li Turchi che Habitano à Venetia, che no' sia fatto").
33. Martin (1993, esp. 26).

who enjoyed no recognized official organizations. Yet the ghettos and the two fondacos also shared important features, chiefly their role in controlling (and more effectively taxing) the shifting merchant populations. As Elisabeth Crouzet-Pavan notes, "the fondaco aided surveillance . . . [and] provided an efficient means for centralizing customs receipts."[34]

Indeed, in the long run the vision of lurking danger behind the fondaco walls, so powerfully articulated in the anonymous motion of 1602, lost out to a competing concern for surveillance and physical containment. These guiding principles, already introduced by Frangia in 1574, underscored the inevitable and odious mixing of Christians and Muslims in the absence of total residential separation. Indeed, the inquisitorial case against Frangia the previous year had revolved very much around the presence of Frangia's wife and children on the premises and their presumed commensality with their Turkish tenants. It was in part this concern about domestic mixing that eventually led to the opening of a fondaco in the former residence of the duke of Ferrara on the Grand Canal in 1621. And once the idea of a fondaco materialized, the previous, long-standing arrangement of Christian-Muslim cohabitation in brokers' houses and private residences throughout the city came not only to be seen as "unnatural" but to captivate subsequent legislators' imagination as the ultimate cause of scandal.[35]

It is thus only fitting that the first regulations for the Fondaco dei Turchi, published by the Board of Trade on May 27, 1621, should systematically conjoin religious rhetoric with reason of state in an effort to maximize the physical separation between the residents of the fondaco and the surrounding neighborhood.[36] At least one-third of the thirty-three regulations were concerned with the obstruction of vision and movement, as well as the creation of internal barriers to prevent vision and movement among the three wings of the house, designated for the residence of Balkan merchants, Anatolian merchants, and the custodian's family, respectively. Among other things, open windows and balconies were to be walled up, doors locked, and access from the outside in (during daytime) and from the inside out (after dusk) carefully monitored by armed guards. The main purpose of the fondaco was to sever its tenants' "scandalous" ties to Venetians—that is, any kind of contact that might go beyond purely economic transactions (see fig. 6.1). The familiarity and intimacy that were believed to grow from physical proximity and the sharing of living space were clearly the main target.

34. Crouzet-Pavan (2002, 121).
35. For a psychological analysis of Venetian fears surrounding the Fondaco dei Turchi, see Özkaya (2003).
36. Cinque Savi, Seconda serie, b. 187, fasc. 3, unpaginated (May 27, 1621). For a partial English translation, see Chambers and Pullan (2001, 350–52).

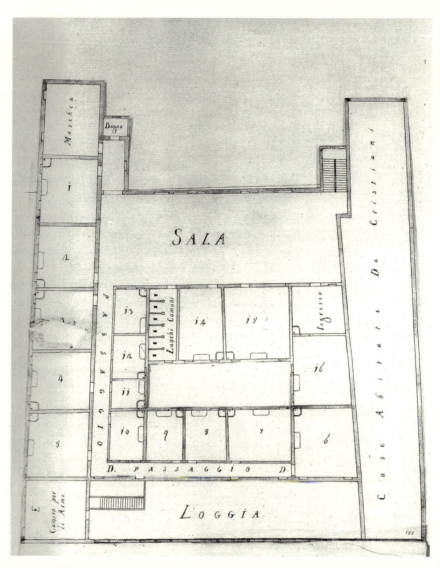

Figure 6.1 *First-floor plan of the Fondaco dei Turchi, drawn by Bernardino Maccaruzzi (1768). A mosque and a bath are at the top left corner and an armory is at the bottom left. A solid wall separates the rooms on the right from the adjacent "Houses inhabited by Christians." ASVe, Miscellanea Mappe, no. 571. Reproduction: Sezione fotoriproduzione dell'Archivio di Stato di Venezia, by permission (num. 17/2011) of Ministero per i Beni e le Attività Culturali.*

These same aspects of merchants' previous living arrangements in brokers' houses made them all the more skeptical of the merits of the new fondaco because forced relocation spelled the potential interruption of important networks. In particular, many merchants and brokers-cum-landlords saw their close ties as mutually beneficial and crucial for their continued prosperity. These ties were part of broad, genuinely trans-imperial networks that often included previously localized Armenian, Greek, and Jewish merchants and brokers and that helped more recently arrived merchants supplement their limited relational resources in the city. Indeed, the complex ties that bound commercial brokers and Ottoman merchants together were not severed entirely even after the latter were ordered to relocate to the fondaco. Repeated legislation before and after 1621 forbidding anyone from lodging Ottoman merchants, and threatening brokers who might do so with a removal from their post, suggests failure to eradicate the practice.[37]

That the tenants of the fondaco themselves were far from content with the obligation to reside there is also made abundantly clear by their constant complaints about the facilities. For example, in 1625 a group of fondaco residents complained that the roof was leaking, the neighbors were mean, and the location of the fondaco, near the Church of San Giovanni Decollato, was too far from the Rialto market.[38] In its response, the Board of Trade dismissed the merchants' allegations as an attempt to evade the requirement to reside in the fondaco. This claim may have had a grain of truth to it because permission to leave the fondaco was granted only sparingly.[39]

The establishment of the fondaco aimed not just to limit the range of possible interactions between Venetian and Ottoman subjects and the types of mediation practiced by trans-imperial commercial brokers. Its changing regulations also served as significant moments in the articulation of categories of Ottoman difference in Venice. The regulations of 1621 recognized the charges of the institution as "Turchi," and further distinguished within that category between "Bosnians and Albanians," on the one hand, and "asiatici," on the other. These categories had been previously introduced into official discourse in preparatory reports commissioned by the Board of Trade from Public Dragomans Michiel Membré and Giacomo de Nores in 1575 and 1620, respectively. Here, again, the dragomans' previous trajectories are vital for understanding their mediation. Both Membré and de Nores had been born on Cyprus and had traveled extensively in the Ottoman and Safavid empires in their youth. In distinguishing

---

37. For example, in 1625, the Board of Trade instituted a fine of 500 ducats on brokers who were found keeping Ottoman and Safavid merchandise in their homes (Cinque Savi, Seconda serie, b. 187, fasc. 3, unpaginated (May 26, 1625)).

38. Cinque Savi, Risposte, b. 146, cc. 212v–213r (Dec. 10, 1625); Senato, Deliberazioni Costantinopoli, reg. 16, cc. 139v–144r (Dec. 14, 1625).

39. Such permission was granted, for example, in 1623, to a sick merchant, Mehmet Celebi from Croia (Kruja, Albania), who asked to temporarily leave the fondaco and move to the house of his friend, Zuanne Trasardo. The board consented, as long as he kept paying rent for his room in the fondaco and without setting a precedent (Cinque Savi, Seconda serie, b. 187, fasc. 3, unpaginated (April 28, 1623)).

Balkan from Anatolian Ottoman Muslims, they seem to have built on a popular Ottoman distinction between "westerners" and "easterners," prevalent among provincial recruits to the imperial administration. In other words, Membré and de Nores seem to have tried to fit this Ottoman regional consciousness (known as *cins*) into the Venetian superordinate category of "Turchi."[40] Regional distinctions among Ottoman subjects were conveniently employed by Anatolian merchants themselves on numerous occasions. In 1579, for instance, they protested their forced relocation to Frangia's hostel, where they were to share their living space with Greeks and Bosnians, suggesting this would inevitably lead to violence. Even in the Ottoman military, they observed, these groups were kept in separate barracks so as to avoid disturbances. On that occasion, the Board of Trade denied their request, warning that accepting it would require opening "as many fondacos as their nations."[41] Indeed, the unwitting recognition by the board of the supplicants' plurality of provenances did little to mitigate an overarching sense of their distinct unity, for "their life, and customs is [sic] very scandalous, and licentious, and in order to continue thus they search in every way to remain separate, much incited and prompted by brokers, and others . . . who benefit handsomely, and give them opportunity to live as they do in contempt of our religion, and as a bad example to the whole city."[42]

Although the board identified the commercial brokers as the main force behind the merchants' demands, it also recognized an essentialized set of habits and customs that distinguished the supplicants. The trope of Turkish licentiousness was, of course, long-standing, part and parcel of early modern racialist discourses about the Turks.[43] The objectification of supplicants' ethnicity was confirmed in a report by Public Dragoman Giacomo de Nores to the Board of Trade in 1620. De Nores observed that, although the majority of Albanian and Bosnian merchants in Venice resided in the house of Frangia's descendants in the parish of San Matteo, the "Asiatic Nation" was dispersed around the city, and was "of different practice and customs" than the rest.[44] A similar logic underwrote the demands set forth by a group of

40. On Ottoman regional consciousness, see (Kunt 1974, esp. 237). See also Kafadar (2007).

41. Cinque Savi, Risposte, b. 136, cc. 130v–131r (March 21, 1579).

42. "La vita, et costumi loro, la qual è molto scandolosa, et licentiosa, et p[er] continuar in essa cercano in ogni modo di star separati, molti instigati, et spenti da sanseri, et altri che p[er] li no[n] honesti officij, che cosi si giova di parlare co[n] la ser[eni]ta V[ostra] che usano di fare co[n] questi, per li quali tragono non mediocre guadagno, dano occasione alli detti di viverre come fano in vilipendio della n[ost]ra religione, et cattivo essempio di tutta la citta." (Cinque Savi, Risposte, b. 136, cc. 130v–131r (March 21, 1579)).

43. On the importance of "customs" and religious difference to medieval and early modern racial thinking, see Braude (1997); Bartlett (2001).

44. Cinque Savi, Seconda serie, b. 187, fasc. 1, unpaginated (Nov. 11, 1620).

Anatolian merchants (many of whom, it was suggested, came from military milieus, where they had served as janissaries and Sipahi elite cavalrymen) in 1625. This time, they forced an Ottoman dignitary to demand on their behalf a new fondaco, where they would be given separate apartments "to distinguish the nations of Bosnia from those of Istanbul and other regions."[45] These examples suggest the convergence of objectifying categories among the (patrician) Board of Trade, the trans-imperial Public Dragomans, and at least some Ottoman merchants themselves.

But despite strong pronouncements about the distinctiveness of Turkish customs and rituals, telling the different groups residing in the fondaco apart sometimes proved rather difficult in actual practice. In 1645, shortly after the outbreak of the War of Crete, a concerned member of the Board of Trade, Girolamo da Ca' da Pesaro, produced a report based on a "reliable source," suggesting that merchants in the fondaco were accumulating weapons and, that

> since the Turks wear clothes that hardly differ from those of Albanians and Bosnians, and since many of them are very experienced in the city, and well instructed in the language, they can and do show up in the shops, and buy directly from them without [the aid of] another interpreter. The other [problem] is that they have close connection with Albanians, people of Perasto, and other people of the armed galleys and ships who buy [weapons] for them, and perhaps we could say that the Jews too buy it to give it to them.[46]

Two entwined problems emerge from Ca' da Pesaro's report. First, there was the difficulty of telling apart the different ethnic groups that resided in the fondaco based on their appearance, and especially distinguishing those that were potential Venetian allies (Bosnians and Albanians) from those that were clearly not (Turks). A related problem had to do with merchants' excessive familiarity with the city and command of the local language, which ostensibly enabled them to

45. Senato, Deliberazioni Costantinopoli, reg. 16, c. 142r (Dec. 19, 1625). That real tensions between Istanbulite and Bosnian merchants existed is also suggested by a petition by Ibrahim Celebi, an Istanbulite janissary-turned-merchant, in which he narrated the difficulties he encountered in his dealings with Abazà, the pasha of Bosnia, in attempting to ship to Venice via Split a great quantity of silk and other kinds of merchandise (Collegio, Risposte di dentro, b. 22, unpaginated (June 21, 1631)).

46. "Li Turchi vestono con habito che poco differisse da quello de Albanesi ò Bossinesi et che molti d'essi prattichi della Città, e ben' instrutti della lingua possino capitar e capitano alle Botteghe, et da loro stessi comprare sen altro interprete; l'altro è che questi han[n]o stretta cognitione con Albanesi, Perastini, et altre genti di Galere e Barche armate che gli le comprano et forse potressimo dire noi, che anco degl'hebrei ne comprino p[er] somministrargliele" (Cinque Savi, Risposte, b. 153, cc. 195v–196v (Dec. 15, 1645)).

interact directly with shop owners, without the mediation and surveillance of brokers and dragomans. Beyond the problem of (mis)recognition thus lurked the deeper problem of misdirected affect. Even those groups previously considered potential Venetian allies, such as the Albanians and the people of Perasto (Perast, Montenegro), or to be unaffiliated, such as the Jews, might be selling weapons to the Turks in clear violation of Venetian trust. Remarkably, the category "Turchi," which was used unproblematically in 1621 to refer to all the intended residents of the fondaco, came to stand only two and a half decades later for a subset thereof, and one whose contours were difficult to establish.

To complicate matters further, several cases of runaway converts who sought to reembrace Islam and return to Ottoman territory, and who found refuge in the fondaco, underscored its jurisdictional and religious alterity at the heart of Venice. In 1622, for example, an unnamed woman convert escaped to the fondaco, declaring her wish to return to Islam twelve years after her (allegedly voluntary) baptism. The Venetian Senate warned her hosts in the fondaco that her departure for Ottoman territory would prompt the government to seek a reciprocal Ottoman gesture toward Christian renegades who wished to return to Christianity. The merchants of the fondaco quickly dropped their support for the woman who was transferred to the Pia Casa dei Catecumeni for further catechization.[47] In another case twenty years later, Lucia, a Bosnian woman, escaped her Muslim husband and kin and arrived in Venice, where she became a servant. Her relatives managed to abduct her into the fondaco and eventually to smuggle her out to Dalmatia on board a ship. She was discovered by the captain, and in her long and convoluted deposition eventually claimed to have always been Christian and to wish to return to Venice.[48] The perceived position of the fondaco as a gateway to the Ottoman Empire for runaway slaves and servants and as a liminal Muslim space at the heart of Venice made it an abomination in the eyes of many Venetians. Indeed, the stakes in establishing and populating the fondaco were so high that it took almost half a century from the moment the Senate authorized its establishment in 1575 until it opened its gates in 1621.

The tension that the fondaco embodied, between a clear-cut Christian-Muslim divide as rehearsed in religious rhetoric, on the one hand, and the complexities of trans-imperial subjects' shifting classifications by a vigilant state, on the other, came to a head in 1662. That year, the Venetian authorities attempted to move all Safavid merchants sojourning in Venice into the fondaco. The case, which triggered successive petitions, official reports, and a number of Senate resolutions during the summer months, involved various trans-imperial groups, including several

47. Senato, Deliberazioni Costantinopoli, reg. 14, cc. 89v–90v (Oct. 9, 1622).
48. AdC, Misc. Penale, b. 343, fasc. 15, cc. 2–15 (Aug. 7, 1642).

generations of Safavid and Ottoman sojourners in Venice; the custodians of the fondaco, all of them descendants of Greek commercial broker Frangia; quite a few Armenian commercial brokers who had lodged Safavid merchants in their houses for decades; Public Dragoman Pietro Fortis, who interpreted between the Safavid merchants and the government; and, of course, patrician members of the Board of Trade and the Senate.

Although Safavid merchants had never been explicitly exempted from the requirement to reside in the fondaco, the ambiguity of the category "Turchi" effectively left them outside it for over four decades. Yet the order of the Board of Trade in 1662 was unequivocal:

> There is no doubt, that the commission of the House of the Fondaco was decreed by the Most Excellent Senate for no other purpose but to have the Mohammedan Nations required to live there separately from Christians, as required by public and private utility and the benefit of Religion, as was considered. And therefore if Persian Muslims would have had the freedom to take shelter wherever they wished, the Fondaco would have been superfluous, as no one would have any longer called himself simply a Muslim, but a Persian Muslim, and to tell them apart and recognize them for what they truly are is not so easy, therefore we consider it necessary to follow the orders established already at the time when the Fondaco was built, so that Muslims of any and all conditions should have to live there.[49]

Using the term "Mohammedan Nations" instead of the far more common but also more ambiguous designation "Turchi," the board insisted that a Muslim was a Muslim, and, furthermore, that its own interpretation was essentially the same as that of legislators forty years earlier, even as it introduced new terminology. It insisted that the fondaco was meant to separate Muslims from Christians and that it was quite hard to tell Turkish and Persian Muslims apart. Here, the semantic ambiguity of the term *Turchi* proved extremely productive once again. Although Venetian authorities were well aware of the fact that not all Ottoman subjects were

---

49. "Non poter cader in dubio, che la deputatione della Casa del Fontico non sia stata dall'Ecc[ellentissi] mo Senato decretata ad'oggetto, che le Nationi Mahomettane in esso havessero ad habitar Separatam[en]te da Christiani, cosi ricercando il publico, e privato Servitio, e q[ue]llo sopra tutto della Religione, com'è stato considerato, onde quando i Turchi Persiani havessero libertà di ricovrarsi, ove meglio volessero, sup[er]fluo sarebbe il Fontico, mentre ogni uno non più semplicem[en]te Turco, ma Turco Persiano si sarebbe denominare, e il far di questi la distintione, e la vera cognitione non è di cosi facile riuscita, che però la esecutione de gli Ordeni già stabiliti nella errretionne del Fontico, stimiamo necessaria, aciò li Turchi di che conditione esser si voglia habbino ad habitare" (Cinque Savi, Seconda serie, b. 187, fasc. 3, unpaginated (June 2, 1662)).

Turks (or Muslims) and that not all Muslims were Turks (or even Ottoman subjects), it was quite logical to suggest that it was hard to tell apart different kinds of Muslims.

Contrary to the claims of the board, evidence suggests that quite a few Safavid merchants did in fact reside outside the fondaco prior to 1662. In 1643, a group of Armenian merchants asked (and were granted) permission from the Board of Trade for two Armenian brokers to continue lodging Armenian and Persian merchants, against a prevailing prohibition on brokers' lodging their clients. They argued that the brokers lived elsewhere and could not be considered "hoteliers" because "they do not provide utensils, nor operate anything the way it is customary for hoteliers, and these nations [Armenian and Persian] come to their houses of their own free will, unlike the Turks in the Fondaco. There is no doubt that if said brokers are obliged to pay hoteliers' taxes, the burden will fall on merchants themselves, who when aggravated by more expenses will much more easily go to other cities."[50] Their request was endorsed.

This was the background to the Safavid merchants' protest in 1662 over the new requirement for them to relocate to the fondaco. Not only was the requirement unprecedented, they suggested, but ritual differences would make it dangerous for them to cohabit with the fondaco Ottoman tenants. Their petition, reproduced here in full, encapsulates some of the major themes of the discourse about foreign merchants articulated by trans-imperial subjects active in the Venetian commercial sphere in the seventeenth century: foreign merchants' presumed helplessness, linguistic incompetence, lack of relational resources, and confusion in the face of multiple magistracies with which they must deal.

Having petitioned Your Serenity on other occasions, we, Muslims of Persia, to let us keep enjoying our old liberty to be able to stay in the houses of our brokers, since the custodian of the Fondaco of the other Muslims unjustly wants to pester us and make us stay with the other Muslims, who are our enemies, opposed to us in law, religion, and Prince, We cannot do that, because we would kill each other, and our King of Persia would have us beheaded, and if we were to enter the Fondaco we would not be able to go back to our country. This [requirement] is a novelty, since we are good

50. "Non prestando utensili, nè operando cosa alcuna, come è ord[ina]rio de albergatori et ricorrono queste nat[io]ni volontieri in d[ett]e Case non altrimenti che fanno li Turchi al Fontigo Ne hà dubbio che se d[et]ti sanseri foss[er]o ubligati all'Allbergaria, l'aggravio saria de stessi mer[it]ti, che quanto più fossero tenuti soccomber à spese, tanto più facilm[en]te capiteriano ad altre scale, con pregiud[iti]o del neg[oti]o di q[ues]ta Città" (Cinque Savi, Risposte, b. 153, c. 90v–91v (Sept. 29, 1643); Cinque Savi, Seconda serie, b. 4, fasc. 47 parte prima, c. 11.3–11.3v (July 9, 1650); Collegio, Risposte di dentro, b. 66 (June 30, 1666)).

friends of this Republic, and if we cannot stay remote and distant from
our Turkish enemies, who dwell in said Fondaco, we would have to go to
trade in other places. And we ask for nothing else but three months to sell
our merchandise, and go away, and give notice to our King. If he concedes
that we go into the Fondaco, we would return to Venice, but if he doesn't
so wish, we would not be able to do so, and would rather go to sleep in
prison for these three months, or where Your Serenity should please, than
in the Fondaco. And we supplicate for piety's sake that you save our lives
in this time, without going to the Fondaco, and suspend an order, that the
Board of Trade has reissued contrary to Your Senate resolution of the 10th
of this month. [This order] wishes, contrary to said resolution, to put us in
the Fondaco by force, without having taken [into consideration] the [nec-
essary] information, and without examination. And then give us a separate
house with a guardian where we Persians could stay, having always come
to Venice with our merchandise, more than to other countries. We could
not present our arguments to the Board of Trade because we do not have
a lawyer, nor a dragoman, nor anyone else, since everyone has abandoned
us out of fear, and we do not know how to speak [Italian]. Therefore we
supplicate Your Excellency not to abandon us, since you are most Pious
masters and in the whole world it is spoken of your good justice.[51]

By repeatedly emphasizing that their life would be jeopardized back home should
they willingly move in with Ottoman subjects, the petitioners also played on

51. "Havendo altre volte suplicato la V[ostra] Ser[eni]ta noi Turchi di Persia di lasciarci godere la
nostra antica liberta di poter star nelle Case delli nostri sanseri, perche il Custode del Fontego di
altri Turchi contro giust[iti]a vol assediarne, et farne star con li altri Turchi, che sono nostri nimici,
contrarij di legge, de Religgione, e di Prencipe, Noi non lo podemo fare, perche si amazzaressimo
fra di noi, et il nostro Re di Persia ne fara butar via la testa, et scauderemo nel fontego non
poderemo piu tornar nella nostra Patria. questa star una novita, che Noi semo boni amici di q[ues]ta
Republica, et quando non potemo star remoti, et lontani dalli nostri nimici Turchi, che sono
in d[ett]o Fontego, per forza bisogna andar a negociar in altre parti, et non volemo altro se non
tre mesi di tempo di vender nostre mercancie, et andar via, et dar parte al Nostro Re, che se lui
concendera, che noi andar in Fontego, noi eseguiremo ancora in Venecia, ma quando lui non vol,
noi non lo potemo fare, et contentemo piu meglio andar in una preggion adormir q[ues]ti tre mesi,
o dove piace alla V[ostra] Ser[eni]ta, ma non in Fontego, la supplichemo per pieta salvarci la vita
in q[ues]to tempo, senza andar in Fontego, et far sospender un proclama, che hano fato li cinq[ue]
Savij di novo contro la vostra parte del Senato delli 10 di q[ues]to mese, che vogliono contro d[ett]a
parte meterci per forza in Fontego, senza haver preso information, et saminar, et poi darci una Casa
separata con un Guardian dove possiamo star Noi Persiani, che seguivano sempre in Vinecia con
nostre mercancie meglio, che in altro paese, Alli 5 Savij noi non potemo trovar nostra ragg[io]ne
p[er]che non havemo un Avocato, ne Dragoman ne nissun altro perche tutti ne hano abbandonato
per paura, et noi non saper parlar, onder supplichemo le V[ostre] E[ccellenze] non abbandonarci
voi, che sete pietissimi sig[no]ri et intutto il Mondo si dice della vostra bona giust[iti]a" (Collegio,
Risposte di dentro, b. 58, unpaginated (June 19, 1662)).

emerging European notions of Oriental despotism.[52] Against a reductive vision of all Muslims as essentially the same, the petitioners insisted on their fundamental difference from Ottoman Muslims. Rather than a religious logic for the confinement of Muslims to a separate residence, they suggested that the historical roots of the fondaco lay in political enmities between the Venetian and Ottoman states. Therefore, given the long-standing alliance between Venice and the Safavid Shah against the common Ottoman enemy, they should not be subjected to similar confinement.

Conversely, the Senate resolution of 1662 also cited a case from 1629 in which special permission had been granted to a Persian to reside outside the fondaco as proof that this had been the exception rather than the rule. More interestingly, it provided some proto-ethnographic observations in support of its resolution:

> These Persian Muslims constantly talk to the other [Muslims] in the Squares, and come to the Fondaco not only on the occasion of the Muslim Bairams [Festivals], but also when someone dies, assisting in their burial rituals and dining and drinking with the Turks, and they even intervene in the negotiation of some of their businesses, or in resolving some other differences; and some of these Persian Muslims have received keys to a room in the Fondaco, and are therefore required to pay rent, although to enjoy the freedom of the others, they reside outside it.[53]

Ultimately, the Senate decided that the half a dozen or so Safavid merchants then present in Venice were expendable and that if they were to take their business elsewhere no real harm to the Venetian economy would ensue. One of the merchants, the board suggested, had been living in Venice for years, without engaging in trade at all. The board was not oblivious to the fact that behind the merchants' petition stood interested commercial brokers, who profited from their close ties to their Safavid lodgers. Here, again, the board based its response on old notions of merchants' lack of relational resources and dependency on brokers, oblivious to the ways in which this very dependency had become a rhetorical tool in the hands of localized trans-imperial subjects themselves.

---

52. On the trope of Oriental despotism in early modern Venice, see Valensi (1990).

53. "Questi Turchi Persiani, pratticano continuam[en]te con gli altri alle Piazze, e capitano al Fontico non solo in ocasione de Bairani de Turchi, ma anche quando alcuno ne muore, assistendo alle funtionj delle loro spolture, e con Turchi mangiano, e bevono, e s'ingeriscono pure ne trattati di alcun loro affarre, ò altro aggiustamto di differenze; e che alcuno di essi Turchi Persiani, havendo riceuto le Chiavi di una Camera del Fontico, resti p[e]rcio obligato all'affitto, benche p[er] godere la libertà degli altri, habiti fuori d'esso." (Cinque Savi, Seconda serie, b. 187, fasc. 3, unpaginated (Aug. 23, 1662)).

7

Levantines

Genealogies of a Category

I n a pathbreaking study over three decades ago, Giorgio Vercellin charted the arc of development of the categories used in the Venetian commercial sphere to refer to Ottoman subjects. According to Vercellin, by the turn of the seventeenth century Venetians distinguished between "Turchi" ("Turks") and those "di nationi suddite turchesche" ("of nations subject to the Turks"). This distinction, he suggested, gave way to the superordinate category "orientali" ("orientals") by the later eighteenth century.[1] To the best of my knowledge, Vercellin's remains the only attempt at a genealogy of categories of Ottoman alterity in early modern Venice (and in Italy, more broadly). Most other studies either have portrayed a pre-Orientalist golden age, during which categories of Venetian and Ottoman belonging were supposedly fluid and inchoate, or have sought to trace a direct line of uncompromising militant rhetoric against "the Turk" from the Middle Ages to the Enlightenment and beyond.[2]

That these two strands of argument still coexist side by side in current scholarship suggests the limits of dialogue between social and intellectual historians. It also reinforces the need to pay closer attention to the different genres in which categories of belonging and alterity were articulated, negotiated, and transformed. Clearly, the emergence and proliferation of superordinate categories that refer to Ottoman subjects should not be reduced to a pre-Orientalist "before"

1. Vercellin (1980, 70).
2. For representative examples, see Dursteler (2006) and Bisaha (2004), respectively.

and an Orientalist "after." As postcolonial scholarship has shown, to understand how ethnolinguistic and geopolitical categories shifted in the wake of imperial expansion, we must not presuppose the overwhelming power of early modern states—themselves in the process of consolidation—to impose unified conceptual schemes. Rather, these very schemes should be understood as emergent, constituted in the process of engaging competing classificatory systems under specific conditions of articulation.[3]

In this vein, I trace in this chapter the haphazard and gradual articulation of the category "Levantini" ("Levantines") in the Venetian commercial sphere to show how its shifting semantic range and prototypical meanings were closely linked to distinct sites and moments of institutionalization: the admission of Levantine Jews to Venice in 1541 and the granting of their first charter of rights in 1589; the establishment of an exchange house for Ottoman-Muslim traders, the Fondaco dei Turchi, in a highly visible edifice on the Grand Canal in 1621; the levying of differential taxes on Jews, Armenians, and other Ottoman and Safavid merchants in the wake of a protracted economic slump in the 1630s; and, finally, the onset of the Venetian-Ottoman War of Crete in 1645. By considering instantiations of the deployment of the term at specific junctures, we see that the category "Levantini" emerged through the ongoing negotiations between trans-imperial subjects and Venetian elites in several institutional frameworks, and specifically through the Venetian Board of Trade. Further, its differing articulations stemmed from the conflation of three distinct, although interrelated, dimensions for understanding difference in the early modern Mediterranean: political jurisdiction, confessional affiliation, and ethnolinguistic identity. I posit that this conflation itself was the result of trans-imperial subjects' efforts to commensurate Venetian and Ottoman (at times conflicting) reasons of state for their own varied strategic purposes.

Given the complex relations between ethnonyms, religious groups, language communities, and imperial jurisdictions and geographies, it is only to be expected that classificatory schemes varied over time and with different genres. It will also not surprise the reader that merchants, brokers, and other trans-imperial subjects affected by state policies were wont to protest their potential inclusion in superordinate categories such as "Levantini" by insisting on their distinctness. At the same time, the designation *Levantini* had several clear advantages. Most obviously, it pointed to a region of immense Venetian commercial interests—the Levant—which, as the Board of Trade recognized in numerous decrees, held the key to the fading economic fortunes of Venice. In addition, unlike "Turks," a category with juridical and ethnolinguistic as well as religious implications, "Levantini"

3. Stoler (1989, 1992); Domínguez (1986); Cohn (1996); Frank (2005).

conveniently elided confessional and ethnolinguistic specificity. "Levantini" some-times designated Venetian and Safavid as well as Ottoman subjects and thus could potentially take the edge off the political and juridical implications of the status of enemy subjects, particularly in wartime. Recognizing trans-imperial subjects' own interests in deploying certain categories and the myriad roles they played in this struggle over definitions thus provides a corrective to the Eurocentric and top-down genealogy of Orientalism. It also underscores the important mediation performed by those claiming to be "in-between" in the process of articulating cat-egories of difference and developing metropolitan practices of boundary-marking and boundary-crossing.

In 1541, the Venetian Senate recognized for the first time the right of *Ebrei Levantini* ("Levantine Jews") to dwell in a newly opened extension of the ghetto, as long as they engaged in "pure mercantile activity."[4] For much of the sixteenth century, the term *Levantini* in Venice, as in other Italian port cities such as Ferrara, Ancona, and later Livorno, typically referred to a subset of diasporic Sephardim. These were Jews who, in the wake of their exile from the Iberian Peninsula in 1492, had settled in the Ottoman Empire and had, as Ottoman subjects, come to enjoy special protections and tax concessions while trading on the Italian penin-sula.[5] Yet, over the course of the next century, the meaning of *Levantini* shifted quite dramatically as it came to refer not only to Jews but also to other Ottoman merchants sojourning in Venice, regardless of their ethnolinguistic identity or confessional affiliation.

The shift in the prototypical meaning of *Levantini* did not end there. By the end of the sixteenth century, it acquired the dual meaning of (1) shifty, even sketchy men and (2) natives of the Levant.[6] With these definitions the paradig-matic focus of the term was no longer on diasporic commercial activity but, rather, on presumed provenance and its attendant character traits. This focus was carried over into French and English as the terms *levantin* and *Levantine* made their first appearances as dictionary headwords at the turn of the eighteenth century and were glossed, first, as "Natives or Inhabitants of the Levant, the Eastern People" and, only second, as "those that are employed on the Mediterranean."[7] The

---

4. A transcript of the Senate decree of June 2, 1541, is available in Arbel (1995b, 197–200). For an English translation by Benjamin Ravid, see Chambers and Pullan (2001, 344).
5. This use of the term *Levantini* to refer to Ottoman Jews was common among contemporary Venetian Jews as well. For an example, see the autobiographical text of seventeenth-century Venetian Rabbi Leon of Modena in Cohen (1988, esp. 120). On the complex relationship between *Ebrei Levantini* and the Venetian state, see also Cooperman (1987).
6. See Florio (1598, 202; 1611, 281).
7. Phillips (1706, unpaginated).

former definition, which ultimately prevailed, presaged the nineteenth-century understanding of "Levantines" as prototypically non-Muslim Ottoman subjects, marked by vaguely "European" habits and sometimes ancestry but corrupted by their surrounding environment into a lifestyle that was not quite European.[8]

These continuities speak to the emergence and gradual consolidation of "the Levant" as a key geopolitical category of inter-imperial discourse, with its attendant ethnolinguistic markers of identity. At the same time, the category "Levantini," like the objects and people it came to denote, witnessed significant variation in both the "class of all things which properly 'fall under' or are described by" it and the shared properties of those members seen as most salient and representative of the class as a whole.[9] To document these decidedly nonlinear and at times contradictory conceptual transformations, I take in this chapter a two-pronged approach. First, I look closely at specific deployments of "Levantini" in Venetian commercial discourse. As in previous chapters, I consider the back-and-forth between the Board of Trade and its trans-imperial interlocutors as important moments during which the category was calibrated and recalibrated through various institutionalized practices of classification. This allows me to show how the term *Levantini* functioned as a strategically deployable shifter, whose "salient interpretation," in the words of linguistic anthropologist Bonnie Urciuoli, "depends on the relation of its user to its audience and so shifts with context."[10] Both trans-imperial subjects and Venetian political elites deployed the term *Levantini* to emphasize the fraught juridical and affective ties that bound diasporic merchants to Venice and its inter-imperial commercial sphere. Few subjects applied the category to themselves as an autonym, but many— often equally "Levantine" in provenance and commercial orientation—applied it to others.[11] By so doing, they strategically situated themselves at the heart of Venice and assumed a metropolitan perspective that projected a Levantine elsewhere. In contests over privileges, "Levantini" thus also served to ultimately

8. On the nineteenth-century category "Levantines," see Schmitt (2005, esp. 57–58). To some extent, a combination of linguistic, sartorial, and affective habits that were "outlandish" and "mixed," marked the Levantini from their emergence as a recognizable category of quasi-ethnic classification in the sixteenth century.

9. This argument builds loosely on semantic prototype theory and specifically on the concepts intension, extension, and prototype (Swartz 1997).

10. Urciuoli defines the *strategically deployable shifter* as "a lexical item or expression deployed in different discursive fields so that, in effect, people using term X in a referring expression in field A are engaged in a different pragmatic activity from those using the formally identical term X in a referring expression in field B. The salient interpretation of the term depends on the relation of its user to its audience and so shifts with context" (2000, unpaginated). See also Silverstein (1976).

11. But see the later discussion of Daniel Rodriga and the tax concessions for Levantine Jews for a specific example in which strategic self-characterization as "Levantini" became useful.

place certain groups and individuals outside the Venetian sphere, both juridically and affectively. This was perhaps the most lasting entailment of the term.

In addition to considering the tangled genealogy of *Levantini* in Venetian commercial discourse, I also trace the uses of the Italian, French, and English cognates *levantino/i*, *levantin(s)* and *Levantine(s)* through a larger (mostly literary) seventeenth-century corpus. This allows me to examine the hypothesis that the shifting articulations of "Levantini" in the Venetian commercial sphere provided the template for other early modern commercial centers, eventually leading to the institutionalization of the category as a proto-Orientalist gloss for Ottoman alterity. At the same time, I document significant differences between Italian and Anglo-French deployments of the category, which relate to the entry of the Atlantic seaboard powers into the Mediterranean in the seventeenth century.

EAST OF WHERE?

By arguing that *Levantini* operated as a strategically deployable shifter that marked those who deploy it as belonging firmly within metropolitan Venice vis-à-vis a foreign Levant, I am also suggesting that the spatial extension of the Levant was given to contestation and inherently depended on a speaker's perspective. In Mediterranean mariners' Lingua Franca, *Levant* signified the eastern wind.[12] As a nautical proper name, from its very emergence the *Levant* thus indicated a direction or orientation projected from a particular vantage point rather than a static location.[13] Yet, over time, the term did come to denote a loose geography. In certain contexts, *the Levant* described the Venetian maritime colonies, sometimes also known by other terms, such as *Oltremare* ("overseas"), a term that dates back to the Crusades period, when it referred to the Holy Land and other Crusader states. By the sixteenth century, the jurisdiction of the Venetian syndics of the Levant came to include the Adriatic coastline (including Istria) as well.[14] This broad use of *the Levant* to refer to the Venetian Stato da Mar in toto was quite prevalent in colonial subjects' petitions as well. For example, in 1629 Stamo Redastama of Corfu petitioned the Senate against the Greek archpriest of the island, who had confiscated a monastery that Redastama had built. His petition described recourse

12. Kahane, Kahane and Tietze (1958, 406: item 603, 276: item 371).
13. I thank Naor Ben-Yehoyada for helping me clarify this point.
14. On the magistracies of "Sindici inquisitori in Levante" and "Provveditore generale del Levante," see Da Mosto (1937, 32, 47, 50, 58, 139, 213); Tiepolo (1994, 919–21); Dudan (1933, 1938); Eufe (2003, 17–19). On Venetian "Romania," see Thiriet (1959, esp. 1–7).

to the Venetian magistrates as "an ordinary and most common thing, not only on Corfu, but in all the Churches of the Levant subject to Your Serenity."[15]

In other contexts, *the Levant* denoted the Ottoman-controlled coastline of the eastern Mediterranean. For example, in 1658 a Neapolitan merchant, Gianlorenzo Santa Chiara, petitioned the Venetian government for an exclusive patent for the importation of coffee, a potion popular, he informed the readers, in the main "cities of the Levant, particularly in Istanbul, Cairo, Izmir, and Alexandria."[16] In the writings of trans-imperial subjects, *the Levant* was sometimes a thinly veiled reference to the Ottoman Empire, particularly after the onset of the War of Crete in 1645 when Ottoman subjecthood could have negative repercussions in Venice.

Yet *the Levant* could also refer to Venetian and Ottoman territories combined. In this use, it at least partially overlapped with *Romania*, a term of much older provenance that denoted regions formerly under Byzantine or eastern Roman rule and, by the fifteenth century, subject to either the Venetians, Mamluks, or Ottomans.[17] An early Venetian Senate decree in 1376 enumerated as parts of the Levant "lower Romania and upwards, that is Cyprus, Romania, Tana, Crete, Alexandria, and Armenia, as well as other places of these regions."[18] Such a combination of Venetian and non-Venetian territories was also the basis for a 1476 Senate act that referred to "The Levant, lower Romania and other areas outside the Gulf [the Adriatic]."[19] Unlike *Romania*, *Levant* was of late medieval coinage and was rooted firmly in the Mediterranean traders' argot. These roots are well attested in its lingering association with diasporic commercial activity, whether that of the Consul in the Levant, who represented the Florentine merchant community in the fifteenth-century Byzantine and later Ottoman capital, or the English Levant Company a century and a half later. Such an expansive, commercially oriented Levant became even more prevalent with the entrance of the Atlantic seaboard powers to the Mediterranean in the seventeenth century—the Levant

15. "Cosa ordinaria, et osservatissima non pure in Corfù, ma in tutte le chiese di Levante sogette à Vostra Serenità" (Collegio, Risposte di dentro, b. 20, unpaginated (March 20, 1629)).

16. Collegio, Risposte di dentro, b. 50, unpaginated (Aug. 23, 1658). It is precisely in this period that Jews of Iberian descent "slowly assimilated or exiled to the borderlands of the Ottoman Empire the native Romaniote Jewry" (Goffman 1990, 78).

17. Although the specific terminology used is unknown, the "Pax Nicephori" negotiations between the eastern (Byzantine) and western (Frankish) empires in the early ninth century already established a region that comprehended Venice and any point east of the Italian Peninsula as the domain of the eastern churches. Wolff (1948) provides a genealogy of *Romania* from late antiquity onward as a self-referential term for the territories of the Roman Empire in the east, through its adoption by Venice in the wake of the Fourth Crusade to refer to formerly Byzantine territories now under Venetian rule, to its eventual extension to encompass Ottoman territory as well and particularly, following Ottoman use, to refer to Asia Minor.

18. Senato, Deliberazioni Miste, reg. 35, cc. 86v–87r (Feb. 12, 1375 m.v.), quoted in Arbel (2001, 78).

19. Senato Mar, reg. 10, c. 104v (Dec. 7, 1476), quoted in Arbel (2001), 75.

Company, after all, was born from the merger of the Turkey Company and the Venice Company in 1592. Thus, in his *relazione* from England in 1618, Venetian Ambassador Pietro Contarini perhaps adopted the perspective of his hosts when he mentioned that, in addition to the East India Company, another English company traded in places "of the Levant, such as Scythia [the lower Danube], Alexandria, Istanbul, Zakynthos, and Venice."[20] The Levant, then, could reach all the way from the Adriatic Sea to the Nile Delta, depending on the changing political and commercial perspective projection. A shifting extension of the term was its hallmark from its late medieval Lingua Franca roots onward.

Unlike the venerable medieval genealogy of the term *Levant*, its derivative adjective (and eventually noun) *Levantine* seems to have appeared only in the sixteenth century and, initially, to have had a significantly more circumscribed semantic range. As mentioned, by the mid-sixteenth century, in Venice *Levantini* referred primarily and paradigmatically to a subset of Sephardic Jewish merchants, namely those who had sojourned in the Ottoman Empire prior to their arrival on the Italian peninsula and who therefore enjoyed the protection of the Porte while away from Ottoman territory. The decidedly commercial setting in which this category emerged in the first several decades of the sixteenth century is significant. According to Benjamin Ravid, Levantini were first singled out from other Jews in Venice in 1541, when the Senate recognized their great contribution to trade and granted them additional rooms for their lodging "so that they shall have greater reason to come to the city to its advantage."[21]

The first half century of Levantini settlement in Venice established many of the features that eventually came to define "Levantine nations" as a whole: internal religious autonomy and collective representation, summary legal procedures under the exclusive jurisdiction of the Board of Trade, and legal nonresidency (and hence nonsubjecthood) on Venetian soil.[22] These were all mirror images of the privileges extended to trade colonies in Byzantium and later in the Ottoman

---

20. "Un'altra compagnia pure negozia per Levante, come Scizia, Alessandria, Costantinopoli, Zante e Venezia" (http://venus.unive.it/riccdst/sdv/strumenti/testi/relazioni/contarini.htm [accessed June 2, 2006]). Similarly, John Evelyn's introduction to the reader in Rycaut's *The History of the Three Late, Famous Impostors, viz. Padre Ottomano, Mahomed Bei and Sabatai Sevi* (1669) mentions "Malta, and other Levantine parts" Evelyn (1669, unpaginated).

21. Ravid (1976, 190).

22. The first consul of the Levantini in Venice was Hayyim Saruq, a prominent Jewish merchant born in the Ottoman Empire, who spent decades in Venice managing business in Zakynthos, Istanbul, and elsewhere (Arbel 1995b, 160). For a study of Jewish consuls in the early modern Mediterranean and their relationship to other forms of consulateship, as well as to notions of community and ethnic distinctness, see Jütte (2011). On Jewish consuls in the Ottoman Empire, see Shmuelevitz (1984, 147–49). For a somewhat dated but still useful overview of British, French, Dutch, and Venetian consuls there, see Steensgaard (1967).

Empire.[23] The very constitution of the Levantini as a "nation," therefore, was modeled on long-standing circum-Mediterranean understandings of the management of ethnolinguistic, religious, and juridical difference in general and of a sovereign's relationship with semi-permanent merchant diasporas in particular. Throughout the sixteenth and seventeenth centuries, Levantini had a strong incentive to preserve their distinctiveness because they were the only Jews (and, for that matter, the only group other than Venetian citizens by birth) to enjoy preferential tax concessions in Venice and the much sought-after privilege of trading directly between Venetian and Ottoman territories. Levantini themselves often emphasized their distinctiveness vis-à-vis the Tedeschi ("German" or Ashkenazi) Jews who had long lived in Venice and who, as moneylenders and traders in secondhand clothes, were quite marginalized economically and politically.

Notably, Venetian officialdom frequently lumped the Levantini together with the Ponentini—Jews of Iberian descent who had settled not in the Ottoman Empire but in Amsterdam and other commercial centers in Atlantic Europe. To be sure, many Levantini and Ponentini were related by kinship or business ties. In a proposed charter drafted in 1589, Daniel Rodriga, the consul of the Ponentini, specifically asked the Venetian authorities to exempt his fellow Ponentini and Levantini from any communal taxation shouldered by the Tedeschi. Because they engaged exclusively in trade, Rodriga's argument went, the Ponentini and Levantini should pay only customs duties.[24] Rodriga's argument helped reinforce the legal fiction of merchants' nonresidence and juridical foreignness, suggesting the role of trans-imperial subjects in mediating for Venetian use what were long-standing Byzantine and Ottoman precedents. Indeed, "Levantini" as a category was premised on the concept of nation as a legally recognizable, autonomous merchant community with its special privileges and immunities, a concept that was itself rooted in well-established circum-Mediterranean mechanisms for dealing with merchant diasporas. In making collective claims in Venice, trans-imperial subjects were thus building on enduring institutional practices for defining the relationship between the marketplace and the state, and between juridically alien subjects and officialdom.

Rodriga's charter was drafted only three years after the Board of Trade had become the Venetian inappellable court for Jewish and Ottoman merchants, and had assumed jurisdiction over all matters concerning Levantine Jewish ritual and residency in the city.[25] In endorsing Rodriga's charter, the board reserved for itself the right to determine membership in the Levantine nation. The charter thus

---

23. On the significance of such enduring arrangements for Ottoman Christians' emergent proto-nationalist group consciousness, see Masters (1987).
24. Ravid (1976, 197–99).
25. Ravid (1976, 199–200).

inaugurated the emergent category "Levantini" for juridical contexts and bolstered the economic and legal standing of those who could claim membership in it. It also empowered the Board of Trade against the claims of competing magistracies, establishing its jurisdiction as the sole arbiter of Levantini status. By basing its decisions on individuals' commercial usefulness the board further institutionalized the link between the category "Levantini" and Venetian-focused mercantile activity in the eastern Mediterranean.

The distinction between the Levantini and other kinds of Jews based on their purported commercial acumen and transience had far-reaching consequences. Sephardic Jews, many of them the descendants of forced converts, were seen as social and religious chameleons par excellence, who notoriously oscillated between Christianity and Judaism while mobilizing an interfaith, inter-imperial network of kin and business associates.[26] Their functioning as the prototypical center of the emergent category thus coupled merchants' physical mobility with the ability to dissimulate their identity as they moved from one environment to another. Confessional ambiguity and geographical mobility thus helped reinforce stereotypic qualities long associated with merchants as shifty people, so that eventually shrewdness and shiftiness, alongside diasporic commercial activity, came to define "Levantines" as a whole.[27]

EMBODYING "LEVANTINI"

The late sixteenth and early seventeenth centuries saw a severe and protracted economic recession, of which contemporary Venetian policymakers were acutely aware. In a sense, the category "Levantini" cohered because it enabled its referents, trans-imperial commercial actors such as Rodriga, to demand, and on occasion obtain, collective concessions from the Venetian government. They were able to do so precisely because the Board of Trade came to perceive such actors as essential for any efforts to resuscitate the economy of the Republic. Starting in the second half of the sixteenth century, Venice found itself in an increasingly weak position vis-à-vis trans-imperial merchants, whose business was vital for its very survival as a commercial empire. Venetian woes were compounded by growing commercial competition from both the Atlantic seaboard powers—the English, the French, and the Dutch—who entered the Mediterranean in this period and from

26. For a classic study of Levantini religious ambiguity confronted by the Venetian inquisitorial search for certainty, see Pullan (1977).
27. As Benjamin Arbel notes, "Shipowning, the phenomenon known as Marranism, and a certain laxity in the observance of religious rules in the economic field seem to have been interrelated" (2000b, 67).

the Portuguese direct maritime trade routes to South and Southeast Asia. Under such circumstances, Venice could ill afford to disregard the demands of merchants engaged in the Levant trade. As they themselves were quick to point out, it would not take much for them to take their lucrative business elsewhere, to Livorno or Amsterdam, to name but two competitors for the increasingly elusive position of Venice as an inter-imperial entrepôt. Finally, some trans-imperial subjects enjoyed especially strong ties to both Ottoman and Venetian officialdom. Through kinship, friendship, or business, merchants who moved across empires could, and at times did, seek patronage from very high officials on one side or on both. They were also quite adept at manipulating different levels of government against one another.

This is the context in which a 1656 Board of Trade report to the Senate concerning the belongings of an Ottoman merchant who had recently died in Venice, a certain Hacı Mehmet, concluded by asserting that the board alone had oversight "in matters pertaining to trade, especially that of Turks, Jews, and others of the Levant."[28] Although the late Mehmet was Muslim, the template for this ruling was emphatically ecumenical, recognizing the multiple confessional groups operating in the Levant trade and subsuming all of them under a unified commercial law. At least in the eyes of Venetian legislators, by the mid-seventeenth century diasporic commercial activity had come to trump other markers of group membership, making trans-imperial merchants active on the Italian peninsula the prototypical center of the incipient category "Levantini."

But how did the category "Levantini" come to extend from Ottoman Jews, first, to all diasporic Ottoman and Safavid merchants in Italian commercial centers, irrespective of confessional affiliation; then, to all those "of the Levant," regardless of confessional affiliation and present location; and, ultimately, to virtually all non-Muslims in the eastern Mediterranean, regardless of juridical status, location, or activity? A few examples from contemporary texts may help elucidate the evolving denotational range and qualities of "Levantini" in the sixteenth century. Some of these examples seek to replicate oral speech and thus give us insight on perceived colloquial use, even if they do not always describe actual speech forms.

Example 1: Alessandro Piccolomini, a Sienese humanist, offered the following words of caution for young women in his *Dialogo de la bella creanza de le donne* (Dialogue on the Politeness of Ladies, 1539):

I confess to you that if it were possible to force nature to create a youth . . . wise and experienced it would have been very well to love him,

---

28. "Nelli affari spettanti alla mercantia, massime de Turchi, ebrei, et altri del Levante" (Cinque Savi, Seconda serie, b. 187, fasc. 3, unpaginated (March 14, 1656)).

but one should not take the risk, for out of a thousand there is not one who is not silly, arrogant, *levantine*, vain, boastful, ostentatious, scandalous, and rude, and therefore a woman should run away as fast as she can, if she does not wish to become in four days the story of Siena.[29]

Example 2: Dalmatian-born Luigi Bassano, in his *Costumi et i modi particolari della vita de' Turchi* (1545) refers to the Turks as wild (*salvatiche*) and lascivious (*lussuriose*) with their own parents-in-law and brothers- and sisters-in-law, as is, he says, "la natione Levantina" in its entirety.[30]

Example 3: The following *Canzona de' Levantini* (Song of the Levantines) was penned by Giovanni Battista dell'Ottonaio (1482–1527), Florentine poet and playwright, and published posthumously in 1559:

> *Although our dress is of a Turk*
> *each of us is a Florentine merchant;*
> *and we have fled from the Levant*
> *with much gold and various merchandise,*
> *which over such a long road*
> *we have carried with infinite fear*
> *of losing [the merchandise] and perhaps also our life.*
> *Because so many have turned against Christians*
> *that, if the leaders of our faith*
> *do not provide aid soon,*
> *all will be seized by the Turks.*
> . . .[31]

29. "Io ti confesso bene che se fusse possibile sforzar la natura che facesse un giovine in quella età savio e pratico sarebbe benissimo di amarlo ma non è da metersi a questo pericolo, che di mille non se ne trova uno che non sia scempio, superbo, levantino, fumoso, vantatore, fastoso, scandoloso, e mal creato, però fuggili una donna più che può se non vuol esser in quattro dì la favola di Siena" (Piccolomini 1539; emphasis added).
30. Bassano (1963 [1545], 22).
31. *Benché di Turco il nostro abito sia,*
   ciascun di noi è Fiorentin mercante;
   e fuggiam di Levante
   con di molto oro e varia mercanzia
   qual per sì lunga via
   condotta abbiàno con paura infinita
   di perder quella e fors'anche la vita.
   Perché contro a' cristian son mossi tanti
   che, se da' capi della nostra fede
   presto non si provede,
   preda sarèn de' Turchi tutti quanti.

Example 4: Also in 1559, Florentine Piero Cimatore's carnival masquerade song, *Canzona delle buttagre* (Song of the Botargo) opened with the following lines:

> *We are dragomans, ladies, Levantines*
> *who bring here from Valona*[32]
> *perfect and tasty botargo*[33]
> *for you, Florentines.*
> *Although it comes from many different countries*
> *ours is superior*
> *because it keeps and preserves better*
> *the goodness and the color.*
> *Enjoy its flavor*
> *women, please,*
> *because this merchandise*
> *is brought as a courtesy by the Levantines.*[34]

Scrivete lor, mercanti:
che, se presto tra lor pace non fanno,
saran forzati a farla con più danno.
Dite che più non voglia ormai nessuno,
se non il suo; tutti a una voce
piglin la santa croce,
vadin lor contro, e seguiràgli ognuno;
dite che là ciascuno
si può far ricco, potente e famoso,
tant'è il paese bel, largo e copioso.
O voi che sete buon cristian, pregate
il ciel ch'unisca in pace i cristian e' regni.
O voi, principi degni,
da sì crudo flagel ne liberate.
Su, d'una volontate,
cerchiàn morir con salute e onore:
e che sia uno ovile e un pastore.
(dell'Ottonaio 1940 [1559], 82–83)

32. The Italian name of Vlorë, an important port city on the Albanian coast.
33. Cured fish roe.
34. *Dragomanni siàn, donne, Levantini,*
che qui dalla Velona
della buttagra assai perfetta e buona
abbiàn per voi portata, fiorentini.
Se ben di più paesi assai ne viene,
la nostra è la migliore,
perché più si conserva e si mantiene
la bontà e 'l colore:
gustate il suo sapore,
donne, per cortesia,

Example 5: A dialogue in Battista Guarini's comedy, *La Idropica* ("The Dropsical Woman," 1583), set in Padua, concerns a mysterious man, whom the speakers, both domestic servants, describe as "dressed as a Levantine" and later as "dressed as a foreigner" and having "the face of a Levantine, and a respectable man."[35]

Example 6: John Florio's Italian-English dictionary, *A World of Words* (1598), defined *Leuantino* as "a lifter, a shifter, a limlifter, a pilferer, an vptaker, a bould bayard. Also one borne in the east countries, an easterling."[36] In the second, much-expanded edition of the dictionary, *Queen Anna's Nevv VVorld of Words* (1611), he reversed the two definitions: "an Easterling, one borne or dwelling in the East. Also as Leuante, a bold vp-taker."[37]

What do these six examples tell us? In Example 1, the adjective *Levantine* has a decidedly pejorative but vague meaning, a sort of generic bad character.

---

perché tal mercanzia
porton per gentilezza i Levantini.
(Cimatore 1936 [1559], 259)

35. "vestito da levantino"; "vestito da forestiero"; "viso di Levantino, e d'uomo di conto" (Guarini 1971 [1583], Act 4, scene 6). Perhaps in an echo of these understandings, on his return to Venice in the early 1630s, Giuseppe Struppiolo, a Venetian physician who had sojourned in the Ottoman Empire for many years and was rumored by some of his neighbors to have "turned Muslim," was reported to have walked around for a while "dressed as a Turk with a cravat, with shoes in the Levantine style." He was now "dressed with a cravat in the Greek style, and a cloak above, and an ordinary black hat on his head." ("Già un'anno fà lui vene à Venetia, vestito da turco, et andò un pezzo vestito da turco con una cravata, con scarpe alla levantina . . . et hora và vestito con una crovata alla greca, et un ferrariol sopra, et in testa capel negro ordinario") (Santo Uffizio, Processi, b. 89, c. 2r (May 6, 1632)). Tellingly, this testimony was by one Pietro Marpegano, a twenty-five-year-old commercial broker. For this young broker, the Levantine sartorial style was neither Turkish nor Greek, but bore a certain affinity to both. Clothes "alla levantina" "di damasco turchino fodrata di canzante con maniche e bavari" ("of deep blue damask lined with iridescent silk with sleeves and collars") were already listed in the inventory of Alfonso II d'Este in 1598 (Battaglia 1973, 1007). Dressing "alla greca" could mean very different things. Sanudo describes a young Venetian nobleman dressed in expensive gilded cloth as "vestito d'oro a la grecha" (Sanudo 1969, I:402). On the other hand, Chris Pastore notes that in late-sixteenth-century Florence "artists working for the Grand Dukes repeatedly conflated contemporary Turks with ancient Greeks and Romans" so that even balloon pants and turbans could be cast as being dressed "alla greca" (2006; 2011). On "exotic" and "oriental" clothes as the marks of foreigners in cinquecento Venice, see also Preto (1975, 119); Newton (1988, 132–44); Wilson (2005).

36. Florio (1598, 202). A few lines above this, under the headword *Leuante*, after the generic definition of the term as "the east winde, the countrey lying toward or in the east," Florio adds, "Also a limlifter, a shifter, an vptaker, a pilfrer, a bold bayard, one that hath learnt his taking vp."

37. The definition of *Levant* in the second edition changed only in that "any country lying East" appeared first, followed by "Also the Sunne-rise. Also the Easterne-winde," and ending with "a lim-lifter, an vp-taker, a bold pilfrer, one that hath learn't his taking vp" (Florio 1611, 281).

In Example 2, in stereotyping his objects as hypersexual and prone to incest, Bassano generalizes from "Turks" to "the Levantine nation," of which, in this context at least, Turks form the paradigmatic members. Significantly, Bassano uses here "the Levantine nation" as a superordinate category, referring to all people living in the Levant, not to merchant diasporas on the Italian peninsula. As we will see shortly, for most other sixteenth-century authors, it was this latter, narrower sense of "Levantini" as diasporic (especially Jewish) merchants trading in Italy that became the most prototypical. In Examples 3 and 4, *the Levant* is contrasted with Florence and Levantines are the link between the two, traversing a great distance and risking their lives to bring Florentines (gendered as feminine consumers) coveted Ottoman goods to enjoy. But note that the actual provenance of the Levantini is elided. Although they wear Turkish clothes, they are also (juridically, at least) "Florentine merchants," making the Levant a place of sojourn rather than of origin. The pairing of Levantini with dragomans in the opening line of Example 4 foregrounds foreignness and Ottoman association, whereas the Christian rhetoric of Example 3 (which is expanded into a true Crusade call later in the poem) reassures the reader of the speakers' religious sameness. In Example 5, "Levantine" stands for a sartorial style and even physiognomy that are clearly foreign yet not easy to pinpoint in space or ascribe to a particular ethnicity. The supposedly offhand comment about the face of "a Levantine and a respectable man" might be an oblique reference to commercial acumen as well. Finally, Example 6 neatly separates provenance from character traits as distinct denotations of *Levantine* and says nothing about mercantile activity at all. Florio is significantly more explicit than Piccolomini in spelling out the Levantine character. That Florio switched the order of his two definitions of *Levantine* in the 1611 second edition of the dictionary may indicate the growing purchase of Levantines' provenance-based, ethnicizing attributes (and the gradual obsolescence of its definition as "pilferer") as the category traveled westward toward the Atlantic, but this tentative conclusion requires further research.[38]

Revealingly, Florio's definition of *Levantine* as a "pilferer" and a "bold bayard" is closely reminiscent not only of Piccolomini's vague warnings in Example 1 but also of the Ottoman term *Levend*, whose morphological similarity to *Levant* some scholars have ascribed to contact with the Mediterranean Lingua Franca. *Levend* emerged in the sixteenth century to denote Ottoman mercenary naval troops, perceived as mobile, unruly, and rebellious (see fig. 7.1). By the seventeenth

---

38. For some suggestive examples of how nineteenth-century British travelers to the West Indies compared Levantine and Afro-Caribbean "hybridity" as part of their evolving system of racial classification, see Sheller (2003, 124–32).

Figure 7.1 *"Levente" (Levend) from Claes Rålamb's Ottoman costume album (c. 1657). National Library of Sweden, MS Rål. 8:0 nr 10, fol.81. Reproduction: National Library, Stockholm, Sweden.*

century, it had acquired also the distinctly sexual connotation of licentious men.[39] Levantines may have been associated with sexual excess earlier, but this association became significantly more pronounced in the nineteenth century.[40]

As these examples suggest, both the class of people subsumed under the category "Levantini" and its properties underwent subtle but important transformations in the course of the sixteenth century. These transformations were never linear, however, and differently positioned actors struggled to deploy the category for their own strategic ends. *Levantini* sometimes referred to Muslim Ottomans; Christian Ottomans; non-Greek, non-Muslim Ottomans; Jewish Ottomans; and so on. This bivalent denotation, neutralizing an important set of confessionally based distinctions in both the Ottoman and Venetian spheres, proved especially productive. This bivalence, furthermore, allowed the term to be used not to point to any precise group of people (or wares) but to mark its context of use as one of inter-imperial commerce, in which speakers reinforced their metropolitan location vis-à-vis a juridically and affectively foreign Levant.[41] This use of *Levantini* as a strategically deployable shifter is particularly evident in the interactions between the Board of Trade and trans-imperial subjects.

TRANS-IMPERIAL SUBJECTS AND THE ARTICULATION OF ALTERITY

To understand how *Levantini* functioned as a strategically deployable shifter in Venetian commercial discourse, it is important to note the key role that trans-imperial subjects played in forging its meanings. As early as 1518, a group of Ottoman Greek merchants negotiated an agreement to lower duties paid in Ancona by "the Levantine merchants, subject to the Turk."[42] By that point, the superordinate category "Levantini," like the merchants themselves, had already circulated across different port cities throughout the Italian peninsula. It was, in fact, caught in the fierce competition among commercial centers to attract the lucrative overland carrying trade from the Ottoman Empire. An early reference to Levantini can be found, for example, in a quotation by Marin Sanudo, a Venetian diarist, from a letter sent in 1533 by Marcantonio Venier, who at the time served

---

39. Peirce (1997, 179–81, 184–85); Laiou (2005–2006). I thank Leslie Peirce for bringing Laiou's study to my attention.

40. For a fascinating discussion of the Ottoman popular shadow-puppet character of Çelebi, who by the nineteenth century was often represented as a Levantine "mösyö," a westernized member of the Istanbul elite and an ardent womanizer, "sporting an elegant fez and a Sherlock Holmes-style checkered coat," see Ze'evi (2006, 136–37).

41. On the strategic use of bivalency, see also Woolard (1998).

42. Quoted in Greene (2010, 39).

as ambassador to the papal court in Ancona. The letter, in Sanudo's rendering, describes how "[in] this city there is great trafficking in merchandise that comes from the west, and especially kersey, which is contracted with Levantines who bring many other wares, like wax, camlets, silks and others of their goods that come from the Levant."[43] Here the literal circulation of the term *Levantini* is made evident, as well as its denotations, through the dual movement of Venetian diplomatic correspondence and trans-imperial commercial actors across the Italian peninsula. Given their mobility and familiarity with both Ottoman and Venetian institutions, it seems plausible that trans-imperial subjects themselves played an important role in giving currency in Venice to this use of *Levantini* as encompassing all Ottoman merchants regardless of confessional affiliation. Anecdotal evidence supports this hypothesis; this denotation is repeated in numerous petitions by trans-imperial subjects to the Board of Trade and other Venetian magistracies throughout the second half of the sixteenth century. In 1561, a group of merchants from Ioannina lodged a complaint against custom officials in Corfu. The petitioners described themselves as "Levantine merchants and subjects of the Signor, Christians, Jews, and Turks."[44] In the following decades, several references to "Levantini" as a superordinate category were made in other petitions by trans-imperial subjects, particularly Cypriot émigrés who aspired to be appointed commercial brokers of the "Levantini." On numerous occasions throughout the 1570s Filippo Emanuel, a Cypriot and the nephew of Public Dragoman Michiel Membré, boasted of his knowledge of "Turkish, Greek, Arabic, and Persian" as grounds for his appointment as a broker of "Levantine merchants." Emanuel had been briefly enslaved in Istanbul prior to his arrival in Venice, and in recognition of his plight the Board of Trade granted him a license to broker trade "with the Levantine nation."[45] Another petition for a similar license was submitted within a week of Emanuel's initial plea by Giulio Torquato, possibly also a Cypriot, on his release from captivity by Maltese corsairs.[46] A third such petitioner was an Armenian named Gioane de Santo, who in 1580 cited his command of Turkish, Armenian, Slavic, and Italian.[47] Finally, a fourth supplicant to invoke the category

---

43. "Si fa in questa città gran facende di merce che vien di ponente et maxime carisee l'è contratà con Levantini che portano altre robe come cere, zambeloti, sede e altre sue mercantie vien di Levante" (Sanuto 1969, 58:11–12).
44. "Noi, mercanti levantini et sudditi del Signor, cosi Christiani come Zudei et Turchi" (Collegio, Risposte di fuori, b. 315, c. 87 (July 11, 1561), quoted in Greene 2008, 23).
45. Collegio, Risposte di dentro, b. 5, c. 200 (Sept. 29, 1573); Cinque Savi, Risposte, b. 136, unpaginated (Jan. 3, 1578).
46. Collegio, Risposte di dentro, b. 5, c. 202 (Oct. 4, 1573). On the Cypriot Torquato family, see Rudt de Collenberg (1982a, 58, 66).
47. "Poter esercitar la Sans[eri]a in rialto con la nacion levantina" (Collegio, Risposte di dentro, b. 6, c. 359 (Oct. 16, 1580)).

"Levantine nation," Francesco, son of Sinan Bey, was a merchant born to an enslaved Cypriot woman and her Muslim Ottoman master. Having converted to Christianity in Venice, he petitioned in 1602 to become a broker "of Jews, Turks, and other Levantine nations."[48]

This denotation of *Levantini* as encompassing all Ottoman merchants in Venice regardless of ethnolinguistic or confessional affiliation was eventually picked up by officialdom, too, for example, in a 1586 decree that referred to "the Levantine merchants who feel themselves discriminated against."[49] Significantly, this example clearly voiced trans-imperial merchants' own perspective and, perhaps, their own categories. Indeed, it is through the ongoing adjudication of trans-imperial subjects' petitions for commercial privileges as merchants engaged in "the Levant trade" and for employment as brokers of such merchants that this extended denotation of *Levantini* seems to have become established in Venetian commercial discourse in the second half of the sixteenth century. This new extension became so commonsense that by 1594 the Board of Trade could claim that the *terzo* had been applied previously "not only to the business of the Turkish nation, but of any other Levantine subject."[50] It is important to remember that the original *terzo* legislation of 1534 had referred simply to "mercanti turchi." In some sense, there were no "Levantines" in Venice in 1534.

In other cases, too, the Board of Trade applied the category "Levantini" retroactively to diasporic merchants who previously had been referred to under multiple categories. In 1599, while assessing the performance of Giacomo de Nores as Public Dragoman, the board mentioned that his predecessor, Michiel Membré, had interpreted for "Turks, Greeks, and other Levantine nations."[51] Yet, to the best of my knowledge, the superordinate category "Levantini" (as distinct from Levantini as Ottoman Jews) does not appear in the documents of the Board of Trade before 1586, thirty-six years into Membré's appointment as Public Dragoman.

Even as the category "Levantini" took root in Venetian commercial discourse toward the end of the sixteenth century, its denotations were neither stable nor necessarily shared. In 1590, the Board of Trade acknowledged the dragoman's difficulties in monitoring unregistered transactions because "Turkish and Levantine merchants close a deal today and the following day set for their travels," implying

48. Cinque Savi, Risposte, b. 141, cc. 30v–31r (Jan. 21, 1602 m.v.).
49. "I mercanti levantini sentono pregiud[iti]o nei loro mercati." (AdC, Misc. Civil, b. 260, fasc. 20, c. 26v (March 10, 1586)).
50. "Non solam[en]te de essa nattione Turchesca, ma de qualsivoglia altro suddito levantino" (Senato Mar, filza 128, unpaginated (Feb. 22, 1594 m.v.)).
51. "Turchi, Greci, et altre nattioni Levantine" (Cinque Savi, Risposte, b. 140, c. 48 (March 31, 1599)).

that "Turks" were not a subset of "Levantines."[52] A similar distinction is evident in a petition to broker the trade of "Turks and Levantines" submitted by Teodoro Dandolo, a Bukhara-born convert, in 1615.[53] In 1620, the review by the Board of Trade of Public Dragoman Giacomo de Nores's request for a salary increase recalled that he had been given permission to "collect a third of the brokerage fees of Greeks, Armenians, and other Levantines, as one collects that of Turks, and Jews."[54] Here, Greeks and Armenians fall under the superordinate category "Levantines," but Turks and Jews apparently do not. A report in 1621 by de Nores concerning the long planned-for Fondaco dei Turchi spoke of "Asiatic Turks, Armenians, and other Levantines, who live scattered around the city."[55] Here both Muslims and Christians, Safavid and Ottoman subjects alike, are considered members of the superordinate category "Levantini," and it is implicitly their sojourn in Venice, away from home, that makes them such. In 1633, the Senate decreed that all legal controversies among "Levantine Turks, and other Turkish subjects" should be referred to the Board of Trade.[56] Here a distinction is made between Turkish and non-Turkish (or perhaps non-Muslim) Ottoman subjects, but the descriptor "Levantine" is attached to the former rather than to the latter.

Part of the appeal of this category as an exonym clearly lay in its ability to foreground its deployers' position in the Venetian metropole vis-à-vis a spatially and juridically distant Levant. This was especially true in the case of émigrés and former colonial subjects who petitioned (now as Venetian residents) to be employed as brokers of Levantines. But what was the appeal of the category as an autonym, invoked by Ottoman merchants as a self-referential term? Here the political-juridical bivalence of the category, premised on a shared Veneto-Ottoman Levant, seems to have been of greater significance, especially during Venetian-Ottoman military conflicts. This bivalence might account for another shift in the meaning of *Levantini* in the wake of the Venetian-Ottoman War of Crete. Starting in the 1640s, Armenian merchants began identifying themselves in notarial deeds and in petitions to the Venetian authorities as either "Levantine Armenians" or "Persian

---

52. "mercanti Turchi, et levantini hoggi fa[n]no un mercato et il giorno seguente si imbarcano per li loro viaggi" (Cinque Savi, Risposte, b. 138, c. 98r (Jan. 13, 1589 m.v.)).

53. Cinque Savi, Risposte, b. 144, cc. 31r–v (Feb. 14, 1614 m.v.); Ufficio della Bolla Ducale, Grazie del Maggior Consiglio, reg. 8, c. 76v (Sept. 23, 1615).

54. "Di riscuoter in publico il terzo delle sansarie de Greci, Armeni, et altri Levantini, come si riscuote quello de' Turchi, et Hebrei" (Cinque Savi, Risposte, b. 145, unpaginated (Sept. 1, 1620)).

55. "Turchi Assiatici, Armeni, et altri Levantini, che habitano sparsi p[er] la Città" (Cinque Savi, Seconda serie, b. 187, fasc. 1, unpaginated (March 29, 1621)).

56. "Controversie vertenti trà Turchi Levantini, et altri sudditi Turcheschi dovessero esser divolute al magistrato dei cinque savij alla mercantia" (Cinque Savi, Seconda serie, b. 4, fasc. 47 part 1, c. 6 (Sept. 12, 1633)).

Armenians."[57] At the time, the Venetian state extended special commercial privileges to Safavid subjects in an attempt to lure them to the city in spite of escalating Venetian-Ottoman hostilities. Under these circumstances, Safavid subjects in Venice had good reasons to distinguish themselves as clearly as possible from Ottoman subjects. This is precisely what emerges from the Venetian notarial archives, where we encounter, first, the neologism *Persian Armenian* and, later and less frequently, *Levantine Armenian*. That Ottoman Armenians were identified as Levantine rather than as Ottoman underscores the productive bivalence of the modifier *Levantine*, deflecting the political implications of *Ottoman*. In this use, *Levantine* simply meant "non-Safavid," but it did not specify Ottoman or other jurisdiction.[58] Significantly, a similar distinction between Persian Armenian sojourners and local (Ottoman) Armenians emerged in Aleppo by the mid-seventeenth century as well.[59]

Given the long-standing claims by the Board of Trade to sole jurisdiction over all Ottoman and Safavid merchants in Venice, it would seem an ideal institution in which the overarching, superordinate category "Levantini" would have solidified as a shorthand for Ottoman and Safavid alterity. Yet a 1645 landmark ruling instead reaffirmed the exclusive jurisdiction of the board over "all the Greek, Armenian, and Levantine and Ponentine Jewish nations, and other subjects of the Grand Turk."[60] Although these groupings could all have fallen under the superordinate category "Levantini," here the board employed its narrower definition, as subset of Jewish merchants operating in Venice under Ottoman protection. This use was not an exception to the rule. In the period 1570–1670, the superordinate category "Levantini" was employed only intermittently and in a distinctly inconsistent fashion. Instead, the board and its trans-imperial interlocutors frequently

---

57. See, for example, Collegio, Risposte di dentro, b. 31, unpaginated (March 29, 1640), b. 37, unpaginated (April 11, 1646); b. 44, unpaginated (March 11, 1653); Cinque Savi, Risposte, b. 154, cc. 19v–20r (April 24, 1646); cc. 129v–131r (late Dec. 1649); Notarile, Atti, b. 8457, c. 105v (Oct. 13, 1648); b. 8458, c. 155v (Dec. 3, 1649); b. 8459, c. 166v (Feb. 3, 1650 m.v.); b. 8460, cc. 151v–152r (Feb. 20, 1651 m.v.); b. 8461, c. 101r (Sept. 7, 1652); b. 8462, cc. 17r–v (March 23, 1653); b. 8464, part II, cc. 1v–2r (March 4, 1656); b. 8846, cc. 52r–v (July 30, 1670).

58. It should be noted that even after the new terminological distinction between "Levantine Armenian" and "Persian Armenian" was introduced, the majority of Venetian documents, including notarial deeds, still identified subjects simply as "Armenians," especially when the case also involved non-Armenian subjects. See, for example, Notarile, Atti, b. 8458, c. 43v (May 14, 1649); b. 8461, c. 129v (Nov. 23, 1652); b. 13563, cc. 317v–318r (Feb. 6, 1656 m.v.); b. 8466, cc. 36v–37r (April 8, 1658); b. 8467, c. 73r (July 1, 1659); b. 8846, c. 20r (June 3, 1670). On the Armenian settlement in Venice in the sixteenth and seventeenth centuries, see Hermet and Cogni Ratti di Desio (1993, esp. chap. 7).

59. Masters (1987, esp. 353).

60. "Tutte le nat[io]ni Greca, Armena, hebrei Levantini, e Ponentini, et altri sudditi del S[igno]r Turco" (Cinque Savi, Risposte, b. 153, unpaginated (Jan. 23, 1644 m.v.)).

used specific ethnonyms (such as *Bosnians, Albanians, Greeks,* and *Armenians*) as well as more narrowly regional or even locale-based terms (e.g., *Dalmatians, Cypriots, Athenians, Perastans,* and *Istanbulites*).

Conversely, when superordinate categories, such as "Subjects of the Turks," and eventually "Levantini," were employed, they often followed a list of confessional and ethnolinguistic groupings, thus foregrounding a Venetian metropolitan perspective that presumably united them all as juridical and commercial diasporas under one law. For example, in 1642, a petition by Nicolò Seguro of Zakynthos asked the Senate to confirm his status as a consul not only of his fellow islanders but of "those of the Nation of Lefkás, Anatolia, Lepanto, and other nearby locations, and also of all the vessels of Mytilene, Panomeria, and other Subjects of the Great Turk."[61] In another case, Giorgio Stampaneo, a clergyman, presented himself to the Venetian authorities in 1664 as "the Chaplain of the Overseas Nation."[62] Although he did not explain who the "Overseas" (*Oltramarini*) were, his past service as emissary in the service of Venetian magistrates in Bar, Shkodër, and Durrës—all communities in the Venetian-Ottoman borderlands in Albania— suggests that they hailed from either Venetian or Ottoman Adriatic territories, similarly to the Oltramarini regiments of the Venetian army.[63] In 1658, a group of merchants who described themselves as "Greeks, Ponentine and Levantine Jews, and Turkish subjects" pleaded the Senate to reaffirm the exclusive jurisdiction of the Board of Trade over their cases.[64] Another petition submitted two years later was signed by "the nation of Greek, Turkish, and Armenian merchants."[65] These

61. "quelli della Nation di S[an]ta Maura, Natolia, Lepanto, et altri lochi circonvicini nec non di tutti li Vasselli Mitilinei, e Panomeriti, et altri Sudditi del Sig[no]r Turco" (Collegio, Risposte di dentro, b. 33, unpaginated (June 21, 1642)).
62. "Capellano della Natione Oltramarina" (Collegio, Risposte di dentro, b. 33, unpaginated (June 21, 1642)).
63. Collegio, Risposte di dentro, b. 63, unpaginated (Nov. 26, 1664). This hypothesis is strengthened by Stampaneo's mention as an abbot in the Mirdita district (Albania) in 1694; see Bartl (2000). On Oltramarini in the seventeenth-century Venetian army, see Del Negro (2001). For their earlier history, see (Mallett and Hale 1984). For an overview of the early modern Venetian colonies "d'oltremare," see Arbel (1996); Ivetic (2000).
64. "Mercanti Greci, Hebrei, Ponentini, e Levantini, et sudditi Turcheschi" (Collegio, Risposte di dentro, b. 48, unpaginated (March 23, 1657)).
65. "La natione de mercanti Greci, Turchi, et Armeni" (Collegio, Risposte di dentro, b. 55, unpaginated (Sept. 1660)). While the use of *nation* in the singular in the petition implies unity, the text does not invoke any category to capture the petitioners' presumably shared status as Ottoman subjects in Venice. Distinctions between Muslim and non-Muslim "people of the book," as well as between Orthodox and Catholic Christians, were carefully observed by the early modern Ottoman state. Whether in this case the specific wording was due to an effort to downplay the petitioners' uneasy status as the subjects of an enemy state or because of their fundamentally different status within Ottoman contexts is hard to gauge. On Ottoman ethnoreligious distinctions, see Goffman (1994).

varying agglomerations of ethnonyms point to two competing tendencies in contemporary Venetian commercial discourse: on the one hand, the proliferation of ethnolinguistic categories referring to the peoples of the Ottoman and Safavid domains, suggesting a growing consciousness of diversity within the previously unitary category "Turks";[66] on the other, a continuing effort to cluster these diverse groupings together under a unifying set of commercial laws and institutional practices, regardless of confessional affiliation or historic ties to Venice.

As these examples suggest, even by the mid-seventeenth century, the category "Levantini" had entered Venetian commercial discourse only partially. The most obvious reason for that was trans-imperial subjects' insistence on their particularity and affinity with Venice, usually on biographical or confessional grounds. In 1636, Luca Miculich, a Bosnian, sought recognition as a Venetian subject (suddito). According to his petition, he had been born a Catholic and had spent many years living as a Franciscan tertiary among friars in Dalmatia and Istria.[67] Implicitly, his well-documented and publicly recognized confessional affiliation made him somehow more suitable to become a Venetian subject, despite his Ottoman roots. Similarly, a year later a group of merchants from the Aegean island of Patmos petitioned the Senate for commercial privileges. Although they were Ottoman subjects, they professed their collective loyalty to Venice, "it being famous, that our island, and also the neighboring ones, are only inhabited by Christians, servants of Your Serenity."[68]

By the 1640s, and especially with the onset of the Venetian-Ottoman War of Crete in 1645, confessional identity had become a particularly common rhetorical tool in the hands of Christian Ottoman supplicants, who sought to foreground their unambiguously Venetian position on the Venetian-Ottoman grid of affect. So, for instance, when a group of silk and wool merchants from Bosnia who found

66. It should be noted, however, that even before the late sixteenth century, certain groups within Ottoman society, especially, Greeks, were sometimes designated in Venice by particular ethnonyms. See, for example, the reference to "Moreiti [inhabitants of the Morea] who are Turkish subjects," in a Senate decision of 1476, referring to non-Turks, or non-Muslims, who are Ottoman subjects in Arbel (2001, 75–76).
67. Collegio, Risposte di dentro, b. 27, unpaginated (May 20, 1636). On Bosnian Catholics, see Fine (1996).
68. "Essendo notorio, che nell'Isola n[ost]ra, & anco le convicine non son habitate, se non da soli C[hristi]ani, servi di V[ost]ra Ser[eni]tà" (Collegio, Risposte di dentro, b. 28, unpaginated (Aug. 26, 1637)). See also Giorgio da Carcusi's petition, in which he repeated the assertion that "the merchants of Patmos are humble servants of Your Serenity, even though they are Turkish subjects" ("Li mercanti Patignoti servi humil[issi]mi della Ser[eni]tà V[ostra] seben suddi Turcheschi") (Collegio, Risposte di dentro, b. 39, unpaginated (July 29, 1648)).

themselves stranded in Venice in early 1646 petitioned for permission to head back home after an eight-month sojourn, they described themselves not simply as "Bosnians" but as "Bosnian Christians."[69] A couple of weeks later, when two Armenian merchants from Transylvania similarly sought permission to leave the city after concluding their business there, they reminded the Senate that the Board of Trade had recently made such concessions "to two other Christian merchants from Transylvania, as are we."[70] A few months later still, three other Bosnian merchants protested that their merchandise had been misidentified (and consequently taxed) as belonging to "Turks" and intimated that "we are Christians, even though subjects [of the Ottomans] and so devoted [to the hope] that God pleases to grant the vows of our hearts for the exaltation of Christianity."[71] Ingeniously, the supplicants did not explicitly name the Ottoman sultan as their sovereign. Rather than an inter-imperial territorial struggle, the conflict over the colony of Crete thus emerges from these and similar petitions as a religious war in which the supplicants, as the champions of Christianity, become the "natural" and unambiguous allies of Venice, not the subjects of an enemy sovereign.

Christian Ottoman subjects were quick to highlight their Christianity on other occasions too, especially when they hoped to involve the Venetian government in their litigations with non-Christian Ottoman subjects. Presumably, they expected confessional affinity to prompt the authorities to take their side. In 1605, an Armenian merchant from Skopje named Murat sought Venetian government assistance in prosecuting two of his Muslim compatriots sojourning in Venice, who, he claimed, had run away after killing his brother Simon. The Board of Trade investigation revealed that, in fact, the two had been tried by Ottoman magistrates and found innocent. In any case, the board concluded, the crimes had been committed on Ottoman soil so there was little ground for Venetian intervention in the matter.[72]

As this example suggests, and as trans-imperial petitioners to the Board of Trade discovered time and again, the appeal to confessional solidarity to trump political and jurisdictional differences was not a foolproof rhetorical strategy. Indeed, when Christian supplicants sought to project an ecumenical Christendom, they were challenged both by shifting Venetian political and commercial exigencies and by a burgeoning consciousness of religious difference among Christian denominations, whether "Levantine" or not. The lacing of religious confession and political subjecthood in the wake of an Age of Confessionalization no doubt contributed to the

---

69. Collegio, Risposte di dentro, b. 37, unpaginated (March 5, 1646).
70. Collegio, Risposte di dentro, b. 37, unpaginated (March 28, 1646).
71. Collegio, Risposte di dentro, b. 37, unpaginated (Aug. 20, 1646).
72. Cinque Savi, Risposte, b. 141, cc. 145r–146v (July 24, 1605).

growing surveillance by the Venetian authorities of all Ottoman and Safavid merchants in Venice *qua* juridical foreigners.[73] This process was further prompted by (and in turn legitimized) the institutionalization of the Fondaco dei Turchi in 1621 as the only state-sanctioned residence for Ottoman Muslim merchants in Venice.

Overall, the use of religious rhetoric to distinguish Christian from Muslim Ottoman and Safavid subjects had only limited purchase in Venetian official discourse because other factors were seen as potentially mitigating any a priori Christian solidarity. In particular, Venetian officials often suspected Armenian subjects' invocations of Christian zeal precisely because of their purported excessive familiarity with "Muslim" languages and customs. Ironically, such stereotypes were often mediated by other trans-imperial subjects, who actively leveled charges of heterodoxy or circulated unflattering rumors against Armenians. For example, in 1571 Marcantonio degli Eletti, a commercial broker of Jewish background (he had converted to Christianity in 1569), denounced to the Holy Office an Armenian named Giacomo as supposedly having vilified the Holy Virgin and having claimed that the Muslim God was better than the Christian one.[74] In 1649, in another case that warrants fuller exploration, Thomas of Aleppo, a Catholic convert and former Armenian prelate and patriarch of Istanbul, accused members of the Venetian Armenian congregation of kidnapping Venetian boys in order to gift them to Muslims in the Ottoman and Safavid empires.[75]

It is hardly surprising that trans-imperial merchants and brokers foregrounded their Christianity in an effort to be exempted from the *terzo*, to extricate themselves from the Fondaco dei Turchi, or to obtain other collective privileges. This was especially true in the mid-seventeenth-century context of a protracted Venetian-Ottoman war, economic recession, and ongoing confessional strife.

73. On the Ottoman Age of Confessionalization, see Krstić (2011).

74. Santo Uffizio, Processi, b. 30, fasc. 32 (Jan. 2, 1571 m.v.); Santo Uffizio, Processi, b. 105, cc. 15r–v (April 3, 1653, testimony of Meliton Armeno).

75. On the struggle within the Venetian Armenian community to rid itself of Thomas, who converted to Catholicism in 1634, was smuggled to Poland, was chased away from Livorno, and ended up in Venice, see Santo Uffizio, Processi, b. 105, unpaginated (Feb. 25, 1649 m.v.–Nov. 17, 1655); Cinque Savi, Risposte, b. 155, cc. 62r–64v (Sept. 24, 1655–Nov. 17, 1655); Cinque Savi, Seconda series, b. 4, fasc. 47, cc. 12r–15r (Sept. 24, 1655); Inquisitori di Stato, b. 527, fasc. 1, c. 10v (April 20, 1656). See also Galanus (1664). Conflicts within the Venetian Armenian community may have been exacerbated, at least in part, by Venetian confusion as to Armenians' relationship to Catholic Orthodoxy. This confusion stemmed from the complex situation of the Armenian Church in the Ottoman and Safavid empires, as well as from missionary attempts to effect the mass conversion of Armenians to Catholicism by converting community leaders in Istanbul and Isfahan in the mid-seventeenth century, efforts in which Venice was implicitly and explicitly involved. See, for example, the 1609 petition by several dozen Catholic Armenians in the Isfahan suburb of New Julfa pleading the pope to dispatch an Italian patriarch and ambassador to educate them in matters of religion and represent them in the shah's court, copied to the Venetian State Inquisitors (Inquisitori di Stato, b. 516, unpaginated (1609)).

What is interesting is how such rhetoric fit into broader contemporary discourses about the Ottomans and especially the plurality of Ottoman ethnolinguistic and confessional groupings, a plurality that was drawn out in numerous popular genres, from travel narratives and costume albums to atlases and bilingual dictionaries.[76] This plurality became essential in the eventual articulation of the category "Levantini." Indeed, this category evolved precisely in the dialectic between the attempts by the Venetian state to devise unified commercial policies, on the one hand, and trans-imperial groups' insistence on their essential difference and particularity, on the other.

TAXING "LEVANTINES"

Although the Board of Trade wielded supreme jurisdiction over foreign merchants in Venice, its policies were clearly shaped by pressure from other actors as well as by the differing and, at times, contradictory agendas of its own membership.[77] The shifting power balance between the Board of Trade and various constituencies among trans-imperial sojourners in Venice is well illustrated by the changing definitions of who was subject to the *terzo,* the tax of one-third of commercial brokerage fees instituted by the Board of Trade in 1534 (see chap. 6). Originally, the tax was levied on all transactions involving "Turkish merchants," ostensibly to finance the activities of a Public Dragoman to protect these merchants from unscrupulous brokers. A century later, in 1636, the board reaffirmed that the tax applied to "the nations of Armenians, Vlachs, Bogodans, Moldavians, Persians, and Bosnians." The same decree also listed the merchandise of Greeks as similarly subject to the *terzo.*[78]

Both juridically and religiously, the ethnonyms agglomerated here—whose shifting denotations merit a study of their own—were of widely varying relationships to the Venetian state and its prescribed Roman Catholicism. Greeks, whether Orthodox or Uniate, were as likely to be Venetian as Ottoman subjects. Moldavians (or *Bogodans,* the obsolete medieval term for Moldavians) and Vlachs were (Christian) subjects of two of the tribute-paying Ottoman principalities, although Vlachs could also be certain inhabitants of Dalmatia.[79] Conversely,

76. On Ottoman understandings of this plurality, see Peirce (2010).
77. The five members of the board, all patricians, were typically appointed for only three-year terms, which did not necessarily overlap, resulting in frequent fluctuations in membership and, consequently, policy.
78. "Le Nationi de Armeni, Valachi, Bogodani, Moldavi, Persiani, et Bossinesi." (Cinque Savi, Seconda serie, b. 147, fasc. 1, unpaginated (May 31, 1636)). See also Collegio, Risposte di dentro, b. 27 (June 20, 1636); Cinque Savi, Risposte, b. 151, cc. 37–38 (Dec. 30, 1636).
79. On the Dalmatian Vlachs, see Roksandic (2009); Wolff (2001).

Bosnians were overwhelmingly Muslim and hailed from one of the sultan's most solidly Ottomanized provinces, whereas Persians were subjects of the arch-rival of the Ottomans, the Safavid shah, who was at war with the sultan throughout much of the period under consideration here. Finally, Armenians could be either Ottoman, Safavid, or indeed Venetian subjects and belonged to any number of confessional groups fiercely antagonistic to one another. In other words, the list encompassed and rendered equal numerous confessional, ethnic, and juridical categories, associated with territories that extended all the way from the western Balkans to central Asia.[80]

Yet the *terzo* legislation of 1636 did omit one category that some insisted should be subject to the tax—Levantine Jews. The long struggle over the exemption of Levantine Jews from the *terzo* revolved around the question of whether they acted essentially as proxies for other Ottoman merchants, particularly Muslims. In these debates, too, trans-imperial subjects took leading roles on both sides. In 1609, Pietro Francolin, a Cypriot émigré to Venice and a former Ottoman captive, submitted a memorandum to the Board of Trade. In it, he claimed that much public revenue had been lost due to tax evasion by scheming merchants. According to Francolin, Jews, who were not subject to the *terzo*, were buying and selling on behalf of Muslim merchants.[81] Francolin's motion to subject the commercial transactions of Jewish merchants to the *terzo* was finally endorsed by the Senate in 1617.[82] But a year later, the legislation was revoked, and the Senate reaffirmed its earlier ruling that the *terzo* was imposed on brokers, not on merchants, and should not be shouldered by merchants under any circumstances.[83] Throughout the following decade, arguments raged on about whether those Jewish merchants who refused to name a broker on releasing their merchandise from the customs office should or should not be required to pay the *terzo* themselves.[84]

---

80. It should be noted, however, that at least in principle the Venetian fiscal regime distinguished between Venetian subjects and the subjects of foreign states. Thus, Greeks, Armenians, and Jews who were Venetian subjects constituted a fiscal category different from their foreign coreligionists. According to Benjamin Arbel (personal communication) this was so obvious in Venice that it was often not explicitly stated in the records.

81. Cinque Savi, Risposte, b. 142, cc. 169v–170r (Jan. 18, 1609 m.v.).

82. Jewish merchants complained about the Senate decree of Nov. 25, 1617 in Cinque Savi, Risposte, b. 144, cc. 151v–152v (Jan. 16, 1617 m.v.). See also the reference to the recent inclusion of Jewish transactions under the *terzo* in the favorable response of the Board of Trade to dragoman Giacomo de Nores's request for a salary increase in early 1618 (Cinque Savi, Risposte, b. 144, c. 149r (Jan. 12, 1617 m.v.)).

83. Cinque Savi, Seconda serie, b. 147, fasc. 1, unpaginated (June 16, 1618). The legislation was endorsed by the Board of Trade on Sept. 15, 1618, and reaffirmed in 1633.

84. Collegio, Risposte di dentro, b. 15, c. 303 (Oct. 24, 1620); Cinque Savi, Risposte, b. 145, cc. 86v–87v (Dec. 16, 1620); cc. 176v–177r (Sept. 28, 1622); Collegio, Risposte di dentro, b. 24, unpaginated (Dec. 30, 1633, including copies of Senate legislation of 1617, 1620, and 1623).

Not surprisingly, those spearheading the efforts to subject Levantine Jews to the tax were members of the brokers' guild, who rightly suspected that much of their business was lost due to illicit brokerage by Levantine Jews and other non-guild members acting in concert with merchants. It is thus interesting to note that soon after submitting his memorandum to the Board of Trade, Francolin became a member of the brokers' guild, inheriting the position of Zorzi of Milos, his aging father-in-law and long-time commercial broker. According to Zorzi's petition on Francolin's behalf, the latter was not only fluent in Turkish and Slavic, which he had acquired during his years in Ottoman captivity, but also well-connected among Ottoman merchants in Venice.[85]

Beyond simple economic competition, the eventual subjection of all Jews to the *terzo* in 1637 could occur only once the tax became an indexical sign of the special foreignness of Ottoman and Safavid merchants, coextensive with the category "Levantines."[86] Indeed, the growing prosperity of Jewish and other Ottoman and Safavid merchants in the early seventeenth century stood in stark contrast to the declining fortunes of the Venetian maritime trade. As the Venetian Empire itself shrank, sojourners from regions previously considered part of a broad Venetian sphere of influence in the eastern Mediterranean increasingly came under scrutiny.

The process by which the transactions of Jews became subject to the *terzo* thus suggests the role of reason of state and political economy in the articulation of early modern ethnolinguistic categories. As discussed in chapter 6, when the *terzo* was first instituted in 1534, its stated purpose was to finance the services of an interpreter, said to be necessary to protect Ottoman merchants' interests vis-à-vis less-than-scrupulous Venetian merchants and brokers. Yet gradually this linguistic and protectionist rationale gave way to a more generalized argument about Levantine merchants' foreignness. That Jewish merchants came to be subject to the *terzo*, even though many if not all of them had resided in Venice for decades, spoke the local dialect fluently, and had no ostensible problem transacting directly with other merchants, was thus both a result of their presumed foreignness as Ottoman subjects and a further mark thereof. Indeed, in a complete reversal of their previous rhetoric, when Levantine Jewish merchants sought exemption from the *terzo* in 1637 they claimed that as residents of Venice they were very experienced and had no need for brokers. They further suggested that, because their merchandise arrived "from the West as well as from the East," it should not be automatically subjected to a tax levied on Levantine goods. Moreover, while they

---

85. Cinque Savi, Risposte, b. 142, cc. 119r–v (March 17, 1609); b. 144, c. 63r (Feb. 5, 1615 m.v.). See also chapter 1.
86. It bears noting that legislation in the matter rarely distinguished Levantine from non-Levantine Jews.

shouldered the tax, other Jewish merchants used false Christian names to avoid an otherwise precarious situation in Spain but, consequently, also evading taxation as Jews in Venice.[87] Remarkably, at this point neither the supplicants nor the Board of Trade addressed merchants' purported need for linguistic assistance as a reason to subject them (or their brokers) to the *terzo*, the stated rationale for imposing a tax on brokerage commissions in the first place. Linguistic incompetence, as we have seen, did figure prominently in other groups' petitions, as well as in Levantine Jews' requests for collective privileges at other times. And although on this occasion the Levantine Jewish merchants did implicitly assert their local residence as the reason they had not employed brokers, they did not mention it as grounds for tax exemption.

The attempts by the Board of Trade to control and tax Jewish merchants soon combined with efforts by the brokers' guild to curb unlicensed brokerage. By early 1637, less than a year after establishing that Jews should not be subjected to the *terzo*, the board decreed that the merchandise of Jews could not be released from the customs office until a licensed commercial broker signed the customs records and paid the tax.[88] The same year, an enterprising customs official, Bartolomeo Guarinoni, suggested a reform that would subject specific commodities to the *terzo*, irrespective of their importer.[89] Another decree, issued in 1642, confirmed that the nations subject to the *terzo* were "Turks, Bosnians, Persians, Armenians, Bogodans, Moldavians, and Jews."[90] The transformation in the criteria for taxation was completed in 1669, when the Board of Trade brought into effect an earlier decree subjecting to the *terzo* any and all merchandise arriving from "Turkish land." But what, exactly, was meant by "Turkish land"? The term used, *paese turchesco*, could just as plausibly be glossed "Muslim land," an ambiguity I return to shortly. The rescript of 1669 emphasized that it applied to merchandise "regardless of nation," but went on to specify the merchandise of "Armenians and other subjects [*soggetti*] of the King of Persia, Levantine and Ponentine Jews, and other subjects [*sudditi*]. . . ."[91] Thus, what marked the wares as taxable here was the identity of their importers after all rather than anything intrinsic to the

---

87. Cinque Savi, Seconda serie, b. 147, fasc. 1, unpaginated (March 28, 1637).
88. Cinque Savi, Seconda serie, b. 147, fasc. 1, unpaginated (Feb. 4, 1636 m.v.).
89. Cinque Savi, Seconda serie, b. 147, fasc. 1, unpaginated (May 23, 1637). Among the goods to be subjected to the *terzo* in Guarinoni's proposal were quicksilver, lambskin, amber, fleece, Bulgarian leather, castor, Cypriot and Syrian phyllites, grain and powder, wolf cloaks, Cypriot and Izmir cotton, musk, orpiment, beaver skins, and Greek sugar.
90. "Tiurchi [*sic*], Valachi, Bossinesi, Persiani, Armeni, Bogodani, Moldavi, et Hebrei." (Cinque Savi, Seconda serie, b. 147, fasc. 2, unpaginated (Feb. 1, 1641 m.v.)).
91. "Che tutte, e cadaune mercantie, che vengono dal Paese Turchesco siano di che ragione, e ritto esser si voglia spettanti à chi si sia anco li Armeni, et altri soggetti al Re di Persia, Hebrei Levantini,

wares themselves. This was a radical break from the original intent of the *terzo* legislation—from a tax levied on brokers and rationalized as financing the assistance to hapless and linguistically incompetent foreign merchants, it came, in effect, to apply to Ottoman and Safavid merchants irrespective of their linguistic competence. The *terzo* legislation thus ultimately undermined distinctions among Ottoman and Safavid Muslim, Jewish, and Christian subjects and between fluent Italian-speaking, long-time residents of Venice and newly arrived sojourners. And although the term *Levantini* was not necessarily used in official deliberations regarding the tax, the new and much expanded boundaries of the group subjected to it suggest the emergence of a new superordinate category. This category—just like "the Levant"—extended to multiple regions east of Venice. And its coherence depended decisively on a metropolitan perspective.

As a coda to this episode, it is revealing to look at arguments put forth by "the Armenian nation" for their exemption from the *terzo* in the mid-seventeenth century. After arguments for exemption based on linguistic competence had failed them in 1650, in early 1663 Armenian merchants petitioned the Senate once again, claiming that their Christian faith should distinguish them from other foreign merchants whose transactions were subject to the tax. They provided the following narrative about the circumstances of the introduction of the tax and its application. The *terzo*, the petitioners suggested, "[o]wed its origins to the entrance to this city of Turkish traders, due to whom, whether in order that they would not be deceived as foreigners, or so that they would not feel extra burden as infidels, the ordinance was established, in which at a later point the Jews were also included."[92] By this account, Jews were subjected to the *terzo* not as an economic measure but almost as an afterthought. The petitioners suggest that the tax was imposed on "Turks" based on religious and juridical rather than linguistic grounds and that it should therefore not be applied to the Christian Armenians. This brief case illustrates the ongoing interactions between state magistracies and trans-imperial groups, through which categories came to be applied in specific contexts. It further suggests that subjects sought to exploit the partial overlaps in meaning (here, the bivalence of "Turk" as a juridical as well as a religious and an ethnolinguistic category) to undermine the regional boundary that was eventually established.

---

e Ponentini, et etiamo Sudditi, debbino per le mercantie capitar in Doana con un Sanser" (Cinque Savi, Seconda serie, b. 147, fasc. 2, unpaginated (Sept. 9, 1669)).

92. "Il terzo delle Sensarie, trasse l'origine dall'ingresso, che in questa Città facevano li Turchi negotianti, à debito de' quali, ò perche non fossero delusi come Forrastieri, ò sentissero maggior aggravio come infideli, fù stabilito l'ordine, in cui posteriormente furono inclusi anco gl'hebrei" (Collegio, Risposte di dentro, b. 59, unpaginated (Jan. 10, 1662)).

"Levantini" as a Traveling Category

To appreciate the novelty of the emerging use of *Levantini* in Venetian commercial discourse and to test the implications of its transformations from an adjective to a noun, it is instructive to compare it with uses in non-Venetian Italian texts as well as with its English and French cognates. In the absence of a full-fledged etymological survey, I suggest, first, that Venetian geography was very much part of the expansive, commercially oriented *Levant* that consolidated in Italian-, French-, and English-language texts by the mid-seventeenth century. For example, a clearly Veneto-centric definition of *the Levant*—one that paradigmatically focused on Venetian colonies in the eastern Mediterranean—was taken up by the English merchant and captain Roger Bodenham, whose account of his "voiage to the Ilands of Candia [Crete] and Chio in the Levant" was published by Richard Hakluyt in 1599.[93] Similarly, the 1658 translation of Nicolas de Bonnefons's *The French Gardiner* by John Evelyn, writer and diarist, asserted that the Italians imported cauliflower seeds "from Candia and other Levantine parts."[94] Evelyn's *Navigation and Commerce, Their Original and Progress* (1674) listed "The *Levantine* parts, *Creete, Rhodes,* and *Cyprus,* &c."[95]

But as we turn our gaze from *Levant* to *Levantine*, we begin to notice a certain departure from Venetian prototypical meanings to French and English ones. In both these latter languages, throughout much of the seventeenth century, *Levantin(e)* was used primarily to refer to people and objects present in a loosely defined region (the Levant) that lay east of France and England (but that potentially included Venice), regardless of their provenance and certainly without an implication of ethnicity, confessional affiliation, or Ottoman juridical status. For example, in his *Epistolae Ho-elianae* (1650), James Howell discusses his intention to bequeath his Italian books "to the worthy company of *Turky* and *Levantine* Merchants, from divers of whom I have received many noble favours." Howell refers here, of course, not to merchants from the Levant but to members of the English Levant Company, who are "Levantine" solely by virtue of their sojourn in the Levant.[96]

The divergence between Venetian (and, more broadly, Italian) and French/English prototypical denotations of *Levantines* became even more pronounced over time. In contrast to the prototypical denotations of *Levantini* in Venetian and other Italian commercial centers as diasporic, largely trans-imperial merchants engaged in the Levant trade, in both French and English a marked shift occurred in

93. Bodenham (1599), 99.
94. Bonnefons (1656, 167–68).
95. Evelyn (1674, 34).
96. Howell (1650, 43). Emphasis in the original.

the late seventeenth century toward a provenance-based definition of *Levantines*. This definition came to operate as a quasi-ethnicity, replete with its characteristic customs, foods, and sartorial and affective styles. Moreover, such an ethnicizing, provenance-based definition of *Levantines* eventually decoupled the category from its earlier, predominantly commercial contexts of use. In this sense, "Levantines" came to be deployed as a marker not so much of its referents' diasporic status nor of a commercial discourse but primarily of authors' globetrotting credentials vis-à-vis a metropolitan readership. This was facilitated, first, precisely by the use of the term as a strategically deployable shifter and, second, by the fact that, unlike their Venetian counterparts, French and English writers encountered "Levantines" primary abroad, either on the Grand Tour in Venice or while sojourning as merchants in the Ottoman Empire.[97]

Levantins/Levantines defined not simply by the referents' current spatial location but by provenance began to appear as headwords in French and English dictionaries at the very end of the seventeenth century. The first French dictionary definition of *Levantin* appeared in Antoine Furetière's 1690 *Dictionnaire universel, contenant généralement tous les mots:* "Someone born in the Levant. The Levantines are for the most part Muslims. Much trade is carried out with the Levantines. Levantine officers are those who command the Mediterranean."[98] This multipart definition nicely captures the complexity of the denotations of the term at that time; it begins with provenance, shifts to confessional affiliation, then to commercial activity, and finally to geopolitics. Such a multiplex understanding eventually gave way to a simpler one, based primarily on nativity. The earliest appearance of *Levantine* as a headword in an English dictionary, John Kersey the Younger's definition from 1702, simply reads, "People that live in the levant."[99] Yet, when the term appeared for the first time in the posthumous revised sixth edition of Edward Phillips's *The New World of Words* (1706), it was glossed as "Natives or Inhabitants of the Levant, the Eastern People."[100]

97. On the place of Venice in the English Grand Tour, see Redford (1996).

98. "Qui est né au Levant. Les *Levantins* sont la plus part Mahometans. Il se fait un grand commerce avec les *Levantins*. Les Officiers *Levantins* sont ceux qui commandent sur la Mediterranée" (Furetière 1690, unpaginated). This definition was soon followed by the 1694 edition of the *Dictionnaire de l'Académie française*, "Natif des pays du Levant. Les peuples Levantins. les nations Levantines" (queried on the Project for American and French Research on the Treasury of the French Language (ARTFL), http://colet.uchicago.edu). The headword *Levantin* does not appear in earlier French dictionaries, such as Jean Nicot's 1606 *Thresor de la langue francoyse*.

99. Based on the corpus available on the Lexicons of Early Modern English (LEME) website (Kersey 1969 [1702], as queried on LEME, http://leme.library.utoronto.ca.myaccess.library.utoronto.ca/lexicons/record.cfm?id=834).

100. Phillips (1706), unpaginated.

Predating by a few decades its dictionary definitions, the noun *Levantines* appeared in English and French print in the second half of the seventeenth century. A notable French precursor appeared in 1603 in Henry Castela's *Le sainct voyage de Hiérusalem et Mont Sinay*, which mentioned that "Levantines do not play [the trumpet] at sea."[101] This use strongly recalls the maritime, Lingua Franca roots of the term; indeed, the term appeared in the context of a description of a naval battle between Venetian and "Levantine" (that is, Ottoman) vessels outside the port of the Cycladic island of Milos in 1600.[102] It seems that over half a century passed before other references to Levantines appeared in either French of English print. These occurrences, too, speak to the shifter qualities of the term.[103] Estienne Cleirac's *Les us, et coutumes de la mer* (1671) referred multiple times to naval terminology used by "les Levantins."[104] Cleirac never defined who the Levantines were, and because all the terms he ascribed to them were in Italianate Mediterranean Lingua Franca, he may have meant mariners operating in the Levant, irrespective of provenance (not unlike Howell's "Levantine merchants"). Around 1675, Jean de La Fontaine opened one of his fables with the framing statement "les Levantins en leur légende disent."[105] The widely read *Recueil de plusieurs relations et traitez singuliers & curieux* (1679) by Jean-Baptiste Tavernier, a French diamond merchant, reported "la conversion de ces Levantins" and proceeded to provide examples of Maronites converting to Catholicism in Aleppo and of a Franciscan friar in Diyarbakır.[106] Later in the same work Tavernier discussed the gardens of Sarajevo, referring to a "Maniere d'appaiser la soif en mangeant toute particuliere aux Levantins" and "Concombres grand ragoût des Levantins."[107] The English translation of Tavernier's slightly earlier work, *The Six Voyages into Persia and the East-Indies* (1677), similarly made repeated use of the new ethnicizing denotation of *Levantines*. It mentioned Levantines at least seven times, discussing their cleanliness and culinary habits, which are frequently contrasted with those of Europeans. Examples are "Certain it is, that the *Europaeans,* more addicted to subtilty and circumvention, than the *Levantines,* and for the most part not endeavouring to be sincere in Commerce, have taught the *Turks* several Cheats, which they were either ignorant of, or did not practice . . ."; "Those Basins are of a fashion more commodious than that of ours, and it is an evident Mark of the

---

101. "Levantins ne sonnent [la trompette] sur mer" (Castela 1603, 483).
102. Ibid.
103. This claim is based on my querying several databases of early modern texts, including Early English Books Online and Gallica, and an extensive search of Google Books.
104. Cleirac (1671, 83, 133, 437, 508, 509, 513, 538, 539).
105. La Fontaine (1678, book VII, fable 3), www.lafontaine.net (accessed June 26, 2006).
106. Tavernier (1679, 90).
107. Tavernier (1679, 502, 554).

cleanliness of the Levantines"; and, as in the French edition, "A way to quench thirst at meals, wholly particular to the Levantines," and the ubiquitous reference to cucumbers, "a fruit of much delicacy amongst the Levantines."[108] That the use of *Levantines* as people originating in the Levant was still somewhat of a neologism to English readers at the end of the seventeenth century is further suggested by Sir Paul Rycaut's 1688 translation of Garcilaso de la Vega's (1539–1616) *The Royal Commentaries of Peru* (first published in Lisbon in 1609). According to the English text, "Levantines" are "the *Greeks* so called in the *Indies*."[109] Later, the translation mentions two soldiers who were "*Levantines,* (or people of the Eastern Countries, called the *Levant*)." These two explicit glosses suggest that, at least for Rycaut, the noun *Levantine* still required explication.[110] It is also worth noting that Rycaut's gloss follows the Venetian prototypical understanding of Levantines as diasporic people. This seems especially significant considering Rycaut's own extensive so-journ in Istanbul and Izmir as a chancellor and later consul of the English Levant Company from 1661 to 1678.[111]

Unfortunately, inquiry into uses of the term *Levantini* in non-Venetian Italian texts is hampered by the heavy literary and humanist bias of the Italian lexico-graphic corpora.[112] Salvatore Battaglia's magisterial *Grande Dizionario della Lingua Italiana* (1961–2002) provides six quotations for *levantino* in the sense of "na-tive, inhabitant of an eastern land."[113] Of these, four use the term as an adjec-tive, applied once each to Levantine Jews, Levantine Christians, a Levantine slave woman, and a Levantine poet. Only two quotations are provided for *Levantino* as a noun. The first is Sanudo's reference to Levantine merchants in Ancona, already discussed. The second is taken from *Le Vite de' pittori, scultori, et architetti moderni* (published in 1672) by Giovanni Pietro Bellori (1613–1696), a Roman antiquar-ian. It thus provides little evidence for the introduction and articulation of this noun in the sixteenth century.[114]

Despite this meager yield from the lexicographic corpora, the term *Levantini* did circulate in diverse Italian contexts at least from the 1520s. The examples cited earlier in the chapter confirm the shifter qualities of the term and illustrate the

---

108. Tavernier (1677, 18, 47, 65, 92). Emphasis in the original.
109. Vega (1688, book 3, chap. 13, 629).
110. Vega (1688, book 5, chap. 28, 814).
111. Anderson (2004).
112. To date, the only Italian lexicographic corpora available online with word lists are the Corpus OVI dell'Italiano antico, with its close to 2,000 texts, and the Archivio Datini. Both extend only to the late fourteenth century and, not surprisingly, do not contain any examples of the word *Levantino* or its derived forms (Corpus OVI dell'Italiano antico, http://gattoweb.ovi.cnr.it [accessed July 19, 2010]).
113. "Oriundo, abitante di un paese orientale" (Battaglia 1973, 1007).
114. Battaglia (1973, 1007).

oscillation in its prototypical referents among Ottoman Jewish subjects of Iberian descent, non-Muslim Ottomans, and all Ottoman and Safavid subjects and between people "in the Levant" and merchants "from the Levant" trading on Italian soil. In most instances in which it was used, *Levantini* could operate as both a noun and an adjective, and it was immediately preceded or followed by its supposed antonym: Ponentini, Spanish, or Portuguese. This use is evident, for example, in a series of laws passed in several Italian port cities in the course of the sixteenth century, which were meant to divert Ottoman trade from the main commercial hubs of Venice, Ancona, and Ragusa. In 1538, Duke Ercole II of Ferrara promised "all Spaniards and Portuguese, Levantines, Slavs, Dalmatians, Greeks, Turks and [people] of every nation, whether Christians or infidels, who will come to live or trade in our lands, cities and any place of our state and dominion," that they could live there according to their customs.[115] A papal brief of 1553 extended to "Portuguese Jews" trading in papal territory the same privileges already conceded to "Jews and Christian believers of the east, called Levantines."[116] In 1572, Duke Emmanuel Philibert of Savoy issued a long charter "for the entire Hebrew nation, of whatever status, condition, and language and for those of that descent, both Italians and Germans, Spanish, Portuguese, Levantine, and from Barbary and Syria."[117] In 1593, the Tuscan Grand Duke Ferdinand I de' Medici issued his "Constitution of Livorno: To all of you merchants of any nation, Levantines, Ponentines, Spaniards, Portuguese, Greeks, Germans, and Italians, Jews, Turks, Moors, Armenians, Persians, and others."[118] These examples of Tuscan, Savoyard, papal, and Ferrarese commercial legislation evidently followed the prototypical Venetian denotation of *Levantini* as merchants of the Jewish Sephardic diaspora under Ottoman protection. At the same time, the category "Levantini" was clearly still in flux, as similar privileges for Levantine merchants to settle in Ancona published in Rome in 1593 listed "Levantini" twice: first as "Levantine Jews" and then as "Jews, Turks, Greeks, and other Levantine merchants."[119] Indeed, in most of these examples, Levantini were included in a long list of ethnonyms that referred

---

115. Ravid (1991, 141–42).
116. "hebreis et Christi fidelibus orientalibus Levantinis nuncupatis" (quoted in Segre 1992, 119).
117. The charter was initiated by a Jewish merchant, Vitale di Sacerdote, and his son Simone, who explicitly cited Florentine, Ferrarese, and papal precedents dating from 1551, 1553, and 1559, respectively (Ravid 1991, 144–45).
118. "Costituzione livornina: A tutti voi mercanti di qualsivoglia nazione, Levantini, Ponentini, Spagnoli, Portoghesi, Greci, Tedeschi, et Italiani, Ebrei, Turchi, Mori, Armeni, Persiani et altri" (quoted in Dermigny 1974, 535). On the Medicean politics of turning Livorno into a "free port," see Trivellato (2009, 74).
119. "Priuilegii d'hebrei leuantini d'ordine dell'ill[ustrissi]mo, & reu[erentissi]mo monsig[nor] cardinal camerlengo per special commissione di N.S. PP. Clemente VIII. Che si osserui quanto da Sisto papa V. de fe[lice]. mem[oria] per sue lettere fu concesso a detti Hebrei, Turchi, Greci & altri

specifically to trade diasporas. The inclusion of Levantini with other ethnonyms long associated with the Levant trade, yet clearly Christian, such as Greeks, Slavs, and Armenians, indicates the gradual shift in the commercial discourse of early modern Italy from confessional to juridical and geopolitical distinctions.[120]

These cursory examples suggest the growing ubiquity of "Levantini"—and the reasons of state that made the category cohere—in late-sixteenth-century Italian commercial discourse. But they do not provide a detailed picture of how the category operated relationally, as a strategically deployable shifter. A more elaborate text, "Argument . . . concerning the trade ordered by Grand Duke Cosimo I between his subjects and the nations of the Levant" (1577) by Filippo Sassetti, a Florentine merchant, allows for an extensive consideration of these relational articulations of the category.[121] Sassetti implicitly organized his text around a series of recursive binary oppositions. At the most obvious level, he contrasts "Levantini (them)" with "Tuscans/Florentines (us)." But whereas the category "Levantini" remains relatively undifferentiated throughout his text, the "us" is soon pluralized and nuanced. At the epicenter of Sassetti's world are Florence and its satellite cities of Pisa and Livorno (the emerging free port of the Tuscan Grand Duchy), as well as the textile hubs of Lucca and Genoa.[122] On another level, the Tuscan urban cluster is contrasted with three rival cities that set its model and point of comparison: Ancona, Venice, and Ragusa. On a broader level still, these Italian entrepôts combined are set against other parts of Europe in whose trade relations with the Levant the Italian peninsula as a whole serves as an intermediary zone: Flanders/Antwerp and France/Marseille. Ultimately, these distinctly commercial zones are juxtaposed with Spain, which provides only raw materials for the Italian textile industry. Other, more remote places are represented by proxy, in the form of merchants sojourning in Venice ("Germans" and "Flemish")[123] and in Antwerp ("English" and "Baltic"). Sassetti thus underscores both the diversity and complexity of trade relations within a Christian oecumene and the unity of this oecumene vis-à-vis the Levant by occasionally glossing it under the collective

---

mercanti leuantini nella citta d'Ancona" (Clemens VIII (1593)). On Portuguese and other Ponentine merchants in Venice, see Da Silva (1987); Kellenbenz (1987); Ruspio (2002, 2007).

120. For a similar argument based on the career of the Greek merchant diaspora in this period, see Greene (2010).

121. "Ragionamento . . . sopra il commercio ordinato dal Granduca Cosimo I tra i sudditi suoi e le nazioni del Levante" (Sassetti 1853 [1577], 171).

122. For a comparative view of the silk industries of Lucca, Genoa, Florence, and Venice, see the numerous contributions in Molà, Mueller, and Zanier (2000). On Livorno, see Trivellato (2009).

123. In the sixteenth and seventeenth centuries, the "Flemish" merchant community of Venice did not distinguish between the northern and the southern Low Countries; the category "Fiamenghi" thus included both "Dutch" and "Flemish" (Van Gelder 2009, esp. 11).

header "Christian merchants." Unlike these Christians (that is, Europeans), the Levantini are never distinguished by geography, ethnolinguistic identity, political subjecthood, relations of center and periphery, or economic function. The only "Levantine" place that Sassetti explicitly mentions is "Gostantinopoli [*sic*]," referred to once as a destination for Tuscan merchants rather than as a place of provenance. The Levantini's religion can be inferred from their interchangeability with "Turchi" and "Turchi e Giudei" throughout the text. "Levantini," in other words, are non-Christian Ottomans. Indeed, Sassetti makes no mention of Christian merchants from the Levant, even though during this period Greeks and Armenians far outnumbered Muslims in the commercial centers of the Italian peninsula and were very much on Venetian and other Italian legislators' minds as they sought to attract Ottoman trade to their ports.[124] Here, the contrast with contemporary Venetian use suggests the novelty of the gradual Venetian extension of "Levantini" to refer to Christian as well as Muslim and Jewish Ottoman and Safavid subjects. It also attests to the initial paradigmatic reference of the term to diasporic merchants trading on the Italian peninsula rather than in their home countries.

E arly modern Venetian official documents only sporadically referred to a superordinate category of "Levantini." More often, confessional, linguistic, and political divides—between and within groups differentially described as Muslims, Christians, and Jews, Armenians and Greeks, Bosnians, Albanians and Moldavians, Ottomans and Safavids—were recognized, although grudgingly, even in unified policies that rendered them all moot. This proliferation of ethnolinguistic categories had the effect of magnifying rather than minimizing the ethnic diversity of the Ottoman Empire in Venetian commercial discourse. At the same time, establishing who was subject to the *terzo* and who was to reside in the Fondaco dei Turchi were two crucial moments in the process whereby a special superordinate category of foreigner was constituted. Trans-imperial subjects, including merchants, brokers, and dragomans operating within and across Venetian and Ottoman state institutional boundaries, played a key role in articulating the category "Levantini" in Venetian commercial discourse and perhaps, although this hypothesis remains to be examined, also in its dissemination to other entrepôts on the Italian peninsula and beyond. From its inception, the category "Levantini" signaled a specific vantage point and perspective and was thus instrumental in marking the position of the speaker as firmly grounded in

124. Stoianovich (1960). But see also an important critique in Kafadar (1996).

the metropole. That the boundaries of this category were not thereby permanently fixed but continued to evolve over the next three centuries attests to the ongoing dialectic between state institutions and trans-imperial subjects. It is this power-laden dialectic that has ultimately naturalized categories of belonging and alterity that, at the outset, were far from natural. And it is shifters such as *Levantini* that lie at the heart of a dynamic that sets the boundary between "here" and "there," between metropolitan society and those deemed foreign to it—a dynamic that continues to this day.

Afterword

S uggestive as it may be, Cornelio Frangipane's embittered comment that "All are foreigners in Venice who aren't Venetians" holds only a partial truth, even for the Venetian myth-makers. Although the juridical status "Venetian" and its attendant political and economic privileges were carefully guarded by a small minority, the contested category "foreigner" was very unevenly applied to and by the majority of the inhabitants and sojourners of the city and its Mediterranean imperial domains. It is hardly by accident that Frangipane's circular statement ultimately leaves unanswered the question of how to tell Venetians and foreigners apart. Who designated whom a foreigner, to what ends, and with what degree of success depended not only on the participants' unique relationship but also on the genre in which the claim was made and on the expected consequences of the acceptance of the claim. More important, although Frangipane conveniently proposed a binary set that included only "Venetian" and "foreigner," a third, intermediary category was clearly at work in the articulation of both, namely trans-imperial subjects. This neologism is a useful analytical category for understanding an intermediary group of individuals, neither fully Venetian nor foreign, who actively engaged a host of Venetian institutions. Trans-imperial subjects made repeated assertions to knowledge of and membership in an elsewhere, but they also exercised membership (and insiders' knowledge) in a range of Venetian metropolitan sites. It was, in fact, this unique position that allowed them to act as effective intermediaries between Venetian and Ottoman elites in the sixteenth and seventeenth centuries.

Although beyond the scope of the current work, the strong intellectual and biographical links between the subjects studied here and their eighteenth-century successors should be acknowledged. The practices of mediation, classification, and demarcation elaborated by early modern trans-imperial subjects constituted important elements in the genealogy of Enlightenment anthropology and the nascent discipline of Orientalism. In particular, eighteenth-century Orientalists, who articulated taxonomies of Mediterranean peoples based on language, ritual, and custom, relied in many ways on the efforts of their trans-imperial forebears in the previous two centuries to institutionalize their specialized knowledge of things Ottoman in several European metropoles.[1] The scientific study of Ottoman culture depended, quite literally, on the development of commercial and diplomatic institutions that facilitated the production and circulation of specific kinds of knowledge across linguistic and political boundaries.

This raises important questions about the location—geographical, textual, and material—of the knowledge produced by trans-imperial subjects, that is, about how the practices and categories they calibrated circulated further and what roles these channels of circulation might have played in the emergence of various publics keenly interested in things Ottoman. The narrative genres most frequently engaged in by trans-imperial subjects—petitions, diplomatic and administrative reports, and court depositions—all circulated only in manuscript and were addressed to a circumscribed readership among primarily metropolitan political and economic elites. Yet, if we consider the interface between the manuscript production of early modern state officialdom and the thriving printing press, it becomes clear that their significance extended much further. Beyond their intended addressees, both manuscript and printed texts often reached broader publics across political and linguistic frontiers. Indeed, the popularity of print culture depended to no small extent precisely on the access it offered to knowledge of distant places and peoples, previously reserved to a smaller group of elite interlocutors.[2] How trans-imperial subjects tapped into the proto-ethnographic curiosity promoted by print culture, nourished it, and participated in shaping its contours is the next step in understanding the role they played in constituting the early modern categories "East" and "West."

1. For a compelling illustration of the special place of Venetian Dalmatia in Enlightenment anthropology, see Wolff (1998, 2005).
2. On print culture in early modern Venice see Wilson (2005). On the conflation of Old and New World taxonomies of difference in early modern print culture see Hall (1995); Schmidt (2001). See also Johns (1998) on the formation of a common public across early modern European centers of literary production as book reproduction became a credible endeavor.

The designation *trans-imperial subjects* already points to these subjects' potential mobility well beyond the Venetian and Ottoman empires. Such subjects and their practices of mediation, classification, conversion, and translation traveled from Venice and the Italian peninsula to the Atlantic seaboard powers, whose interactions with Mediterranean societies increased dramatically precisely during this period. There they interacted with other social groups and their cultural categories.[3] Of particular interest in this context is the merging of notions of Ottoman and Muslim alterity with conceptions of race, religion, and indeed civilization, developed in the wake of European imperial expansion and missionary efforts in the Americas, Africa, and South and East Asia.[4] At the same time, the well-attested presence in south and southeastern Europe of trans-imperial subjects from the Venetian-Ottoman borderlands (including many descendants of the Latin families of Pera and the colonial nobility of Venetian Istria and Dalmatia) calls for further investigation into their role in the articulation of Occidentalist, proto-nationalist, and anti-Ottoman discourses there. To address these questions, a broader comparative framework is needed that will engage not only Venetian archival and narrative sources but Ottoman ones as well. Such a framework will allow scholars to develop a more finely tuned picture of the multiple interactions among various trans-imperial cadres, their intellectual genealogies and milieus, and their links to other groups in Ottoman society and beyond.

As we have seen, dragomans' notions of loyalty and competence, commercial brokers' understandings of foreignness and locality, and converts' and their patrons' ideas about converthood, personal transformation, and indeed Christian subjectivity itself were all shaped by and in turn helped shape Venetian institutions. These ideas were also informed by subjects' prior life trajectories and the cultural categories they had acquired in diverse Ottoman and Venetian milieus. Recent Ottomanist scholarship on early state-formation, on tensions between metropolitan and provincial administrative and legal practices, and on the processes of religious conversion in the Balkans, Istanbul, and the Arab provinces have already alerted us to some of the rewards of approaching the Ottoman archives from a comparative perspective.[5] Bringing the Ottoman archives to bear on broader early modern historiographical debates continues to challenge and refine our conceptual vocabulary for understanding practices of imperial subject-making

3. For illuminating examples of such trans-imperial subjects in an early modern Iberian context, see Al-Hajari (1997); García-Arenal and Wiegers (2003).
4. On the changing scales of Venetian cartography of "the East" in the wake of European Atlantic expansion, see the suggestive comments in Lestringant (1994, 1–3).
5. Makdisi (1997, 2005); Deringil (2000); Peirce (2003); Barkey (2008); Casale (2010); Krstić (2011). See also Goffman (1990, 147–54) for insightful comments on the potential of Ottoman official registers for the study of early modern foreign presence in Istanbul and the provinces.

and the maintenance of social boundaries. Integrating the Ottomans more fully into early modern historical narratives is a crucial antidote not only to visions of European pre-Enlightenment innocence but also to equally problematic and Eurocentric postcolonial assumptions about a linear European imperial expansion as the main driving force of early modern history.

Further, it would be useful to explore the applicability of the concept trans-imperial subject to other kinds of intermediaries and intermediary practices in the Venetian-Ottoman borderlands, as well as to other periods and regions. Much is to be gained by thinking of the early modern Mediterranean world as cohering around a set of genres and institutions that are dialogically related in complex ways and that defy classification along simple political lines. This book has focused on the commercial and diplomatic spheres and their paradigmatic trans-imperial subjects—primarily brokers, converts and their patrons, and dragomans. But other institutions, genres, and social groups clearly played important roles in constituting Mediterranean spaces of encounter as well. The growing scholarship on pilgrims, travelers, scholars, missionaries, merchant diasporas, mariners, soldiers, slaves, servants, and itinerant laborers in the medieval and early modern Mediterranean has already provided ample materials for conceptual synthesis. Such synthesis would not only refine the concept trans-imperial subject but help give better chronological precision to the semiotic contributions made by the specific groups I have studied in this book.

Finally, the concept trans-imperial subjects raises important questions about prevailing notions of early modern coloniality, citizenship, and subjecthood more generally. To the extent that trans-imperial subjects operated within a multiplex sociopolitical context, how were their trajectories and categories constitutive of broader discourses about place, subjecthood, and social membership? How do their performances of mediation challenge not only a bifurcated vision of metropole and colony, self and other, but the very mapping of social positionality onto geographical space? Venice and Istanbul, the two important early modern centers of cultural production examined here, can only be understood as nodes along mutually constituted networks of trade, kinship, religious ties, circulating texts, and migration, around which categories of inclusion and exclusion were formed. The centrality of trans-imperial subjects to processes of boundary-making in the early modern Mediterranean underscores the extent to which sociocultural systems in the region interpenetrated and overlapped over their long histories. Understanding the trans-imperial dimensions of early modern cultural mediation thus helps document the emergence of boundaries now so ingrained that their very historicity is often forgotten. It also calls into question the motivations of those who benefited—and still do—from naturalizing the boundaries that, at the beginning of the period under study, were anything but natural.

Appendixes

APPENDIX 1.1

Petition by Zuan Giacomo (1563)

Limmensa benignita di V[ost]ra Sub[limi]ta, che sempre aiuta tutti gli suoi fideli sudditi, et poveri opressi da adversita, et travagli di quest mondo, et massime, quelli poverini che essendo nelle mani del Diavolo privi del vero lume della fede del n[ost]ro Dolciss[m]o S[igno]r m[esse]r jesu cristo redentor n[ost]ro illuminati dal lume del spirito santo humilmente vengono all'agua del S[antissi]me Battesemo Lassando ogni loro sustantia, et inascendo nel sangue di me jesu cristo, si come ho fatto jo povero Zuan Giac[om]o fatto di Ebreo cristiano, et p[ri]ma nominato jacob dalla baldora, et essendomi Batteggiato, et rimasto senza susta[n]tia alcuna ridotto p[er] gra[zia] di Jddio in casa delli m[agnifi]ci m[esser] Andrea, et Gier[ola]mo Contarini et fratelli su del cl[arissi]mo me[sser] Dario p[er] l'amor d'Jddio fino a' tanto che di qualche aiuto cristiano mi p[ro]veda, et se ben io son rimasto senza beni di sorte alcuna, mi e' pero restata la gra[zia], et speranza del somo redentor n[ost]ro, et la clementia infinita di v[ost]ra Ser[eni]ta. Pero getatomi à piedi sui humiliss[imamen]te, come fideliss[imo] suo schiavo supp[li]co sua celtitudine sia contenta di farmi gra[zia], ch'io possi essercitar l'off[izi]o di sensaro in ogni luoco, si come à de gl'altri in tal cassi sono sta concessi fino à tanto che venga l'occasione, che si facia sanseri ordenarii, accio con questo favore, et gra[zia] di V[ostra] S[ereni]ta, et del mio s[igno]r m[esser] jesu cristo possa sustentar la mia povera vita, et pregar il somo jddio p[er] la felicita, et esaltatione di V[ostra] S[ereni]ta, et del suo feliciss[im]o D[omi]nio, et cossi humilm[en]te alla sua benignita, et clementia mi racc[omand]o:

Source: ASVe, Collegio, Risposte di dentro, b. 1, c. 7 (Sept. 27, 1563).

APPENDIX 1.2

Reply by the Board of Trade to Samuel Spiera's Petition (1641)

Conoscendo le [Eccellenze] V[ostre] di quanta importanza fosse al neg[ozi]o di quela Piazza, che le sansarie del trafico de mer[ca]to fossero contrattate col mezo di p[er]sone Civili, e degne di fede, decretò sin l'anno 1503, che queste dovessero passare p[er] mano de soli Venetiani Originarij, e ne insditui l'università di 190 sanseri ord[ina]ri di Rialto, à quali approprio questo affare delle sansarie, obligandoli à non potersi applicare al altro essercitio, et prohibiendo nell'istesso tempo, che alcun' altro non potesse far sansarie, et par[ticularmen]te gl'hebrei, sotto pene severissime; Ben secondo le occorenze sono stati gratiati alcuni benemeriti poter essercitare come sopra numerarij; et ad alcuni hebrei concesso il poter far sansarie in ghetto, e di strazzaria, che non hanno che fare colle sansarie di Rialto; et del 1532 ult[im]o Zuno pare che gli meriti del S. Meir Maurogonato le fosse delli Ecc[elentissi]mi S[igno]ri Capi dell'ecc[elentissim]o Cons[igli]o di X. li concesso con suoi discendenti, oltre gl'altri privilegi, questo ancora di poter essercitar una sansaria in ghetto, et fuori di ghetto. Nelle quali equivostre parole forse fondando il ser[enissim]o Samuel Spiera le sue insdanze, supplica la S[erenità] V[ostra] col mezo dell' ecc[elentissi]mo sig[no]r Bailo compiacersi habilitarlo con quattro fig[lio]li ad essercitare una sansaria in Rialto commune con tutte le nation; il che saria p[er] n[ost]ro senso rive[rentemen]te un contravenire à tanti publici decreti, e terminationi de mag[istra]ti delegati in questo affare; Che però non mancando modi alla pub[lic]a munifficenza di consolare q[ue]llo che col'impiego fruttuoso di se stessi in vantagio le publici interessi prourano di rendersi degni della pub[lic]a gratia, come hà fatto il su[pradet]to Spiera, massime nelle ultime congiunture in Cost[antinopo]li et ne fà pieno attestato l'ecc[elentissi]mo s[igno]r Bailo Cont[ari]ni rimett[end]o ogni n[ost]ro senso al sapientiss[im]o volere di V[ostra] S[erenit]a.

Source: ASVe, Cinque Savi, Risposte, b. 152, cc. 194r–v (July 12, 1641).

APPENDIX 1.3

Petition by Lorenzo Capessich (1621)

Havendo io Lorenzo Capessich da Sebenico tratenutomi in Turchia per occasione de negoci l'intiero corso d'anni dodeci hò apreso perfettamente la lingua turca, in modo ch aggiunta alla schiava, et Italiana le quali benissimo posiedo, mi rendono atto di potermi adoperarre ad utilità publica, et privata nel comercio, massime che havendo io aquistato molti amici nel paese, li ho' conservando perche dependenze de quali han[n]o con la nostra casa in Sebenico, dove hò potuto rendermi fruttuoso suddito, et servo di V[ostra] S[erenit]à in diversi negocij, nè quali sono stato adoperato da Ill[ustrissi]mi Pub[li]ci Rapp[resentan]ti nelli abbocamenti con li S[ignor]i Sanzachi, et nelle trattationi con ministri turchi; et perche io hò dessegnato di fermarmi in q[ue]sta Alma Città per poter con honesta utilità tratenermi in essa, che è Patria Universale à tutte le gente et à me particolarm[en]te nato de Parenti benemeriti, et di madre della famiglia Vegici spatafora di Napoli di Romania, che con la perdita di quella fed[elissi]ma Città perde molte richezze; supp[lic]o riv[erentemen]te V[ostra] S[ereni]tà che si degni di farmi gratia, ch'io sia creato Sansale ord[ina]rio, che non manchero di faticarmi in q[ue]sto impiego per sempre antepore co'l servitio publico la sodisfatione de mercanti per achrescimento del comercio. Gr[ati]e.

Source: ASVe, Collegio, Risposte di dentro, b. 16, c. 135 (Nov. 13, 1621).

APPENDIX 2.1

Inventory of the Archives of the Guild of Commercial Brokers (1493–1807)

Note: The following is based on an inventory produced by the staff of the ASVe but updated to reflect actual current content, as necessary.

517 517.1 1493–1664 *Capitolare dell'Arte dei Senseri* (appellatione, ordine, parte)
Copies of decrees by various magistracies (Senate, Provveditori di Comun, UaM, Governatori delle Intrade, Cinque Savi alla Mercanzia) in matters of brokers, guild resolutions, elections, lists of guild members, officials elected
517.2 1670–1740 Capitolare dell'Arte dei Senseri perg.
517.3 1670–1740 Copia dello stesso

518 518.1 *Coppie d'Instrumenti seguiti tra la Scola di S[an]ta Catarina di questa Oltre da una & il Rev[eren]do Monast[eri]o delle M[ol]te R[iveren]de Madre d'essa S[an]ta dall'altra olin governata dalli Sanseri del Fontico de Todeschi, et hora possessà dalli Sanseri Ordinari di Rialto. in vigor dell'unione tra loro Seguit[o]*
(copy made in the second half of the eighteenth century)
[518.alt] 1555–1591 Terminazioni de' Magistrati, Provveditori sopra Camere e Camera d'Imprestidi, nonchè d'altre Magistrature, relative ai Senseri. Sembra essere il Capitolare (e Notatorio) A delle amere degli Imprestiti, dove essiste analogo Capitolare
Transferred to Ufficiali agli imprestiti 8 Bis
518.2 1763–1806 Terminazioni delli Sanseri Rimasti Principia 1762 usque

519 519.1 1661 Raspa
Lists of guild members convicted by the guild tribunal
519.2 1705 Libro intitolato Mare, ove sono descritti tutti li Sanseri, Ordinarij di Rialto, & Fontico; Restaurato di nuovo dà mè Gio:Battista Paludi, Nodaro dell'Offitio medesimo; In tempo delli Spettabili Signori Presidenti infrascritti, Gio:Batt[ist]a Asinelli, Giacomo Gavazzi, Paulo Astori, Presidenti attuali
On the frontispiece: a copy of a license issued by the Provveditori di Comun on August 1, 1705, to appoint new guild member brokers in place of deceased ones. The alphabetical register that follows specifies the date of appointment,

the appointee's full name (including his father's first name), name of the deceased broker in whose place he was appointed, and the new broker that eventually replaced him.

519.3 1740 Repertorio di tutti i Libri, e Carti dell'Officio de Senseri stabilito sotto la reggenza de Sig[no]ri Bortolo Gariboldi, Gaetano Trentin, Antonio Cornoldi. Pressid[en]ti.

Alphabetical-chronological listings for the following rubrics: secret denunciations, criminal trials with conviction, nonexpedited criminal trials, expedited verdicts, criminal trials without conviction, defenses without trial, sentences without trial, sworn statements of entering brokers, debtors' certificates, account books, misc. books, index.

520 *520.1 1680 Somario delli sottoscriti undeci libri de Parte del p[rese]nte Offitio di Senseri Ordinarij di Rialto segnati come segue cioe + A B C D E F G H I L. Quali principiano dall'anno di n[ost]ra Salute 1531 sino al p[rese]nte. Con una Rubrcia in fine copisisima p[er] Alfabetto di tutto quello contiene il p[rese]nte Somario. Fatto da me Gio: Antonio dall Aglio Fidelissimo Quadernier del p[rese]nte Offitio d'ordine delli S'pli Sig[no]ri Presidenti infrascritti. / Guglielmo Corandi / Zuanne Bortoletti / Z. Batt'a Carminati / Honorandi Pressid[en]ti / Finito l'Anno MDCLXXX [1680]*

Details the decisions of the confraternity on elections to various offices, expenditures (such as new books, paintings), rulings in matters of illicit brokers, charity to poor members.

520.2 1682 Somario Delli cinque Capitoli che s'attrovano al p[rese]nte nell'OFFITIO de SANSERI ORDENARII DI RIALTO dovendossi per l'avenire secondo si andara registrando le parti nel Capitolar S[opradet]to novissimo, cossi si dovera ponerle nel p[rese]nte Somario, e fornito che sarà se li farà nel fine una Rubrica per Alfabetto di tutto quello che contenira lo stesso. / Fatto da me Gio: Domenio dall'Aglio Fedellissimo Quadernier del p[rese]nte Offitio d'ordine delli Sp'ti sig[no]ri Gio: Maria Mutti, Gio: Batt'a Carminati, Giacomo Joanis Honorandi Pres[iden]ti / MDCLXXXII

520.3 1752 Tavola di tutti li Decreti Leggi Parti, e Terminazioni che si contengono nelli due Capitolari Vecchio, e Nuovo del Spett[ant]e Officio de S[igno]ri Sanseri Ordinarj di Rialto e nelli Libri delli Cap'li del medemo Officio principiando dal libro + sino al libro O avvertendo che le due Lettere unite .V. vorranno dinotare il Capitolar Vecchio e le due lettere unite C.N. vorranno dinotare il Capitolar Novo e così pure le lettere sole +. A. B. Ecc. Voranno dinotare il Libro de Capitoli + libro A et il numero seguente vorra' dinotare le cartadura Parimenti le Lettere unite C3.o dintano Cap. Terzo ★ Fatta per ordine de Sp. Sp. Signori Antonio Cornoldi Carlo M[ari]a Ruberti Lorenzo Damiani ONORANDI PRESSIDENTI L'ANNO MDCCLII

Organized thematically, with very brief entries.

521 A) 1560–1566 (mostly lists of members, some resolutions in cases of members, with index at end)

B) 1570–1570 *Libro de parte*

[unnumbered] 1621–1672 *Libro di Capitoli de Sanseri di Fontico,*

H) 1655–1665

L) 1677–1683 *Libro de Capitoli*

[unnumbered] 1677–1683 *Libro de Capitoli*—not same as above

[unnumbered] 1700–1712 *Libro di Capitoli segnato*

522–524 1713–1802 *Riduzioni di Congregazioni di Capitoli Generali come sopra*

525   *525.1* 1596–1598

           525.2 1608–1609 *Libro delle Denontie*

           Presidents: Mattio Bon, Giovanni Biopanditi, Vallerio Lolletti.

           Approximately 400 pages, about half unnumbered.

           525.3 1613–1614 *Libro delle Denontie*

           Presidents: Bastian di Martini, Francesco Lenerin, Diomede Vercelli.

           525.4 1643 *Libro de Denontie e Processi*

           Presidents: Eugenio Lamanedi, Lorenzo Bianchi, Antonio Cargnion.

526–530 1590s–1670s *Processi*

           Trial transcripts are copied in individual notebooks; now ordered alphabetically, they seem initially to have been ordered chronologically. Several are marked as A, B, etc.

531   1799–1801 *Processi definiti*

532–537 1675–1800 *Processi*

538   1640s–1680s trials, legislation

539–542 1745–1793 *Suppliche dell'Arte dei Senseri*

543   *543.1* 1626–1640 [1658] *Multorum*

           543.2 1640–1691 *Multorum*

           543.3 1676–1678 *Intimationi p[er] il Giuramento et Consegne delle Carte de nomi de Senseri*

           543.4 1722–1744 *Multorum*

544–548 1724–1807 *vari registri* [esecuzioni contra debitori, etc.]

549–550 1786–1807 *Giornale di cassa*

Source: ASVe, Arti, bb. 517–50.

APPENDIX 3.1

Deposition of Abdone q. Giovanni of Aleppo (1616, Excerpted)

Essendo io nato christiano in Aleppo, et battezzato. dopo 10 anni in c[irc]a sono stato fatto turco et per d[et]to tempo visuto alla turchesca. et son circonciso. et hora essendo capitato à Venetia, et volendo lassar d[et]ta setta de turchi et esser buon cat[toli]co mi son in questo loco per far quanto mi sarà ordinato

Int. che dica con che occ'one abbandonasse la fede cat[toli]ca et si facesse turco.

R.t Io caminai da giovine, et in un certo tempo che seida territorio di Tripoli alcuni turchi si erano ribellati, io andai tra di loro, et mi posi un turbante in testa, et loro mi accettorono ricercandomi chi ero, et io li risposi che ero turco. et li dissi che da picolo era uscito fuori di casa mia, et che per questo non era tagliato, et all'hora poi mi fecero circoncider. ma io li disi cosi perche se li havesse detto che era christiano, mi haverebbero fatto rinegar per forza ò che mi haverebbero ammazzato, et per questo io li dissi che ero turco. Et mi lassai poi anco tagliar per l'istesso timor, perche loro se ne accorsero che non ero tagliato.

Int. per qual c'a andò cosi à seida fra turchi, et non andò fra christiani.

R.t io era stato in Gierusalem à visitar il s[an]to sepolcro come Pelegrino, et nel ritorno passai da seida non sapendo dove andar, et cosi mi compagnai fra loro, perche era anco un gran bisogno.

Int R.t avanti che io andasse in Gerusalem q'n stava à casa io tessevo delli ormesini

Int R.t q'n mi tagliorono et mi fecero turco mi chiamorono Ebraim. Et sevì come soldato per un anno un capitano che si chiamava Magiar Mustaffa che era capo delli ribelli. Et passato poi l'anno andai nel gran Cairo, et per che niuno sapeva che io era stato turcho, mi vesti da christiano et steti fra christiani per sette anni. dopo andando verso Constantinopoli à Borsa, vi fù un turco che mi conobbe ch ero stato turco, et accio non mi scoprisse, mene fuggi nelli confini dell'ongaria per venir in queste arti della X'pianità, ma da un barbier mi fù detto che li passi non erano sicuri, che saria stato preso come spione, et cosi per timore tornai indietro et per altre strade poi son venuto al seraglio della Bossina. Et da seraglio con alcuni mercanti turchi son venuto à Venetia, et mentre son stato con loro hò fatto alla turca, perche loro mi tenevano per turco, et credevano ch'io fosse uno di quei loro santoni che vano à cercando.

Int R.t Io non son tornato à star in Aleppo perche là si era saputo che mi era fatto turco, et non saria stato sicuro longam[en]te se bene vi son stato una volta cosi per passaggio doi mesi, et andava in chiesa come Christiano.

Source: ASVe, Santo Uffizio, Processi, b. 71, fasc. "Abdone q. Giovanni Sensale d'Aleppo" (April 14, 1616).

APPENDIX 3.2

Deposition of Pierre Blanche (1631)

[. . .] Io ho seguitato la vita di mio padre nutrito et allevato nella setta et heresie di calvino . . . et essendo io partito dal mio paese l'anno passato del mese di ott[ob]re mi trattenuti nel Piamonte alcuni mesi, medicando secondo la mia p[ro]fess[io]ne et finalm[en]te già 5 mesi in c[irc]a veni à venetia, et son stato al lazareto vechio c[irc]a tre mesi, et poi in Venetia, et doppio che io son partito di francia, hò sempre havuto in pensiero di lasciare quella setta heretica di calvino, et farmi cat[toli]co perche in franza viddi alcuni miracoli et altrove più in Italia, fatti dalla B[eat]a Vergine, onde mi risolsi determinatam[en]te di farmi Cat[toli]co anzi feci voto di andar à Roma, et andarò a Genova à far contum[ati]a et alli giorni passati andai à S. franc[esc]o di Paola dal P. Confessore che è qui p[rese]nte et ostendit p[er]sona supti' P. Ignatio Correctore Percio conoscendo io di essa stato in errore graviss[im]o havendo tenuto osservato et creduto tutto quello che tiene vede et osserva la setta calvinista, et conoscendo esser vera la fede cat[toli]ca et ap[ostoli]ca Rom[an]a instantam[en]te dimando à q[uest]o s[antissi]mo trib[una]le di esser reconsiliato alla s[an]ta chiesa cat[toli]ca et ap[ostoli]ca Rom[an]a.

Source: ASVe, Santo Uffizio, Processi, b. 88 (Oct. 16, 1631).

APPENDIX 3.3

Deposition of Maddalena q. Melin Turca (1647)

Jo son nata nel territorio della città de clini, sopra sebenico tre giornate, di padre, et m[ad]re christiani, mio padre si chiamava melin contadino e soldato, mia m[ad]re chiamavasi chiarana; ambedue morsero. Jo non sò che nome mi fù imposto, q[uand]o fui battezzata, et maddalena mia sorella che non sò se sia viva ò morta, mi disse che fui battezzata. Et son stata con mio padre sino alla mia età de 10 anni in c[irc]a Et corrigens se ipsam, dixit. Steti con mio p[ad]re sino alla età di 5 anni, che all'hora fui levata dalli parenti di mio p[ad]re turchi, e mi condussero à Zemonico, dove fui allevata, e chiamata p[er] nome Rachima, et mi fecero vivere secondo la legge turchesca, et mi maritorono da un turco chiamato Fasula, che non sò se sia vivo ne morto, ma non hò havuto fig[lio]li. Et hò 50 anni in c[irc]a. et per tutto questo tempo hò vissuto alla turchesca. et mi conformai à quelli riti maometani. Hora essendo capitata in q[uest]a Citta Cat[toli]ca essendo stata amaestrata per 40 giorni circa nella casa de catecumeni nelli a[arti]c[o]li della s[an]ta fede cat[toli]ca vedo che N. S. Giesù c[risto] sia dio, nato di maria vergine. che vi siano 3 p[er]sone divine. che siano 7 li savi' della chiesa. et universalm[en]te tengo e credo tutto quello che tiene e crede la s[anta] m[adre] chiesa. Et perciò son pronta ad abiurare, e vivere e morire in questa s. fede [christ]iana.

Source: ASVe, Santo Uffizio, Processi, b. 103, fasc. "Madalena q. Melin Turca" (June 4, 1647).

APPENDIX 3.4

Deposition of Anna Frais (1630)

Son comparsa in q[uest]o s[an]to off[iti]o à denontiar me stessa, come essendo nata, nutrita et allevata da padre et m're et in paesi de luterani, hò sempre tenuto et creduto tutto quello che insegua la setta di lutero eccettando che hò creduto vi sia il purgatorio, et anco la intercessione de santi. Finalui che essendo venuta in cognit[ion]e del mio errore per le prediche et essortationi del P. fra Giacomo sud[et]to mi son risoluta di ridarmi al grembo della s[an]ta Chiesa Cat[toli]ca, detestando in tutto et per tutto, tutto quello che contradite à d[et]ta s[an]ta Chiesa, confermo p[ro]posito di credere per l'avvenire et osservare quello che tiene, crede et insegna la s[an]ta m[ad]re Chiesa Cat[toli]ca. Perciò humilm[en]te supplico q[uest]o s[an]to tribunale à volermi reconciliare à d[et]ta s[an]ta m[ad]re chiesa.

Source: ASVe, Santo Uffizio, Processi, b. 88 (June 4, 1630).

APPENDIX 3.5

Deposition of Marco Lombardo (1632)

Già sei ani in c[irc]a ritrovandomi in Alessandria nell vassello di Pelegrin di Rossi nel quale ero come nobile, et ricercando le mie frage mi fò dato un schiaffo, all'hora che i turchi mi presero p[er] salvarmi et mi condussero seco al castello ove stei 4 mesi in c[irc]a et ivi osservai le ceremonie maometane usandomi violenza con imbicagarmi con aqua di vita, et violentem[en]te mi circoncisere, et mi fecero per forza parlar turchezo, et confessai di esser turco per paura della morte che mi minacciavano, io però havevo continuam[en]te nel core Iddio, la vergine et li santi, quali sempre honorai con le mie or'oni di giorni et di notte. et senza haver fatto altre ceremonie, quello che feci lo feci con l'esterior et non mai col core. Qu[ando] poi hò veduto il tempo opportuno mi son trasferito in Nazaret et qui hò trovato un Pre[te] di S. Fran[cesc]o il quale mi hà reconciliato nella maniera che si puo vedere dalla fede dalla lui fattami, qual hora p'nto nel s.[ant]o off[iti]o. Hora dolente et pentito dimando à dio p[er]dono et à q[uest]o s[antissi]mo trib[una]le di esser reconciliato alla s[an]ta fede p[ro]mettendo di viver p[er] l'avvenire da buono et vero cat[toli]co et sono pochi giorni che son ritornato à Ven[eti]a cioè 15 giorni in c[irc]a, et doppo che son fugito dalli turchi son sempre vissuto alla Cat[toli]ca et mi son confessato et co[mun]icato in Nazaret 3 volte in 8 giorni che dimorai di Nazaret, et un'altra ritrovandomi al Zante.

Source: ASVe, Santo Uffizio, Processi, b. 88 (Nov. 8, 1632).

APPENDIX 4.1

Translation of Antonio Giustiniano's Alms-Collecting Patent (1619)

By order of the Most Illustrious and Reverend Bishop.
It is entrusted to you, Reverend heads of Monasteries, both of men and of women, and to all the Vicars, Vicar Foranes, Archpriests, and Curates of the Cities, Castles, and Villages of our jurisdiction, that the Pia Casa of Venice has suspended and annulled all the Patents, or mandates previously conceded to several infidels who had come to the Holy Fountain, which allowed them to search for alms everywhere, that from now on in no way shall it be allowed, that in the Villages, and locales subject to the said Territory may they search any longer by virtue of the aforesaid Patents, but the only one who may do so or have it done is Antonio Giustiniano, formerly a Jew turned Christian, bearer of our present mandate, as elected by the lords Governors of the aforesaid Pia Casa, to be permitted once a year starting August 15, day of the Blessed Virgin, to hold (conforming to his order) one general alms-collecting [campaign] in all the Cities, Lands, and places of the Most Serene Dominion, for the sustenance of all those who every day come to [receive] Holy Baptism, to whom we beseech you to give with charity all favors and accompany him to all the Houses, and Farms, so that he receives from all the devotees of Christ our Lord grains, wine, money, and other [goods] to be able to provide for the necessities of that Pia Casa, and since it could be that those who have until now collected alms in virtue of the aforesaid patents may be upset by that prohibition, you should persuade them to come to the aforesaid Pia Casa their mother, assuring them that they will be provided for by the aforesaid lords Governors, as is their intention and thought.
You are required to publicize this mandate in your Churches eight days before the above-said feast of the Blessed Virgin, so that all the faithful prepare to make this holy alms-giving.

Source: ASPV. Sezione antica, Catecumeni, Documenti diversi, b. 2, reg. 1, c. 95 (July 1, 1619).

APPENDIX 5.1

Petition by Giacomo de Nores (1594)

Poiche è piacciuto à nostro Sig[no]re Dio chiamar à miglior vita il Sig[no]r Michele Membré, doppo una lunga sua servitù che ha prestato d'interprete alla Ser[eni]ta, è parso à me Giacomo de Nores consapevole tra me stesso di non esser à gli altri servitori, et sudditi suoi di fideltà, ne di devotione punto inferiore, d'humilissimamente presentarmi à suoi piedi, et come servitore non inhabile per tal carrico, che essendo incontrato dalla somma sua clemenza, et pieta io non potessi essercitarlo supplicai riverentemente la Ser[eni]ta V[ostra] che si degni in questa occasione accettar la mia servitù, et divottione co'l farmi gratia, che come particolare suo servitore e suddito io possa per l'avenire maggiormente mostrare la prontezza, et fedeltà mia, servendola in carico maggiore, et più importante, che questo mio non è. Sapendo pure, che se giova il non esser nato di sangue Vile io son figliuolo primogenito, et successore nel feudo del q[uondam] s[igno]re Pietro de Nores Cav[alie]re, et feudatario di Vostra] Ser[eni]ta nel Regno di Cipro soggetto de conditioni tali, che meglio la Ser[eni]ta le puo conoscere di quello si convenga à me il raccontarle, et che havendo dedicato et dato la vita sua combattendo in servitio di questa Ser[enissi]ma Republica co'l sangue sparso nell'ultima Guerra, la reso certa testimonianza della divottione sua verso questo felicissimo stato, à garra della famiglia Materna Podocattara, non meno della Paterna in suo servitio afflitta, et dessolata. Se gli incommodi della vita passata pono dar loco & merito, io ne lo sentiti tali, e tanti che non si possono provare di maggiori, quando che nelle fascie restai misera preda di gente Turca privio non solamente d'ogni sostanza, et del sangue proprio e di parenti, ma della memoria anco, et cognitione della Patria dove ero nato: Ho girato per molti, et molti anni in varie, et diverse fortune, et Paesi, nella Turchia, nella Persia, et in Babilonia con tutti quei disaggi et incontri, che in servitù tale sogliono rissultate. Et se è neccessaria, come pur è neccessarissima una compita intelligenza della lingua Turchesca dovendosi di quella farne professione, io dico alla Ser[eni]ta V[ostra] come mi sento cosi Padrone di quella, che non solo mi è facilissimo il leggere, il scrivere, il compore et tradure in quell'Idioma, ma l'insegnare anco q[u]ando ne fosse l'occasione mi sarebbe non men facile aggiongio à questo altrotanta cognitione della lingua Araba, et della Persiana da me solo forsi non da altri in questa Città intesa, delle quali io posso cosi facil[men]te valermi, come della Turchesca, et queste lingue q[u]anto giovino all'offitio d'interprete in servitio suo, à lei più, che à me è facile il conoscerlo, et perche non meno è giovevole à tal carrico la pratica de costumi de Turchi delle inclinationi loro, et delle maniere di trattare molto diverse dalle nostre facilmente puo la Ser[eni]ta V[ostra] persuadersi, che essendo io, posso dire, nato tra queste genti, et à mio mal grado notrito, et allenato, havendo praticato per molti anni i negocij loro, et girato per molto, et diverse Provincie, et Paesi qua, et la di maniera io potrei valermi nelle occasioni, che alla giornata s'appresentassero, et da lei mi fussero commesse, che ne resterebbe come spero apieno servita, et sodisfatta. Corre percio l'ottavo anno che io servo questo feliciss[im]o stato per esposit[o]re di queste genti all'offitio de gli Ill[ustrissi]mi Sig[no]ri cinque savij sopra la mercantia con sodisfattione, cred'io, di quel gravissimo magistratto, et quello, che più importa ho havuto il carrico di tradure molte, et importantissime lettere publiche cosi di quelle, che veniano di fuori, come di quelle che di qui erano mandati altrove, et cio credo d'haver io fatto con tanto compiacim[en]o di chi mi commetteva questo offitio quanto desidero che informandosi la Ser[eni]ta V[ostra] intenda godendo io haver quello per testimonio delle fatiche mie, a cui ho immediatamente servito, et ubedito accompagnando dunque Ser[enissi]mo Principe li meriti della casa mia non mediocri per le smarite facolta, perdita della Patria, et sangue sparso in servitio di q[u]esta Ser[enissi]ma Republica, le stenti, le fattiche i disagi, i tormenti miei di tanti anni d'insoportabil servitù con una cognitione compita della lingua non solo Turchesca, ma dell'Araba, et Persiana, ardisco, torno a dire, d'humiliss[imamen]te comparer a i piedi della Ser[eni]ta V[ostra] et riverentemente supplicarla che si degni collocarmi nel loco già vaccante per la morte di esso sig[no]r Michel Membré, q[u]al gratia oltre che sara conferita in persona fedelissima, et non inetta per tal carrico dedicata già tanto tempo al solo servitio suo, tralasciando ogni altri essercitio à cui potrebbe essersi applicata per poter con ispirito più espedito servir la Ser[eni]ta V[ostra] sara anco accettissima à S[ua] D[ivina] Maestà dovendosi per tal via sostenere la povera mia Madre due infelicissime Cugine et trattenere una poverissima casa che è in colmo d'ogni disaggio la q[u]ale meco insieme alla clemenza, et bontà della Ser[eni]ta V[ostra] humilissimamente raccommando.

Translation

Since it has pleased our Lord God to call to a better life Mr. Michele Membré, after the long service he has rendered to the Serenity as an interpreter, it is my role, Giacomo de Nores, knowing myself not to be inferior to your other servants and subjects in either loyalty or devotion, to humbly present myself at your feet, and as a servant not unqualified for said task, that being encountered by your utmost clemency, and piety . . . to petition reverently Your Serenity that it deign accept in this occasion my servitude, and devotion by granting me the favor, that as its special servant and subject I could in the future demonstrate even more my readiness, and loyalty, by serving in an even greater, and more important task than mine. Knowing as well, that enjoying not having been born of vile blood I am the firstborn son and heir to the estate of the late lord Pietro de Nores, knight and feudatory of Your Serenity in the Kingdom of Cyprus, a subject of such conditions that the Serenity could better recognize than I could recount, and that having dedicated and given his life fighting in the service of this Most Serene Republic with the blood shed in the last war, I give sure testimony of his devotion toward this Most Happy State, and also of the maternal family Podocattara, no less afflicted and desolate in your service than the paternal one. If the inconveniencies of the past life can give place and merit, I have experienced so many of those that cannot be proven any greater, when in the swaddles I was left the wretched prey of Turkish people and was deprived not only of all sustenance, and of my own and my relatives' blood, but of memory as well, and of the recognition of the homeland where I was born: I have traveled for many, many years in various and diverse circumstances and countries, in Turkey, in Persia, and in Babylonia with all those misfortunes and encounters that must result from servitude. And if it is necessary, as indeed is very much the case, to give proof of competent knowledge of the Turkish language, I say to Your Serenity how I feel so much the Master of that [language], that it is not only most easy for me to read, and write, compose and translate in that idiom, but also to teach it when given the opportunity it would be easy for me, adding to it also knowledge of the Arabic language, and the Persian, which perhaps I alone understand in this city, of which [languages] I can avail myself so easily as of Turkish, and it is easier for you than for me to recognize the benefits of these languages for the office of interpreter in your service, and since it is no less useful for that task to be familiar with the customs of the Turks, their inclinations and their manner of negotiation, which are very different from ours, Your Serenity can easily be convinced, that being, I might say, born among these people, and to my bad fortune raised and educated [there], having been involved in their affairs for many years, and traveled in many and diverse provinces and lands here and there I could make use of the opportunities that the day would present me, and that you would give me, which I hope would make you well served and fully satisfied. It is the eighth year that I serve this most happy state introducing these people to the office of the illustrious masters Cinque Savij sopra la mercantia with satisfaction, I believe, of that most important magistrate and, more importantly, that I have had the task of translating many and most important public letters both incoming and outgoing, and this I believe to have done with great satisfaction of those who entrusted me with that office as I would like that, once informed, Your Serenity will enjoy having this as testimony of my efforts, for which I have immediately served, and obeyed, having thus enjoined most Serene Prince the not-insubstantial merits of my house for the lost wealth, the loss of the homeland, and blood shed in service of this Most Serene Republic, my privations, efforts, misadventures, and torments of many years of insufferable servitude with complete knowledge of not only the Turkish language, but also Arabic and Persian, I dare, so to speak, to appear most humbly at the feet of Your Serenity and petition you reverently that you deign place me in the position made vacant for the death of said Mr. Michel Membré, which favor, beyond being granted to a person most loyal and not inept for that task, already dedicated for a long time solely to your service, forsaking any other employment to which he might have applied himself to be able to serve Your Serenity with the promptest sprit, will also be most agreeable to His Divine Majesty to be able in this way to support my poor mother [and] two most unhappy cousins and to keep a most impoverished house which is full of every hardship, and which along with me appeals most humbly to the clemency and kindness of Your Serenity.

Source: ASVe, Senato Mar, filza 128, unpaginated (Dec. 13, 1594).

APPENDIX 5.2

Petition by Andrea Negroni (1594)

Supplico Io Andrea Negroni Humilissimo servo, et publico suo Dragomano, che ella sia contenta di concedermi il luocho vacante per la morte de mr Michiel Membré non per la sua grattia, et benigna promessa et l'utile, e fedele servitio da me 15 anni in circa prestato, ma per la sua simplice benignità, et gratia à questo dono veramente perche conviene, che concora la sufficienza mia per questa, e non per altra ragione sarà licito à me alcune cose racordare l'una, è oltra il cotidiano servitio che nella occasione della presa d'uscochi del vassello di Mercanti Bosenesi di grossi cavedeli diede à v[ost]ra Ser[eni]tà tanto disturbo poiche Io scrivendo l'Arze de Sinan Bassà andai di ordine suo à Liesena, et fatte le consignationi di quelle mercantie scrivendo li riceveri, et quietanze con segni, marche, et sigilli de cadauno di essi Turchi con grande avantaggio, et riputatione p[ub]lica posi fine, et perpetuo silentio, et tronchata ogni difficultà, et oltra ciò, che nell'importante, et scandoloso negocio mosso da Turchi di voler fabrichare una fortezza da novo per mezo la fortezza di Zara portando con ogni altra preparatione sette canoni grossi da 50 et una Colombrina ponendo quelli in salvo in la Città di Clina lontan delli Confini vinti miglia pretendendo essi Turchi, che alcuni luochi insieme con la fortezza di Verpoglia fussero nelle giurisditione, et dentro delli confini del Sig[no]r Turcho, onde per tal caso son stato mandato dalla Ser[eni]ta V[ost]ra per una fregata di Cattaro, et poi per via de Scardona co[n] il sig[no]r Alessandri andassemo dal Sig[no]r Bassà, l'onde io fece quello, che conveniva alla mia fidelità, et con viva voce contra li Turchi Adverssarij quali pretendavano nei confini della Ser[eni]tà V[ost]ra chi case, et campi, et chi molini o stabilite, et formate le due Arze à me ordinate, et quelle dal Sig[no]r Bassà sottoscritte, et sigilate à laude del Sig[no]r Iddio fù quietato ancora quel scandoloso negocio, et rivocato ogni ordine de ditta innovatione, ommetto d'haver sospito anco il travaglioso scandalo di sciavusi dell' Apaltatore del gran Sig[no]re poiche, et di quello, et da altra varia servitù con benigne dimostrationi si è mostrata V[ost]ra Ser[eni]tà Ottimamente contenta, altra cosa, ch'io debo dire opportuna al presente proposito è che alla lingua, et scrittura Turchesca, et d'altri dodeci sorte de carateri orientali de scritture io mi trova grandemente perito, et sarà licito dire, che io non conosco altri più sufficienti di me per stare in certa accostumata modestia imperoche non bastando il parlare, et lo scrivere mà il prudentemente fare questo, et quello con il quale i più intendenti e versati con singulare discretione possino conservare il decoro del suo Principe, e non offender l'orgoglio per aventura d'altro grande Sig[no]re con cui occora negotiare, et nello spiegare in scrittura po occorer che torni à bene mostrare vigoria, et ardimento, et congiontamente bona mente, et rispetto nella quale sola distrezza consiste la perfetione di negotij. Questa gran discretione con grandissime pene si acquista, però torno à ricordar à V[ost]ra Ser[eni]ta che io son povero con padre, Madre, moglie, et tre figliolini, che con nove soli ducati al mese di stipendio ho sempre fidelmente servito, ne mai molestai punto le orecchie sue di darmi augumento di sorte nisuna, ma sempre con pacientia, et speranza succeder all'offitio sopradetto, l'onde di novo Io supplico, che io li sia raccomandato q'ando il Sig[no]r Iddio per la publica felicità, et gloria etc.

Translation
I, Andrea Negroni, Your most humble servant, and public dragoman, petition that you be content to grant me the position vacated due to the death of Mr. Michiel Membré, neither by force of your kind promise, nor as a recompense for the useful and loyal service I have rendered for about 15 years, but rather for your simple kindness and favor. This gift, however, should be accompanied by my own skill, and for that reason alone I should be permitted to make note of certain things. First of all, besides [my] unusual service, on the occasion of the capturing by the Uskoks of the ship of the Bosnian merchants and a great amount of capital, which caused Your Serenity great inconvenience, which is why, having written the *arz* [decree] of Sinan Pasha, I went on his instructions to Lesina [Hvar, an island off the shores of Dalmatia], and handled the surrendering of those goods, writing down what was received and noting the receipts with marks, stamps, and seals of each one of these Turks [so that] with great advantage, and public reputation, I put an end and perpetual silence [to their complaints], and stopped any trouble. Moreover, that in the important and scandalous affair prompted by the Turks' wish to build a new fortress near the fortress of Zadar, carrying in addition to all the other preparations seven large canons of fifty and one culverin bringing them safely to the city of Clina [Koljane, Croatia], twenty miles from the border, these Turks pretending that some places, including the fortress of Verpoglia [Vrpolje, Croatia], were under the jurisdiction and within the borders of the Grand Turk, for which occasion I was sent by Your Serenity onboard a frigate to Kotor, and then through Scardona along with Mr. Alessandri we went to the Pasha, where I did what befit my loyalty, and stated clearly against the Turkish adversaries, who lay claims to either houses, or fields, or mills and structures within the borders of Your Serenity. And once the two *arz* [decrees] that I requested were ready and signed by the Pasha and sealed to the Glory of God, this scandalous affair too was silenced, and any order of that innovation was revoked. I omit the troubling scandal of the *messangers* of the Grand Signor's leaseholder, since on both this matter and on the occasion of other various services Your Serenity has proven highly satisfied. Another thing I should say regarding the current issue is that I am well versed in the Turkish language and writing, and in twelve other types of Oriental alphabets, and it would be legitimate to say that I don't know anyone better suited than me, with all due modesty. Because it is not enough to speak it and write it, but to do so prudently, which is that with which those [persons] who possess the greatest understanding and utmost discretion are able to maintain the dignity of their Prince and avoid offending the pride,

as it happens, of another great potentate with whom they negotiate. And in explaining in writing it may end up being useful to demonstrate vigor, and boldness, and at the same time good attention and respect, in the ambit of which alone consists the perfection of affairs. This great discretion is acquired with the greatest pain. But I turn to remind Your Serenity that I am poor with father, mother, wife and three children, that with a salary of only 9 ducats a month I have always served loyally, and have never bothered your ears to give me a raise of any sort, but always [served] patiently with the hope of succeeding the above mentioned office, for which I again petition that I be recommended, to the glory of God and public felicity, etc.

Source: ASVe, Senato Mar, filza 128, unpaginated (Dec. 9, 1594).

Bibliography

MAIN ARCHIVAL SERIES AND MANUSCRIPT SOURCES

Archivio Storico del Patriarcato di Venezia (ASPV).
    Sezione Antica, Catecumeni
    Sezione Antica, Examinum Matrimoniorum
Archivio delle Istituzioni di Ricovero e di Educazione (AIRE).
    CAT A 1 (Capitoli et Ordeni per il buon Governo delle Pie Case de' Cattecumeni di
        Venezia, 1737)
    CAT B 4 (Notatorio, 1592–1599)
    CAT B 6 (Notatorio, 1610–1619)
    CAT C 1 (Catastico, 1504–1695)
    CAT C 2 (Catastico, 1557–1718)
    CAT E 8 (Commisaria Mocenigo, 1636–1665)
    CAT G 1 (Misc., 17th century)
    CAT G 3 (Serie dei Priori del Pio Logo de Catecumeni)
    CAT G 5 (Serie dei Priori del Pio Logo de Catecumeni)
Archivio di Stato di Venezia (ASVe).
    Avvogaria di Comun, Miscellanea Civil
    Avvogaria di Comun, Miscellanea Penale
    Avvogaria di Comun, Misto
    Avvogaria di Comun, Processi per nobiltà
    Arti, Sensali
    Atti diversi, manoscritti
    Bailo a Costantinopoli, Cancelleria
    Capi del Consiglio dei Dieci, Lettere di Ambasciatori, Costantinopoli

Cattaver
Cinque Savi alla Mercanzia, Risposte
Cinque Savi alla Mercanzia, Seconda serie
Collegio, Notatorio, Filze
Collegio, Notatorio, Registri
Collegio, Risposte di dentro
Collegio, Suppliche commesse ai Savi
Collegio, Suppliche di fuori
Compilazione Leggi
Consoli dei mercanti
Dieci Savi alle decime, Catastici
Dieci Savi alle decime, Condizioni di decima
Documenti Turchi
Esecutori contro la bestemmia, Raspe sentenze
Notarile, Atti
Notarile, Testamenti
Ospedali e luoghi pii diversi
Provveditori alla sanità
Provveditori sopra ospedali e luoghi pii
Quarantia Criminale
Santo Uffizio, Processi
Senato, Deliberazioni Costantinopoli, Filze
Senato, Deliberazioni Costantinopoli, Registri
Senato, Dispacci, Costantinopoli
Senato, Dispacci, Provveditori da Terra et da Mar
Senato Mar, Filze
Senato Mar, Registri
Senato Terra, Filze
Ufficio della Bolla Ducale, Grazie del Maggior Consiglio, Filze
Ufficio della Bolla Ducale, Grazie del Maggior Consiglio, Registri
Biblioteca Nazionale Marciana (BNM).
MSS. Italiani
Museo Civico Correr (MCC).
Cod. Cicogna
MSS Morosini-Grimani
MSS PD

PUBLISHED WORKS

Abercrombie, Thomas A. 1998. *Pathways of Memory and Power: Ethnography and History among an Andean People.* Madison: University of Wisconsin Press.
Abisaab, Rula J. 2004. *Converting Persia: Religion and Power in the Safavid Empire.* New York: Tauris.

Abulafia, David. 1993. *Commerce and Conquest in the Mediterranean, 1100–1500.* Variorum Collected Studies Series. Aldershot, UK: Ashgate.

Abulafia, David, and Nora Berend, eds. 2002. *Medieval Frontiers: Concepts and Practices.* Burlington, Vt.: Ashgate.

Adanir, Fikret. 2003. "Religious Communities and Ethnic Groups under Imperial Sway: Ottoman and Habsburg Lands in Comparison." In *The Historical Practice of Diversity: Transcultural Interactions from the Early Modern Mediterranean World to the Postcolonial World,* ed. Dirk Hoerder, Christiane Harzig, and Adrian Shubert, 54–86. New York: Berghahn Books.

Adelman, Jeremy, and Stephen Aron. 1999. "From Borderlands to Borders: Empires, Nation-States, and the Peoples in Between in North American History." *American Historical Review* 104(3): 814–41.

Agmon, Danna. In progress. "An Uneasy Alliance: Traders, Missionaries and Tamil Intermediaries in Eighteenth-Century French India." Unpublished PhD dissertation, University of Michigan.

Ago, Renata. 1999. "Una giustizia personalizzata. I tribunali civili di Roma nel XVII secolo." *Quaderni Storici* 34(2): 389–412.

Ágoston, Gábor. 2007. "Information, Ideology, and Limits of Imperial Policy: Ottoman Grand Strategy in the Context of Ottoman-Habsburg Rivalry." In *The Early Modern Ottomans: Remapping the Empire,* ed. Virginia H. Aksan and Daniel Goffman, 75–103. New York: Cambridge University Press.

Aguilar Moreno, Manuel. 2002. "The Indio Ladino as a Cultural Mediator in the Colonial Society." *Estudios de cultura nahuatl* 33: 149–84.

Aikema, Bernard, and Dulcia Meijers. 1989. *Nel regno dei poveri: Arte e storia dei grandi ospedali veneziani in età moderna, 1474–1797.* Venice: Arsenale.

Aksan, Virginia H. 1995. *An Ottoman Statesman in War and Peace: Ahmed Resmi Efendi 1700–1783.* Leiden and New York: Brill.

Albèri, Eugenio. 1839. *Relazioni degli ambasciatori veneti al Senato.* Florence: Società editrice fiorentina.

——. 1855. *Relazioni degli ambasciatori veneti al Senato.* Florence: Società editrice fiorentina.

Algazi, Gadi. 1997. "Giborei Tarbut v'Avodat Giborim" [Culture heroes and heroes' cult]. *Zmanim* 58: 40–47. [In Hebrew.]

——. 2005. "Diversity Rules: A Review of *The Corrupting Sea: A Study of Mediterranean History* by Peregrine Horden and Nicholas Purcell." *Mediterranean Historical Review* 20(2): 227–45.

Al-Hajari, Ahmad ibn Qasim. 1997. *The Supporter of Religion against the Infidels.* Trans. P. S. van Koningsveld, Qasim Samarra'i, and Gerald A. Wiegers. Madrid: Consejo Superior de Investigaciones Científicas.

Allegra, Luciano. 1991. "Modelli di conversione." *Quaderni Storici* 26(78): 901–15.

——. 1996. "L'ospizio dei catecumeni di Torino." In *Identità in bilico: Il ghetto ebraico di Torino nel Settecento,* 54–110. Turin: S. Zamorani.

Allerston, Patricia A. 1996. "The Market in Second-Hand Clothes and Furnishings in Venice, c1500–c1650." Unpublished PhD dissertation, European University Institute.

——. 1999. "Reconstructing the Second-Hand Clothes Trade in Sixteenth- and Seventeenth-Century Venice." *Costume* 33: 46–56.

——. 2000. "Clothing and Early Modern Venetian Society." *Continuity and Change* 15(3): 367–90.

Ambrosini, Federica. 2000. "Between Heresy and Free Thought, between the Mediterranean and the North: Heterodox Women in Seventeenth-Century Venice." In *Mediterranean Urban Culture 1400–1700*, ed. Alexander Cowan, 83–94. Exeter, UK: University of Exeter Press.

Amman, Hans Jacob. 1677–1678. *Reisz in das Gelobte Land*. Zürich: In Verlegung Ioh. Wilhelm Simlers und Ioh. Rudolff Rhanen, Bey Michael Schauffelbergers, Seligen Erben, Durch Iohannes Bachmann.

Anderson, Sonia P. 2004. "Rycaut, Sir Paul (1629–1700)." *Oxford Dictionary of National Biography*. Oxford: Oxford University Press, www.oxforddnb.com.myaccess.library.utoronto.ca/view/article/24392.

Appuhn, Karl R. 2009. *A Forest on the Sea: Environmental Expertise in Renaissance Venice*. Baltimore: Johns Hopkins University Press.

Arbel, Benjamin. 1989a. "The Cypriot Nobility from the Fourteenth to the Sixteenth Century: A New Interpretation." *Mediterranean Historical Review* 4(1): 175–97.

——. 1989b. "Résistance ou collaboration?: Les Chypriotes sous la domination vénitienne." In *Etat et colonisation au Moyen Age et à la Renaissance,* ed. Michel Balard, 131–43. Lyon: La Manufacture.

——. 1991. "Salomone Ashkenazi: Mercante e armature." In *Il mondo ebraico: Gli ebrei tra Italia nord-orientale e Impero asburgico dal Medioevo all'Eta contemporanea,* eds. Giacomo Todeschini, and Pier Cesare Ioly Zorattini, 111–28. Pordenone: Studio Tesi.

——. 1995a. "Regime colonial, colonisation et peuplement: Le cas de Chypre sous la domination Venitienne." *Travaux Historiques* 43–44: 95–103.

——. 1995b. *Trading Nations: Jews and Venetians in the Early-Modern Eastern Mediterranean*. Leiden and New York: Brill.

——. 1996. "Colonie d'oltremare." In *Storia di Venezia dalle origini alla caduta della serenissima, vol. 5: Il Rinascimento: Societa ed economia,* eds. Alberto Tenenti and Ugo Tucci, 947–85. Rome: Istituto della Enciclopedia Italiana.

——. 2000a. *Cyprus, the Franks and Venice, 13th–16th Centuries*. Aldershot, UK: Ashgate.

——. 2000b. "Shipping and Toleration: The Emergence of Jewish Shipowners in the Early Modern Period." *Mediterranean Historical Review* 15(1): 56–71.

——. 2001. "Jews in International Trade: The Emergence of the Levantines and Ponentines." In *The Jews of Early Modern Venice*, eds. Robert C. Davis and Benjamin Ravid, 73–96. Baltimore: Johns Hopkins University Press.

——. 2002a. "Maps of the World for Ottoman Princes?: Further Evidence and Questions Concerning 'the "Mappamondo" of Hajji Ahmed.'" *Imago Mundi* 54(1): 19–29.

——. 2002b. "Roman Catholics and Greek Orthodox in the Early Modern Venetian State." In *The Three Religions: Interdisciplinary Conference of Tel Aviv University and Munich*

University, Venice, October 2000, eds. Nili Cohen and Andreas Heldrich, 73–86. Munich: Herbert Utz Verlag.

——. 2004. "Opening Comments." Presented at the workshop Trade, Colonies, and Intercultural Contacts in the Venetian World, 1400–1650. Venice International University, Venice, Italy, May 27–28.

——. 2008. "Operating Trading Networks in Times of War: A Sixteenth-Centruy Venetian Patrician Between Public Service and Private Affairs." In *Merchants in the Ottoman Empire,* ed. Suraiya Faroqhi and Gilles Veinstein, 23–34. Paris: Peeters.

——. 2009. "Cyprus on the Eve of the Ottoman Conquest." In *Ottoman Cyprus: A Collection of Studies on History and Culture,* ed. Matthias Kappler and Eftihios Gavriel, 37–48. Wiesbaden: Harrassowitz.

——. In press. "Translating the Orient for the Serenissima: Michiel Membrè in the Service of Sixteenth-Century Venice." In *La frontière méditerranéenne,* ed. Albrech Fuess and Bernard Heyberger. Tours: Centre d'Études Supérieures de la Renaissance.

Arvanitakis, Dimitris, ed. 2000. *Le relazioni dei provveditori venezini di Zante (XVI–XVIII Sec.).* Venice: Istituto Elenico.

Asad, Talal. 1996. "Comments on Conversion." In *Conversion to Modernities: The Globalization of Christianity,* ed. Peter van der Veer, 263–73. New York: Routledge.

Ashtor, Eliahu. 1975. "Ebrei cittadini di Venezia?" *Studi Veneziani* 17–18: 145–57.

——. 1983. *Levant Trade in the Later Middle Ages.* Princeton: Princeton University Press.

Ashtor, Eliyahu and Benjamin Z. Kedar. 1992. *Technology, Industry and Trade: The Levant versus Europe, 1250–1500.* Variorum Collected Studies Series. Hampshire, UK: Ashgate.

Aslanian, Sebouh David. 2010. *From the Indian Ocean to the Mediterranean: The Global Trade Networks of Armenian Merchants from New Julfa.* Berkeley: University of California Press.

Astorri, Antonella. 1988. "Il 'Libro delle senserie' di Girolamo di Agostino Maringhi (1483–1485)." *Archivio Storico Italiano* 146(3): 389–408.

Austen, Ralph A., and Jonathan Derrick. 1999. *Middlemen of the Cameroons Rivers: The Duala and Their Hinterland, C.1600–c.1960.* New York: Cambridge University Press.

Babaie, Sussan, Kathryn Babayan, Ina Baghdiantz McCabe, and Massumeh Farhad. 2004. *Slaves of the Shah: New Elites of Safavid Iran.* London, New York: I. B. Tauris.

Baer, Marc D. 2001. "Honored by the Glory of Islam: The Ottoman State, Non-Muslims, and Conversion to Islam in Late Seventeenth-Century Istanbul and Rumelia." Unpublished PhD dissertation, University of Chicago.

——. 2004. "Islamic Conversion Narratives of Women: Social Change and Gendered Religious Hierarchy in Early Modern Ottoman Istanbul." *Gender & History* 16(2): 425–58.

——. 2007. *Honored by the Glory of Islam.* New York: Oxford University Press.

Bakhtin, Mikhail M. 1981. "Forms of Time and of the Chronotope in the Novel." In *The Dialogic Imagination: Four Essays,* 84–258. Austin: University of Texas Press.

Balard, Michel. 1978. *La Romanie génoise: XIIe–début du XVe siécle.* Rome: École française de Rome.

——, ed. 1989. *Etat et colonisation au Moyen Age et à la Renaissance*. Lyon: La Manufacture.

Balard, Michel, and Alain Ducellier, eds. 2002. *Migrations et diasporas méditerranéennes (Xe–XVIe siècles)*. Paris: Publications de la Sorbonne.

Balcı, Sezai. 2006. "Osmanlı devleti'nde tercümanlık ve bab-ı ali tercüme odası." Unpublished PhD dissertation, Ankara University, Ankara.

Bareille, G. 1908. "Catéchuménat." In *Dictionnaire de théologie catholique, contenant l'exposé des doctrines de la théologie catholique leurs preuves et leur histoire*, ed. Alfred Vacant and E. Mangenot, 1968–87. Paris: Letouzey et Ané.

Barker, William. 2002. "Alciato's Emblems and the Album Amicorum: A Brief Note on Examples in London, Moscow, and Oxford." www.mun.ca/alciato/album.html.

Barkey, Karen. 2008. *Empire of Difference: The Ottomans in Comparative Perspective*. New York: Cambridge University Press.

Barth, Fredrik. 1969. *Ethnic Groups and Boundaries: The Social Organization of Culture Difference*. Boston: Little, Brown and Company.

Bartl, Peter. 2000. "Die Diözese Alessio während der Türkenzeit im Spiegel der geistlichen Visitationsberichte." In *Krishterimi ndër Shqiptarë. Simpozium Ndërkombëtar Tiranë, 16–19 Nëntor 1999*, 235–249. Shkodër: Qendra e Studimeve Shqiptare "Ernest Koliqi" Shkodër & Bashkimi Katolik i Publicistëve Shqiptarë, http://www.kulturserver-hamburg.de/home/shkodra/simpoziumi/simpoziumi_sek4_art07.html.

Bartlett, Robert. 1993. *The Making of Europe: Conquest, Colonization, and Cultural Change, 950–1350*. Princeton: Princeton University Press.

——. 2001. "Medieval and Modern Concepts of Race and Ethnicity." In *Race and Ethnicity in the Middle Ages*. Special issue of *Journal of Medieval and Early Modern Studies* 31(1): 39–56.

Bassano, Luigi. 1963 [1545]. *Costumi et i modi particolari della vita de' Turchi*. Ed. Franz Babinger. Munich; M. Hueber.

Battaglia, Salvatore. 1973. "Levantino." In *Grande dizionario della lingua italiana*, vol. 8, 1006–7. Turin: Unione tipografico-editrice torinese.

Beck, Hans G., Manoussos Manoussacas, and Agostino Pertusi, eds. 1977. *Venezia, centro di mediazione tra Oriente e Occidente, secoli XV–XVI: Aspetti e problemi*. Florence: L. S. Olschki.

Becker, Howard. 1940. "Constructive Typology in the Social Sciences." In *Contemporary Social Theory*, ed. Harry E. Barnes, Howard Paul Becker, and Frances Bennett Becker, 17–46. New York: Appleton-Century.

Beg, Muhammad Abdul Jabbar. 1977. "The Status of 'Brokers' in Middle Eastern Society in the Pre-Modern Period." *Muslim World* 67(2): 87–90.

Bellavitis, Anna. 2001. *Identité, mariage, mobilité sociale: Citoyennes et citoyens à Venise au XVIe siècle*. Rome: École française de Rome.

Beltrami, Daniele. 1954. *Storia della popolazione di Venezia dalla fine del secolo XVI alla caduta della Republica*. Padua: CEDAM.

Bennassar, Bartolomé. 1988. "Conversion ou reniement?: Modalités d'une adhésion ambiguë des chrétiens à l'Islam (XVIe–XVIIe siècles)." *Annales ESC* 6: 1349–66.

——. 1996. "Conversions, esclavage et commerce des femmes dans les peninsules ibe-rique, italienne ou balkanique aux XVIe et XVIIe siecles." In *Conversioni nel Mediter-raneo*. Special issue of *Dimensioni e problemi della ricerca storica* 2: 101–9.

Bennassar, Bartolomé, and Lucile Bennassar. 1989. *Les chrétiens d'Allah: L'Histoire ex-traordinaire des renégats, XVIe et XVIIe siècles*. Paris: Perrin.

Berktay, Halil. 1998. "Studying 'Relations' or Studying Common Problems in Compara-tive Perspective." In *Chrétiens et musulmans à la Renaissance,* eds. Bartolomé Ben-nassar and Robert Sauzet, 313–16. Paris: H. Champion.

Bernos, Marcel. 2003. "Le baptême d'enfants juifs; un cas de conscience pour les théolo-giens." In *Identités juives et chrétiennes: France méridionale XIVe–XIXe siècle. Etudes offertes à René Moulinas,* eds. René Moulinas and Gabriel Audisio, 113–23. Aix-en-Provence: Publications de l'université de Provence.

Bertelè, Tommaso. 1932. *Il palazzo degli ambasciatori di Venezia a Constantinopoli e le sue antiche memorie ricerche storiche con documenti inediti*. Bologna: Apollo.

Bertolini, Dario. 1881. "Prezzi di alcune derrate in Venezia e altrove nel secolo XV." *An-nali di Statistica*, serie 2a 19: 132–44.

Biddick, Kathleen. 2000. "Coming Out of Exile: Dante on the Orient(alism) Express." *American Historical Review* 105(4): 1234–49.

Bierman, Irene A. 1991. "The Ottomanization of Crete." In *The Ottoman City and Its Parts: Urban Structure and Social Order,* ed. Irene A. Bierman, Rifa'at Ali Abou-El-Haj, and Donald Preziosi, 53–75. New Rochelle: Aristide D Caratzas.

Biggs, Michael. 1999. "Putting the State on the Map: Cartography, Territory, and Eu-ropean State Formation." *Comparative Studies in Society and History* 41(2): 374–405.

Biow, Douglas. 2002. *Doctors, Ambassadors, Secretaries: Humanism and Professions in Renaissance Italy*. Chicago: University of Chicago Press.

Bisaha, Nancy. 1999. "'New Barbarian' or Worthy Adversary?: Humanist Constructs of the Ottoman Turks in Fifteenth-Century Italy." In *Western Views of Islam in Medi-eval and Early Modern Europe: Perception of Other,* ed. David R. Blanks and Michael Frassetto, 185–205. New York: St. Martin's Press.

——. 2004. *Creating East and West: Renaissance Humanists and the Ottoman Turks*. Phil-adelphia: University of Pennsylvania Press.

Bitterli, Urs. 1989. *Cultures in Conflict: Encounters between European and Non-European Cultures, 1492–1800*. Stanford: Stanford University Press.

Bizzocchi, Roberto. 1995. "Church, Religion, and State in the Early Modern Period." *Jour-nal of Modern History* 67: S152–65.

Black, Christopher F. 2000. "The Development of Confraternity Studies over the Past Thirty Years." In *The Politics of Ritual Kinship: Confraternities and Social Order in Early Modern Italy,* ed. Nicholas Terpstra, 9–29. New York: Cambridge University Press.

——. 2001. *Early Modern Italy: A Social History*. New York: Routledge.

——. 2004. "The Public Face of Post-Tridentine Italian Confraternities." *Journal of Reli-gious History* 28(1): 87–101.

Blalock, Hubert M. 1967. "Middleman Minorities." In *Toward a Theory of Minority-Group Relations,* 79–84. New York: John Wiley.

Blanks, David R., and Michael Frassetto. 1999. *Western Views of Islam in Medieval and Early Modern Europe: Perception of Other.* New York: St. Martin's Press.

Boccato, Carla. 1974. "La disciplina delle Sansarie nel ghetto di Venezia." *Giornale Economico* 6: 27–37.

Boccazzi Mazza, Barbara. 2005. "Governare i 'luoghi pii': La casa delle zitelle." *Studi Veneziani* 50: 293–99.

Bodenham, Roger. 1599. "The voyage of M. *Roger Bodenham* with the great Barke Aucher to *Candia* and *Chio,* in the yeere 1550." In *The principal nauigations, voyages, traffiques and discoueries of the English nation made by sea or ouer-land, to the remote and farthest distant quarters of the earth, at any time within the compasse of these 1600. yeres,* vol. 2, ed. Richard Hakluyt, 99–101. London: By George Bishop, Ralph Newberie, and Robert Barker.

Boerio, Giuseppe. 1960 [1829]. *Dizionario del dialetto veneziano.* Turin: Bottega d'Erasmo.

Boettcher, Susan R. 2004. "Confessionalization: Reformation, Religion, Absolutism, and Modernity." *History Compass* 2: 1–10.

Bolognesi, Dante. 2000. "Fiere, mercati e sensali a Ravenna in età moderna." *Romagna arte e storia* 20(60): 75–96.

Bombaci, Alessio. 1948. "Una lettera turca in caratteri latini del dragomanno ottomano Ibrahim al veneziano Michele Membrè (1567)." *Rocznik Orjentalistyczny* 15: 129–44.

Bonacich, Edna. 1973. "A Theory of Middleman Minorities." *American Sociological Review* 38(5): 583–94.

Bonnefons, Nicolas de. 1656. *The French Gardiner.* Trans. John Evelyn. London: Printed by J. C. for John Crooke.

Bono, Salvatore. 1998. "Conversioni di musulmani al cristianesimo." In *Chrétiens et musulmans à la Renaissance: Actes du 37e colloque international du CESR (1994),* ed. Bartolomé Bennassar and Robert Sauzet, 429–45. Paris: H. Champion.

———. 1999. *Schiavi musulmani nell'Italia moderna: Galeotti, vu' cumprà, domestici.* Naples: Edizioni scientifiche italiane.

Borgherini-Scarabellin, Maria. 1925. *Il Magistrato dei Cinque Savi alla Mercanzia dalla istituzione alla caduta della Repubblica: Studio storico su documenti d'archivio.* Venice-Padua: Milani.

Bornstein-Makovetsky, Leah. 1989. "Jewish Brokers in Constantinople during the 18th Century According to Hebrew Documents." In *The Mediterranean and the Jews: Banking, Finance and International Trade (XVI–XVIII Centuries),* ed. Ariel Toaff and Simon Schwarzfuchs, 75–104. Ramat Gan, Israel: Bar-Ilan University Press.

Bossy, John. 1970. "The Counter-Reformation and the People of Catholic Europe." *Past and Present* 47: 51–70.

Bouwsma, William J. 1968. *Venice and the Defense of Republican Liberty: Renaissance Values in the Age of the Counter Reformation.* Berkeley: University of California Press.

Bowd, Stephen D. 2000. "'The Tune Is Marred': Citizens and People in Gasparo Contarini's Venice." *European Review of History* 7(1): 83–97.

Bracewell, Wendy. 1992. *The Uskoks of Senj: Piracy, Banditry, and Holy War in the Sixteenth-Century Adriatic*. Ithaca: Cornell University Press.

———. 2005. "Orientalism, Occidentalism and Cosmopolitanism: Balkan Travel Writings on Europe." Bulgarian Society for 18th Century Studies' International Interdisciplinary Conference on Occidentalism, www.bulgc18.com/occidentalism/bracewell_en.htm.

Brady, Thomas A., Jr. 2004. "Confessionalization—The Career of a Concept." In *Confessionalization in Europe, 1555–1700: Essays in honor and memory of Bodo Nischan*, ed. J. M. Headley, Hans J. Hillerbrand, and Anthony J. Papalas, 1–20. Burlington, Vt.: Ashgate.

Brătianu, George Ioan, ed. 1927. *Actes des notaires génois de Péra et de Caffa de la fin du treizième siècle (1281–1290)*. Bucarest: Cvltvra Natională.

Braude, Benjamin. 1997. "The Sons of Noah and the Construction of Ethnic and Geographical Identities in the Medieval and Early Modern Periods." *William and Mary Quarterly* 54(1): 103–42.

Braude, Benjamin, and Bernard Lewis, eds. 1982. *Christians and Jews in the Ottoman Empire: The Functioning of a Plural Society*. New York: Holmes & Meier.

Braudel, Fernand. 1972 [1949]. *The Mediterranean and the Mediterranean World in the Age of Philip II*. New York: Harper & Row.

Brockey, Liam Matthew. 2007. *Journey to the East: The Jesuit Mission to China, 1579–1724*. Cambridge, Mass.: Belknap Press, Harvard University Press.

Brotton, Jerry. 1997. *Trading Territories: Mapping the Early Modern World*. London: Reaktion Books.

———. 2002. *The Renaissance Bazaar: From the Silk Road to Michelangelo*. New York: Oxford University Press.

Brown, Horatio. 1900. "Preface." In *Calendar of State Papers and Manuscripts, Relating to English Affairs Existing in the Archives and Collection of Venice, and in Other Libraries of Northern Italy*, ed. Rawdon Brown, lxii–lxix. London: Longman, Roberts, and Green.

Brown, Patricia Fortini. 1996. *Venice and Antiquity: The Venetian Sense of the Past*. New Haven: Yale University Press.

Brummett, Palmira J. 1994. *Ottoman Seapower and Levantine Diplomacy in the Age of Discovery*. Albany: SUNY Press.

———. 2007a. "Visions of the Mediterranean: A Classification." *Journal of Medieval and Early Modern Studies* 37(1): 9–55.

———. 2007b. "The Renegade in Ottoman Space: A Taxonomy." Paper presented to the Annual Meeting of the Middle East Studies Association, Montreal, Canada, November 17–20.

Buganza, Gianni. 1998. *Le complessità dell'ordine: Il processo penale veneziano e le ragioni del principe tra diritto, società e destino*. Venice: Marsilio.

Burke, Peter. 1980. "Did Europe Exist before 1700?" *History of European Ideas* 1(1): 21–28.

Burkholder, Mark A. 1998. "Bureaucrats." In *Administrators of Empire*, 77–103. Aldershot, UK Ashgate.

Byars, Jana L. 2005. "Concubinage in Early Modern Venice." Unpublished PhD dissertation, Pennsylvania State University.

Caffiero, Marina. 2003. "'La caccia agli ebrei': Inquisizione, Casa dei Catecumeni e battesimi forzati nella Roma moderna." In *Le inquisizioni cristiane e gli ebrei*, 503–37. Rome: Accademia nazionale dei Lincei.

Campanini, Antonella. 1996. "L'identità coatta: La Casa dei catecumeni a Bologna." In *Verso l'epilogo di una convivenza: Gli ebrei a Bologna nel XVI secolo,* ed. Maria G. Muzzarelli, 155–76. Florence: Giuntina.

Carlebach, Elisheva. 2001. *Divided Souls: Converts from Judaism in Germany, 1500–1750.* New Haven: Yale University Press.

Carmichael, Ann G. 1986. *Plague and the Poor in Renaissance Florence.* New York: Cambridge University Press.

Carrier, James G. 1995. *Occidentalism: Images of the West.* New York: Oxford University Press.

Casale, Giancarlo L. 2004. "The Ottoman Age of Exploration: Spices, Maps and Conquest in the Sixteenth-Century Indian Ocean." Unpublished PhD dissertation, Harvard University.

——. 2005. "Two Examples of Ottoman Discovery Literature from the Mid-Sixteenth Century." Paper presented at the Ottoman and Atlantic Empires in the Early Modern World Conference, Istanbul, October 2005, www.wm.edu/oieahc/conferences/otto man/papers/Casale.pdf

——. 2010. *The Ottoman Age of Exploration.* New York: Oxford University Press.

Casini, Matteo. 2002. "Fra città-stato e stato regionale: Riflessioni politiche sulla repubblica di Venezia nella prima età moderna." *Studi Veneziani* 44: 15–36.

Cassidy, Tanya M. 2000. "'Race to the Park': Simmel, the Stranger and the State." *Irish Communications Review* 8: 14–20.

Castela, Henry. 1603. *Le sainct voyage de Hiérusalem et Mont Sinay, faict en l'an du grand Jubilé, 1600. . . .* Paris: L. Sonnius.

Cavallo, Sandra. 1995. *Charity and Power in Early Modern Italy: Benefactors and Their Motives in Turin, 1541–1789.* New York: Cambridge University Press.

Cavazza, Silvano. 1998. "Frangipane Cornelio." In *Dizionario Biografico degli Italiani,* vol. 50, 227–30. Rome: Enciclopedia italiana.

Cerutti, Simona. 1995. "Giustizia e località a Torino in età moderna: Una ricerca in corso." In *Cittadinanze,* Special issue of *Quaderni Storici* 89: 445–86.

Chakrabarty, Dipesh. 2000. *Provincializing Europe: Postcolonial Thought and Historical Difference.* Princeton: Princeton University Press.

Chambers, David. 1970. *The Imperial Age of Venice, 1380–1580.* London: Thames & Hudson.

Chambers, David, and Brian S. Pullan, eds. 2001. *Venice: A Documentary History, 1450–1630.* Toronto: University of Toronto Press.

Charney, Paul. 1991. "The Implications of Godparental Ties between Indians and Spaniards in Colonial Lima." *Americas* 47(3): 295–313.

Chatterjee, Indrani. 1999. *Gender, Slavery, and Law in Colonial India.* New Delhi: Oxford University Press.

Chittolini, Giorgio. 1995. "The 'Private,' the 'Public,' the State." *Journal of Modern History* 67: S34–61.

Chojnacka, Monica. 2001. *Working Women of Early Modern Venice.* Baltimore: Johns Hopkins University Press.

Chojnacki, Stanley. 1994. "Social Identity in Renaissance Venice: The Second *Serrata.*" *Renaissance Studies* 8(4): 341–58.

——. 2000. *Women and Men in Renaissance Venice: Twelve Essays on Patrician Society.* Baltimore: Johns Hopkins University Press.

Christ, Georg. 2006. "Konflikt am Schnittpunkt von Orient und Okzident: Ein venezianischer Konsul im mamlukischen Alexandria 1418–1420." Unpublished PhD dissertation, Universität Basel.

Çiçek, Kemal. 2002. "Interpreters of the Court in the Ottoman Empire as Seen from the Sharia Court Records of Cyprus." *Islamic Law and Society* 9(1): 1–15.

Cimatore, Pietro. 1936 [1559]. "Canzona delle buttagre." In *Canti carnascialeschi del rinascimento,* ed. Charles. S. Singleton, 259–60. Bari: Laterza.

Çirakman, Aslı. 2001. "From Tyranny to Despotism: The Enlightenment's Unenlightened Image of the Turks." *International Journal of Middle East Studies* 33(1): 49–68.

——. 2002. *From the "Terror of the World" to the "Sick Man of Europe": European Images of Ottoman Empire and Society from the Sixteenth Century to the Nineteenth.* New York: Peter Lang.

Cleirac, Estienne. 1671. *Les us, et coutumes de la mer.* Rouen: Chez Jean Bethelin.

Clemens VIII. 1593. *Priuilegii d'hebrei leuantini d'ordine dell'ill.mo, & reu.mo monsig. cardinal camerlengo per special commissione di N.S. PP. Clemente VIII. . . .* Rome: Appresso Paolo Baldo.

Cline, Sarah. 1993. "The Spiritual Conquest Reexamined: Baptism and Christian Marriage in Early Sixteenth-Century Mexico." *Hispanic American Historical Review* 73(3): 453–80.

Cochrane, Eric W., and Julius Kirshner. 1975. "Deconstructing Lane's Venice." *Journal of Modern History* 47(2): 321–34.

Cohen, Jeremy D. 2003. "Cultural and Commercial Intermediaries in an Extra-Legal System of Exchange: The *Practicos* of the Venezuelan Littoral in the Eighteenth Century." *Itinerario* 27(2): 105–24.

Cohen, Mark R., ed. 1988. *The Autobiography of a Seventeenth-Century Venetian Rabbi: Leon Modena's Life of Judah.* Princeton, N.J.: Princeton University Press.

——. 2005. *Poverty and Charity: Judaism, Christianity, and Islam.* Special Issue of *Journal of Interdisciplinary History* 35(3).

Cohn, Bernard S. 1996. *Colonialism and Its Forms of Knowledge: The British in India.* Princeton: Princeton University Press.

Coleman, David. 2003. *Creating Christian Granada: Society and Religious Culture in an Old-World Frontier City, 1492–1600.* Ithaca: Cornell University Press.

Colin, Georges S., and Carl Heinrich Becker. 1999. "Dallāl." In *Encyclopaedia of Islam,* vol. 2, 102b. Leiden: Brill.

Colzi, Francesco. 1998. "'Per maggiore facilita del commercio': I sensali e la mediazione mercantile e finanziaria a Roma nei secoli xvi–xix." *Roma Moderna e Contemporanea* 6(3): 397–425.

Conley, Thomas. 2002. "The Speech of Ibrahim at the Coronation of Maximilian II." *Rhetorica* 20(3): 263–73.

Constable, Olivia R. 2001. "Funduq, Fondaco, and Khān in the Wake of Christian Commerce and Crusade." In *The Crusades from the Perspective of Byzantium and the Muslim World,* ed. Aneliki E. Laiou and Roy P. Mottahedeh, 145–56. Washington, D.C.: Dumbarton Oaks Research Library and Collection.

———. 2003. *Housing the Stranger in the Mediterranean World: Lodging, Trade, and Travel in Late Antiquity and the Middle Ages.* New York: Cambridge University Press.

Cooper, Frederick. 2005. *Colonialism in Question: Theory, Knowledge, History.* Berkeley: University of California Press.

Cooperman, Bernard D. 1987. "Venetian Policy toward Levantine Jews and Its Broader Italian Context." In *Gli ebrei e Venezia, secoli XVI–XVIII,* ed. Gaetano Cozzi, 65–84. Milan: Edizioni Communita.

Corazzol, Gigi. 1994. "Varietà notarile: Scorci di vita economica e sociale." In *Storia di Venezia dalle origini alla caduta della serenissima,* vol. 6, *Dal Rinascimento al Barocco,* ed. Gaetano Cozzi and Paolo Prodi, 775–91. Rome: Istituto della Enciclopedia Italiana.

Cornet, Enrico. 1859. *Paolo V. e la repubblica veneta. Giornale dal 22. ottobre 1605–9. giugno 1607. Corredato di note e documenti tratti dall'I. R. Biblioteca in Vienna, dalla Marciana, dal museo Correr, e dall'archivio ai Frari in Venezia.* Vienna: Tendler & comp.

Coronil, Fernando. 1996. "Beyond Occidentalism: Toward Nonimperial Geohistorical Categories." *Cultural Anthropology* 11(1): 51–87.

Corpis, Duane J. 2001. "The Geography of Religious Conversion: Crossing the Boundaries of Belief in Southern Germany, 1648–1800." Unpublished PhD dissertation, New York University.

Cortelazzo, Manlio. 1989a. "Il veneziano, lingua ufficiale della Repubblica?" In *Venezia, il Levante e il mare,* 99–113. Pisa: Pacini Editore.

———. 1989b. "Arabismi di Pisa e arabismi di Venezia." In *Venezia, il Levante e il mare,* 447–49. Pisa: Pacini Editore.

Coryate, Thomas. 1611. *Coryats crudities. . . .* London: Printed by W. S.

Costa, Pietro. 1999. *Civitas: Storia della cittadinanza in Europa.* 4 vols. Rome-Bari: Laterza.

Costantini, Massimo. 1996. "Le strutture dell'ospitalità." In *Storia di Venezia dalle origini alla caduta della serenissima,* vol. 5: *Il Rinascimento: Societa ed economia,* ed. Alberto Tenenti and Ugo Tucci, 881–911. Rome: Istituto della Enciclopedia Italiana.

Costantini, Vera. 2004. "La loi du sultan débarque à Chypre: L'installation ottomane à partir d'une analyse des bilans." In *Insularités Ottomanes,* ed. Nicolas Vatin and Gilles Veinstein, 111–20. Paris: Maisonneuve & Larose, Institut français d'études anatoliennes.

Cowan, Alexander. 1999. "Patricians and Partners in Early Modern Venice." In *Medieval and Renaissance Venice,* ed. Ellen E. Kittell and Thomas F. Madden, 276–93. Urbana: University of Illinois Press.

———. 2000. "Foreigners and the City: The Case of the Immigrant Merchant." In *Mediterranean Urban Culture 1400–1700,* 45–55. Exeter, UK: University of Exeter Press.

———. 2003. "Mogli non ufficiali e figlie illegittime a Venezia nella prima età moderna." *Quaderni Storici* 38(3): 849–65.

Cozzi, Gaetano. 1994. "Fortuna e sfortuna della Compagnia di Gesù a Venezia." In *I gesuiti e Venezia: Momenti e problemi di storia veneziana della Compagnia di Gesù: Atti del convegno di studi, Venezia, 2–5 ottobre 1990,* ed. Mario Zanardi, 58–88. Venice, Padua: Giunta regionale del Veneto.

Cristellon, Cecilia. 2003. "L'ufficio del giudice: mediazione, inquisizione e confessione nei processi matrimoniali veneziani (1420–1532)." *Rivista Storica Italiana* 115(3): 851–98.

Crouzet-Pavan, Elisabeth. 2002. *Venice Triumphant: The Horizons of a Myth.* Trans. Lydia G. Cochrane. Baltimore: Johns Hopkins University Press.

Curtin, Philip D. 1984. "Overland Trade of the Seventeenth Century: Armenian Carriers between Europe and East Asia." In *Cross-Cultural Trade in World History,* 179–206. New York: Cambridge University Press.

Curto, Diogo R., and Anthony Molho, eds. 2002. *Commercial Networks in the Early Modern World.* Badia Fiesolana: European University Institute.

Da Mosto, Andrea. 1937. *L'Archivio di stato di Venezia.* Rome: Biblioteca d'arte editrice.

Da Silva, José G. 1987. "Les Juifs portugais entre Lisbonne et Venise: Une autre vision de la Méditerranée e de l'éeconomie, XVIe–XVIIIe siècles." In *Gli ebrei e Venezia, secoli XVI–XVIII,* ed. Gaetano Cozzi, 117–35. Milan: Edizioni Communita.

Dal Borgo, Michela. 1997. "Neo-convertiti aspiranti sensali (1569)." *Quaderni di Studi Arabi* 15: 163–65.

Daniel, Norman. 1960. *Islam and the West: The Making of an Image.* Edinburgh: Edinburgh University Press.

Dankoff, Robert. 2004. *An Ottoman Mentality: The World of Evliya Çelebi.* Leiden, Boston: Brill.

Dannenfeldt, Karl H. 1955. "The Renaissance Humanists and the Knowledge of Arabic." *Studies in the Renaissance* 2: 96–117.

Das Gupta, Ashin. 1991. "The Broker at Mughal Surat, c.1740." *Review of Culture* (Macao) 13–14: 173–80.

Davidoff, Leonore, and Catherine Hall. 1987. *Family Fortunes: Men and Women of the English Middle Class, 1780–1850.* London: Hutchinson.

Davis, James C., ed. 1970. *Pursuit of Power: Venetian Ambassadors' Reports on Spain, Turkey, and France in the Age of Philip II, 1560–1600.* New York: Harper & Row.

Davis, Natalie Zemon. 1987. *Fiction in the Archives: Pardon Tales and Their Tellers in Sixteenth-Century France*. Stanford: Stanford University Press.

——. 2001. "Polarities, Hybridities: What Strategies for Decentering?" In *Decentering the Renaissance: Canada and Europe in Multidisciplinary Perspective, 1500–1700*, ed. Germaine Warkentin and Carolyn Podruchny, 19–32. Toronto: University of Toronto Press.

——. 2006. *Trickster Travels: A Sixteenth-Century Muslim between Worlds*. New York: Hill and Wang.

Davis, Robert C. 1991. *Shipbuilders of the Venetian Arsenal: Workers and Workplace in the Preindustrial City*. Baltimore: Johns Hopkins University Press.

——. 1994. *The War of the Fists: Popular Culture and Public Violence in Late Renaissance Venice*. New York: Oxford University Press.

——. 2003. *Christian Slaves, Muslim Masters: White Slavery in the Mediterranean, the Barbary Coast, and Italy, 1500–1800*. New York: Palgrave Macmillan.

Davis, Robert C., and Benjamin Ravid, eds. 2001. *The Jews of Early Modern Venice*. Baltimore: Johns Hopkins University Press.

De Boer, Wietse. 2001. *The Conquest of the Soul: Confession, Discipline, and Public Order in Counter-Reformation Milan*. Leiden, Boston: Brill.

——. 2003. "Social Discipline in Italy: Peregrinations of a Historical Paradigm." *Archiv für Reformationsgeschichte* 94: 294–306.

de Certeau, Michel. 1986. *Heterologies: Discourse on the Other*. Minneapolis: University of Minnesota Press.

——. 1988. *The Practice of Everyday Life*. Berkeley: University of California Press.

De Maria, Blake. 2003. "The Merchants of Venice: A Study in Sixteenth-Century Cittadino Patronage." Unpublished PhD dissertation, Princeton University.

De Matteo, Luigi, and Maria C. Schisani. 1999. "Stockbrokers and Stock Exchange Brokerage in Naples from the Decade of French Rule to Post-Unification." In *Guilds, Markets and Work Regulations in Italy, 16th–19th Centuries*, ed. Alberto Guenzi, Paola Massa, and Fausto Piola Castelli, 323–39. Milan: FrancoAngeli.

De Pelsmaeker, P. 1905. "Le Courtage à Ypres Aux XIIIe et XIVe siècles." *Bulletin de la Commission Royale d'Histoire* 64: 439–84.

De Vivo, Filippo. 2004. "The Diversity of Venice and Her Myths." *Historical Journal* 47(1): 169–77.

——. 2007. *Information and Communication in Venice: Rethinking Early Modern Politics*. Oxford: Oxford University Press.

Degler, Carl N. 1991. *In Search of Human Nature: The Decline and Revival of Darwinism in American Social Thought*. New York: Oxford University Press.

Degli Avogadro, Jacopo. 1857. *Notizie storiche dell'istituto de' Catecumeni in Venezia*. Venice: G. B. Merlo.

Del Negro, Piero. 2001. "Il leone in campo: Venezia e gli oltramarini nelle guerre di Candia e di Morea." In *Mito e antimito di Venezia nel bacino adriatico (secoli XV–XIX)*, ed. Sante Graciotti, 323–44. Rome: Il Calamo.

Del Torre, Giuseppe. 1992. "Stato regionale e benefici ecclesiastici: Vescovadi e canonicati nella terraferma veneziana all'inizio dell'età moderna." *Atti dell'Istituto Veneto di Scienze Lettere e Arti, Classe di Scienze Morali, Lettere ed Arti* 151: 1171–236.

Dell'Ottonaio, Giovanni Battista. 1940 [1559]. "Canzona de' Levantini." In *Nuovi canti carnascialeschi del rinascimento con un Apendice: tavola generale dei canti carnascialeschi editi ed. inediti*, ed. Charles S. Singleton, 82–83. Modena: Società tipografica modenese.

Denny, Walter B. 1970. "A Sixteenth-Century Architectural Plan of Istanbul." *Ars Orientalis: The Arts of Islam and the East* 8: 49–63.

Denton, John. 1998. "Renaissance Translation Strategies and the Manipulation of a Classical Text: Plutarch from Jacques Amyot to Thomas North." In *Europe et Traduction*, ed. Michel Ballard, 67–78. Ottawa: Presses de l'Université d'Ottawa.

Deringil, Selim. 2000. "'There Is No Compulsion in Religion': On Conversion and Apostasy in the Late Ottoman Empire: 1839–1856." *Comparative Studies in Society and History* 42(3): 547–75.

Dermigny, Louis. 1974. "Escales, échelles et ports francs au moyen age et aux temps modernes." *Les grandes escales* 3(34): 213–644.

Derosas, Renzo. 1981. "Moralità e giustizia a Venezia nel '500–'600: Gli esecutori contro la bestemmia." In *Stato, società e giustizia nella Repubblica Veneta (sec. XV–XVIII)*, ed. Gaetano Cozzi, 431–528. Rome: Jouvence.

Dictionnaire de l'Académie française. 1694. Paris: Veuve de J. B. Coignard & J. B. Coignard.

Dilis, Emile. 1910. "Les courtiers anversois sous l'ancien régime." *Annales de l'Académie Royale d'Archéologie de Belgique* 62(2): 299–462.

Dimmock, Matthew. 2005. *New Turkes: Dramatizing Islam and the Ottomans in Early Modern England*. Aldershot, UK: Ashgate.

Dirlik, Arif, Vinay Bahl, and Peter Gran. 2000. *History after the Three Worlds: Post-Eurocentric Historiographies*. Lanham, Md.: Rowman & Littlefield.

Domínguez, Virginia R. 1986. *White by Definition: Social Classification in Creole Louisiana*. New Brunswick: Rutgers University Press.

Donazzolo, Pietro. 1928. *I viaggiatori veneti minori: Studio bio-bibliografico*. Rome: Alla sede della Società.

Dooley, Brendan M. 1999. *The Social History of Skepticism: Experience and Doubt in Early Modern Culture*. Baltimore: Johns Hopkins University Press.

Dorsey, Peter A. 1998. "Going to School with Savages; Authorship and Authority among the Jesuits of New France." *Willam and Mary Quarterly* 55(3): 399–420.

Doumerc, Bernard. 2002. "Les Vénitiens confrontés au retour des rapatriés de l'empire colonial d'outre-mer (fin XVe–début XVIe siècle)." In *Migrations et diasporas méditerranéennes (Xe–XVIe siècles)*, ed. Michel Balard and Alain Ducellier, 375–98. Paris: Publications de la Sorbonne.

Dubois, Laurent. 2004. *A Colony of Citizens: Revolution & Slave Emancipation in the French Caribbean, 1787–1804*. Chapel Hill: University of North Carolina Press.

Dudan, Bruno. 1933. *Il diritto coloniale veneziano e le sue basi economiche*. Rome.

——. 1938. *Il dominio veneziano di Levante*. Bologna: N. Zanichelli.

Dureau, Yona. 2001. "The Role of Converts in Cultural Exchanges in Europe in the 16th and 17th Century." In *Troubled Souls: Conversos, Crypto-Jews, and Other Confused Jewish Intellectuals from the Fourteenth through the Eighteenth Century*, ed. Charles Meyers and Norman T. Simms, 32–41. Hamilton, New Zealand: Outrigger Publishers.

Dursteler, Eric R. 2000. "Identity and Coexistence in the Early Modern Mediterranean: The Venetian Nation in Constantinople, 1573–1645." Unpublished Ph.D. dissertation, Brown University.

——. 2006. *The Venetians in Constantinople: Nation, Identity, and Coexistence in the Early Modern Mediterranean*. Baltimore: Johns Hopkins University Press.

——. 2011. *Renegade Women: Gender, Identity, and Boundaries in the Early Modern Mediterranean*. Baltimore: Johns Hopkins University Press.

Eickhoff, Ekkehard, and Rudolf Eickhoff. 1970. *Venedig, Wien und die Osmanen: Umbruch in Südosteuropa 1645–1700*. Munich: Callwey.

Eisenbichler, Konrad. 1997. "Italian Scholarship on Pre-Modern Confraternities in Italy." *Renaissance Quarterly* 50: 567–80.

Eldem, Edhem. 1999. "Istanbul: From Imperial to Peripherialized Capital." In *The Ottoman City Between East and West: Aleppo, Izmir, and Istanbul*, by Edhem Eldem, Daniel Goffman and Bruce Alan Masters, 135–206. New York: Cambridge University Press.

Ellero, Giuseppe. 1987. *L'Archivio I.R.E. Inventari dei fondi antichi degli opsedali e luoghi pii di Venezia*. Venice: IRE.

Elson, Christina M., and R. Alan Covey, eds. 2006. *Intermediate Elites in Pre-Columbian States and Empires*. Tucson: University of Arizona Press.

Emerson, Caryl, and Michael Holquist. 1981. "Glossary." In *The Dialogic Imagination: Four Essays*, 423–34. Austin: University of Texas Press.

Epstein, Steven A. 2006. *Purity Lost: Transgressing Boundaries in the Eastern Mediterranean, 1000–1400*. Baltimore: Johns Hopkins University Press.

Eufe, Rembert. 2003. "Politica linguistica della Serenissima: Luca Tron, Antonio Condulmer, Marin Sanudo e il volgare nell'amministrazione veneziana a Creta." *Philologie im Netz* 23: 15–43. www.fu-berlin.de/phin/phin23/p23t2.htm.

——. 2005. "Vicende coloniali e usi linguistici. I veneziani ed il volgare a Creta e a Venezia." In *Lingue, istituzioni, territori. Riflessioni teoriche, proposte metodologiche ed esperienze di politica linguistica*, ed. Cristina Guardiano, Emilia Calaresu, Cecilia Robustelli and Augusto Carli, 193–206. Rome: Bulzoni.

Evelyn, John. 1669. *The History of the Three Late, Famous Impostors, viz. Padre Ottomano, Mahomed Bei and Sabatai Sevi*. Savoy: Printed for Henry Herringman.

——. 1674. *Navigation and Commerce, Their Original and Progress . . .* London: Printed by T. R. for Benj. Tooke.

Fabris, Antonio. 1989. "Note sul mappamondo cordiforme di Haci Hamed di Tunisi." *Quaderni di Studi Arabi* 7: 3–17.

Fallers, Lloyd. 1955. "The Predicament of the Modern African Chief: An Instance from Uganda." *American Anthropologist* 57(2): 290–305.

Farolfi, Bernardino. 1998. "Brokers and Brokerage in Bologna from the Sixteenth to the Nineteenth Centuries." In *Guilds, Markets and Work Regulations in Italy, 16th–19th Centuries,* ed. Alberto Guenzi, Paola Massa, and Fausto Piola Castelli, 306–22. Aldershot, UK: Ashgate.

Faroqhi, Suraiya. 1986. "The Venetian Presence in the Ottoman Empire (1600–1630)." *Journal of European Economic History* 22: 345–84.

Favero, Giovanni, and Francesca Trivellato. 2004. "Gli abitanti del ghetto di Venezia in età moderna: Dati e ipotesi." *Zakhor: Rivista di storia degli ebrei d'Italia* 7: 9–48.

Fedalto, Giorgio. 1991. "Greci e Armeni." In *Patriarcato di Venezia,* ed. Bruno Bertoli and Silvio Tramontin, 303–21. Gregoriana libreria editrice. Padua: Giunta regionale del Veneto.

———. 2002. "La comunità greca, la chiesa di Venezia, la chiesa di Roma." In *I Greci a Venezia: Atti del Convegno internazionale di studio, Venezia, 5–7 novembre 1998,* ed. Maria F. Tiepolo and Eurigio Tonetti, 83–102. Venice: Istituto Veneto de Scienze, Lettere ed Arti.

Feldman, Martha. 1995. *City Culture and the Madrigal at Venice.* Berkeley: University of California Press.

Fenlon, Iain A. 2006. "Lepanto: Music, Liturgy, and Memorialization." Paper presented to the 52nd Annual Meeting of the Renaissance Society of America, San Francisco, March 23–25.

———. 2008. *The Ceremonial City: History, Memory and Myth in Renaissance Venice.* New Haven: Yale University Press.

Fernández-Armesto, Felipe, ed. 1987. *Before Columbus: Exploration and Colonization from the Mediterranean to the Atlantic, 1229–1492.* Philadelphia: University of Pennsylvania Press.

Ferraro, Joanne M. 2001. *Marriage Wars in Late Renaissance Venice.* New York: Oxford University Press.

Ferro, Marco. 1779. *Dizionario del diritto comune e veneto.* Venice: Presso P. Savioni.

Fine, John. 1996. "The Medieval and Ottoman Roots of Modern Bosnian Society." In *The Muslims of Bosnia-Herzegovina: Their Historic Development from the Middle Ages to the Dissolution of Yugoslavia,* ed. Mark Pinson, 1–21. Cambridge, Mass.: Harvard University Press.

Finlay, Robert. 1999. "The Immortal Republic: The Myth of Venice during the Italian Wars (1494–1530)." *Sixteenth Century Journal* 30(4): 931–44.

Fleischer, Cornell H. 1986. *Bureaucrat and Intellectual in the Ottoman Empire: The Historian Mustafa Ali (1541–1600).* Princeton: Princeton University Press.

———. 1992. "The Lawgiver as Messiah: The Making of the Imperial Image in the Reign of Suleyman." In *Soliman le Magnifique et son temps,* ed. Gilles Veinstein, 159–78. Paris: Documentation française.

Fleming, Kate E. 2007. "Two Rabbinic Views of Ottoman Mediterranean Ascendancy: The *Cronica de los Reyes Otomanos* and the *Seder Eliyahu Zuta.*" In *A Faithful Sea: The Religious Cultures of the Mediterranean, 1200–1700,* ed. Adnan A. Husain and K. E. Fleming, 99–120. Oxford: Oneworld.

Flood, F. Barry. 2009. *Objects of Translation: Material Culture and Medieval "Hindu-Muslim" Encounter*. Princeton: Princeton University Press.

Flores, Jorge. 2009. "Empires and Cultural Brokers: The Social World of Native Interpreters in Imperial Goa." Paper presented at the Center for Historical Studies, Northwestern University, May 7.

Florio, John. 1598. *A Worlde of Wordes, or Most Copious and Exact Dictionarie in Italian and English*. London: printed by Arnold Hatfield for Edw. Blount.

——. 1611. *Queen Anna's New World of Words, or, Dictionarie of the Italian and English Tongues*. London: Printed by Melch. Bradwood for Edw. Blount and William Barret.

Foa, Anna, and Lucetta Scaraffia. 1996. "Introduzione: Le conversioni fra costruzione dell'identità e intrecci di culture." In *Conversioni nel Mediterraneo (atti del convegno—Roma, 25–27 marzo 1996)*. Special issue of *Dimensioni e problemi della ricerca storica* 2: 7–14.

Fois, Mario. 1994. "Ignazio di Loyola, la Compagnia di Gesù e Venezia tra Riforma e Controriforma." In *I gesuiti e Venezia: Momenti e problemi di storia veneziana della Compagnia di Gesù*, ed. Mario Zanardi, 181–232. Gregoriana libreria editrice. Venice: Giunta regionale del Veneto.

Folkemer, Lawrence D. 1946. "A Study of the Catechumenate." *Church History* 15(4): 286–307.

Fondazione "Giorgio Cini." 1971. *Venti anni di attività della Fondazione Giorgio Cini*. Venice: Per i tipi della Stamperia.

Foucault, Michel. 1977. *Discipline and Punish: The Birth of the Prison*. New York: Pantheon Books.

Fourrier, Sabrine, and Gilles Grivaud, eds. 2006. *Identités croisées en un milieu méditerranéen: Le cas de Chypre (antiquité-Moyen Âge)*. Mont-Saint-Aignan: Universités de Rouen et du Havre.

Franco, Ivana. 1995. "L'emigrazione da Premana (Como) e da Grosio (Sondrio) a Venezia nel periodo 1800–1850 indagata attraverso gli Examina Matrimoiorum." In *Le Alpi, il Trentino e il lavoro dell'uomo*. Special issue of *SM Annali di San Michele*: 8: 79–111.

Frangipane, Cornelio. 1858 [c. 1555]. *I forestieri in Venezia. Lettera inedita*. Venice: Antonelli.

Frank, Andrew. 2005. *Creeks and Southerners: Biculturalism on the Early American Frontier*. Lincoln: University of Nebraska Press.

Fraser, Nancy. 1991. "Rethinking the Public Sphere: A Contribution to the Critique of Actually Existing Democracy." In *Habermas and the Public Sphere*, ed. Craig J. Calhoun, 109–42. Cambridge, Mass.: MIT Press.

Frazee, Charles A. 1983. *Catholics and Sultans: The Church and the Ottoman Empire, 1453–1923*. New York: Cambridge University Press.

Fubini Leuzzi, Maria. 1994. "'Dell'allogare le fanciulle degli Innocenti': Un problema culturale ed economico, 1577–1652." In *Disciplina dell'anima, disciplina del corpo e disciplina della società tra medioevo ed età moderna*, ed. Paolo Prodi and Carla Penuti, 863–99. Bologna: Mulino.

Fuchs, Barbara. 2001. *Mimesis and Empire: The New World, Islam, and European Identities.* New York: Cambridge University Press.

———. 2006. "Traveling Epic: Translating Ercilla's *La Araucana* in the Old World." *Journal of Medieval and Early Modern Studies* 36(2): 379–95.

Furetière, Antoine. 1690. *Dictionnaire universel, contenant généralement tous les mots,* Vol. 2. The Hague and Rotterdam: Chez Arnout & Reinier Leers.

Furnivall, John S. 1944. *Netherlands India: A Study of Plural Economy.* New York: Macmillan.

Fusaro, Maria. 2000. "The English Mercantile Community in Venice, 1570–1670." Unpublished Ph.D. dissertation, Cambridge University.

———. 2002. "Coping with Transition: Greek Merchants and Ship Owners between Venice and England in the Sixteenth Century." Presented at the XIIIth Economic History Congress, Buenos Aires, www.eh.net/XIIICongress/cd/papers/10Fusaro90.pdf.

———. 2003. "Les Anglais et les Grecs: Un réseau de coopération commerciale en Méditerranée vénitienne." *Annales: Histoire, Sciences Sociales* 58(3): 605–25.

Gager, Kristin E. 1997. "Women, Adoption, and Family Life in Early Modern Paris." *Journal of Family History* 22(1): 5–25.

Gal, Susan. 2002. "A Semiotics of the Public/Private Distinction." *differences* 13(1): 77–95.

Gal, Susan, and Judith T Irvine. 1995. "The Boundaries of Languages and Disciplines: How Ideologies Construct Difference." *Social Research* 62(4): 967–1001.

Galanus, Clemens. 1664. *Epistola pro libris suis Armeno-Latinis Apologetica ad R. P. D. Thomam Sersalem Clericorum Regularium Consultorem.* Munich: Typis Ioannis Iæclini, Typograph Electoral.

Galtarossa, Massimo. 2002. "La formazione burocratica del segretario veneziano: Il caso di Antonio Milledonne." *Archivio Veneto* 158: 5–64.

———. 2003. "Cittadinanza e Cancelleria ducale a Venezia (XVI–XVIII sec.)." *Storia di Venezia—Rivista* 1: 147–52. www.storiadivenezia.it/rivista/0103/sdvnumerouno.pdf.

García-Arenal, Mercedes, ed. 2001. *Conversions islamiques: Identités religieuses en islam méditerranéen.* Paris: Maisonneuve et Larose.

García-Arenal, Mercedes, and Gerard A. Wiegers. 2003. *A Man of Three Worlds: Samuel Pallache, a Moroccan Jew in Catholic and Protestant Europe.* Baltimore: Johns Hopkins University Press.

Gasparini Silvia. 1994 [2005]. "Giving a Rule to Accounting: Public Works and Bookkeeping in a Venetian Law of 1755." Paper presented at the 17th Annual Congress of the European Accounting Association, Venice, Italy, April 6–8, http://147.162.217.112:90/prospero/Accounting.htm.

Gavitt, Philip. 1990. *Charity and Children in Renaissance Florence: The Ospedale Degli Innocenti, 1410–1536.* Ann Arbor: University of Michigan Press.

Geertz, Clifford. 1960. "The Javanese Kijaji: The Changing Role of a Cultural Broker." *Comparative Studies in Society and History* 2(2): 228–49.

Gelderblom, Oscar, and Joost Jonker. 2003. "Amsterdam as the Cradle of Modern Futures and Options Trading, 1550–1650." Economy and Society of the Low Countries in the Pre-industrial Period Working Paper no. 9. www.iisg.nl/~lowcountries/2003-9.pdf.

Genot-Bismuth, Jacqueline. 1993. "The Università Degli Ebrei and the Nationi of the Venice Ghetto (1516–1630): A Reconsideration of Some Presuppositions of Contemporary Jewish Historiography." In *New Horizons in Sephardic Studies,* ed. Yedida K. Stillman and George K. Zucker, 15–35. Albany: SUNY Press.

Gentilcore, David. 1999. "Figurations and State Authority in Early Modern Italy: The Case of the Sienese Postmedicato." *Canadian Journal of History* 34(3): 359–83.

Georgopoulou, Maria. 1996. "Mapping Religious and Ethnic Identities in the Venetian Colonial Empire." *Journal of Medieval and Early Modern Studies* 26(3): 467–96.

——. 2001. *Venice's Mediterranean Colonies: Architecture and Urbanism.* New York: Cambridge University Press.

Geraci, Robert P., and Michael Khodarkovsky, eds. 2001. *Of Religion and Empire: Missions, Conversion, and Tolerance in Tsarist Russia.* Ithaca: Cornell University Press.

Gerbi, Antonello. 1985. *Nature in the New World: From Christopher Columbus to Gonzalo Fernandez De Oviedo.* Pittsburgh: University of Pittsburgh Press.

Ghobrial, John-Paul. 2010. "A World of Stories: Information in Constantinople and Beyond in the Seventeenth Century." Unpublished PhD dissertation, Princeton: Princeton University.

Gilroy, Paul. 1993. *The Black Atlantic: Modernity and Double Consciousness.* Cambridge, Mass.: Harvard University Press.

Ginzburg, Carlo. 1980. *The Cheese and the Worms: The Cosmos of a Sixteenth-Century Miller.* Baltimore: Johns Hopkins University Press.

——. 1983. *The Night Battles: Witchcraft & Agrarian Cults in the Sixteenth & Seventeenth Centuries.* Baltimore: Johns Hopkins University Press.

Giovanni Leone Africano. 1967 [1550]. "Della descrittione dell'Africa et delle cose notabli che ivi sono." In *Primo volume delle navigationi et viaggi,* ed. Giovanni Battista Ramusio. Venice: Giunti.

Gleason, Elizabeth G. 1993. *Gasparo Contarini: Venice, Rome, and Reform.* Berkeley: University of California Press.

Glixon, Jonathan E. 2003. *Honoring God and the City: Music at the Venetian Confraternities, 1260–1807.* New York: Oxford University Press.

Goffman, Daniel. 1990. *Izmir and the Levantine World, 1550–1650.* Seattle: University of Washington Press.

——. 1994. "Ottoman Millets in the Early 17th Century." *New Perspectives on Turkey* 11: 135–58.

——. 1998. *Britons in the Ottoman Empire 1642–1660.* Seattle: University of Washington Press.

——. 2002. *The Ottoman Empire and Early Modern Europe.* New York: Cambridge University Press.

——. 2007. "Negotiating with the Renaissance State: The Ottoman Empire and the New Diplomacy." In *The Early Modern Ottomans: Remapping the Empire,* ed. Virginia Aksan and Daniel Goffman, 61–74. Cambridge, UK: Cambridge University Press.

Goffman, Daniel, and Christopher Stroop. 2004. "Empire as Composite: The Ottoman Polity and the Typology of Dominion." In *Imperialisms: Historical and Literary*

Investigations, 1500–1900, ed. Balachandra Rajan, Elizabeth Sauer, and Anthony Pagden, 129–45. New York: Palgrave Macmillan.

González de Lara, Yadira. 2001. "Institutions for Contract Enforcement and Risk-sharing: From Debt to Equity in Late Medieval Venice." Universita' degli Studi de Brescia, www.eco.unibs.it/~segdse/paperseminari/th_paper.pdf.

Goody, Esther N. 1982. *Parenthood and Social Reproduction: Fostering and Occupational Roles in West Africa*. New York: Cambridge University Press.

Goody, Jack. 1969. "Adoption in Cross-Cultural Perspective." *Comparative Studies in Society and History* 11(1): 55–78.

Gourdin, Philippe. 2004. "Pour une réévaluation des phénomènes des colonisation en Méditerranée occidentale et au Maghreb pendant le Moyen Âge et le début des Temps Modernes." In *Chemins d'outre-mer: études d'histoire sur la Méditerranée médiévale offertes à Michel Balard*, ed. Damien Coulon, 411–23. Paris: Publications de la Sorbonne.

Grabar, Oleg. 2003. "Review of Maria Georgopoulou, *Venice's Mediterranean Colonies: Architecture and Urbanism*; Deborah Howard, *Venice and the East: The Impact of the Islamic World on Venetian Architecture 1100–1500*; Lisa Jardine and Jerry Brotton, *Global Interests: Renaissance Art Between East and West*; Rosamund Mack, *Bazaar to Piazza: Islamic Trade and Italian Art, 1300–1600*." *Art Bulletin* 85(1): 189–92.

Graciotti, Sante. 2006. "La Fondazione Cini e l'Europa orientale." Fondazione Giorgio Cini, http://www.cini.it/pdf/istituti/europaorientale.pdf.

Graizbord, David L. 2004. *Souls in Dispute: Converso Identities in Iberia and the Jewish Diaspora, 1580–1700*. Philadelphia: University of Pennsylvania Press.

Green, Arnold W. 1947. "A Re-Examination of the Marginal Man Concept." *Social Forces* 26(2): 167–71.

Greenblatt, Stephen. 1991. *Marvelous Possessions: The Wonder of the New World*. Oxford: Clarendon Press.

Greene, Molly. 2000. *A Shared World: Christians and Muslims in the Early Modern Mediterranean*. Princeton: Princeton University Press.

——. 2002. "Beyond the Northern Invasion: The Mediterranean in the Seventeenth Century." *Past & Present* 174(1): 42–71.

——. 2007. "Trading Identities: The Sixteenth-Century Greek Moment." In *A Faithful Sea: The Religious Cultures of the Mediterranean, 1200–1700*, ed. Adnan A. Husain and Kate E. Fleming, 121–48. Oxford: Oneworld.

——. 2008. "The Italian Connection: Ottoman Merchants in Italy." Unpublished paper, www.usc.edu/schools/college/crcc/private/ierc/conference_registration/papers/Greene_final.pdf.

——. 2010. *Catholic Pirates and Greek Merchants: A Maritime History of the Mediterranean*. Princeton: Princeton University Press.

Greer, Allan. 2005. *Mohawk Saint: Catherine Tekakwitha and the Jesuits*. New York: Oxford University Press.

Grendi, Edoardo. 1983. "Sistemi di carita." *Quaderni Storici* 53(2): 383–577.

——. 1987. "La pratica dei confini fra comunità e stati: Il contesto politico della cartografia." In *Cartografia e Istituzioni in età moderna*, 133–45. Rome: Libreria dello Stato.

——. 1993. "Storia di una storia locale: Perché in Liguria (ed in Italia) non abbiamo avuto una 'local history'?" *Quaderni Storici* 82: 141–97.

Grendler, Paul F. 1977. *The Roman Inquisition and the Venetian Press, 1540–1605*. Princeton: Princeton University Press.

Grewal, Inderpal. 1996. *Home and Harem: Nation, Gender, Empire, and the Cultures of Travel*. Durham: Duke University Press.

Grosrichard, Alain. 1998. *The Sultan's Court: European Fantasies of the East*. London: Verso.

Grubb, James S. 1986. "When Myths Lose Power: Four Decades of Venetian Historiography." *Journal of Modern History* 58(1): 43–94.

——. 1994. "Memory and Identity: Why Venetians Didn't Keep *Ricordanze*." *Renaissance Studies* 8: 375–87.

——. 1996. *Provincial Families of the Renaissance: Private and Public Life in the Veneto*. Baltimore: Johns Hopkins University Press.

——. 2000. "Elite Citizens." In *Venice Reconsidered: The History and Civilization of an Italian City-State, 1297–1797*, ed. John R. D. Martin, 339–64. Baltimore: Johns Hopkins University Press.

——. 2002. "Introduction." In *Family Memoirs from Verona and Vicenza (15th–16th Centuries)*, v–xxxix. Rome: Viella.

Guarini, Battista. 1971 [1583]. *Opere di Battista Guarini*. 2nd ed. Ed. Marziano Guglielminetti. Turin: Unione tipografico-editrice torinese.

Gudeman, Stephen. 1975. "Spiritual Relationships and Selecting a Godparent." *Man* n.s. 10(2): 221–37.

Hagen, Gottfried. 2004. "Ottoman Understandings of the World in the Seventeenth Century." In *An Ottoman Mentality: The World of Evliya Çelebi*, ed. Robert Dankoff, 215–56. Leiden: Brill.

——. 2006. "Review of Gabriel Piterberg, *An Ottoman Tragedy: History and Historiography at Play*." H-Turk, H-Net Reviews, www.h-net.org/reviews/showrev.cgi?path=8331153159749.

Hall, Kim F. 1995. *Things of Darkness: Economies of Race and Gender in Early Modern England*. Ithaca: Cornell University Press.

Hamilton, Alastair. 1994. "An Egyptian Traveller in the Republic of Letters: Josephus Barbatus or Abudacnus the Copt." *Journal of the Warburg and Courtauld Institutes* 57: 123–50.

Hampton, Timothy. 2006. "The Diplomatic Moment: Representing Negotiation in Early Modern Europe." *Modern Language Quarterly* 67(1): 81–102.

Hankins, James, ed. 2000. *Renaissance Civic Humanism: Reappraisals and Reflections*. New York: Cambridge University Press.

Hanks, William F. 2010. *Converting Words: Maya in the Age of the Cross*. Berkeley: University of California Press, 2010.

Harmless, William. 1995. *Augustine and the Catechumenate.* Collegeville, Minn.: Liturgical Press.

Harris, William V., ed. 2005. *Rethinking the Mediterranean.* New York: Oxford University Press.

Hay, Denys. 1957. *Europe, the Emergence of an Idea.* Edinburgh: Edinburgh University Press.

Head, Randolph C. 1990. "Religious Boundaries and the Inquisition in Venice: Trials of Jews and Judaizers, 1548–1580." *Journal of Medieval and Renaissance Studies* 20(2): 175–204.

Hermet, Aleramo, and Paola Cogni Ratti di Desio. 1993. *La Venezia degli Armeni: Sedici secoli, tra storia e leggenda.* Milan: Mursia.

Herzog, Tamar. 2003. *Defining Nations: Immigrants and Citizens in Early Modern Spain and Spanish America.* New Haven: Yale University Press.

Hess, Andrew C. 1972. "The Battle of Lepanto and Its Place in Mediterranean History." *Past and Present* 57: 53–73.

Ho, Engseng. 2004. "Empire through Diasporic Eyes: A View from the Other Boat." *Comparative Studies in Society and History* 46(2): 210–46.

Hodgen, Margaret T. 1964. *Early Anthropology in the Sixteenth and Seventeenth Centuries.* Philadelphia: University or Pennsylvania Press.

Hoerder, Dirk, Christiane Harzig, and Adrian Shubert, eds. 2003. *The Historical Practice of Diversity: Transcultural Interactions from the Early Modern Mediterranean World to the Postcolonial World.* New York: Berghahn Books.

Höfert, Almut. 2003. *Den Feind beschreiben: "Türkengefahr" und europäisches Wissen über das Osmanische Reich 1450–1600.* Frankfurt: Campus Verlag.

Horden, Peregrine, and Nicholas Purcell. 2000. *The Corrupting Sea: A Study of Mediterranean History.* Malden, Mass.: Blackwell.

Horodowich, Elizabeth. 2008. *Language and Statecraft in Early Modern Venice.* Cambridge, UK: Cambridge University Press.

Housley, Norman. 1996. "Frontier Societies and Crusading in the Late Middle Ages." In *Intercultural Contacts in the Medieval Mediterranean,* ed. Benjamin Arbel, 104–19. London: F. Cass.

Howard, Deborah. 2000. *Venice & the East: The Impact of the Islamic World on Venetian Architecture 1100–1500.* New Haven: Yale University Press.

Howell, James. 1650. *Epistolae Ho-elianae: Familiar Letters Domestic and Forren.* London: Printed by W. H. for Humphrey Mosely.

Howorth, Henry H. 1880. *History of the Mongols from the 9th to the 19th Century. Part 3: The Mongols of Persia.* London: Longmans, Green, and Co.

Hudon, William V. 1996. "Religion and Society in Early Modern Italy—Old Questions, New Insights." *American Historical Review* 101(3): 783–804.

Hughes, Diane Owen. 1983. "Sumptuary Law and Social Relations in Renaissance Italy." In *Disputes and Settlements: Law and Human Relations in the West,* ed. John Bossy, 69–99. New York: Cambridge University Press.

Hughes, Everett C. 1952. "Social Change and Status Protest: An Essay on the Marginal Man." In *Where Peoples Meet: Racial and Ethnic Frontiers*, ed. Everett C. Hughes and Helen M. Hughes, 188–99. Glencoe, Ill.: Free Press.

Husain, Adnan A. 2007. "Introduction." In *A Faithful Sea: The Religious Cultures of the Mediterranean, 1200–1700*, ed. Adnan A. Husain and K. E. Fleming, 23. Oxford: Oneworld.

Husain, Adnan A., and Kate E. Fleming, eds. 2007. *A Faithful Sea: The Religious Cultures of the Mediterranean, 1200–1700*. Oxford: Oneworld.

Imber, Colin. 2002. *The Ottoman Empire, 1300–1650: The Structure of Power*. Houndmills, UK: Palgrave Macmillan.

Imber, Colin, Keiko Kiyotaki, and Rhoads Murphey, eds. 2005. *Frontiers of Ottoman Studies: State, Province, and the West*. 2 vols. New York: Tauris.

Imhaus, Brünehilde. 1997. *Le minoranze orientali a Venezia 1300–1510*. Rome: Il Veltro.

Inalcık, Halil, and Cemal Kafadar, eds. 1993. *Süleymân the Second and His Time*. Istanbul: Isis Press.

Infelise, Mario. 1997. "Professione reportista: Copisti e gazzettieri nella Venezia del '600." In *Venezia: Itinerari per la storia della città*, ed. Stefano Gasparri, Giovanni Levi, and Pierandrea Moro, 183–209. Bologna: Mulino.

——. 2001. "The War, the News and the Curious: Military Gazettes in Italy." In *The Politics of Information in Early Modern Europe*, ed. Brendan M. Dooley and Sabrina A. Baron, 216–36. New York: Routledge.

——. 2002. "Roman *Avvisi*: Information and Politics in the Seventeenth Century." In *Court and Politics in Papal Rome, 1492–1700*, ed. Gianvittorio Signorotto and Maria A. Visceglia, 212–28. New York: Cambridge University Press.

Ingersoll, Richard Joseph. 1985. "The Ritual Use of Public Space in Renaissance Rome." Unpublished PhD dissertation, University of California, Berkeley.

Ioly Zorattini, Pier Cesare. 1972. "Note e documenti per la storia dei marrani e giudaizzanti nel veneto del seicento." *Michael: On the History of the Jews in the Diaspora* 1: 326–41.

——. 1998. "Domenico Gerosolimitano a Venezia." *Sefarad* 58(1): 107–15.

——. 2000. "Derekh Teshuvah; la via del ritorno." In *L'identità dissimulata: Giudaizzanti iberici nell'Europa cristiana dell'età moderna*, 195–248. Florence: L. S. Olschki.

——. 2008. *I nomi degli altri: Conversioni a Venezia e nel Friuli veneto in età moderna*. Florence: Leo S. Olschki.

Irvine, Judith T., and Susan Gal. 2000. "Language Ideology and Linguistic Differentiation." In *Regimes of Language: Ideologies, Polities, and Identities*, ed. Paul V. Kroskrity, 35–83. Santa Fe: School of American Research Press.

Isom-Verhaaren, Christine. 2004. "Shifting Identities: Foreign State Servants in France and the Ottoman Empire." *Journal of Early Modern History* 8(1–2): 109–35.

Israel, Jonathan. 1990. "The Amsterdam Stock Exchange and the English Revolution of 1688." *Tijdschrift voor geschiedenis* 103(3): 412–40.

Istituto italiano di cultura di Istanbul, ed. 1995. *Yuzyillar Boyunca Venedik Ve Ýstanbul Görünümleri—Vedute di Venezia ed Istanbul attraverso i secoli dalle collezioni del Museo Correr-Venezia e Museo del Topkapi-Istanbul.* Istanbul: Güzel Sanatlar.

Ivetic, Egidio. 2000. *Oltremare: L'Istria nell'ultimo dominio veneto.* Venice: Istituto Veneto di scienze, lettere ed arti.

Jacobson, Matthew Frye. 1998. *Whiteness of a Different Color: European Immigrants and the Alchemy of Race.* Cambridge, Mass.: Harvard University Press.

Jacoby, David. 1987. "Venice and the Venetian Jews in the Eastern Mediterranean." In *Gli ebrei e Venezia, secoli XVI–XVIII,* ed. Gaetano Cozzi, 29–58. Milan: Edizioni Communita.

——. 1997. *Trade, Commodities and Shipping in the Medieval Mediterranean.* Variorum Collected Studies Series. Brookfield, Vt.: Ashgate.

——. 1999. "Cretan Cheese: A Neglected Aspect of Venetian Medieval Trade." In *Medieval and Renaissance Venice,* ed. Ellen E. Kittell and Thomas F. Madden, 49–68. Urbana: University of Illinois Press.

Jager, Patrick. 1993. "Les limites orientales de l'espace européen." *Dix-hutième siècle* 25: 11–21.

——. 1995. "Comment peut-on être arabe?: Regards des voyageurs sur les nations levantines." In *Studies on Voltaire and the Eighteenth Century, vol. 335: Nations and Nationalisms: France, Britain, Ireland and the Eighteenth-Century Context,* ed. Michael O'Dea and Kevin Whelan, 323–34.. Oxford: Voltaire Foundation.

Janos, Damien. 2006. "Panaiotis Nicousios and Alexander Mavrocordatos: The Rise of the Phanariots and the Office of Grand Dragoman in the Ottoman Administration in the Second Half of the Seventeenth Century." *Archivum Ottomanicum* 23: 177–96.

Jardine, Lisa, and Jerry Brotton. 2000. *Global Interests: Renaissance Art between East and West.* Ithaca: Cornell University Press.

Jasanoff, Maya. 2005. *Edge of Empire: Lives, Culture, and Conquest in the East, 1750–1850.* New York: Alfred A. Knopf.

Jennings, Ronald C. 1993. *Christians and Muslims in Ottoman Cyprus and the Mediterranean World, 1571–1640.* New York: New York University Press.

Johns, Adrian. 1998. *The Nature of the Book: Print and Knowledge in the Making.* Chicago: University of Chicago Press.

Johnson, James H. 2005. "Deceit and Sincerity in Early Modern Venice." *Eighteenth-Century Studies* 38(3): 399–415.

Jones, Ann Rosalind, and Peter Stallybrass. 2000. *Renaissance Clothing and the Materials of Memory.* New York: Cambridge University Press.

Jütte, Daniel. 2011. "The Jewish Consuls in the Early Modern Mediterranean and Holy Roman Empire: A Study in Economic and Diplomatic Networks (1500–1800)." In *Cosmopolitan Networks in Commerce and Society, 1660–1914,* ed. Andreas Gestrich and Margrit Schulte Beerbühl. London: German Historical Institute.

Kafadar, Cemal. 1986. "A Death in Venice (1575): Anatolian Muslim Merchants Trading in the Serenissima." *Journal of Turkish Studies* 10: 191–218.

——. 1996. *Between Two Worlds: The Construction of the Ottoman State*. Berkeley: University of California Press.

——. 2007. "A Rome of One's Own: Reflections on Cultural Geography and Identity in the Lands of Rum." *Muqarnas* 24: 7–25.

Kahane, Henry R., Renée Kahane, and Andreas Tietze. 1958. *The Lingua Franca in the Levant: Turkish Nautical Terms of Italian and Greek Origin*. Urbana: University of Illinois.

Karapidakis, Nicolas, 1992. *Civis fidelis: L'Avènement et l'affirmation de la citoyenneté corfiote (XVIème–XVIIème siècles)*. Frankfurt am Main: Peter Lang.

Kayserling, Meyer, Yosef Hayim Yerushalmi, J. S. da Silva Rosa, and M. Weisz. 1971. *Biblioteca Española-Portugueza-Judaica and Other Studies in Ibero-Jewish Bibliography*. New York: KTAV Publishing House.

Keane, Webb. 1997. "From Fetishism to Sincerity: Agency, the Speaking Subject, and Their Historicity in the Context of Religious Conversion." *Comparative Studies in Society and History* 39(4): 674–93.

——. 2002. "Sincerity, 'Modernity,' and the Protestants." *Cultural Anthropology* 17(1): 65–92.

Kedar, Benjamin Z. 1997. "Multidirectional Conversion in the Frankish Levant." In *Varieties of Religious Conversion in the Middle Ages*, ed. James Muldoon, 191–99. Gainesville: University Press of Florida.

Kellenbenz, Hermann. 1987. "I Mendes, i Rodrigues d'Evora e i Ximenes nei loro rapporti commerciali con Venezia." In *Gli ebrei e Venezia, secoli XVI–XVIII*, ed. Gaetano Cozzi, 143–61. Milan: Edizioni Communita.

——. 1996. "Introduction to De La Vega's *Confusión de confusiones*." In *Extraordinary Popular Delusions and the Madness of Crowds*, ed. Martin S. Fridson, 125 –46, New York: John Wiley.

Kersey, John [J. K.]. 1969 [1702]. *English Dictionary: Or, a Compleat: Collection Of the Most Proper and Significant Words, Commonly Used in the Language. . . .* Edinburgh: Scolar Press facsimile.

Kertzer, David I. 1997. *The Kidnapping of Edgardo Mortara*. New York: Alfred Knopf.

——. 2002. "The Montel Affair: Vatican Jewish Policy and French Diplomacy under the July Monarchy." *French Historical Studies* 25(2): 265–93.

Kettering, Sharon. 1986. *Patrons, Brokers, and Clients in Seventeenth-Century France*. New York: Oxford University Press.

Kirshner, Julius. 1973. "Civitas Sibi Faciat Civem: Bartolus of Sassoferrato's Doctrine on the Making of a Citizen." *Speculum* 48(4): 694–713.

——. 1979. "Between Nature and Culture: An Opinion of Baldus of Perugia on Venetian Citizenship as Second Nature." *Journal of Medieval and Renaissance Studies* 9(2): 179–208.

——, ed. 1996. *The Origins of the State in Italy, 1300–1600*. Chicago: University of Chicago Press.

Klapisch-Zuber, Christiane. 1985. *Women, Family, and Ritual in Renaissance Italy*. Chicago: University of Chicago Press.

——. 1999. "L'adoption impossible dans l'Italie de la fin du Moyen Âge." In *Adoption et fosterage*, ed. Mireille Corbier, 321–37. Paris: De Boccard.

Kleinlogel, Cornelia. 1989. *Exotik-Erotik: Zur Geschichte des Türkenbildes in der deutschen Literatur der frühen Neuzeit (1453–1800)*. Frankfurt am Main: Peter Lang.

Krstić, Tijana. 2004. "Narrating Conversions to Islam: The Dialogue of Texts and Practices in Early Modern Ottoman Balkans." Unpublished PhD dissertation, University of Michigan.

——. 2009. "Illuminated by the Light of Islam and the Glory of the Ottoman Sultanate: Self-Narratives of Conversion to Islam in the Age of Confessionalization." *Comparative Studies in Society and History* 51(1): 35–63.

——. 2011. *Contested Conversions to Islam: Narratives of Religious Change in the Early Modern Ottoman Empire*. Stanford: Stanford University Press.

Kunt, Metin Ibrahim. 1974. "Ethnic-Regional (Cins) Solidarity in the Seventeenth-Century Ottoman Establishment." *International Journal of Middle East Studies* 5(3): 233–39.

Kuper, Hilda. 1969. "'Strangers' in Plural Societies: Asians in South Africa and Uganda." In *Pluralism in Africa*, ed. Leo Kuper and Michael G. Smith, 247–82. Berkeley: University of California Press.

Kyrris, Costas P. 1968. "Cypriote Scholars in Venice in the XVI and XVII Centuries with Some Notes on the Cypriote Community in Venice and Other Cypriote Scholars Who Live in Rome and the Rest of Italy in the Same Period." In *Ho hellenismos eis to exoterikon: Über Beziehungen des Griechentums zum Ausland in der neueren Zeit*, ed. Johannes Irmscher and Marika Mineemi, 183–272. Berlin: Akademie-Verlag.

——. 1969. "Further Documents Relating to Cypriote Immigrants in Venice (XVI–XVII) Centuries." *Epeteris* 3: 145–65.

——. 1970. "The Cypriote Family of Soderini and Other Cypriotes in Venice (XVI–XVII Centuries)." *Neo-Hellenika* 1: 58–78.

——. 1989. "Modes de survivance, de transformation et d'adaptation du régime colonial latin de Chypre après la conquête ottomane." In *Etat et colonisation au Moyen Age et à la Renaissance*, ed. Michel Balard, 153–65. Lyon: La Manufacture.

La Fontaine, Jean de. 1678. *Fables choisies mises en vers*, vol. 2. Paris: Thierry and Barbin.

Laiou, Sophia. 2005–2006. "The Levends of the Sea in the Second Half of the 16th Century: Some Considerations." *Archivum Ottomanicum* 23: 233–47.

Lamont, Michèle, and Virág Molnár. 2002. "The Study of Boundaries in the Social Sciences." *Annual Review of Sociology* 28: 167–95.

Lanaro, Paola, ed. 2006. *At the Centre of the Old World: Trade and Manufacturing in Venice and on the Venetian Mainland (1400–1800)*. Toronto: Centre for Reformation and Renaissance Studies.

Lanaro Sartori, Paola. 1999. *I mercati nella Repubblica veneta: Economie cittadine e stato territoriale (secoli XV–XVIII)*. Venice: Marsilio.

Landa, Janet T. 1983. "The Political Economy of the Ethnically Homogeneous Chinese Middleman Group in Southeast Asia: Ethnicity and Entrepreneurship in a Plural

Society." In *The Chinese in Southeast Asia*, ed. Linda Lim, 86–116. Singapore: Maruzen Asia.

——. 1994. *Trust, Ethnicity, and Identity: Beyond the New Institutional Economics of Ethnic Trading Networks, Contract Law, and Gift-Exchange*. Ann Arbor: University of Michigan Press.

Lane, Frederic C. 1973. *Venice, a Maritime Republic*. Baltimore: Johns Hopkins University Press.

Lane, Frederic C., and Reinhold C. Mueller. 1985. *Money and Banking in Medieval and Renaissance Venice*. Baltimore: Johns Hopkins University Press.

Langbein, John H. 1974. *Prosecuting Crime in the Renaissance: England, Germany, France*. Cambridge, Mass.: Harvard University Press.

Lattes, Alessandro. 1884. *Il diritto commerciale nella legislazione statutaria delle città italiane*. Milan: Hoepli.

Lattes, Andrea Yaakov. 1999. "Gli ebrei di Ferrara e le imposte per i catecumeni." *Rassegna Mensile di Israel* 65(3): 41–54.

Laughran, Michelle A. 1998. "The Body, Public Health and Social Control in Sixteenth-Century Venice." Unpublished PhD dissertation, University of Connecticut.

Lawrance, Benjamin N., Emily Lynn Osborn, and Richard L Roberts. 2006. *Intermediaries, Interpreters, and Clerks: African Employees in the Making of Colonial Africa*. Madison: University of Wisconsin Press.

Lazar, Lance G. *Working in the Vineyard of the Lord: Jesuit Confraternities in Early Modern Italy*. Toronto: University of Toronto Press.

——. 2004. "Negotiating Conversions: Catechumens and the Family in Early Modern Italy." In *Piety and Family in Early Modern Europe–Essays in Honor of S. Ozment*, ed. Marc R. Forster and Benjamin J. Kaplan, 152–77. Aldershot, UK: Ashgate.

Lestringant, Frank. 1994. *Mapping the Renaissance World: The Geographical Imagination in the Age of Discovery*. Trans. David Fausset. Berkeley: University of California Press.

Lesure, Michele. 1983. "Michel Cernivic <<explorator secretus>> à Constantenople (1556–1563)." *Turcica* 15: 127–54.

"Levantine, *a.* and *n.*" 1989. *The Oxford English Dictionary*. 2nd ed. OED Online, http://dictionary.oed.com.proxy.lib.umich.edu/cgi/entry/50132326?single=1&query_type=word&queryword=levantine&first=1&max_to_show=10.

Leybourn, William. 1693. *Panarithmologia Being a Mirror, Breviate, Treasure, Mate, for Merchants, Bankers, Tradesmen, Mechanicks, and a Sure Guide for Purchasers, Sellers, or Mortgagers of Land, Leases, Annuities, Rents, Pensions, &c.* London: Printed by T. J. for John Dunton . . . and John Harris.

Libby, Lester J. 1978. "Venetian Views of the Ottoman Empire from the Peace of 1503 to the War of Cyprus." *Sixteenth Century Journal* 9(4): 103–26.

Lo Basso, Luca. 2001a. "Reclutamento dei galeotti e gestione dell'armata ottomana tra XVI e XVII secolo." Paper presented at the conference *Armi del Sovrano*, Rome, www.assostoria.it/Armisovrano/Lo%20Basso.pdf.

——. 2001b. "Schiavi, forzati e buonevoglie. La gestione dei rematori delle galere dell'Ordine di Santo Stefano e della Repubblica di Venezia. Modelli a confronto." In *L'Ordine di Santo Stefano e il mare*, 169–232. Pisa: ETS.

Lomperis, Linda. 2001. "Medieval Travel Writing and the Question of Race." In *Race and Ethnicity in the Middle Ages*. Special issue of *Journal of Medieval and Early Modern Studies* 31(1): 147–64.

Luebke, David M. 2005. "How to Become a Loyalist: Petitions, Self-Fashioning, and the Repression of Unrest (East Frisia, 1725–1727)." *Central European History* 38(3): 353–83.

Lupprian, Karl-Ernst. 1978. *Il Fondaco dei Tedeschi e la sua funzione di controllo del commercio tedesco a Venezia*. Venice: Centro Tedesco di Studi Veneziani.

Luria, Keith P. 1996. "The Politics of Protestant Conversion to Catholicism in Seventeenth-Century France." In *Conversion to Modernities the Globalization of Christianity*, ed. Peter van der Veer, 23–46. New York: Routledge.

——. 2005. *Sacred Boundaries: Religious Coexistence and Conflict in Early-Modern France*. Washington, D.C.: Catholic University of America Press.

Luzzatto, Gino. 1995 [1961]. *Storia economica di Venezia dall'XI al XVI secolo*. Venice: Marsilio.

Lybyer, Albert H. 1913. *The Government of the Ottoman Empire in the Time of Suleiman the Magnificent*. Cambridge, Mass.: Harvard University Press.

MacCormack, Sabine. 2007. *On the Wings of Time: Rome, the Incas, Spain, and Peru*. Princeton: Princeton University Press.

Machiavelli, Niccolò. 1965. *The Prince*. Trans. W. K. Marriott. London: Dent.

Mack, Rosamond E. 2002. *Bazaar to Piazza: Islamic Trade and Italian Art, 1300–1600*. Berkeley: University of California Press.

Mackenney, Richard. 1987. *Tradesmen and Traders: The World of the Guilds in Venice and Europe, c. 1250–c. 1650*. London: Croom Helm.

Mackie, Louise. 2001. "Italian Silks for the Ottoman Sultans." Proceedings of the 11th International Congress of Turkish Art. *Electronic Journal of Oriental Studies* 4(31): 1–21.

MacLean, Gerald, ed. 2005. *Re-Orienting the Renaissance*. London: Palgrave Macmillan.

Macrides, Ruth. 1987. "The Byzantine Godfather." *Byzantine and Modern Greek Studies* 11: 139–62.

——. 1990. "Kinship by Arrangement: The Case of Adoption." *Dumbarton Oaks Papers* 44: 109–18.

——. 1999. "Substitute Parents and Their Children." In *Adoption et fosterage*, ed. Mireille Corbier, 307–19. Paris: De Boccard.

Magni, Cornelio. 1682. *Quanti di più curioso e vago ha potuto raccorre C. M. nel primo biennio da esso consumato in viaggi e dimore per la Turchia, parte I*. Venice: Appresso Abondio Menafoglio.

Makdisi, Ussama. 1997. "Reclaiming the Land of the Bible: Missionaries, Secularism, and Evangelcial Modernity." *American Historical Review* 102(3): 680–713.

——, ed. 2005. *Beyond the Clash of Civilizations: Missionaries, Conversion, and Tolerance in the Ottoman Empire*. Special issue of *Archaeology & History in the Lebanon* 22.

Malkiel, David J. 1991. *A Separate Republic: The Mechanics and Dynamics of Venetian Jewish Self-Government (1607–1624)*. Jerusalem: Magnes Press.

Mallett, Michael E., and John R. Hale. 1984. *The Military Organization of a Renaissance State: Venice, c. 1400 to 1617*, New York: Cambridge University Press.

Manno, Antonio. 1995. *I mestieri di Venezia: Storia, arte e devozione delle corporazioni dal XIII al XVIII secolo*. Cittadella: Biblos.

Marino, John A. 2002. *Early Modern History and the Social Sciences: Testing the Limits of Braudel's Mediterranean*. Kirksville, Mo.: Truman State University Press.

Martin, John. 1993. *Venice's Hidden Enemies: Italian Heretics in a Renaissance City*. Berkeley: University of California Press.

——. 1996. "Spiritual Journeys and the Fashioning of Religious Identity in Renaissance Venice." *Renaissance Studies* 10(3): 358–70.

Martin, John, and Dennis Romano, eds. 2000. *Venice Reconsidered: The History and Civilization of an Italian City-State, 1297–1797*. Baltimore: Johns Hopkins University Press.

Martínez-Fernández, Luis. 2000. "Marriage, Protestantism, and Religious Conflict in Nineteenth-Century Puerto Rico." *Journal of Religious History* 24(3): 263–78.

Masi, Gino, ed. 1941. *Statuti delle colonie fiorentine all'estero (secc. Xv–Xvi)*. Milano: Giuffrè.

Masters, Bruce. 1987. "Trading Diasporas and 'Nations': The Genesis of National Identities in Ottoman Aleppo." *International History Review* 9(3): 345–67.

Matar, Nabil I. 1998. *Islam in Britain, 1558–1685*. New York: Cambridge University Press.

Mattingly, Garrett. 1955. *Renaissance Diplomacy*. London: Cape.

Matuz, Josef. 1975. "Die Pfortendolmetscher zur Herrschaftszeit Süleymân des Prächtigen." *Südost-Forschungen* 24: 26–60.

Mavroidi, Fani. 1989. *Aspetti della società veneziana del '500: La Confraternita di S.Nicolo dei Greci*. Ravenna: Diamond Byte.

McClintock, Anne. 1995. *Imperial Leather: Race, Gender and Sexuality in the Colonial Contest*. New York: Routledge.

McKee, James B. 1993. *Sociology and the Race Problem: The Failure of a Perspective*. Urbana: University of Illinois Press.

McKee, Sally. 2000. *Uncommon Dominion: Venetian Crete and the Myth of Ethnic Purity*. Philadelphia: University of Pennsylvania Press.

——. 2007. "The Implications of Slave Women's Sexual Service in Italy." In *Unfreie Arbeit: Ökonomische und kulturgeschichtliche Perspektiven*, ed. M. Erdem Kabadayi and Tobia Reichardt, 101–14. Hildesheim: Olms.

McNeill, William. 1974. *Venice: The Hinge of Europe*. Chicago: Chicago University Press.

Membré, Michele. 1969. *Relazione di Persia (1542)*. Ed. Giorgio R. Cardona. Naples: Istituto Universitario Orientale.

Ménage, Victor L. 1958. "The Map of Hajji Ahmed and Its Makers." *Bulletin of the School of Oriental and African Studies* 21(1–3): 291–314.

Meserve, Margaret. 2000. "Medieval Sources for Renaissance Theories on the Origins of the Ottoman Turks." In *Europa und die Türken in der Renaissance*, ed. Bodo Guthmüller and Wilhelm Kühlmann, 409–36. Tübingen: Max Niemeyer.

———. 2006. "News From Negroponte: Politics, Popular Opinion, and Information Exchange in the First Decade of the Italian Press." *Renaissance Quarterly* 59(2): 440–80.

———. 2008. *Empires of Islam in Renaissance Historical Thought*. Boston: Harvard University Press.

Metcalf, Alida C. 2005. *Go-Betweens and the Colonization of Brazil, 1500–1600*. Austin: University of Texas Press.

Migliardi O'Riordan, Giustiniana. 2001. "Présentation des archives du Baile à Constantinople." *Turcica* 33: 339–67.

Mignolo, Walter D. 1995. *The Darker Side of the Renaissance: Literacy, Territoriality, and Colonization*. Ann Arbor: University of Michigan Press.

Milano, Attillo. 1970. "Battesimi di Ebrei a Roma dal cinquecento all'ottocento." In *Scritti in memoria di Enzo Sereni saggi sull'ebraismo romano*, ed. Daniel Carpi and Renato Spiegel, 133–67. Jerusalem: Fondazione Sally Mayer.

Miller, William. 1908. *The Latins in the Levant, a History of Frankish Greece (1204–1566)*. London: Murray.

Millet, Hélène, ed. 2003. *Suppliques et requêtes: Le gouvernement par la grâce en Occident (XIIe–XVe siècle)*. Rome: École Française de Rome.

Mills, Kenneth, and Anthony Grafton, eds. 2003. *Conversion: Old Worlds and New*. Rochester: University of Rochester Press.

Minkov, Anton. 2000. "Conversion to Islam as Reflected in Kisve Bahası Petitions: An Aspect of Ottoman Social Life in the Balkans, 1670–1730." Unpublished PhD dissertation, McGill University.

———. 2004. *Conversion to Islam in the Balkans: Kisve Bahası Petitions and Ottoman Social Life, 1670–1730*. Leiden: Brill.

Mintz, Sidney W. 1985. *Sweetness and Power: The Place of Sugar in Modern History*. New York: Viking.

Mintz, Sidney W., and Eric R. Wolf. 1950. "An Analysis of Ritual Co-Parenthood (Compadrazgo)." *Southwestern Journal of Anthropology* 6: 341–68.

Mishkova, Dianna. 2008. "Symbolic Geographies and Visions of Identity: A Balkan Perspective." *European Journal of Social Theory* 11(2): 237–56.

Mitchell, Timothy. 1988. *Colonising Egypt*. New York: Cambridge University Press.

Molà, Luca. 1994. *La comunità dei lucchesi a Venezia: Immigrazione e industria della seta nel tardo Medioevo*. Venice: Istituto veneto di scienze, lettere ed arti.

———. 1997. "The Silk Industry of Renaissance Venice: The Challenge of Innovation in a Mercantilist Economy." Unpublished Ph.D. dissertation, Johns Hopkins University.

———. 2000. *The Silk Industry of Renaissance Venice*. Baltimore: Johns Hopkins University Press.

Molà, Luca, Reinhold C. Mueller, and Claudio Zanier, eds. 2000. *La seta in Italia dal Medioevo al Seicento: Dal baco al drappo*. Venice: Marsilio.

Molho, Anthony. 1998. "The Italian Renaissance, Made in the USA." In *Imagined Histories: American Historians Interpret the Past,* ed. Anthony Molho and Gordon S. Wood, 263–94. Princeton: Princeton University Press.

Montanari, Daniele. 1987. *Disciplinamento in terra veneta: La diocesi di Brescia nella seconda metà del XVI secolo.* Bologna: Mulino.

Monter, E. William, and John Tedeschi. 1986. "Toward a Statistical Profile of the Italian Inquisitions, Sixteenth to Eighteenth Centuries." In *The Inquisition in Early Modern Europe: Studies on Sources and Methods,* ed. Gustav Henningsen, John Tedeschi, and Charles Amiel, 130–57. Dekalb: Northern Illinois University Press.

Morrison, Kenneth M. 1985. "Discourse and the Accommodation of Values: Toward a Revision of Mission History." *Journal of the American Academy of Religion* 53: 365–82.

Morton, A. H. 1993. "Introduction." In *Mission to the Lord Sophy of Persia (1539–1542),* by Michele Membré, vii–xxviii. London: School of Oriental and African Studies, University of London.

Mueller, Reinhold C. 1972. "Charitable Institutions, the Jewish Community and Venetian Society." *Studi Veneziani* 14: 37–81.

——. 1997. *The Venetian Money Market: Banks, Panics, and the Public Debt, 1200–1500.* Baltimore: John Hopkins University Press.

Mueller, Reinhold C., and Stefano Piasentini. n.d. "Cives: Privilegi di cittadinanza veneta, 1250–1500." http://venus.unive.it/riccdst/cives.htm.

Muir, Edward. 1981. *Civic Ritual in Renaissance Venice.* Princeton: Princeton University Press.

——. 1995. "The Italian Renaissance in America." *American Historical Review* 100: 1095–118.

——. 2007. *The Culture Wars of the Late Renaissance: Skeptics, Libertines, and Opera.* Cambridge, Mass.: Harvard University Press.

Muldoon, James. 1999. *Empire and Order: The Concept of Empire, 800–1800.* New York: St. Martin's Press.

Müller, Joseph, ed. 1966 [1879]. *Documenti sulle relazioni delle città toscane coll' Oriente cristiano e coi Turchi fino all' anno mdxxxi.* Rome: Società Multigrafica.

Murphey, Rhoads. 1993. "The Ottoman Resurgence in the Seventeenth-Century Mediterranean: The Gamble and Its Results." *Mediterranean Historical Review* 8(2): 186–200.

——. 2001. "Suleyman I and the Conquest of Hungary: Ottoman Manifest Destiny or a Delayed Reaction to Charles V's Universalist Vision." *Journal of Early Modern History* 5(3): 197–221.

Nardi, Giuseppe. 1967. *Opere per la conversione degli schiavi a Napoli.* Naples: Ufficio catechistico diocesano.

Necipoğlu, Gülru. 1989. "Sultan Süleyman and the Representation of Power in a Context of Ottoman-Hapsburg-Papal Rivalry." *Art Bulletin* 71(3): 401–27.

——. 1991. *Architecture, Ceremonial, and Power: The Topkapi Palace in the Fifteenth and Sixteenth Centuries.* New York: Architectural History Foundation.

Neck, Rudolf. 1950. "Andrea Negroni: Ein Beitrag zur Geschichte der österreichisch-türkischen Beziehungen nach dem Frieden von Zsitvatorok." *Mitteilungen des österreichischen Staatsarchivs* 3: 166–95.

Neff, Mary. 1981. "A Citizen in the Service of the Patrician State: The Career of Zaccaria De' Freschi." *Studi Veneziani* 5: 33–61.

——. 1985. "Chancellery Secretaries in Venetian Politics and Society, 1480–1533." Unpublished PhD dissertation, University of California, Los Angeles.

Neumann, Iver B., and Jennifer M. Welsh. 1997. "'The Turk' as Europe's Other." In *Cultural Politics and Political Culture in Postmodern Europe*, ed. J. Peter Burgess, 291–320. Amsterdam: Rodopi.

Newton, Stella M. 1988. *The Dress of the Venetians, 1495–1525*. Aldershot, UK: Scolar Press.

Nicol, Donald M. 1988. *Byzantium and Venice: A Study in Diplomatic and Cultural Relations*. New York: Cambridge University Press.

Nicolaou-Konnari, Angel. 2006. "L'identité en diaspora: Vies et oeuvres de Pierre de Nores (avant 1570?–après 1646) et Georges de Nores (1619–1638)." In *Identités croisées en un milieu méditerranéen: Le Cas de Chypre (antiquité-Moyen Âge)*, ed. Sabrine Fourrier and Gilles Grivaud, 329–53. Mont-Saint-Aignan: Universités de Rouen et du Havre.

Nicot, Jean. 1606. *Thresor de la langue francoyse*. Paris: David Douceur.

Nirenberg, David. 1996. *Communities of Violence: Persecution of Minorities in the Middle Ages*. Princeton: Princeton University Press.

Nubola, Cecilia, and Andreas Würgler, eds. 2002. *Suppliche e "gravamina": Politica, amministrazione, giustizia in Europa, secoli XIV–XVIII*. Bologna: Il mulino.

O'Connell, Monique. 2001. "Sinews of Rule: The Politics of Officeholding in Fifteenth-Century Venetian Crete." *Renaissance Studies* 15(3): 256–71.

——. 2004. "The Venetian Patriciate in the Mediterranean: Legal Identity and Lineage in Fifteenth-Century Venetian Crete." *Renaissance Quarterly* 57(2): 466–93.

——. 2009. *Men of Empire: Power and Negotiation in Venice's Maritime State*. Baltimore: Johns Hopkins University Press.

Oestreich, Gerhard. 1968. "Strukturprobleme des Absolutismus." *Vierteljahrschrift für Sozial- und Wirtschaftgeschichte* 55: 329–47.

Ortiz, Fernando. 1995 [1940]. *Cuban Counterpoint, Tobacco and Sugar*. Durham: Duke University Press.

Outler, Albert C. 1955. "Introduction." In *Confessions and Enchiridion, by St. Augustine*, 13–25. London: SCM Press.

Özkaya, Belgin T. 2003. "Theaters of Fear and Delight: Ottomans in the Serenissima." In *Thamyris/Intersecting: Place, Sex and Race, vol. 10: After Orientalism: Critical Entanglements, Productive Looks*, ed. Inge E. Boer, 45–61. New York: Rodopi.

Paci, Renzo. 1971. *La scala di Spalato e il commercio veneziano nei Balcani fra Cinque e Seicento*. Venice: Deputazione di storia patria per le Venezie.

Pagden, Anthony. 2002. *The Idea of Europe: From Antiquity to the European Union*. New York: Cambridge University Press.

Paraskevas, Konortas. 1999. "From Ta'ife to Millet: Ottoman Terms Concerning the Ottoman Greek Orthodox Community." In *Ottoman Greeks in the Age of Nationalism,* ed. Dimitri Gondicas and Charles Issawi, 169–79. Princeton: Darwin Press.

Pardo, Osvaldo F. 2004. *The Origins of Mexican Catholicism: Nahua Rituals and Christian Sacraments in Sixteenth-Century Mexico.* Ann Arbor: University of Michigan Press.

Park, Robert E. 1928. "Human Migration and the Marginal Man." *American Journal of Sociology* 33(6): 881–93.

Parkes, Peter. 2003. "Fostering Fealty: A Comparative Analysis of Tributary Allegiances of Adoptive Kinship." *Comparative Studies in Society and History* 45(4): 741–82.

Parry, V. J. 1962. "Renaissance Historical Literature in Relation to the Near and Middle East (With Special Reference to Paolo Giovio)." In *Historians of the Middle East,* ed. Bernard Lewis and Peter M. Holt, 277–89. New York: Oxford University Press.

Pastore, Christopher J. 2003. "Expanding Antiquity: Andrea Navagero and Villa Culture in the Cinquecento Veneto." Unpublished PhD dissertation, University of Pennsylvania.

——. 2006. "Re: [Serenissima] Dressed in Gold like a Greek." serenissima@yahoogroups.com [Listserv], July 5, http://groups.yahoo.com/group/serenissima/message/2929.

——. 2011. "Bipolar Behavior: Ferdinando I De'Medici and the East." In *The "Turk" and Islam in the Western Eye 1453–1750,* ed. James Harper, 129–54. Aldershot, UK: Ashgate.

Pearson, Michael N. 1988. "Brokers in Western Indian Port Cities: Their Role in Servicing Foreign Merchants." *Modern Asian Studies* 22(3): 455–72.

Pecchioli, Renzo. 1983. *Dal "Mito" di Venezia al' "Ideologia Americana."* Venice: Marsilio.

Pedani, Maria Pia. 1994. *In nome del Gran Signore: Inviati ottomuni a Venezia dalla caduta di Costantinopoli alla guerra di Candia.* Venice: Deputazione editrice.

——. 1997. "Simbologia ottomana nell'opera di Gentile Bellini." *Atti—Istituto Veneto di Scienze, Lettere ed Arti* 155(1): 2–29.

——. 2002. *Dalla frontiera al confine.* Venice: Herder Editrice.

Pederin, Ivan. 1990. "Die Wichtigen Ämter der Venezianischen Verwaltung in Dalmatien und der Einfluss Venezianischer Organe auf die Zustände in Dalmatien." *Studi Veneziani* 20: 303–57.

Peirce, Leslie. 1993. *The Imperial Harem: Women and Sovereignty in the Ottoman Empire.* New York: Oxford University Press.

——. 1997. "Seniority, Sexuality, and Social Order: The Vocabulary of Gender in Early Modern Ottoman Society." In *Women in the Ottoman Empire: Middle Eastern Women in the Early Modern Era,* ed. Madeline C. Zilfi, 169–96. Leiden, New York: Brill.

——. 2003. *Morality Tales: Law and Gender in the Ottoman Court of Aintab.* Berkeley: University of California Press.

——. 2004. "Changing Perceptions of the Ottoman Empire: The Early Centuries." *Mediterranean Historical Review* 19(1): 6–28.

——. 2010. "Polyglottism in the Ottoman Empire: A Reconsideration." In *Braudel Revisited: The Mediterranean World, 1600–1800*, ed. Gabi Piterberg, Teofilo F. Ruiz, and Geoffrey Symcox, 76–98. Toronto: Toronto University Press.

Pels, Peter. 1997. "The Anthropology of Colonialism: Culture, History, and the Emergence of Western Governmentality." *Annual Review of Anthropology* 26(1): 163–83.

Pergher, Roberta. 2007. "Impero immaginato, Impero vissuto: Recenti sviluppi nella storiografia del colonialismo italiano." *Ricerche di Storia Politica* 10(1): 53–66.

Peri, Vittorio. 1975. *Chiesa romana e rito greco: G. A. Santoro e la Congregazione dei Greci (1566–1596)*. Brescia: Paideia.

Pertile, Antonio et al, eds. 1894. *Storia del diritto italiano dalla caduta dell'Impero romano alla codificazione, vol. 4: Storia del diritto privato*. Turin: Unione tipografico-editrice.

Pertusi, Agostino, ed. 1966. *Venezia e l'Oriente fra tardo Medioevo e Rinascimento*. Florence: Sansoni.

——, ed. 1973. *Venezia e il Levante fino al secolo XV*. Florence: Olschi.

Petkov, Kiril. 1997. *Infidels, Turks, and Women: The South Slavs in the German Mind, ca. 1400–1600*. New York: Peter Lang.

Petta, Paolo. 1996. *Stradioti: Soldati albanesi in Italia, sec. XV–XIX*. Lecce: Argo.

Petti Balbi, Giovanna, ed. 2001. *Comunità forestiere e "nationes" nell'Europa dei secoli XIII–XVI*. Naples: Liguri.

Pfister, Manfred. 2005. "Inglese Italianato-Italiano Anglizzato: John Florio." In *Renaissance Go-Betweens: Cultural Exchange in Early Modern Europe*, ed. Andreas Höfele and Werner von Koppenfels, 32–54. Berlin: Walter de Gruyter.

Pfister, Max. 1993. "Grenzbezeichnungen im Italoromanischen und Galloromanischen." In *Grenzen und Grenzregionen*, ed. Wolfgang Haubrichs and Reinhard Schneider, 37–50. Saarbrücken: Saarbrücker Druckerei und Verlag.

Phillips, Edward. 1706. *The New World of Words:* or, Universal English dictionary.... 6th ed., ed. John Kersey. London: printed for J. Phillips; H. Rhodes; and J. Taylor.

Piccolomini, Alessandro. 1539. *Dialogo de la bella creanza de le donne*. Venice: per Curzio Navò e fratelli. www.bibliotecaitaliana.it/xtf/view?docId=bibit001201/bibit001201.xml.

Pilidis, Giorgio I. 1999. "Morire per honor di la Signoria: Gli stradioti greci a Venezia." In *Demosia ilaria: Pubblica celebrazione: 500 anni dalla fondazione della Comunita dei greci ortodossi di Venezia, 1498–1998*, 25–46. Venice: Istituto ellenico di studi bizantini e postbizantini di Venezia.

Piterberg, Gabriel. 2003. *An Ottoman Tragedy: History and Historiography at Play*. Berkeley: University of California Press.

Pitt-Rivers, Julian A. 1977. *The Fate of Shechem or, The Politics of Sex: Essays in the Anthropology of the Mediterranean*. New York: Cambridge University Press.

Pocock, J. G. A. 1997. "What Do We Mean by Europe?" *Wilson Quarterly* 31: 12–29.

Post, Gaines. 1974. "Medieval and Renaissance Ideas of Nation." In *The Dictionary of the History of Ideas*, ed. Philip P. Wiener, vol. 3, 318–24. New York: Scribner.

Pratt, Mary L. 1992. *Imperial Eyes: Travel Writing and Transculturation*. New York: Routledge.

Press, Irwin. 1969. "Ambiguity and Innovation: Implications for the Genesis of the Culture Broker." *American Anthropologist* 71(2): 205–17.

Preto, Paolo. 1975. *Venezia e i turchi*. Florence: G. C. Sansoni.

———. 1986. "La guerra segreta: Spionagio, sabotaggi, attentati." In *Venezia e la difesa del Levante: Da Lepanto a Candia, 1570–1670*, ed. Donatella Calabi, Giovanna Cecconi, and Ennio Concina, 79–85. Venice: Arsenale.

———. 1994. *I servizi segreti di Venezia*. Milan: Il Saggiatore.

Prodi, Paolo, and Carla Penuti. 1994. *Disciplina dell'anima, disciplina del corpo e disciplina della società tra medioevo ed età moderna*. Bologna: Mulino.

Prodi, Paolo, and Wolfgang Reinhard. 1996. *Il Concilio di Trento e il moderno*. Bologna: Mulino.

Prosperi, Adriano. 1982. "'Otras Indias': Missionari Della Contrariforma Fra Contadini e Selvaggi." In *Scienze, credenze occulte, livelli di cultura*, 205–34. Florence: L. S. Olschki.

———. 1990. "Ortodossia, diversità, dissenso: Venezia e il governo della religione intorno alla metà del Cinquecento." In *Andrea Palladio, nuovi contributi*, ed. André Chastel and Renato Cevese, 27–31. Milano: Electa.

———. 1992. "L'inquisizione in Italia." In *Clero e società nell'Italia moderna*, ed. Mario Rosa, 275–320. Rome-Bari: Editori Laterza.

Pullan, Brian S. 1971. *Rich and Poor in Renaissance Venice: The Social Institutions of a Catholic State, to 1620*. Cambridge, Mass.: Harvard University Press.

———. 1977. "'A Ship with Two Rudders': 'Righetto Marrano' and the Inquisition of Venice." *Historical Journal* 20(1): 25–58.

———. 1983. *The Jews of Europe and the Inquisition of Venice, 1550–1670*. Totowa, N.J.: Barnes & Noble.

———. 1999. "'Three Orders of Inhabitants': Social Hierarchies in the Republic of Venice." In *Orders and Hierarchies in Late Medieval and Renaissance Europe*, ed. Jeffrey H. Denton, 147–68. Toronto: University of Toronto Press.

Purcell, Nicholas. 2003. "The Boundless Sea of Unlikeness?: On Defining the Mediterranean." *Mediterranean Historical Review* 18(2): 9–29.

Pym, Anthony. 1998. *Method in Translation History*. Manchester, UK: St. Jerome.

Qaisar, A. Jan. 1974. "The Role of Brokers in Medieval India." *Indian Historical Review* 1(2): 220–46.

Rafael, Vicente L. 1988. *Contracting Colonialism: Translation and Christian Conversion in Tagalog Society under Early Spanish Rule*. Ithaca: Cornell University Press.

Raines, Dorit. 2006. *L'invention du mythe aristocratique: L'image de soi du patriciat vénitien au temps de la Sérénissime*. Venice: Istituto veneto di scienze lettere ed arti.

Raj, Kapil. 2007. *Relocating Modern Science: Circulation and the Construction of Knowledge in South Asia and Europe, 1650–1900*. Houndmills, UK: Palgrave Macmillan.

Ramaswamy, Sumathi. 2007. "Conceit of the Globe in Mughal Visual Practice." *Comparative Studies in Society and History* 49(4): 751–82.

Rapp, Richard T. 1976. *Industry and Economic Decline in Seventeenth-Century Venice.* Cambridge, Mass.: Harvard University Press.

Ravid, Benjamin. 1976. "The First Charter of the Jewish Merchants of Venice, 1589." *AJS Review* 1: 187–222.

——. 1982. "The Socioeconomic Background of the Expulsion and Readmission of the Venetian Jews, 1571–1573." In *Essays in Modern Jewish History a Tribute to Ben Halpern,* ed. Phyllis C. Albert and Frances Malino, 27–55. London: Fairleigh Dickinson University Press.

——. 1983. "*Contra Judaeos* in Seventeenth-Century Italy: Two Responses to the Discorso of Simone Luzzatto by Melchiore Palontrotti and Giulio Morosini." *AJS Review* 78: 301–51.

——. 1991. "A Tale of Three Cities and Their Raison d'Etat: Ancona, Venice, Livorno, and the Competition for Jewish Merchants in the Sixteenth Century." *Mediterranean Historical Review* 6(2): 138–62.

——. 1999. "Curfew Time in the Ghetto of Venice." In *Medieval and Renaissance Venice,* ed. Ellen E. Kittell and Thomas F. Madden, 237–75. Urbana: University of Illinois Press.

——. 2001. "The Forced Baptism of Jewish Minors in Early-Modern Venice." *Italia* 13–15: 259–301.

——. 2003. *Studies on the Jews of Venice, 1382–1797.* Variorum Collected Studies Series. Aldershot, UK: Ashgate.

Redford, Bruce. 1996. *Venice & the Grand Tour.* New Haven: Yale University Press.

Richter, Daniel K. 1988. "Cultural Brokers and Intercultural Politics: New York-Iroquois Relations, 1664–1701." *Journal of American History* 75: 40–67.

——. 2001. "Native Voices in a Colonial World." In *Facing East from Indian Country: A Native History of Early America,* 110–50. Cambridge, Mass.: Harvard University Press.

Riesenberg, Peter N. 1992. *Citizenship in the Western Tradition: Plato to Rousseau.* Chapel Hill: University of North Carolina Press.

Rietbergen, Peter. 1989. "A Maronite Mediator between Seventeenth-Century Mediterranean Cultures: Ibrahim al Hakilani, or Abraham Ecchellense (1605–1664)." *Lias* 16: 13–42.

Riley, Patrick. 2004. "Augustine's *Confessions* and the Paradoxes of Conversion." In *Character and Conversion in Autobiography: Augustine, Montaigne, Descartes, Rousseau, and Sartre,* 24–59. Charlottesville: University of Virginia Press.

Robinson, David. 2000. *Paths of Accommodation: Muslim Societies and French Colonial Authorities in Senegal and Mauritania, 1880–1920.* Athens: Ohio University Press.

Rocciolo, Domenico. 1998. "Catecumeni e neofiti a Roma tra '500 e '800; provenienza, condizioni sociali e 'padrini' illustri." In *Popolazione e società a Roma dal Medioevo all'età contemporanea,* ed. Eugenio Sonnino, 711–24. Rome: Il calamo.

Rochard, Patricia. 1992. *Türkei: Abendland begegnet Morgenland, 16.–18. Jahrhundert.* Internationale Tage Ingelheim. Mainz: H. Schmidt.

Rodrigue, Aron. 1996. "Difference and Tolerance in the Ottoman Empire. Interview by Nancy Reynolds." *Stanford Electronic Humanities Review* 5 (1). www.stanford.edu/group/SHR/5–1/text/rodrigue.html.

Roksandic, Drago. 2009. "The Dinari Vlachs/Morlachs in the Eastern Adriatic from the Fourteenth to the Sixteenth Centuries: How Many Indentities?" In *Balcani occiden-tali, Adriatico e Venezia fra XIII e XVIII secolo,* ed. Oliver J. Schmitt and Gherado Ortalli, 271–86. Vienna: Austrian Academy of Sciences.

Roland, Ruth A. 1999. *Interpreters as Diplomats: A Diplomatic History of the Role of Inter-preters in World Politics.* Ottawa: University of Ottawa Press.

Romano, Dennis. 1987. *Patricians and Popolani: The Social Foundations of the Venetian Renaissance State.* Baltimore: Johns Hopkins University Press.

——. 1991. "The Regulation of Domestic Service in Renaissance Venice." *Sixteenth Cen-tury Journal* 22(4): 661–77.

——. 1993. "Aspects of Patronage in Fifteenth- and Sixteenth-Century Venice." *Renais-sance Quarterly* 46(4): 712–33.

——. 1996. *Housecraft and Statecraft: Domestic Service in Renaissance Venice.* Baltimore: Johns Hopkins University Press.

Rota, Giorgio. 2004. "Religious Conversion and Professional Rivalry in Venice: Two Cases from the 17th Century." Unpublished paper presented at the 29th Deutscher Orientalistentag, Halle, Germany, September 20–24.

Roth, Cecil. 1936. "Forced Baptisms in Italy: A Contribution to the History of Jewish Persecution." *Jewish Quarterly Review* n.s. 27(2): 117–36.

Rothman, E. Natalie. 2006. "Between Venice and Istanbul: Trans-Imperial Subjects and Cultural Mediation in the Early Modern Mediterranean." Unpublished PhD disserta-tion, University of Michigan, Ann Arbor.

——. 2009a. "Interpreting Dragomans: Boundaries and Crossings in the Early Modern Mediterranean." *Comparative Studies in Society and History* 51(4): 771–800.

——. 2009b. "Self-Fashioning in the Mediterranean Contact Zone: Giovanni Battista Sal-vago and His *Africa Overo Barbaria* (1625)." In *Renaissance Medievalisms,* ed. Kon-rad Eisenbichler, 123–43. Toronto: Centre for Reformation and Renaissance Studies.

——. 2010. "Genealogies of Mediation: 'Culture Broker' and Imperial Governmentality." In *Anthrohistory: Unsettling Knowledge, Questioning Discipline,* ed. Edward Murphy, David W. Cohen, Chandra D. Bhimull, Fernando Coronil, Monica Eileen Patterson, and Julie Skurski, 67–79. Ann Arbor: University of Michigan Press.

——. 2011. "Conversion and Convergence in the Venetian-Ottoman Borderlands." *Iden-tity and Religion in the Medieval and Early Modern Mediterranean,* ed. John J. Mar-tin. Special issue of *Journal of Medieval and Early Modern Studies* 41(3): 601–33.

Rouillard, Clarence D. 1941. *The Turk in French History, Thought, and Literature (1520–1660).* Paris: Boivin.

Rowan, Steven W. 1975. "Ulrich Zasius and the Baptism of Jewish Children." *Sixteenth Century Journal* 6(2): 3–25.

Rubiés, Joan Pau. 2000. *Travel and Ethnology in the Renaissance: South India through European Eyes, 1250–1625.* New York: Cambridge University Press.

——. 2005. "Oriental Despotism and European Orientalism: Botero to Montesquieu." *Journal of Early Modern History* 9(1–2): 109–80.

Rudt de Collenberg, Wipertus H. 1982a. "Les litterae hortatoriae accordees par les papes en faveur de la rédemption des Chyrpriotes captives des Turcs (1570–1597) d'Apres les fonds de l'Archivo Segreto Vaticano." *Epeteris* 11: 13–167.

——. 1982b. "Le pape et ses cousines sultanes: Clement VIII Aldobrandini et sa parente chypriote." In *XVe Congrès international de généalogie et d'héraldique, Madrid, 1982, Acta*, 455–71. Madrid: Imprenta Saez.

——. 1983. "Recherches sur quelques familles chypriotes apparentées au pape Clément VIII Aldobrandini (1592–1605): Flatro, Davila, Sozomenoi, Lusignan, Bustron et Nores." *Epeteris* 12: 5–68.

——. 1986. "Le baptême des juifs à Rome de 1614 à 1798 selons les Registres de la <<Casa dei Catecumeni>>" *Archivum historiae pontificiae* 24: 91–231.

——. 1987. *Esclavage et rancons des chretiens en Mediterranee: 1570–1600: D'apres les Litterae Hortatoriae de l'Archivio Segreto Vaticano*. Paris: Leopard d'or.

——. 1989. "Le baptême des musulmanes esclaves à Rome aux XVIIe et XVIIIe siècles." *Mélanges de l'École française de Rome* 101(1): 9–181; 101(2): 519–670.

——. 1990. "Les <<custodi>> de la Marciana Giovanni Sozomenos et Giovanni Matteo Bustron: Relation familiales, sociales, culturelles et politiques au sein de la communauté chypriote." *Miscellanea Marciana* 5: 9–76.

——. 1993. "Les premiers Podocataro: Recherches basées sur le testament de Hugues (1452)." *Thesaurismata* 23: 130–82.

Ruggiero, Guido. 1993. *Binding Passions: Tales of Magic, Marriage and Power at the End of the Renaissance*. New York: Oxford University Press.

——. 1999. "The Abbot's Concubine." In *Medieval and Renaissance Venice*, ed. Ellen E. Kittell and Thomas F. Madden, 166–80. Urbana: University of Illinois Press.

——. 2001. "The Strange Death of Margarita Marcellini: *Male*, Signs, and the Everyday World of Pre-Modern Medicine." *American Historical Review* 106(4): 1141–58.

Ruspio, Federica. 2002. "Una comunità di marrani a Venezia." *Zahor: Rivista di storia degli ebrei in Italia* 5: 53–85.

——. 2007. *La nazione portoghese: Ebrei ponentini e nuovi cristiani a Venezia*. Turin: S. Zamorani.

Ryan, James D. 1997. "Conversion vs. Baptism?: European Missionaries in Asia in the Thirteenth and Fourteenth Centuries." In *Varieties of Religious Conversion in the Middle Ages*, ed. James Muldoon, 146–67. Gainesville: University Press of Florida.

Sabbadini, Roberto. 1995. *L'acquisto di una tradizione: Tradizione aristocratica e nuova nobiltà a Venezia*. Udine: Istituto editoriale veneto friulano.

Sacerdoti, Alberto. 1937. "Introduzione." In *<<Africa overo Barbarìa>>. Relazione al doge di Venezia sulle reggenze di Algeri e di Tunisi*, by Giovanni Battista Salvago, i–xiv. Padua: Cedam.

Sagredo, A., and Federico Berchet. 1860. *Il Fondaco dei Turchi a Venezia. Studi storici ed artistici*. Milan: G. Civelli.

Sahlins, Marshall D. 1995. *How "Natives" Think about Captain Cook, for Example*. Chicago: University of Chicago Press.

Sahlins, Peter. 1989. *Boundaries: The Making of France and Spain in the Pyrenees*. Berkeley: University of California Press.

Said, Edward W. 1978. *Orientalism*. New York: Pantheon Books.

Santosuosso, Antonio. 1973. "Relgious Orthodoxy, Dissent, and Suppression in Venice in the 1540s." *Church History* 42(4): 476–85.

Sanuto, Marino. 1969. *I diarii di Marino Sanuto*. Bologna: Forni Editore.

Sarti, Raffaella. 1991. "Obbedienti e fedeli: Note sull'istruzione morale e religiosa di servi e serve tra Cinque e Settecento." *Annali dell'Istituto storico italo-germanico in Trento* 17: 91–120.

——. 2001. "Bolognesi schiavi dei 'Turchi' e schiavi 'turchi' a Bologna tra Cinque e Settecento: Alterità etnico-religiosa e riduzione in schiavitù." *Quaderni Storici* 107: 437–74.

Sarton, George. 1936. "The Unity and Diversity of the Mediterranean World." *Osiris* 2: 406–63.

Sassetti, Filippo. 1853 [1577]. "Ragionamento sopra il commercio ordinato dal Granduca Cosimo I tra i sudditi suoi e le nazioni del Levante." *Archivio Storico Italiano: Appendice* 9: 165–88.

Sbriziolo, Lia. 1968. "Per la storia delle confraternite veneziane: Dalle deliberazioni miste (1310–1476) del Consiglio dei Dieci. Scolae comunes, artigiane e nazionali." *Atti dell'Istituto Veneto di Scienze, Lettere ed Arti* 126: 405–42.

Scannell, T. B. 2003 [1908]. "Catechumen." In *Catholic Encyclopedia*. New York: Appleton. www.newadvent.org/cathen/03430b.htm.

Scarabelli, Luciano. 1847. "Prefazione." In *Storia della Guerra di Paolo IV Sommo Pontefice contro gli Spagnuoli*, by Pietro Nores, ix–xxvii. Florence: G. P. Vieusseux.

Scaraffia, Lucetta. 2002. *Rinnegati: Per una storia dell'identità occidentale*. Rome: Laterza.

Scarcia, Gianroberto. 1969. "Presentazione." In *Relazione di Persia (1542)*, by Michele Membré, ed. Giorgio R. Cardona, xi–lxx. Naples: Istituto universitario orientale.

Schermerhorn, Richard A. 1970. "Colonization and Pluralism." In *Comparative Ethnic Relations: A Framework for Theory and Research*, 148–63. New York: Random House.

Schmidt, Benjamin. 2001. *Innocence Abroad: The Dutch Imagination and the New World, 1570–1670*. New York: Cambridge University Press.

Schmitt, Oliver J. 2001. *Das venezianische Albanien (1392–1479)*. Munich: Oldenbourg.

——. 2004. "'De le novelle de Albania adviso Vostre Excellentie . . .': Milanese and Mantuan *dispacci* and the Political History of the Venetian Overseas Empire in the Second Half of the 15th Century." Paper presented at the workshop on Trade, Colonies, and Intercultural Contacts in the Venetian World, 1400–1650, Venice International University, Venice, May 27–28.

——. 2005. *Levantiner: Lebenswelten und Identitäten einer ethnokonfessionellen Gruppe im osmanischen Reich im "langen 19.Jahrhundert."* Munich: Oldenbourg.

Schmitter, Monika. 2004. "Virtuous Riches: The Bricolage of *Cittadini* Identities in Early Sixteenth-Century Venice." *Renaissance Quarterly* 57(3): 908–69.

Schmutz, Jürg. 2000. *Juristen für das Reich: Die deutschen Rechtsstudenten an der Universität Bologna 1265–1425.* Basel: Schwabe.

Schulz, Juergen. 2004. *The New Palaces of Medieval Venice.* University Park, Pa.: Pennsylvania State University Press.

Schutte, Anne Jacobson. 2001. *Aspiring Saints: Pretense of Holiness, Inquisition, and Gender in the Republic of Venice, 1618–1750.* Baltimore: Johns Hopkins University Press.

Schwartz, Stuart B., ed. 1994. *Implicit Understandings: Observing, Reporting, and Reflecting on the Encounters between Europeans and Other Peoples in the Early Modern Era.* New York: Cambridge University Press.

Schwoebel, Robert. 1967. *The Shadow of the Crescent: The Renaissance Image of the Turk (1453–1517).* Nieuwkoop: B. de Graaf.

Seed, Patricia. 1995. *Ceremonies of Possession in Europe's Conquest of the New World, 1492–1640.* New York: Cambridge University Press.

Segre, Renata. 1975. "Neophytes during the Italian Counter-Reformation: Identities and Biographies." In *Proceedings of the Sixth World Congress of Jewish Studies, 13–19 August 1973,* 131–42. Jerusalem: World Union of Jewish Studies.

——. 1992. "Sephardic Settlements in Sixteenth-Century Italy: A Historical and Geographical Survey." In *Jews, Christians, and Muslims in the Mediterranean World after 1492,* ed. Alisa Meyuhas Ginio, 112–37. London: Cass.

Sella, Domenico. 1961. *Commerci e industrie a venezia nel secolo XVII.* Venice: Istituto per la Collaborazione Culturale.

Selwood, Jacob. 2003. "Making Difference: Aliens, Strangers and Others in Early Modern London, 1580–1680." Unpublished PhD dissertation, Duke University.

Sénac, Philippe. 2000 [1983]. *L'Occident médiéval face à l'islam: L'Image de l'autre.* Paris: Flammarion.

Sermoneta, Giuseppe B. 1993. "Il mestiere del neofito nella Roma del settecento." In *Shlomo Simonsohn Jubilee Volume,* ed. Aharon Oppenheimer, 213–43. Tel Aviv: Tel Aviv University.

Setton, Kenneth M. 1984. *The Papacy and the Levant (1204–1571).* Philadelphia: American Philosophical Society.

Sheller, Mimi. 2003. *Consuming the Caribbean: From Arawaks to Zombies.* New York: Routledge.

Shmuelevitz, Aryeh. 1984. *The Jews of the Ottoman Empire in the Late Fifteenth and the Sixteenth Centuries: Administrative, Economic, Legal and Social Relations as Reflected in the Responsa.* Leiden: Brill.

Shuval, Tal. 2000. "The Ottoman Algerian Elite and Its Ideology." *International Journal of Middle East Studies* 32(3): 323–44.

Siegmund, Stefanie. 2005. "Gender-Specific Conversion Narratives in Sixteenth-Century Italian Archival Sources." Unpublished paper presented at the 119th Annual Meeting of the American Historical Association, Seattle.

——. 2006. *The Medici State and the Ghetto of Florence: The Construction of an Early Modern Jewish Community.* Stanford: Stanford University Press.

Silverblatt, Irene M. 2004. *Modern Inquisitions: Peru and the Colonial Origins of the Civilized World.* Durham: Duke University Press.

Silverman, David J. 2005. "Indians, Missionaries, and Religious Translation: Creating Wampanoag Christianity in Seventeenth-Century Martha's Vineyard." *William and Mary Quarterly* 62(2): 141–74.

Silverstein, Michael. 1976. "Shifters, Linguistic Categories, and Cultural Description." In *Meaning in Anthropology,* ed. Keith H. Basso and Henry A. Selby, 11–55. Albuquerque: University of New Mexico Press.

Simmel, Georg. 1971. "The Stranger." Trans. Robert Park and Ernest Burgess. In *On Individuality and Social Forms,* ed. Donald N. Levine, 143–49. Chicago: Chicago University Press.

Simonsen, D. 1903. "Giulio Morosinis Mitteilungen über seinen Lehrer Leo da Modena und seine jüdischen Zietgenossen." In *Festschrift zum siebzigsten Geburtstage A. Berliner's gewidmet von Freunden und Schülern,* ed. A. Freimann and Meier Hildesheimer, 337–44. Frankfurt am Main.

Simonsfeld, Henry. 1968. *Der Fondaco dei Tedeschi in Venedig und die deutsch-venetianischen Handelsbeziehungen.* Aalen: Scientia Verlag.

Simonsohn, Shlomo. 1989. "Some Well-Known Jewish Converts during the Renaissance." *Revue des études juives* 148: 17–52.

Skilliter, Susan A. 1982. "The Letters of the Venetian 'Sultana' Nur Banu and Her Kira to Venice." In *Studia Turcologica memoriae Alexii Bombaci dicata,* ed. Aldo Gallotta and Ugo Marazzi, 515–36. Naples: Herder.

Soykut, Mustafa. 2001. *Image of the "Turk" in Italy: A History of the "Other" in Early Modern Europe, 1453–1683.* Berlin: K. Schwarz.

Sperling, Jutta. 1999a. *Convents and the Body Politic in Late Renaissance Venice.* Chicago: University of Chicago Press.

——. 1999b. "The Paradox of Perfection: Reproducing the Body Politic in Late Renaissance Venice." *Comparative Studies in Society and History* 41(1): 3–32.

Spuler, Bertold. 1935. "Die europäische diplomatie in Konstantinopel bis zum Frieden von Belgrad (1739). 3. Teil." *Jahrbücher für Kultur und Geschichte der Slaven* 11(3/4): 313–66.

Steensgaard, Neils. 1967. "Consuls and Nations in the Levant from 1570 to 1650." *Scandinavian Economic History Review* 15: 13–55.

Stephen, S. Jeyaseela. 2008. *Caste, Catholic Christianity, and the Language of Conversion: Social Change and Cultural Translation in Tamil Country, 1519–1774.* Delhi: Kalpaz Publications.

Stergios, James. 2006. "Language and Nationalism in Italy." *Nations and Nationalism* 12(1): 15–33.

Stoianovich, Traian. 1960. "The Conquering Balkan Orthodox Merchant." *Journal of Economic History* 20: 234–313.

Stoler, Ann L. 1989. "Rethinking Colonial Categories: European Communities and the Boundaries of Rule." *Comparative Studies in Society and History* 31: 134–61.

———. 1992. "Sexual Affronts and Racial Frontiers: European Identities and the Cultural Politics of Exclusion in Colonial Southeast Asia." *Comparative Studies in Society and History* 34(3): 514–51.

———. 2001. "Tense and Tender Ties: The Politics of Comparison in North American History and (Post) Colonial Studies." *Journal of American History* 88(3): 829–65.

———. 2002. *Carnal Knowledge and Imperial Power: Race and the Intimate in Colonial Rule.* Berkeley: University of California Press.

———. 2004. "Affective States." In *A Companion to the Anthropology of Politics,* ed. David Nugent and Joan Vincent, 4–20. Oxford: Blackwell.

Stoler, Ann L., and Frederick Cooper. 1997. "Between Metropole and Colony: Rethinking a Research Agenda." In *Tensions of Empire: Colonial Cultures in a Bourgeois World,* 1–56. Berkeley: University of California Press.

Stonequist, Everett V. 1961 [1937]. *The Marginal Man: A Study in Personality and Culture Conflict.* New York: Russell & Russell.

Stouraiti, Anastasia. 2003. "Costruendo un luogo della memoria: Lepanto." *Storia di Venezia—Rivista* 1: 65–88.

Stow, Kenneth R. 1976. *Catholic Thought and Papal Jewry Policy, 1555–1593.* New York: Jewish Theological Seminary of America.

———. 1993. "A Tale of Uncertainties: Converts in the Roman Ghetto." In *Shlomo Simonsohn Jubilee Volume,* ed. Aharon Oppenheimer, 257–81. Tel Aviv: Tel Aviv University.

———. 2001. *Theater of Acculturation: The Roman Ghetto in the Sixteenth Century.* Seattle: University of Washington Press.

———. 2002. "'Neofiti' and Their Families; Or, Perhaps, the Good of the State." *Leo Baeck Institute Year Book* 47: 105–13.

Stringham, Edward. 2003. "The Extralegal Development of Securities Trading in Seventeenth-Century Amsterdam." *Quarterly Review of Economics and Finance* 43: 321–44.

Subrahmanyam, Sanjay. 1997. "Connected Histories: Notes towards a Reconfiguration of Early Modern Eurasia." *Modern Asian Studies* 31(3): 735–62.

———. 2006. "A Tale of Three Empires: Mughals, Ottomans, and Habsburgs in a Comparative Context." *Common Knowledge* 12(1): 66–92.

———. 2007. "Holding the World in Balance: The Connected Histories of the Iberian Overseas Empires, 1500–1640." *American Historical Review* 112(5): 1359–85.

Suriano, Francesco. 1900 [1484]. *Il trattato di terra santa e dell'Oriente.* Ed. Girolamo Golubovich. Milan: Artigianelli.

Swartz, Norman. 1997. "Definitions, Dictionaries, and Meanings." Simon Fraser University, www.sfu.ca/philosophy/swartz/definitn.htm

Szepe, Helena. 2006. "Lepanto in Venetian Family Archives." Paper presented to the 52nd Annual Meeting of the Renaissance Society of America, San Francisco, March 23–25.

Targhetta, R. 1994a. "Falier, Domenico." *Dizionario biografico degli Italiani,* vol. 44, 423–24.

——. 1994b. "Falier, Luca." *Dizionario biografico degli Italiani,* vol. 44, 426–27.

Tassini, Giuseppe. 1887. *Curiosità veneziane, ovvero origini delle denominazioni stradali di Venezia.* Venice: Alzetta e Merlo.

Taussig, Michael T. 1986. *Shamanism, Colonialism, and the Wild Man: A Study in Terror and Healing.* Chicago: University of Chicago Press.

Tavakoli-Targhi, Mohamad. 2001. *Refashioning Iran: Orientalism, Occidentalism, and Historiography.* New York: Palgrave Macmillan.

Tavernier, Jean-Baptiste. 1677. *The Six Voyages of John Baptista Tavernier, Baron of Aubonne through Turky, into Persia and the East-Indies, for the space of forty years. . . .* London: Printed by William Godbid for Robert Littlebury.

——. 1679. *Recueil de plusieurs relations et traitez singuliers & curieux.* Paris: Clouzier.

Taylor, Jean G. 1983. *The Social World of Batavia: European and Eurasian in Dutch Asia.* Madison: University of Wisconsin Press.

——. 1992. "Women as Mediators in VOC Batavia." In *Women and Mediation in Indonesia,* ed. Sita van Bemmelen, 249–63. Leiden: KITLV Press.

Tedeschi, John. 1990. "Inquisitorial Law and the Witch." In *Häxornas Europa 1400–1700: Early modern European Witchcraft Centres and Peripheries,* ed. Bengt Ankarloo and Gustav Henningsen, 83–118. Oxford: Clarendon Press.

Tenenti, Alberto. 1955. "Gli schiavi di Venezia alla fine de Cinquecento." *Rivista storica italiana* 67(1): 52–69.

——. 1973. "The Sense of Space and Time in the Venetian World of the Fifteenth and Sixteenth Centuries." In *Renaissance Venice,* ed. John R. Hale, 17–46. London: Faber and Faber.

Terpstra, Nicholas. 1994. "Apprenticeship in Social Welfare: From Confraternal Charity to Municipal Poor Relief in Early Modern Italy." *Sixteenth Century Journal* 25(1): 101–20.

——, ed. 2000. *The Politics of Ritual Kinship: Confraternities and Social Order in Early Modern Italy.* New York: Cambridge University.

Tezcan, Baki. 2009. "The Second Empire: The Transformation of the Ottoman Polity in the Early Modern Era." *Comparative Studies of South Asia, Africa and the Middle East* 29(3): 556–72.

Theunissen, Hans. 1999. "Cairo Revisited (I): Four Documents Pertinent to the Ottoman-Venetian Treaty of 1517." *Electronic Journal of Oriental Studies* 2(7): 1–29.

Thiriet, Freddy. 1959. *La Romanie vénitienne au Moyen Age: Le développement et l'exploitation du domaine colonial vénitien, 12e–15e siècles.* Paris: E. de Boccard.

Tiepolo, Maria F. 1973. *La Persia e la Repubblica di Venezia: Mostra di documenti dell'Archivio di Stato e della Biblioteca Marciana di Venezia.* Tehran: Biblioteca Centrale dell'Università di Tehran.

——. 1986. *Mestieri e arti a Venezia 1173–1806.* Venice: L'Archivio.

——. 1994. "Archivio di Stato di Venezia: Antichi regimi." In *Guida generale degli archivi di Stato italiani,* ed. Piero D'Angiolini and Claudio Pavone, vol. 4, 857–1014. Ufficio centrale per i beni archivistici. Rome: Ministero per i beni culturali e ambientali.

Tinguely, Frédéric. 2000. *L'écriture du Levant à la Renaissance Enquête sur les voyageurs français dans l'empire de Soliman le Magnifique.* Geneva: Droz.

Todorov, Tzvetan. 1984. *The Conquest of America: The Question of the Other.* New York: Harper & Row.

Todorova, Maria N. 1997. *Imagining the Balkans.* New York: Oxford University Press.

Tolan, John V. 2008. *Sons of Ishmael: Muslims through European Eyes in the Middle Ages.* Gainesville: University of Florida Press.

Trebbi, Giuseppe. 1980. "La cancelleria veneta nei secoli XVI e XVII." *Annali della Fondazione Luigi Einaudi* 14: 65–125.

——. 1986. "Il segretario veneziano." *Archivio Storico Italiano* 144(527): 35–73.

Trexler, Richard C. 1994. *Public Life in Renaissance Florence.* Ithaca: Cornell University Press.

Trivellato, Francesca. 2009. *The Familiarity of Strangers: The Sephardic Diaspora, Livorno, and Cross-Cultural Trade in the Early Modern Period.* New Haven: Yale University Press.

Trouillot, Michel-Rolph. 1991. "Anthropology and the Savage Slot: The Politics and Poetics of Otherness." In *Recapturing Anthropology: Working in the Present,* ed. Richard G. Fox, 17–44. Santa Fe: School of American Research Press.

——. 1995. *Silencing the Past: Power and the Production of History.* Boston: Beacon Press.

Tucci, Ugo. 1957. "Mercanti Veneziani in India all fine del secolo XVI." In *Studi in onore di Armando Sapori,* 1089–112. Milan: Istituto Editoriale Cisalpino.

——. 1973. "The Psychology of the Venetian Merchant in the Sixteenth Century." In *Renaissance Venice,* ed. John R. Hale, 346–78. London: Faber and Faber.

——. 1985. "Tra Venezia e mondo turco: I mercanti." In *Venezia e i Turchi,* ed. Gino Benzoni, 38–55. Milan: Electra.

Turan, Ebru. 2007. "The Sultan's Favorite: Ibrahim Pasha and the Making of the Ottoman Universal Sovereignty in the Reign of Sultan Suleyman (1516–1526)." Unpublished PhD dissertation, University of Chicago.

Tymoczko, Maria. 2003. "Ideology and the Position of the Translator: In What Sense Is a Translator 'In-Between'?" In *Apropos of Ideology: Translation Studies on Ideology,* ed. María Calzada Pérez, 181–201. Ideologies in Translation Studies. Manchester, UK: St. Jerome.

Urban Padoan, Lina. 1990. *Venezia e il "foresto". Situazioni avventure, "meraviglie", quando anche i re alloggiavano in locande: Hosterie, locande e alberghi dal XIII al XIX secolo.* Venice: Centro internazionale dlla grafica.

Urciuoli, Bonnie. 2000. "Strategically Deployable Shifters In College Marketing, or Just What Do They Mean by 'Skills' and 'Leadership' and 'Multiculturalism'?" Language & Culture Working Paper, Symposium 6,Binghamton University, http://language-culture.binghamton.edu/symposia/6/

Valensi, Lucette. 1990. "The Making of a Political Paradigm: The Ottoman State and Oriental Despotism." In *The Transmission of Culture in Early Modern Europe,* ed. Anthony Grafton and Ann Blair, 173–203. Philadelphia: University of Pennsylvania Press.

——. 1993. *The Birth of the Despot: Venice and the Sublime Porte.* Ithaca: Cornell University Press.

——. 2001. "Intercommunal Relations and Changes in Religious Affiliation in the Middle East: Seventeenth to Nineteenth Centuries." In *The Construction of Minorities: Cases for Comparison across Time and around the World,* ed. André Burguière and Raymond Grew, 99–120. Ann Arbor: University of Michigan Press.

Van Boxel, Piet. 1998. "Dowry and the Conversion of the Jews in Sixteenth-Century Rome: Competition between the Church and the Jewish Community." In *Marriage in Italy, 1300–1650,* ed. Trevor Dean and Kate J. P. Lowe, 116–27. New York: Cambridge University Press.

Van der Veer, Peter. 1994. "Syncretism, Multiculturalism, and the Discourse of Tolerance." In *Syncretism/Anti-Syncretism: The Politics of Religious Synthesis,* ed. Charles Stewart and Rosalind Shaw, 196–211. New York: Routledge.

Van Gelder, Maartje. 2004. "Supplying the *Serenissima*: The Role of Flemish Merchants in the Venetian Grain Trade during the First Phase of the *Straatvaart.*" *International Journal of Maritime History* 16(2): 39–60.

——. 2009. *Trading Places: The Netherlandish Merchants in Early Modern Venice.* Leiden: Brill.

Van Houtte, J. A. 1936. "Les courtiers au Moyen âge. Origine et caractéristiques d'une institution commerciale en Europe occidentale." *Revue historique de droit français et étranger* 15: 105–41.

Vanzan, Anna. 1996. "In Search of Another Identity: Female Muslim-Christian Conversions in the Mediterranean World." *Islam and Christian-Muslim Relations* 7(3): 327–33.

——. 1997. "La Pia Casa dei Catecumeni in Venezia: Un tentativo di devshirme cristiana." In *Donne e Microcosmi Culturali,* ed. Adriana Destro, 221–55. Bologna: Patron Editore.

Vatin, Nicolas, and Gilles Veinstein, eds. 2004. *Insularités ottomanes.* Paris: Maisonneuve & Larose.

Vega, Garcilaso de la. 1688. *The royal commentaries of Peru.* Trans. Sir Paul Rycaut. London: Printed by Miles Flesher for Richard Tonson.

Veinstein, Gilles, ed. 1992. *Soliman le Magnifique et son temps.* Paris: Documentation française.

Vercellin, Giorgio. 1979. "Mercanti turchi a Venezia alla fine del Cinquecento: Il *Libretto dei contratti turcheschi* di Zuane Zacra sensale." *Il Veltro* 23: 243–76.

——. 1980. "Mercanti turchi e sensali a Venezia." *Studi Veneziani* 4: 45–78.

Verlinden, Charles. 1954. *Précédents medievaux de la colonie en Amerique.* Mexico City: Comisión de Historia del Instituto Panamericano de Geografica e Historia.

——. 1970. *The Beginnings of Modern Colonization: Eleven Essays with an Introduction.* Trans. Yvonne Freccero. Ithaca: Cornell University Press.

Vickery, Amanda. 1998. "Golden Age to Separate Spheres?: A Review of the Categories and Chronology of English Women's History." In *Gender & History in Western Europe,* ed. Robert V. M. Shoemaker, 197–225. London: Arnold.

Vigiano, Valentina. 2001. "I <<mezzani>> nella Palermo della prima metà del cinquecento: Norme, pratiche, modelli aggregativi e reti fiduciarie." In *Le regole dei mestieri e delle professioni secoli XV–XIX*, ed. Marco Meriggi and Alessandro Pastore, 347–63. Milan: F. Angeli.

Viswanathan, Gauri. 1998. *Outside the Fold: Conversion, Modernity, and Belief*. Princeton: Princeton University Press.

Vitali, Achille. 1992. *La moda a Venezia attraverso i secoli: Lessico ragionato*. Venice: Filippi editore.

Vitkus, Daniel J. 2003. *Turning Turk: English Theater and the Multicultural Mediterranean, 1570–1630*. New York: Palgrave Macmillan.

Voigt, Lisa. 2002. "Captivity, Exile, and Interpretation in *La Florida Del Inca.*" *Colonial Latin American Review* 11(2): 251–73.

Vovard, André. 1959. *Les turqueries dans la littérature française: Le cycle barbaresque*. Paris: Privat.

Wansbrough, John E. 1996. *Lingua Franca in the Mediterranean*. Richmond, UK: Curzon Press.

White, Luise. 2000. "'A Special Danger': Gender, Property, and Blood in Nairobi, 1919–1939." In *Speaking with Vampires: Rumor and History in Colonial Africa*, 151–74. Berkeley: University of California Press.

White, Richard. 1991. *The Middle Ground: Indians, Empires, and Republics in the Great Lakes Region, 1650–1815*. New York: Cambridge University Press.

Williams, Eric E. 1994 [1944]. *Capitalism & Slavery*. Chapel Hill: University of North Carolina Press.

Wilson, Bronwen. 2003. "Reflecting on the Face of the Turk in Sixteenth-Century Venetian Portrait Books." *Word & Image* 19(1–2): 38–58.

——. 2004. "Reproducing the Contours of Venetian Identity in Late Sixteenth-Century Costume Books." *Studies in Iconography* 25: 1–54.

——. 2005. *The World in Venice: Print, the City and Early Modern Identity*. Toronto: University of Toronto Press.

——. 2006. "Allies and Adversaries: Print, Venice, and the *Teatro della guerra.*" Paper presented to the 52nd Annual Meeting of the Renaissance Society of America, San Francisco, March 23–25.

——. 2007. "*Foggie diverse di vestire de' Turchi*: Turkish Costume Illustration and Cultural Translation." *Journal of Medieval and Early Modern Studies* 37(1): 97–139.

Wolf, Eric R. 1956. "Aspects of Group Relations in a Complex Society: Mexico." *American Anthropologist* 58(6): 1065–78.

——. 1982. *Europe and the People without History*. Berkeley: University of California Press.

——. 1994. "Perilous Ideas: Race, Culture, People." *Current Anthropology* 35(1): 1–12.

Wolff, Robert Lee. 1948. "Romania: The Latin Empire of Constantinople." *Speculum* 23(1): 1–34.

Wolff, Larry. 1994. *Inventing Eastern Europe: The Map of Civilization on the Mind of the Enlightenment*. Stanford: Stanford University Press.

——. 1997. "Venice and the Slavs of Dalmatia: The Drama of the Adriatic Empire in the Venetian Enlightenment." *Slavic Review* 56(3): 428–55.

——. 1998. "The Enlightened Anthropology of Friendship in Venetian Dalmatia: Primitive Ferocity and Ritual Fraternity among the Morlacchi." *Eighteenth-Century Studies* 32(2): 157–78.

——. 2001. *Venice and the Slavs: The Discovery of Dalmatia in the Age of Enlightenment.* Stanford: Stanford University Press.

——. 2005. "The Adriatic Origins of European Anthropology." *Cromohs* 10: 1–5. www.cromohs.unifi.it/10_2005/wolff_adriatic.html.

Woodhead, Christine. 2008. "Consolidating the Empire: New Views on Ottoman History 1453–1869." *English Historical Review* 123(503): 973–87.

Woolard, Kathryn A. 1998. "Simultaneity and Bivalency as Strategies in Bilingualism." *Journal of Linguistic Anthropology* 8(1): 3–29.

Woolfson, Jonathan. 1998. *Padua and the Tudors: English Students in Italy, 1485–1603.* Cambridge, UK: James Clarke.

Wright, Anthony D. 1996. "Republican Tradition and the Maintenance of 'National' Religious Traditions in Venice." *Renaissance Studies* 10: 405–16.

Wright, Diana G. 2000. "Bartolomeo Minio: Venetian Administration in 15th Century Nauplion." *Electronic Journal of Oriental Studies* 3(5): 1–235. www.let.uu.nl/oosters/EJOS/EJOS-III.5.html.

——. 2006. "The First Venetian Love Letter?: The Testament of Zorzi Cernovich." *Electronic Journal of Oriental Studies* 9(2): 1–20.

Zanardo, Andrea. 1996. "'Lor colpa fu d'essere sedotti': Un processo dell'inquisizione modenese ad ebrei e neofiti." *Nuova Rivista Storica* 80(3): 525–92.

Zannini, Andrea. 1993. *Burocrazia e burocrati a Venezia in età moderna: i cittadini originari (sec. XVI–XVIII).* Venice: Istituto veneto di scienze, lettere ed arti.

Ze'evi, Dror. 2004. "Back to Napoleon?: Thoughts on the Beginning of the Modern Era in the Middle East." *Mediterranean Historical Review* 19(1): 73–94.

——. 2006. *Producing Desire: Changing Sexual Discourse in the Ottoman Middle East, 1500–1900.* Berkeley: University of California Press.

Zele, Walter. 1990. "Alī bey, un interprete della Porta nella Venezia dell '500." *Studi Veneziani* 19: 187–224.

Zenner, Walter P. 1991. "Middleman Minority Theories." In *Minorities in the Middle: A Cross-Cultural Analysis*, 1–26. Albany: SUNY Press.

Zernatto, Guido. 1944. "Nation: The History of a Word." *Review of Politics* 6: 351–66.

Zerubavel, Eviatar. 1981. *Hidden Rhythms: Schedules and Calendars in Social Life.* Chicago: University of Chicago Press.

Zimmerman, Bénédicte. 2008. "Histoire croisée and the Making of Global History." Paper presented at the summer school on Comparative and Trans-national History: Theories, Methodology and Case Studies, European University Institute, www.eui.eu/HEC/ResearchTeaching/20082009-Autumn/SS-reading-Zimmermann.pdf.

Županov, Ines G. 2005. *Missionary Tropics: The Catholic Frontier in India (16th–17th Centuries).* Ann Arbor: University of Michigan Press.

Index

Note: Page numbers in *italics* indicate illustrations; those with a *t* indicate tables.